CURRENT ASSET MANAGEMENT

WILEY PROFESSIONAL BANKING AND FINANCE SERIES
EDWARD I. ALTMAN, Editor

THE STOCK MARKET, 4TH EDITION
Richard J. Teweles and Edward S. Bradley

TAX SHELTERED FINANCING THROUGH THE R&D LIMITED PARTNERSHIP
James K. La Fleur

CORPORATE FINANCIAL DISTRESS: A COMPLETE GUIDE TO PREDICTING, AVOIDING, AND DEALING WITH BANKRUPTCY
Edward I. Altman

CREDIT ANALYSIS: A COMPLETE GUIDE
Roger H. Hale

CURRENT ASSET MANAGEMENT: CASH, CREDIT, AND INVENTORY
Jarl G. Kallberg and Kenneth L. Parkinson

Current Asset Management

Cash, Credit, and Inventory

JARL G. KALLBERG

KENNETH L. PARKINSON

New York University,
Graduate School of Business Administration

A Wiley-Interscience Publication

JOHN WILEY & SONS

New York • Chichester • Brisbane • Toronto • Singapore

Library of Congress Cataloging in Publication Data:

Kallberg, Jarl G.
　Current asset management.

　(Wiley professional banking and finance series)
　"A Wiley-Interscience publication."
　Includes bibliographical references and index.
　1. Cash management.　2. Credit management.
3. Inventory control.　4. Accounts receivable.　5. Working capital.　I. Parkinson, Kenneth L.　II. Title.
III. Series.

HG4028.C45K34　1984　　　658.1'5244　　　83-21687
ISBN 0-471-87090-0

Printed in the United States of America

10　9　8　7　6　5　4　3　2　1

To Peggy and Erik

To Brenda and Jeff

Contributors

This book contains three contributions:

Float Studies, by Susan Hinko of Merrill, Lynch, Pierce, Fenner and Smith;

Integrating the Cash Management Function, by David Spiselman of the Manhattan Management Consulting Group;

Forecasting Cash Flows at a Credit Union, by Professor Gordon Sick of the University of Alberta.

These sections contain insightful comments and viewpoints on topics of current interest.

Preface

This book is concerned with the modern techniques of management in the three major components of current assets: cash, inventory, and accounts receivable. Because of its relevance to each of the preceding areas, and to the firm's overall planning, the fundamentals of short-term forecasting techniques are also developed.
We believe that a unified treatment of this subject is important for a wide variety of reasons.

Higher interest rates have forced a closer examination of the performance of current assets and the escalating costs of investment in them.

An economic climate of retrenchment rather than growth has placed a greater emphasis on operational efficiency and has highlighted the need for liquidity.

The pervasiveness of the computer (and generally increasing managerial technical skills) has allowed more firms of all sizes to adopt automated information and management techniques.

The regulatory environment has changed the impact of traditional policies, especially in the areas of cash and credit management.

There are also a number of other reasons for considering the components of current assets in the aggregate. As the firm's cash flow cycle indicates, these assets are intimately linked; decisions made in one area impact each of the other areas. Cash management is interlinked with receivables and inventory management in that it shares common goals with these functions. It is also the likely recipient or the point at which the major impact of changes in either area are likely to be recognized. For example, improved receivables management typically results in accelerated collections and consequently more cash. Furthermore, the whole area of forecasting is applicable throughout these areas with techniques of applications that are developed for one, having further utility in the adjoining areas.

Finally, it is clear that policy making in current asset management is made difficult by the problem of evaluating the costs and benefits of alternative strategies. These are best evaluated by analyzing the firm's overall performance, rather than the performance of any subarea.

Since the basic goals of current asset management are to ensure the adequate liquidity of the firm and the efficient utilization of assets, we can use several key ratios to measure the liquidity and current asset performance of a firm. A sample of these is given in Exhibit P.1. Case 5.2 illustrates their usage.

EXHIBIT P.1   WORKING CAPITAL RATIOS

Liquidity	Current ratio = current assets/current liabilities Quick ratio (acid test) = (current assets − inventory)/current liabilities
Turnover ratios*	Receivables turnover = credit sales/receivables Inventory turnover = cost of goods sold/inventory Cash turnover = sales/cash
Days sales outstanding†	Receivables × average daily sales
Aggregate measure‡	Conversion cycle = DSO(receivables) + DSO(inventory) + DSO(cash)

*Note the number of possible variations on these definitions. For example, "receivables" could mean (1) an end-of-year figure, (2) an average of end-of-year and start-of-year, or (3) an average over all the 12 months.

†This ratio is also usable for other current assets, so that we have days sales outstanding (DSO) for inventory or cash as well. Its relationship with the turnover ratios should be clear.

‡Another important measure of aggregate performance (related to prediction of bankruptcies) is the Altman Z-score discussed in Section 7.6.

This book addresses itself to the solution of the types of working capital problems that can be uncovered by financial statement analysis or otherwise. This process of problem and solution is given in Exhibit P.2.

EXHIBIT P.2   Working Capital Problems and Possible Solutions

Relevant chapters are given in parentheses.

Problem	Possible Solutions
Illiquidity	Increase short-term financing (3, 4, 5, 6) Speed "asset conversion" (1, 4, 5, 6, 7) Slow payables (1, 2) Speed collections (1, 2, 4, 5) Decrease short-term investment (1, 3, 7) Better management of cash position (1, 2, 3, 7)
Slow receivables turnover	Factor (or "bulk finance") (5) Change credit terms (5) Change credit standards (5)

EXHIBIT P.2 (*Continued*)

Relevant chapters are given in parentheses.	
Problem	Possible Solutions
Slow inventory	Change order sizes (6)
turnover	Dump obsolete and slow-moving items (6)
	Change safety stocks (6, 7)
	Change service level (6)
	Change supplier (6)
	Change distribution system (6)

This exhibit serves as an overview of this text and again highlights the interactions among the components of current assets.

The reader may have observed that we have not explicitly mentioned strategies for the management of current liabilities. There are two basic reasons for this. First, we feel that there is not a developed methodology for the solution of these types of problems. Second, and most important, within our discussion of current asset management many of the most important aspects of current liability management will be covered.

JARL G. KALLBERG
KENNETH L. PARKINSON

New York, New York
February 1984

Acknowledgements

We owe a special thanks to our friends who have commented on earlier versions of this work: Harry Grammatikos and Ram Rao of New York University, Richard Norgaard of the University of Connecticut, Aviva Rice of Manufacturer's Hanover Trust, and John Langeler of the Bank of New York. We gratefully acknowledge the assistance of Duen-Li Kao, Peggy Kallberg, and Robert Ching in the preparation of the manuscript. Our MBA classes in working capital management and corporate cash management practices at New York University's Graduate School of Business Administration have contributed much to the content and exposition of this material. Finally, we thank the staff at John Wiley for their excellent work on this manuscript and our editors Stephen Kippur of Wiley and Professor Edward Altman of New York University who have been essential to the completion of this work. All of the above are absolved of any responsibility for remaining errors; for these each author credits the other.

CONTENTS

CURRENT ASSET MANAGEMENT

1 The Cash Management Environment

Corporate cash management represents one of the newer areas of financial management. As such, it has taken time to develop basic concepts or fundamental techniques. For a long time, it was virtually ignored, relegated to a rather obscure segment of corporate finance. A glance at historic literature or texts will confirm this position. However, in recent years it has emerged from this subdued position to assume an ever-increasing role in the financial activities of corporations.

The principles and techniques discussed in this section have originated and been developed in a U.S. context. This development does not preclude the application of cash management fundamentals to other countries or areas of corporate finance. While there may be differences in the payment methods and banking systems in other countries, the basic concepts of corporate cash management are universal. As is the case with other financial disciplines, the basic concepts must be tailored to suit the particular environment or the individual requirements of any one country.

Cash management, then, can be viewed as the major driving force of corporate treasury. Its title may sound somewhat limited or circumscribed, but it actually encompasses a wide range of financial activities.

The overall effectiveness of the corporate treasury function will be determined by the successful establishment of a comprehensive cash management system. The functional effectiveness of a corporate cash management system will be determined by the development and interaction of many diverse components. This will entail recognizing the basic environmental and organizational factors that tend to make one company act differently from another. Also, better control and analysis of the essential cash flows are essential ingredients in the cash management function. This must be coupled with sound bank compensation methods and efficient management of appropriate information. Short-term liquidity considerations, including borrowing as well as investing, together with the effective forecasting and scheduling of short-term cash flows can lead to better control over the firm's cash management. Finally, the firm must continue to look ahead to prospective developments that may have substantial effects on the firm's cash management systems or offer opportunities for extending the firm's existing systems to newer areas or locations.

These aspects of corporate cash management will be explored in further detail in the following chapters. The first chapter will deal with the different environments of cash management as well as the basic flows of cash for the corporation. The second chapter will deal with basic analytical tools and bank compensation techniques. The next chapter will consider liquidity, forecasting, and control. The fourth will discuss future developments and offer case problems and exercises.

Corporate cash management is affected by the various organizational and environmental factors within and outside the firm. The structure of the treasury area is extremely important in dividing the workload efficiently and establishing effective checks and balances over the different functions of cash management. These functions, in turn, are affected by various factors that determine or at least influence the size and scope of the central treasury area. Externally, the banking system plays a significant role in creating the operating environment for the corporation's cash management activities. In this section the fundamental functions of cash management will be discussed in terms of their respective places within the treasury organization. In addition, environmental factors, both internal and external to the corporation, will be discussed, and their influence on the overall corporate cash management function or organization will be described.

SECTION 1.1   OVERVIEW OF CASH MANAGEMENT

The management of cash has taken on a broader and integral role in corporate financial management in recent years. For years this aspect of corporate treasury was considered to be of little importance to a company's financial functions, and the treasurer and his staff were largely ignored. Indeed, with consistently stable and low rates of interest, there appeared to be little to be gained in paying an undue amount of attention to cash balances and the establishment of newer systems or techniques to improve the control or even the concentration of the company's cash. The management of cash, such as it was, was usually relegated to local operating units that tended to select nearby banks for their cash management services, based on convenience and familiarity and an absence of an overall corporate banking network. There was very little contact with central treasury staff, whose role was essentially that of securing adequate bank credit and collecting "dividends" to the parent from each local operating unit. These "dividends" represented the upstreaming of profits, internal debt repayments, or extremely large excesses of funds, and they, in turn, created a pool of corporate cash that could be used to fund those other operations that were periodically or even chronically short of cash or to be invested prudently in the money markets by the so-called staff experts.

Cash balances, whether those managed locally or at central treasury, were managed in accounting terms; that is, the balances shown on the company's own cash ledger were generally viewed and accepted as the true cash balance of the company. Large balances were regarded as satisfactory performance and desirable as an indicator of adequate corporate liquidity. In fact, most corporations and banks alike would take special actions at regular quarterly reporting intervals to inflate their accounting cash balances and thereby demonstrate substantial liquidity. This window dressing was quite commonplace and, of course, led to grossly misrepresented cash positions as shown in company financial statements. This accounting-oriented approach discouraged any great degree of coordination between the local operating units and the central treasury staff and typically created substantial cash balances at the lead operational banks, usually unknown to and probably unmeasured by anyone from the company.

Not much consideration was given to bank compensation for other than credit services. Companies tended to maintain numerous lines of credit with many banks throughout the country, although the more significant lines were usually clustered at the larger banks located near corporate headquarters as well as the banks located in the major money centers. These banks were usually included because they had much larger legal lending limits than the smaller regional banks. Compensation was in the form of "free" collected balances in amounts ranging from 10 to 15% of the overall line of credit. These compensating balances were typically kept in a separate corporate account so as not to be confused with any other operating accounts, which, in turn, were expected to generate sufficient balances on the bank's books to provide that institution with a respectable return. The corporate treasurer or cash manager (if the title even existed) received very little quantitative information from his banks and could expect those bankers who experienced inadequate levels of balances to bring such situations to his attention in order to correct the deficit. Indeed, the attitude of the commercial banker condoned this approach, and those companies leaving the largest excess balances, even at levels far beyond the agreed-upon amounts, were considered the bank's best customers and were assured by the banker that the company would always receive the best rates and considerations in credit crunches. Several of the largest commercial banks went so far as to negotiate excess balances from their corporate customers as a kind of extra compensation for the bank and added insurance for the company in case of tight credit constraints. It should be noted that most of these negotiations were handled as gentlemen's agreements, and these informal arrangements were seldom noted on the company's public financial statements. Even when they were, they were worded rather ambiguously.

Companies who played the float game were usually viewed with some disdain by their fellow treasurers from larger firms and their banking counterparts. Only companies that were in trouble would ever attempt to take advantage of the system or try to reduce the level of good-will balances in the bank. Besides, the bank balances were the surest sign of corporate liquidity, and the maintenance of bank lines of credit through these balances was considered a form of financial insurance.

As far back as the late 1940s and early 1950s, some corporations convinced their banks to assist them in their receipts processing by receiving checks in the mail from customers of the corporations. This was attractive not because of any great realization or concern over mail float but because the firms wanted to relieve the processing workload on their local offices, which were handling the incoming checks and depositing them in their local banks. The RCA Corporation is generally acknowledged as the first corporation to establish lock box arrangements. This was arranged in the late 1940s with several of the firm's banks in New York City, Chicago, and Los Angeles. However, much in the way of further innovation was absent until the later 1960s and 1970s, when the stability and predictability of interest rates disappeared, thereby creating increased interest and activity in improved cash management.

Companies began to take note of the differences between cash balances that were recorded on their own books and on those of their banks. In addition, commercial banks began to recognize noncredit services as a means of establishing a relationship with a corporation. Meanwhile, the Federal Reserve Bank (or the "Fed") provided a major impetus by announcing its Regional Check Processing Center (RCPC) network and with it guaranteed check availability of 0, 1, or 2 days to banks using the Fed for check clearing.[1] This development had great implications from two different aspects. First of all, it established a "worst case" availability schedule for check clearance, and a bank could, therefore, establish a defined, routine check clearing process for its corporate customers. This would enable banks to compete for corporate business, and the banks that were able to offer attractive mail times began to develop substantial corporate lock box business. Banks now knew that they could do no worse than the Fed's schedule, provided they made local deadlines and were able to apply the availability to each item. They could also develop "what if" types of analyses in order to evaluate alternative clearing methods, such as sending larger checks directly to the bank(s) on which the items were drawn or to major correspondent banks in the local areas to obtain better availability. These direct-send networks had been established prior to the Fed's conversion to fixed availability, since many banks found that they could easily beat the Fed availability by using direct sends. The larger Chicago banks were pioneers in establishing far-reaching direct send networks, even after the Fed's changeover since their geographic location, advanced processing systems, and large amount of corporate business permitted them to develop the required volumes or economies of scale to offer improved availabilities over the Fed. With these developments it became extremely important for corporations to study or have studied for them their cash collections in order to compare carefully and evaluate alternative lock box services.

The other major implication of the Fed's enhanced availability was the guaranteed nature of it; that is, the availability was given to the bank by the Fed and, in turn, was usually passed on to large corporate customers regardless of whether the checks cleared by that time period or not. This difference between the availability given and the actual clearing back or "presentment" of the item has led to the creation of "Fed float," or the amount of check clearance (usually measured in dollars) advanced by the Fed by granting availability that differed from the actual clearance. It should be noted, also, that this float is virtually always positive; that is, the Fed never seems to beat the float figure it grants. The U.S. banking system functions such that this float works for the benefit of the writer of the check in that funds do not actually have to be in the writer's bank account until the time the check clears. Legally speaking, of course, the check writer must not write a check without funds in his or her account, or the result can be check kiting. However, kiting is extremely difficult to prove, especially in the corporate setting, since the check writer must have no intention of funding his or her bank account for kiting to occur. Since this is not the case with most corporate disbursements, check kiting in corporate situations is rare and typically only occurs in criminal cases. In any case, corporate cash managers noted that they could delay funding their accounts for some time after their checks were mailed and continue to have use of the funds that would otherwise have been deposited in their disbursement accounts. With this realization and related actions created by it corporate cash management had come of age!

In fairly rapid-fire fashion corporations and banks studied this new concept and gave birth to a myriad of innovative noncredit bank services and improved corporate cash management techniques. During the 1975–1980 time period such new services and techniques as remote (later controlled) disbursing,[2] zero balance banking, concentration accounts, depository transfer checks, automated lock boxes, and a vast array of bank balance reporting systems were introduced or implemented throughout U.S. corporations. The challenge of corporate cash management has become the integration of these services and techniques into the general working capital area of a company, with the treasury function assuming a more significant and active role in corporate financial matters than ever before.

What, then, is the context for corporate cash management? That is, what are its objectives and major areas to be considered in establishing an effective system for corporate cash management? What internal and external factors affect it most heavily? What analytical tools or techniques are available to be used in evaluating present practices or in assessing the feasibility of modified procedures or alternative banking services or arrangements? How does a company define the scope of its cash management function and establish effective control over this function? Furthermore, what lies ahead in newer horizons for corporate cash management?

To begin with, it has become fairly common to regard corporate cash management as a system with interrelationships between a company and its banks as well as between the different operating units and the central treasury staff of the firm itself. To be sure, the extent of the latter is essentially determined by the size of the company, the number and location of its operating units, and the degree to which funds are or are not managed centrally. In any case, corporate cash management will usually have the following essential objectives:

To control and track cash flows.

To optimize internal sources and uses of cash.

To provide adequate external sources of liquidity for the firm.

To manage, in a prudent fashion, external short-term borrowing and/or investment activities.

Thus the scope of corporate cash management encompasses or interacts with many areas of financial management. Among these areas are receivables, disbursements, forecasting, short-term investing and/or borrowing, and general corporate accounting. Different corporations may create varying environments or approaches to these areas, but the common threads remain in each case.

The handling of receivables is often split between the treasury and controller (or accounting) functions of a corporation. The former is concerned with the acceleration and reporting of receipts information, whereas the latter is involved with the recording and resolution of receivables transactions. Through the use of automated statistical models, a company's receipts can be analyzed and optimal collection points determined. Directing customer check payments to bank lock boxes in locations determined in this manner can then decrease the time delays in receiving and clearing these items. Accompanying payment information such as invoices being paid or statements describing the payments in further detail can then be transferred physically or electronically to the accounting users of these data. At the same time the amount of the deposit and the expected clearance time for the checks deposited can be reported or transmitted to the cash manager or corporate cash concentration service. This system mobilizes the company's cash in a simplistic, routine fashion.

Optimizing disbursements has provided great benefits in improving corporate cash management, in both a financial and a control sense. By utilizing various disbursement techniques such as zero balance arrangements, controlled disbursing, or even delayed or staggered funding, a corporation can minimize the amount of excess operating balances existing in the payables and payroll disbursement accounts maintained with its banks. Again, automated models can provide direction in establishing an effective network for this funding function. Just as important is gaining control over these flows so that funds do not remain needlessly in any particular location when they can be utilized elsewhere or invested in short-term money market instruments.

Cash management also entails varying degrees of forecasting. To manage receivables collections and the funding of disbursements effectively, a reliable forecast is required. Most corporations perform some type of forecasting, whether recognized as such or not. Cash management needs for forecasting purposes differ because of timing requirements and the magnitude of the cash flows. In most cases, short-term scheduling of cash, the projection of anticipated cash inflows and outflows for periods ranging from one day up to one month, provides a satisfactory guideline in formulating short-term cash management strategies and planning activities in the money markets. Longer forecasts, which often employ various statistical techniques and approaches, tend to be for longer periods of time than cash scheduling and may have more impact on longer-term financial decisions than day-to-day cash management.

The precision of a company's forecasting activity and its system for managing cash flows impact its short-term borrowing and investment decisions as well. For corporations that are generally in a net borrowing position, optimal use of internally generated funds can forestall additional external borrowings. This can be extremely important in times of higher interest rates. For those firms in excess cash positions, effective scheduling of cash can increase the amount of and usually the return from short-term investments. This area, then, often demonstrates the fruits of labor for cash management to the overall corporation.

Finally, corporate cash management interacts very heavily with general corporate accounting, providing details on the many types of transactions so that they can be properly recorded on the company's books. This interaction has historically had one of the greatest influences on corporate cash management procedures and practices and yet has been one of the least understood areas. The more systematic and automated a cash management function becomes, the simpler and more straightforward are the accounting audit and reporting requirements. The treasury and accounting areas must work together in harmonious fashion in order to avoid serious and frequent internal operating problems.

SECTION 1.2   FUNCTIONAL TREASURY ORGANIZATION

Figure 1.1 illustrates a functional treasury organization for a typical large corporation. Although organizations may differ from firm to firm, the essential treasury functions are represented in the figure. The individual boxes shown represent the treasury functions, not necessarily the actual number of individual staff members involved throughout the activities. The functions connected by solid lines represent those that typically report directly to the treasurer's area while the ones connected by the broken lines represent those areas influenced very heavily by the treasury function. These areas may not be included in the typical treasury organization of a firm but often report to

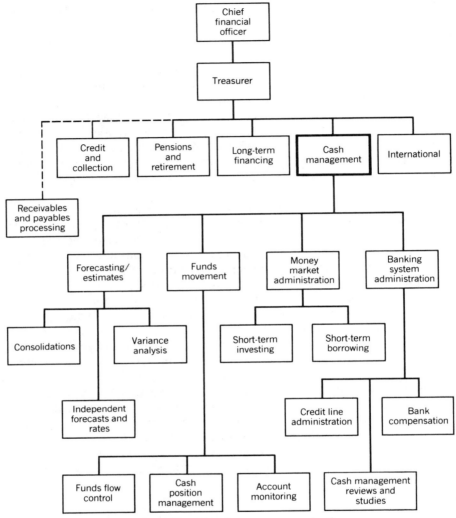

Fig. 1.1   Functional treasury organization.

another operating area of finance such as accounting. The different functional areas reporting directly include pension and retirement fund administration, long-term or special financing and investments, cash management, and international treasury. One or more of these functional areas may be combined, depending on many of the factors discussed below. Our discussion will focus on the cash management area specifically.

The cash management function usually has as its basic activities forecasting, funds movement, money market administration, and banking system administration. Again, depending on the individual corporation, these activities may be combined.

Forecasting involves coordinating and consolidating short-term projections of cash needs and surpluses from the major users and providers of cash throughout the organization. It usually also includes preparing or obtaining independent estimates of future interest rates or other critical factors. The analysis of the variance between actual results and prior estimates is also an important task for this area in order to pinpoint forecasting problems or those factors that have exerted major influence on the precision of the forecast. The standard output provided by forecasting is often viewed as a guide for the other areas of cash management, one that assists in the daily planning for cash management activities. In Section 3.3, we will distinguish between cash forecasting and cash scheduling, but for the purposes of looking at the typical organization the term *forecasting* will encompass both activities.

Funds Movement is often the main nerve center of cash management, entailing the daily cash position maintenance for the corporation, monitoring and controlling key operating bank accounts, and regulating the flow of funds to, from, and within the corporation. This area interacts with the corporation's banking network as well as with the local operating units and other financial areas as appropriate. It may also be involved with the international units by processing funds transfers to and from overseas points. Its activities are influenced by other areas of cash management in that it utilizes the cash forecasts to anticipate or plan for major cash flows; provides funds for or requests funds from money market administration, depending on the net cash position; uses the banking network established by banking system administration; and maintains the target balances for compensation purposes set by banking system administration.

Money market administration functions as the provider of short-term funds when needed or the investor of short-term excesses when available. In the past, this function was considered the primary and perhaps only role of corporate cash management, especially at the central staff location. Today, of course, the entire scope of cash management has been expanded much further. In many corporations the money market activity may not be of sufficient size to require a separate staff and, consequently, may be incorporated into the funds movement activity. In other companies, however, this function is very important and is a separate activity that must interact and coordinate with the daily cash position management for the firm.

Banking system administration provides the liaison between the corporation and its banks for administrative and analytical purposes. General levels of bank compensation, whether paid by fees or balances or for credit or noncredit services, are established here and translated into target balance levels for each bank. It is safe to assume that some level of target balance will remain for each bank even if compensation for services is on a fee basis. This is particularly true for operating banks where maintenance of zero balances is usually extremely difficult if not impossible. This area also conducts special cash management studies that involve the review, evaluation, or modification of existing banking arrangements or daily cash management practices. Such studies can be performed by in-house staff, by the use of outside consultants, or by a combination of the two. By establishing this function as a separate area, the corporation can obtain objective and more timely analyses of its cash management function. This may not be possible if assigned to the other operating areas that cannot devote sufficient time or independent perspective to reviewing ongoing practices or services. It can also serve as a practical and effective entry point into the corporate treasury function for newer staff members to learn the fundamental aspects of the corporate system.

All these functions and their relative structure within the corporate treasury organization are by no means ironclad. In any given situation, any one function may take on a larger, more significant role, thereby determining the appropriate organization. On the other hand, one or more of these functions may be combined under the same treasury area and will be treated on a concurrent or part-time basis. The individual functions are not any less important whatever the individual corporate situation. The functions have to be completed efficiently for sound cash management practices to be maintained.

SECTION 1.3   FACTORS INFLUENCING THE CASH MANAGEMENT FUNCTION

There are a number of additional internal company-related factors that influence, to a large extent, the structure and scope of the firm's cash management function. There are, as well, several key external factors. For purposes of this discussion, the factors will be considered individually. In practice, however, they are quite interrelated.

Company size, in terms of sales and the extent of operations, provides the order of magnitude for cash management. While it may be arguable that smaller corporations have the same problems as larger firms but on a lesser scale, larger corporations are usually able to cost-justify changes in their cash management practices because of the size of their funds flow and resultant savings through system improvements. These firms also tend to deal with far more banks, require more substantial bank credit facilities, and have numerous operating locations. Such situations create the need for an active, specialized cash management function, whereas smaller firms may not possess such concerns, dealing with a relative handful of banks and having few operating locations as a rule. Corporate cash managers will often find more common interests with their counterparts from companies of similar size than in ones of much smaller size within their same industry.

Of course, this does not mean that the *business characteristics* or *mix* of the company is not a major factor. For instance, cash-intensive businesses generate large amounts of funds and usually have large short-term excesses. This requires more cash mobilization and short-term investment activity. Companies whose business encompasses a great deal of retail sales will have different cash management problems and concerns than companies whose major businesses comprise manufacturing and distribution, for example.[3] In cases of department stores or supermarkets, the handling of local store deposits—whether predominantly cash, checks, or credit cards—is a common concern, almost regardless of company size. Only in the smallest of such corporations, where very few retail outlets are involved, will the same concerns with money movement and deposit control not be important. Furthermore, the number of product lines or the presence of a wide variety of types of products can create different problems because of individual characteristics or recurring seasonal peaks and valleys. Companies with a single product or a homogeneous group of products may have stronger tendencies toward centralized cash management, whereas others with a wider mix or those that have grown through merger and acquisition may lean more toward decentralized organizations.

The *centralization* or *decentralization* of the company's operations will probably have a similar effect on the treasury organization as well. It is usually the case in such instances for central staff to be looked on as the provider of the "bare essentials," and cash management has not typically been viewed as one of these. However, many large corporations have discovered that some degree of centralized cash management, if only for funding cash needs and investing or borrowing in the short term, can be extremely effective for the total corporation. Thus we have seen substantial interest in and growth of corporate cash management at most corporations, regardless of the decentralized nature of their operations. In many cases this change has not been easy, as the local operations have been unwilling to relinquish control over their cash management activities. There is no doubt that cash management changes are more difficult and require more time to implement the more decentralized the firm.

The *global scope* of the corporation's operations also influences its cash management activities. The necessary movement of funds to and from overseas points, whether to the company's subsidiary locations or from export customers, affects the overall cash management operations. However, this aspect of cash management (i.e., the global nature of the field) is essentially undeveloped at present and does not exert a major influence on overall corporate cash management. Most corporations have not yet addressed the same issues of organization, reporting, and so on, for international as they have for domestic (U.S.) cash management. To date, most corporations have concentrated only on the foreign exchange and exposure management aspects of international cash management, and they have reflected this in their organizations. This status seems to be slowly changing as the scope of corporate cash management is broadening and the role of the cash manager is becoming wider in geographic terms.

The final internal influence is that exerted on corporate cash management by the *accounting/audit function*. Note that for the purposes of this discussion we have combined the accounting and audit functions. In many cases these areas are separate entities, but we can safely consider them as one. Accounting may often play a leading role in establishing documentation standards between the corporation and its banks, as well as usually performing the reconciliation function for all transactions affecting the cash account on the company's books. Historically, accounting's figure for cash was the only one considered or even monitored on any kind of periodic basis, and much of the cash management function was contained within this area. Sometimes the accounting function can unwittingly influence the cash management greatly. For example, in one company the local, decentralized financial managers possessed a great deal of control over the reporting of financial figures monthly. This was not a major problem for the accounting function as their role was essentially one of consolidating all the financial reports from the different operating units. However, it did pose problems for the treasury function in that information was extremely difficult to obtain, and its accuracy was suspect. For some time, the international cash manager had attempted to obtain current information relating to the banking arrangements overseas and to the levels of excess cash or short-term borrowings. Each subsidiary was fully responsible for its short-term investments and borrowings, and the amount of information reported to corporate staff was minimal at best. In any case, one year all this changed. The accounting department decided that each subsidiary should create an artificial staff entity that would assume all responsibility for short-term investments, borrowings, interest income and expense, and dividend remittances. This change was incorporated into the annual accounting procedures manual update and came as quite a surprise to both the foreign subsidiaries and the international cash manager. Suddenly, the corporate treasury staff was given the responsibility for all cash, investments, and borrowings on a worldwide basis without any change in its authority. In other words, the international cash manager was responsible for investing or borrowing cash and had no authority to do so. The cash manager faced a dilemma; he did not want to receive a telex from his overseas units asking, "What did you want me to do with your cash *yesterday*?" Thus his job was extremely delicate in establishing a standard set of procedures for the local managers to follow, even though they might not receive any direct benefit from their actions. In this case, the treasury function had been saddled with a responsibility that could have been uncontrollable if the foreign financial managers had been unwilling to cooperate readily to assure that effective cash management procedures and practices were followed.

External Factors

Equally important are the external factors. These factors are determined basically by the U.S. banking system and the presence of different types of float with which the cash manager must cope. These factors have been researched by different organizations, and a major part of the education of the typical cash manager has been the understanding of these systems and their relationship or impact on the corporation.

The *banking system* used to be incredibly difficult to comprehend. Each state exerted some amount, however small, of individuality, or so it seemed. With little documentation or obvious overall plan for a nationwide system, corporate cash managers were left to their own devices to cope with the banks around the country. However, as cash management became more popular and both banks and corporations began to develop effective cash management practices, this cloud of mystique that surrounded U.S. banking began to disappear. To be sure, a corporation doing business with banks throughout the country still may encounter difficulties on the local level, but that same corporation has probably been able to develop effective cash management procedures that obviate the need for major interaction with a large number of small, local banks. The breadth of services offered by virtually every major regional bank has made this transition possible. The presence and role of the Fed has also been a major determining factor in this evolutionary process.

Clearly, the most substantial influence the banking system has for the corporate cash manager lies in the check clearing process. Both the Fed and individual banks, through their direct-send programs, are influential factors in check clearance and related availability of funds to the corporation. These two tracks are outlined in Figure 1.2. The basic advantage of the direct send branch is better availability of funds than would be possible through the Fed's branch. Accordingly, the former branch tends to be used for larger dollar items. These clearing processes have aided greatly in streamlining the check clearing performance of the U.S. banking system. In past years the Fed's performance had been somewhat erratic, with the result that the availability it granted to participating banks was better than its actual ability to accomplish. This led to the creation of Fed float, which at times approximated $6 billion.[4] In recent years, however, this gap has been significantly narrowed, with Fed float now in the $2 billion range and dropping.

Much of the overall external influence on cash management is evidenced in the generation of one type of *float* or another. The various types of float affect the corporate cash manager in one or more ways, slowing the collection of checks deposited or delaying the clearing of checks mailed out to vendors. The different types of float are shown schematically in Figure 1.3.

The major types of float shown are mail, processing, check clearance, disbursement, and Fed. The types of float overlap in the sense that one party's mail, processing, and check clearance floats are contained in another's disbursement float. Each corporate cash manager works at reducing the different floats that work against his or her company and, at least to some extent, at extending the float(s) that work for the company. The measurement or estimation of the various floats is the basis for many of the analytical techniques available to the corporate cash manager. As far as any individual

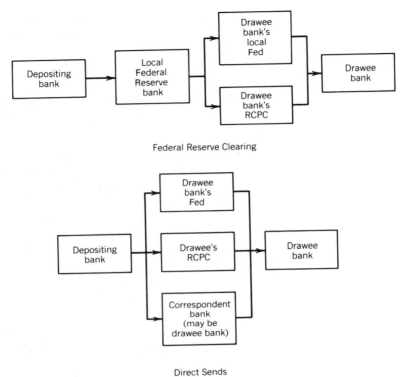

Federal Reserve Clearing

Direct Sends

Fig. 1.2 Check clearance tracks.

cash manager is concerned, disbursement float appears to be the largest type of float involved in cash management. This is due to the manner in which the different types of float are measured on an operating, or normal, basis as opposed to their measurement on an analytical, or opportunity, basis. By this we mean that one type of float may be measured more fully than another type on an operating basis, even though the differential may not be as great on an opportunity basis. A good example of this is evidenced in typical collection studies. Without any empirical study, the only float that is actually measured is check clearance float in that the funds deposited will not be available to the company until they have cleared or have been collected. However, this ignores the mail and processing floats, which, when combined with the clearance float, comprise the major portions of disbursement float. Disbursement float, on the other hand, is measured from the time funds are mailed out or are placed in the company's bank accounts. In this case, the measurement comprises the extent of the float. Accordingly, disbursement float may appear to be far greater than collection float, and many cash

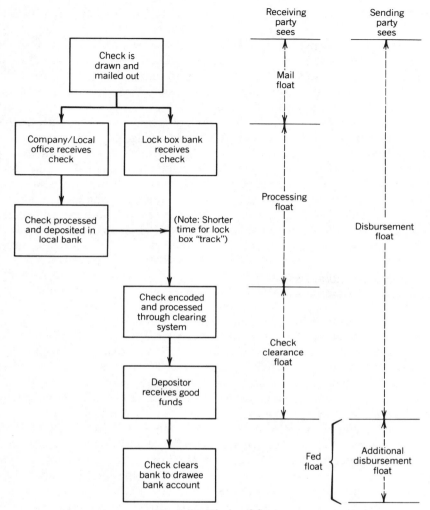

Fig. 1.3   Kinds of float.

managers or treasurers may be misled into concentrating more on this area than on the full spectrum of cash management.[6]

In summary, the influences and roles of internal and external factors affect the overall cash management function of every corporation. The corporate cash manager must coexist with many diverse forces, some of which can be controlled or affected directly by his or her actions. Others will be much more independent, causing more direct effects than the other way around. The knowledgeable cash manager must recognize these differences and devise ways to cope with them on an effective basis.

SECTION 1.4 CASH GATHERING—MANAGING CASH INFLOWS

The corporate cash manager must manage the flows to, from, and within the firm. It is often helpful to view the overall cash flow of a corporation in terms of a pipeline, such as the one shown in Figure 1.4.

At its center is the reservoir, the cash pool. This is the center of the corporation's liquidity, into which and from which all cash should flow. Cash flows in from many sources, such as the collection of accounts receivable remittances from customers, short-term borrowings from banks or other external sources as required, internal company transfers such as subsidiary dividends or loan repayments, proceeds from long-term financial transactions or equity issues, and the liquidation of marketable securities. Cash flows out of the central pool to pay for operating and manufacturing expenses, purchases or additions to long-term assets, employee payroll, income and other taxes, debt and interest as scheduled, dividends to corporate shareholders, and marketable securities. Cash management involves the structuring (in some cases even the erection), regulating, and streamlining of the pipeline. In addition, it requires various tools and techniques to deal with the clogs and leaks in the pipeline that would otherwise affect the smooth flow of the system.

Cash gathering entails the collection of customer remittances and the movement of these receipts to a primary corporate concentration bank. This mobilization and concentration of funds is important insofar as this process creates the cash pool available for satisfying the cash requirements of the firm, such as disbursement funding or investing in short-term money market instruments. The more centralized cash management systems tend to have fewer such concentration points.

Figure 1.5 shows the basic flow of cash receipts. The two essential methods of handling customer payments and entering them into the check clearing system are direct deposit by a company employee at a local bank and the utilization of a bank lock box service. Note that the lock box could also receive mail from company locations. Some firms do this in order to have all remittances deposited through the same bank or group of banks. However, it usually adds to the mail float for those items as well as the bank processing charge. As the figure shows, the deposit "track" depends on the dollar size, volume, and operating location, and the method of concentration depends on the size of the deposit and other factors.

Historically, companies tended toward local deposits, and this method still prevails in smaller corporations, for small local payments, or for very decentralized operations, especially retail department stores, supermarkets, and fast food chains. However, the use of bank lock box services has proliferated in recent years so much that the corporate lock box network of most large firms have become quite far-reaching and sophisticated.

In general, a lock box accelerates collections over local deposits by reducing the mail and local office processing time as well as improving the

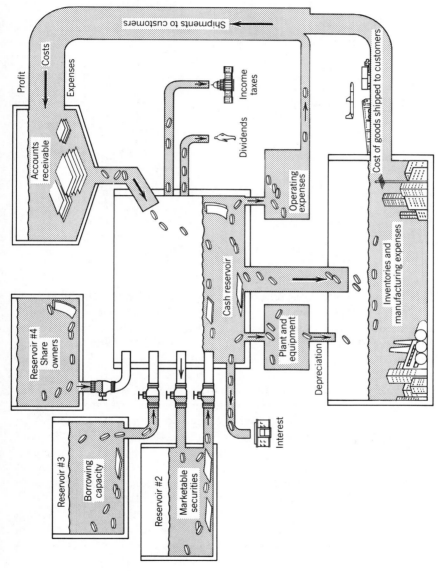

Fig. 1.4 The cash flow pipeline.

Profit

Costs

Expenses

Accounts receivable

Shipments to customers

Income taxes

Dividends

Operating expenses

Cost of goods shipped to customers

Reservoir #4
Share owners

Cash reservoir

Plant and equipment

Inventories and manufacturing expenses

Depreciation

Reservoir #3
Borrowing capacity

Reservoir #2
Marketable securities

Interest

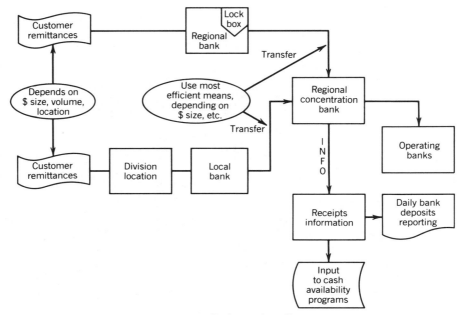

Fig. 1.5 Cash receipts flow.

time required to collect the checks through the clearing system. This is accomplished by instructing customers to send their remittances to a specific point that has been strategically selected. At each point, the corporation will have established a post office box that is accessed by a local bank. These points are usually located in major cities where the Federal Reserve Bank has a major district or branch bank (see Figure 1.6).

It is interesting to note that the first lock boxes were established as individual corporate post office boxes while most current ones are "phantom" boxes. The U.S. Postal Service does not fine sort the mail to the individual boxes but just sorts all boxes for each particular bank together. The bank then does the fine sorting. A unique zip code, favored by many regional and a few money center banks, has the same effect. Many of the "old-timers" in cash management felt that the fine-sort post office box gave them more flexibility in that the bank could be changed without changing the box number. However, they were quite chagrined to find that the Postal Service considered the box as belonging to the bank anyway, thereby eliminating the expected benefit of flexibility. Habit has a way of transcending understanding.

The so-called Fed City points typically offer better mail services; they represent major collection centers for the Postal Service and improved availability in check collection as they can readily access the Fed's clearance system at a minimum. In many of the major centers where a few extremely

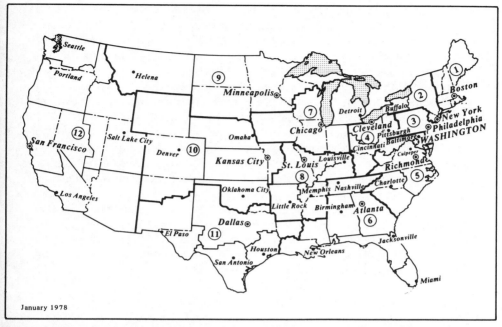

January 1978

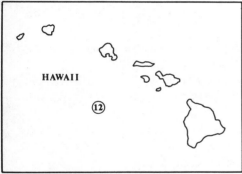

HAWAII

ALASKA

LEGEND

—— Boundaries of Federal Reserve Districts

—— Boundaries of Federal Reserve Branch
Territories

⭐ Board of Governors of the Federal
Reserve System

⊙ Federal Reserve Bank Cities

• Federal Reserve Branch Cities

· Federal Reserve Bank Facility

Fig. 1.6 Boundaries of Federal Reserve Districts and their branch territories.

large commercial banks account for the majority of corporate deposit activity, correspondent banking arrangements are utilized to clear checks faster than the Fed. These direct-send networks have become an important means of check clearance and have permitted many banks outside the major money centers to offer attractive corporate deposit services.

Optimal points are usually selected by reviewing typical remittance data. Occasionally, if the vast majority of payments originate from a narrow geographic area, establishing a lock box nearby requires little analysis other than good common sense. On the other hand, many cash managers may not have the time or inclination to review or analyze detailed data or make clearcut choices. In such instances, a lock box study, such as those offered by most major banks, will be required. These studies are discussed in greater detail in Chapter 2.

In any case, the result is the identification of one or more potential lock box locations. Some of the lock box models also pinpoint specific banks as well, but the selection of the ultimate lock box bank is usually left up to the company. There are a number of major criteria that can prove to be quite helpful in selecting a new lock box location. They include:

The type of lock box service desired (i.e., retail, wholesale, etc.).

Cost of services.

The bank's availability schedule(s) for the mix of items to be sent to the box.

Overall bank relationship (i.e., existing services with the bank, including past experience with the bank's lock box area especially).

Existence of accelerated collection methods such as direct-send arrangements, and whether improved availability is passed on routinely to corporate customers.

Processing cutoffs for reporting deposits and processing daily check receipts.

Number and frequency of daily mail pickups.

Method of assessing float (i.e., whether actual float is assigned to each item, whether it is assigned to each deposit, or whether some sort of float "factor" is used).

Error rates (e.g., percentage of errors as compared with total items handled). Also, the means by which errors are detected and relayed to the company.

Most of these criteria deal with each potential bank objectively and suggest different measures of the sophistication and quality of the respective bank's service. This is quite evident in the criteria dealing with the processing, availability, direct-send programs, float assessment, and error rates. In cases where new relationships are being established, these factors are extremely critical. If a cash manager discovers major discrepancies or deficiencies after initiating a new lock box, it is quite cumbersome and usually somewhat costly to change to another bank. The time required to convert most of the company's customers to sending their remittances to a new lock box configuration usually is in the 60–120-day range, and the decision to switch to another bank adds this amount of time again. Thus it is absolutely critical that the cash manager does his or her "homework" to identify and select the optimal mix of banks for the company's collection system.

Many companies have surveyed potential banks to determine the best bank for a new lock box. However, this procedure is certainly not foolproof in that banks may not provide accurate or sufficient answers to questions that will allow the cash manager to make an effective decision. For instance, a corporation conducted a survey of most major banks throughout the U.S. to document their lock box services. The responses were in the form of completed written questionnaires, and the responses were used to select a bank in a location where no existing bank relationship existed. (A sample of the questionnaire is shown in Exhibit 1.1).

In one far western point a bank was selected because it "offered" actual float on items, and most items came from its regional area rather than the area where the existing lock box was located. However, by monitoring the actual operation and availability obtained through the lock box, it was noted that the bank was not offering actual availability but was using a gross float factor. Thus an ineffective point was established on the basis of the survey, but the expected gain was not realized. In the end, the lock box was shifted, and the bank was viewed with a great deal of suspicion thereafter. The bank–corporation relationship was significantly damaged, and the bank could not expect to be an important operating bank to the firm afterward. More discussion on the means of monitoring bank performance is included in later sections.

The cost of the service can, of course, be an important factor in selecting a bank for lock box services, but for many cases it will only be a minor influence. In these cases the volume of items tends to be relatively small while the size of the individual items is quite large. The major benefit of the lock box comes from the faster check clearance, and this improvement usually far exceeds the differences in the costs for the services among several banks. In other cases where item volume is extremely large and the individual item's value is quite small, lock box cost will be a very important factor and, in fact, may effectively dictate the choice of bank or even whether to use a lock box at all.

In any case, the type of lock box service needed is of major importance. We will consider several types of lock boxes and discuss the special characteristics of each type. The major types are wholesale, retail, automated, and small company lock boxes.

Wholesale lock boxes are characterized by relatively lower volume levels but higher value per item. A typical wholesale lock box would include 500 checks per month with an average value of $5000 per check. The main

EXHIBIT 1.1   LOCK BOX QUESTIONNAIRE

Bank Name _____   Date _____
Lock Box Contact Officer _____
Telephone _____

I. **Mail Pickup**
    Attach or describe your schedule for weekdays.
    _____

    — Any weekend pickups?   ☐ Yes   ☐ No
    — If so, what is the schedule?_____
    — Unique zip code?   ☐ Yes   ☐ No
    — Who fine sorts mail?   ☐ Bank   ☐ Post Office
    — Latest mail pickup time included in current deposit: _____

II. **Processing**
    — Weekday schedule: _____

    — Number of shifts: _____
    — 24-hour processing?   ☐ Yes   ☐ No
    — Weekend schedule: _____   ☐ None
    — Holiday schedule: _____   ☐ None
    — How would processed payment details be delivered?
    _____
    _____

    — Any special delivery arrangements?   ☐ Yes   ☐ No
    — If so, please describe. _____
    _____

    — Do you have different methods of handling retail versus wholesale lock boxes? ☐ Yes   ☐ No
    — If so, please describe. _____
    _____

    — Do you offer data transmission facilities?   ☐ Yes   ☐ No
    — If so, please describe. _____
    _____
    _____

    — Can you process OCR documents?   ☐ Yes   ☐ No
    — If so, describe limitations and/or requirements. _____
    _____

    — Can you process pre-punched cards?   ☐ Yes   ☐ No
    — If so, describe any limitations. _____
    _____

objectives in establishing this type of lock box are optimizing the mail time for receiving customer checks as well as improving the time required to clear these checks and provide the firm with good funds. This float improvement usually far outweighs bank charges, and, accordingly, location and availability schedules are more important decision factors. Envelopes, payment details such as invoice copies or statements and copies of all checks are sent by the bank to the company to permit further processing of the receipts. Such lock boxes are usually located at Fed City points, and companies tend to arrange a network of wholesale lock boxes at strategic, regional points, depending on the geographic spread of the customer base.

EXHIBIT 1.1   *(Continued)*

— Do you offer the following types of lock box output?
(Check all that apply)

☐ Check Photo   ☐ Magnetic Tape (our format)
☐ Punch Cards   ☐ Typed List of Checks
☐ Tapes of MICR Data   ☐ Other (Specify) _____
☐ Paper Tape of Remittances
                                     ☐ Other (Specify) _____

— Describe procedures for handling adjustment: _____
_____
_____
_____
_____
_____

— When are adjustments credited to our account? _____
— Current lock box volume (Monthly): _____ items.
                                     _____ accounts.

III.   **Availability & Reporting**

— How is it determined?   ☐ Actual (per item)
☐ Factor   ☐ Other (Specify)
— If factors are used, how are they set?
☐ By Account   ☐ Overall Factor
— Please attach or describe your most current availability schedule (if appropriate).
_____
_____
_____

— Do you pass along direct send availability?
☐ Yes   ☐ No   ☐ Partial
— Do you currently provide deposit information to:
☐ NDC   ☐ TIP (GE)   ☐ Neither
— What is your cutoff time for reporting same day activity? _____ (local time)
— Can you provide monthly account analysis?   ☐ Yes   ☐ No
— If not, how frequently can they be obtained? _____
_____
_____

IV.   **Pricing**

— Please attach a complete list of standard lock box charges.
— Do you offer the option of direct fees versus compensating balances?   ☐ Yes   ☐ No
— If so, how are fees determined? _____
_____
_____
_____
_____

The next type is the *retail* lock box. Its primary purpose is the efficient processing of high-volume, low-dollar checks, in many cases replacing in-house processing of the items. Examples of retail lock boxes are credit card payments, mail order business payments, or utility bill payments. Typical volumes for retail lock boxes can exceed 100,000 items per month, and typical average item size can be as low as $5–10 per item. Bank charges for retail lock box services are usually quite important, since companies often establish only one such arrangement. Given the smaller dollar size of each item, float considerations are of lesser concern. Many banks do not offer this type of lock box on a manual processing basis as the labor costs can be prohibitive. Usually any enclosed details and only check copies from "exception" items; that is, those items that cannot be routinely processed by the bank according to the company's standard instructions (otherwise considered as "clean" items) are returned to the company. Increasingly, retail lock boxes are being transformed to automated lock boxes by incorporating a machine-readable turnaround document in the billing procedures or by instituting machine capture (even if by manual entry) at the bank.

This introduces the next type, the *automated* lock box. This type of lock box service offers acceleration in the receivables processing as relevant customer remittance data such as customer number, invoice number(s), and dollar amount can be captured in machine-readable form at the bank and transmitted electronically to the company ready to be processed further by the company's computerized data processing systems. Bank charges for this type of service will vary, depending on whether machine-readable documents are utilized or whether manual key entry of receipt data is required. Many banks will not offer this service at all or only in limited fashion as the investment in sophisticated scanning equipment or in many manual key operators is quite substantial and requires significant volumes of data to be economically feasible. Those banks that do offer it may also only choose to use this sort of processing for retail lock box volume levels since wholesale levels can often be handled quite effectively on a manual basis. Lately, however, a few banks have begun to convert most of their lock box processing to this type, because of the rapid increase in labor costs or the scarcity of skilled personnel.[6]

The last type of lock box is an increasingly common one being offered by many banks to their local customers, especially smaller companies in close proximity to the bank. This service entails the bank's receiving customer payments and processing the checks for smaller companies that may not have sufficient internal resources to handle the checks properly on a timely and accurate basis. The bank may also offer this service in conjunction with other services such as accounts receivable processing or cash concentration and automatic investment of excess funds. Clearance and mail float times are not significant, as the items tend to be smaller and drawn on the local area, and the small local company will tend to look to its major bank (if it has more than one bank) for such a service without shopping around. This type of lock box service is offered by many banks throughout the country, even those smaller ones in remote locations as part of the overall services provided or offered by these banks to their local customers.

The essential steps in manual lock box processing are shown in Figure 1.7. The bank accesses a post office box, usually around the clock. In many cities this is a phantom box in that the bank has arranged with the local postal service to reserve a block of lock box numbers for its customers. All mail for this block of numbers is sorted together by the postal service and is picked up by the bank. The bank then fine-sorts the mail down to individual corporate lock boxes and processes the items. In this way, the bank can

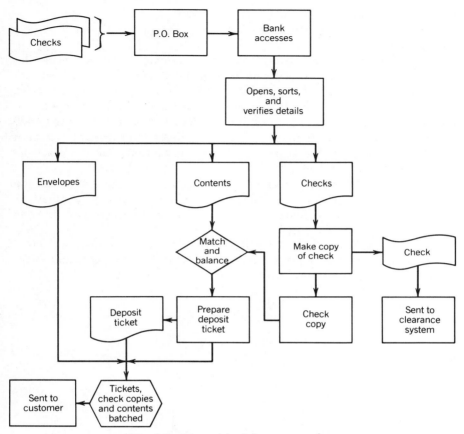

Fig. 1.7   Manual lock box processing.

obtain the mailed items sooner than if the postal service were to sort the items down to individual box numbers. Thus the processing cycle can be accelerated. Some banks also accomplish this acceleration by establishing a unique zip code for the bank. In this case all mail for the bank, including the lock box inputs and post office box numbers, are sorted together by the postal service and fine-sorted by the bank's mail room. The remaining steps in lock box processing are fairly straightforward and really do not vary significantly from bank to bank. A common variation that has diminished in occurrence in recent years entailed the manner in which the bank processed the lock box inputs for each customer. Some banks used to organize the lock box processing on an "assembly line" basis, with each "station" providing a common work step for many customers, other banks used one work station to process all steps for individual or groups of the same customers. Each type naturally felt that its way was better. Today most banks have moved away from the assembly line approach and offer a common work station or group of operating staff to handle a company's receipts on a continual basis.

In establishing a lock box arrangement a company must be certain that processing instructions are acceptable, formalized, and understood between it and the lock box processing staff of its bank so that processing errors are minimized. Often it is essential for the company cash manager and accounts receivable personnel to visit the prospective lock box bank in order to review procedures and ensure that service requirements and procedures are completely understood. This is especially true in the case of a new bank or when special procedures are involved.

Once checks have been received and deposited at a company's bank, the *concentration* of cash must be considered. There are two major methods used by corporations to achieve the concentration of funds—*wire transfers* and *depository transfer checks* (DTC's).

As shown in Figures 1.8 and 1.9, there are a few variations in each method. Regardless of these variations, there are several major aspects and differences that will affect the selection of either basic method:

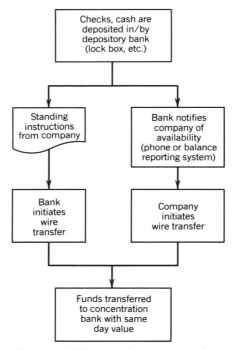

Fig. 1.8   Wire transfer concentration.

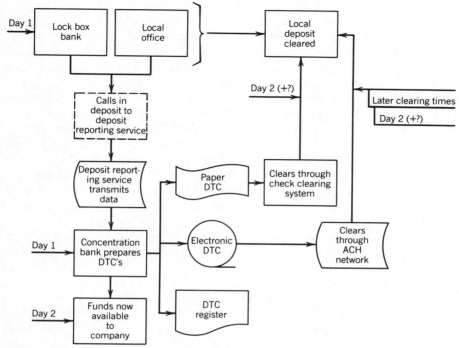

Fig. 1.9   DTC system.

Aspects	Differences
Costs	DTC's significantly cheaper, usually 10–15% of wires.
Control	DTC's offer more timely information in reportable format; wires may depend on sending bank's initiation, thereby creating errors and resulting loss of use of funds.
Reliability	Major problems with wires as compared with DTC's.
Accuracy	No appreciable differences.
Availability of funds	Wires are same-day value; DTC's are one or two days; DTC's may create "dual" balances.
Best Uses	DTC's for many reporting points, especially for smaller amounts; wires for very large amounts or for same-day concentration of funds.

In summary, then, DTC's offer significant cost savings in that much smaller amounts of funds can be concentrated economically. This advantage, coupled with the possible creation of "dual" balances (i.e., good funds in both the sending location and concentration point at the same time) tend to make DTC's considerably more attractive. This has been evident in their increased use by most corporations. The dual balance situation has existed for some time and has been viewed as a key attraction by many corporations in using DTC's. The balances are created when the DTC's take longer to clear back against the depository account than the availability given to the corporation by the concentration bank. This is due to delays in the check clearing process and is essentially underwritten by the Fed. Often, however, this situation is unpredictable, and companies have been unaware of its existence while it occurs but notice it historically. Balance reporting systems can be used to monitor key accounts, but if large numbers of depository accounts are involved, this becomes impractical or too costly. As a result, many companies choose to use any dual balances for compensation purposes, rather than attempt actually to use the funds twice. As the Fed's clearance system has improved, the creation of dual balances has been reduced. Also, the conversion to electronic DTC's will tend to reduce this phenomenon as well, as its existence is due to the paper-based clearance system for the most part. We should note, though, that some companies utilizing electronic DTC's have reported the same situation at many regional banks that do not have an effective electronic interface with their local automated clearing house. In such cases, the banks must prepare a paper entry to clear the electronic DTC, thereby creating a similar situation to paper DTC's. In any case, the dual balance possibility can not be overlooked in assessing the cost–benefit advantages of alternative cash concentration systems. However, it may be extremely difficult to do so quantitatively unless a company has had comparable experience over a suitable period of time with both the depositing location(s) and the concentration point.

It should be noted that wire transfers do offer advantages in special cases where large amounts of funds clear the same day and would otherwise be unavailable to the corporation until the next business day. Although these funds could be used for compensation purposes, many corporations may want to use the funds centrally, especially if the amount of funds exceeds the level required for compensation or if the corporation wishes to pay for its bank services on a fee basis. Many banks can report such same-day clearances in time for the good funds to be moved to the company's concentration point that day. Obviously, if the depositing point also happens to be a major concentration point, the funds can be easily moved and utilized the same day.

The choice of a concentration system depends on many factors, as cited earlier. Once chosen and established, it becomes routine and automatic, a regular procedure or aspect of the overall corporate cash management system. A company does not normally switch concentration systems often,

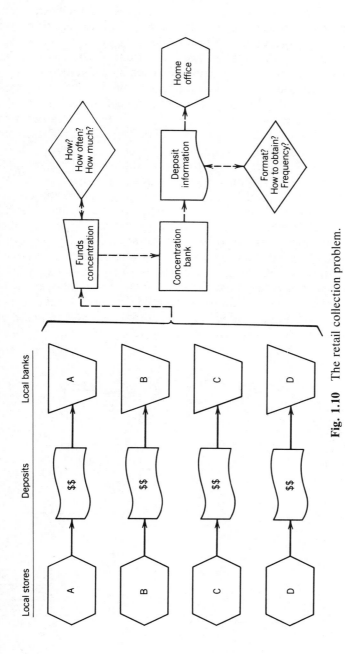

Fig. 1.10 The retail collection problem.

since the disruption to routine, standard operating systems and procedures is apt to cause more problems and resultant loss of funds than could be gained otherwise. The choice of DTC or wire transfer is not optional for each deposit on any given day. This should not be overlooked in the establishment of a funds concentration system. Wire transfers can be effectively used as a backup in emergency situations such as when errors occur in the transmission of deposit information and funds would be left at the depositing location for another day or more. However, if such situations should occur very frequently, there may be serious problems with the structure of the concentration system or the performance of the depositing points in reporting accurately and on a timely basis.

An illustration of funds concentration is shown by the *retail collection problem* (Figure 1.10). With many local deposits at various banks, the concentration of funds centrally can be a major problem for the corporation. Such considerations as the means of transfer, frequency of transfer, maintenance of local balances, availability of funds, and reporting of deposit information are important. Another consideration may be the presence of larger amounts of cash than checks. This is often the case in large supermarket chains, for example. In such cases, these amounts may be too small to warrant wire transfer concentration, yet central control over the funds is desired. Another consideration is the handling of funds on the weekends.

A typical solution to the retail collection problem is shown in Figure 1.11, an *automated DTC system*. The system offers increased control and the

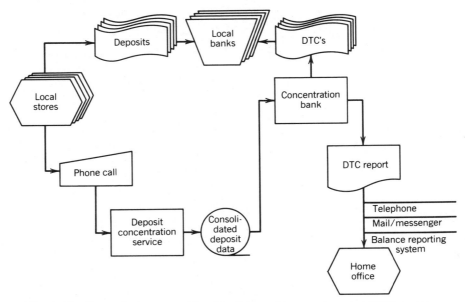

Fig. 1.11 One solution to retail collection problem: automated DTC system.

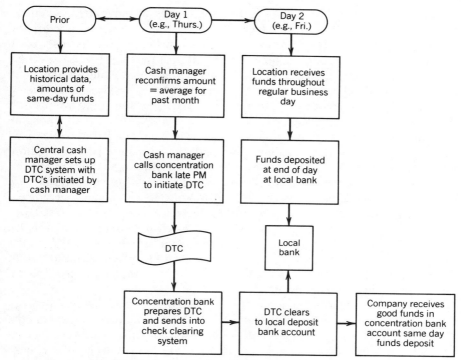

Fig. 1.12 Typical anticipatory DTC system.

automatic upstreaming of funds from many local points. The frequency of DTC preparation is determined by the amount of local deposits and expected clearance times and corresponding availability of funds. As far as the presence of high percentages of cash in the local deposit is concerned, the system can be used on an "anticipatory" basis, creating DTC's prior to actual local deposit so that the funds will clear the same day. For instance, this is feasible for many supermarkets as their business volume is fairly predictable and the flow of funds is sufficient to offset minor differences between actual and anticipated amounts. In such cases, the interchange of information between local points and a central cash management function is critical to the success of the concentration system. This type of anticipatory system is often utilized for weekend deposits as well. A typical anticipatory DTC system is shown in Figure 1.12.

SECTION 1.5 DISBURSEMENT FUNDING AND CASH POSITION MANAGEMENT

Cash disbursing is the next flow that is important to the corporate cash manager, and, for the most part, his or her involvement with the disbursing function will entail the funding of the company's disbursement accounts. Very rarely does the cash manager have any daily responsibility for the actual preparation and distribution of corporate disbursements as this usually resides within the accounting function and often at the local level. However, the corporate cash manager's role in managing the funding of the bank accounts on which normal disbursements are drawn is very important in establishing an efficient cash management system for the company overall. If left to the local managers, disbursement funding will usually become uncontrolled and generate significant operating balances at the banks used for disbursing. These balances are normally far in excess of any required levels, and, given the tendency toward fee compensation methods at present times, they may represent substantial unused funds to the corporation.

There are three basic approaches to funding disbursement accounts— delayed or staggered funding, controlled disbursements, and zero balance account arrangements. Each technique has its own distinct characteristics and application to the corporate cash management system. In addition, the three may exist simultaneously in any corporation, reflecting the different levels of development of cash management expertise or the most optimal method for the circumstances.

The simplest means of funding disbursement accounts is *delayed or staggered funding*. Originally, it was one of the most commonly used methods, as nothing else was available, and astute corporate cash managers noticed that they did not have to fund their disbursements on the day the checks were mailed but could do so some time later. Accordingly, staggered funding was developed. The approach, shown in Figure 1.13, utilizes a formula for transferring funds to the disbursement account, usually based on historical clearing patterns. To the extent that clearing patterns are predictable, this technique can be quite effective in reducing operating balances and extremely simple to implement. In the illustration shown, the disbursement accounts are funded on a percentage basis each business day. Typical applications of this method of funding are still utilized in funding local payrolls, for example. Especially in the case of weekly salary payroll accounts, the pattern of check clearance does not vary substantially from one payroll period to another. Accordingly, the corporate cash manager can utilize this method of funding if payroll accounts are to be maintained locally in order to control the level of balances in outlying bank accounts. This type of funding routine is also applicable to corporate dividend accounts, which also exhibit a fairly predictable clearing pattern. In any case, a corporate cash manager would be interested in this method of funding if he or she were unable to implement any other form or were constrained by corporate organizational or political impediments from taking full control of disbursement funding. A problem can arise if the cash manager does not have an effective cash projection and reporting system for accounts that can be stagger-funded. The local financial manager may not be cognizant of the benefits of delaying the funding or may consider the method a form of check kiting. In such cases, the cash manager

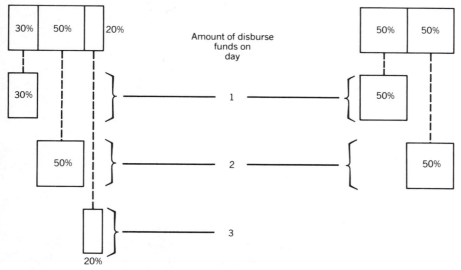

Fig. 1.13   Delayed or staggered funding.

will face an educational challenge with the local manager and may need to enlist the help of his legal staff or bank cash management experts to resolve any problems. The key distinction of a potential kiting situation is the honoring of company or personal checks with the payment of uncollected funds. A staggered funding scheme or other disbursement funding techniques does not utilize uncollected funds but, rather, delays the actual transfer of collected funds to cover the daily check clearings. Furthermore, since the intent of the cash manager is not to create funds or take advantage of the bank's inability to differentiate between collected and uncollected funds, check kiting schemes are extremely rare in occurrence. If present at all, such schemes tend to occur in personal checking accounts.

While staggered funding offers some benefits, it is a fairly crude technique and may not be very effective if the clearing patterns are not very predictable. This is often the case for major disbursement accounts, and some other form of funding is usually necessary. *Controlled disbursing*, shown in Figure 1.14, is such a technique. Originally, this type of funding was only available at banks with remote branches or those that were located in a remote section of the country. Consequently, this technique was first termed *remote disbursing*. As such it was not enthusiastically embraced by most major corporations, which did not want to pay major disbursements from a geographical point with which they had no connection or wished to avoid the disreputable image of taking unfair advantage of the check processing system.[7] However, most corporations were not really interested in elongated disbursement float, but they were interested in controlling that float. This was evidenced in the popular acceptance of controlled disbursing when the latter method was

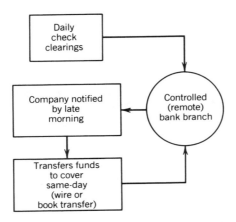

Fig. 1.14 Controlled disbursements.

offered by major money center banks. The basic technique is simple; disbursement accounts are not funded until the day checks are presented against the account, and the controlled disbursement account is located in an isolated branch such that the clearance can be funded on the same day. In fact, most current controlled disbursement points can provide this information by late morning (usually no later than 11 A.M.) so that the corporation can still access the short-term credit markets if necessary. This type of funding can be implemented for any number of corporate accounts, all of which can be funded with one transfer of funds.[8]

With or without the availability of controlled disbursing, one of the major developments in corporate cash management has been the *zero balance account* arrangement. By utilizing this technique, the corporate cash manager has been able to lace together many diverse accounts at the same bank and establish an automatic control of funds flow to and from these accounts and a central concentration account. A typical zero balance account arrangement is shown in Figure 1.15. In this illustration note that accounts can be zero-balanced either way; that is, deposit accounts can automatically upstream funds and disbursement accounts can be funded automatically. The main advantages of such an arrangement are the elimination of excess balances in the operating accounts, the elimination of misguided transfers among various operating accounts, and the reduction of local bank balance monitoring efforts. Zero balance arrangements are effective tools in consolidating cash management activities at a specific bank, and they alter the target balance levels in that they transfer all activity to one central account. This, however, is not an unpleasant situation for most cash managers as they tend to target by bank rather than by individual account. Zero balance accounts (ZBA's) help fine-tune this approach.

If controlled disbursement accounts are not available, it is still possible to establish an effective funding routine, based on the amount of clearings from the previous day. The latter figure is usually the one most commonly

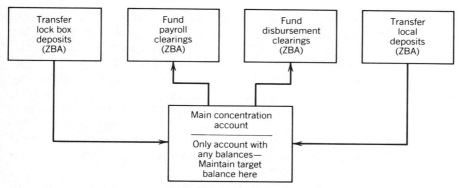

Fig. 1.15   Zero-balance account arrangement.

reported through bank balance reporting systems. It should be noted that this type of funding routine will not be very effective if the corporation does not maintain significant balances with the bank involved. If sufficient balances are maintained and the amount of any daily disbursement clearing does not vary significantly from day to day (this margin should not exceed the overall level of balances that must be maintained at a minimum), a simple funding procedure can be established. First, the company determines its average daily clearance from historical records, a simple task. Next, it transfers that amount into its disbursement account on the day that the funding procedure is to begin. After this, the amount of funds cleared and reported through the bank's balance reporting system will be funded one day later. On average, the account will be properly funded, and the only thing the cash manager has to determine is whether the average amount of clearing has changed over time. If so, a transfer for the difference, especially if it represents an additional deposit into the disbursement account, should be made as appropriate.

In the early days of cash management many companies and knowledgeable consultants recommended the use of *payable-through-drafts* to improve disbursement control and improve the company's disbursement float. Such drafts appear similar in form to checks but are payable by the individual firm, not its bank. The drafts clear back to an issuing bank that, in turn, presents them to the issuing firm for review and approval before any payments are completed. This review period is typically 24 hours. Because drafts are not checks but a form of corporate obligation to pay, they should not be treated as checks by commercial banks. As a result, they would offer little in the way of disbursement float improvement. However, in the past drafts were often treated as checks, thereby offering the issuer extended float as well as improved control over corporate funds. Today, most banks have improved their internal systems so that these mistakes do not occur.

There are, of course, situations in which these drafts can be utilized as effective tools. In instances where local issuance of payments are involved, they can offer effective control over the dispensation of corporate funds. Local insurance agents or salesmen may be the issuers of such items, and a system of review and control may be necessary. In any case, drafts should not be used or recommended for use by corporate cash managers for normal cash disbursements. These items should rightfully be treated as *collection items* by the depositing bank with the lack of credit to the receiving customer until the item clears back to the issuing party and is approved. Thus, the receiving party has not really received payment until the actual review period has expired. This may affect the regular collection process and cause credit problems for the issuer if drafts are used.

A bank service related to disbursements is *account reconciliation*. This service is offered by most banks and is useful for accounts with relatively high volumes of check disbursing activity such as payroll or regular disbursement accounts. It is also used when the company does not have sufficient staff to perform the function in-house. The basic process is very simple. The company sends a record of its checks drawn to the bank, and the bank matches them with the checks that have cleared. Much of this data-matching is done by computer. The company usually receives a listing of all checks paid and those issued but not yet cleared. These reports are used by the accounting function. There are some variations in the type of service, but these normally represent a portion of the overall service described earlier. Companies may be interested in these partial reconciliations when they have their own in-house routines and only need check clearance data from the bank. Some banks can calculate the average clearance time for a company's checks in the reconciling process. This can be useful in establishing funding patterns or in providing cash estimates. However, the computation is dependent on accuracy of the issue date submitted by the company to the bank. Often this field is not carefully completed, with the result that the clearance times are invalid.

Another aid in disbursement funding is the *direct electronic deposit of payroll* (Figure 1.16). This type of arrangement is relatively new and is part of the Electronic Funds Transfer System (EFTS) development. For companies with many diverse employee locations, payrolls have been a tough operating problem. Drawing paychecks on local banks has been the alternative used most often, and the cash manager or local financial manager transfers funds to these accounts by payday or on a staggered funding scheme. With a great number of these accounts, this type of process is inefficient at best and usually creates substantial excess balances in these small local banks. Some companies have consolidated their payrolls into one major bank to keep the excess funds in one central place and utilize other forms of disbursement funding. However, local paycheck cashing privileges must be arranged, and they usually require compensating balances or the equivalent. Direct deposit of payroll offers an electronic alternative to either of these.

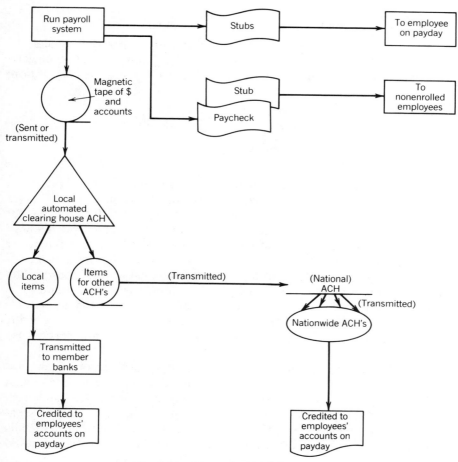

Fig. 1.16   Direct deposit of payroll.

The payroll system run generates data that are transmitted through the Automated Clearing House (ACH) network to the individual employee's bank account. Obviously, the employee's bank must be a member of an ACH somewhere, but the end points are tested thoroughly prior to any real transmissions. This service is attractive to the company with many widespread paying locations, with employees who travel frequently and are not always at one location permanently, or with a need to transfer payrolls to local employees quickly and at relatively low cost. The company does give up the disbursement float generated by the paper-based paychecks, but this may be unproductive for the firm in any case if it remains in local payroll accounts. The cash manager should decide whether the benefits outweigh the costs for his or her particular firm.[9]

Fund Transfers

Although it could be considered as a part of both cash gathering and disbursing, *fund transfers* are significant activities for most cash managers. There are three major reasons for fund transfer activities by the corporation:

Target Balance Maintenance.
Operational Coverage or Concentration.
Internal Company Funding Requests.

Maintaining target balances at major banks often requires a daily decision as to whether funds should be moved in or out of key accounts at each major bank. Similarly, operating banks usually require daily transfer decisions for covering clearings of payroll and accounts payable disbursement fundings or for concentrating deposits at a major bank. Short-term investments or debt repayments require fund transfers as well. Internally, local plant operating or payroll accounts are often funded by local request, rather than by the central corporate cash manager overseeing the local operation. In some companies subsidiaries may run their own cash management systems autonomously from corporate staff, only requesting funds or transferring excess funds daily to the corporate treasury. International transfers can also be an active fund transfer area.

In all, then, the cash manager typically faces a myriad of reasons for transferring funds and requires effective tools to do so. The most common method has been the wire transfer, and it is also the service that many cash managers had the most problems with in dealing with their banks. Essentially, the cash manager telephoned his or her bank to transmit the details of the transfer. This set off a chain reaction of paperwork that resulted ultimately in an electronic transfer being made. Volume in this area has grown dramatically recently, and many banks and corporations have worked together to improve the electronic transfer capabilities available to the cash manager. Today the cash manager can initiate routine, repetitive transfers from his or her main bank account to predetermined receiving points at other banks by sitting down at a timeshare terminal and inputting the data. This can be accomplished for nonroutine transfers as well. For high volumes of transfers this service is quite effective, replacing the makeshift procedures devised by some banks and companies in the past. One such system utilized telecopy machines to transmit written transfer instructions between the cash manager and the bank. While effective to some extent, the terminal-based services are easier to use and have proved to be highly accurate and responsive in use.

The key objective in any funds transfer system is the avoidance of lost or erroneous transfers. Although these errors can never be totally eliminated, the use of terminal-based transfer systems offered by most banks can aid the cash manager greatly. Many cash managers utilize these systems for repetitive transfers only, reverting to the regular telephone method for non-repetitive transfers.

Lost or erroneous transfers pose more than operating headaches for the cash manager. The loss of funds created by the erroneous transfer must be resolved. If the problem has arisen because of the bank's handling or mis-handling of the transfer, the corporate customer can usually obtain compensation from his bank. This compensation is typically figured at the bank's cost of funds (e.g., the Federal Funds rate) for the number of days, including weekends if appropriate, the corporate customer did not have use of the funds. The firm's bank may, in turn, settle in a similar manner with one of its correspondents if the latter bank actually created the error. Obviously, the development and use of more effective transfer systems is attractive to both banks and their corporate customers in order to avoid this painful procedure of compensation.

Other types of transfers exist in addition to the regular wire transfers discussed earlier. DTC's were discussed previously in the cash-gathering section and offer a low-cost concentration method. The use of the ACH network for fund transfers is beginning to be explored. This type of service would handle repetitive transfers, especially those that the cash manager knows about well in advance. The transfers would be "warehoused" in the ACH system and released on the day the funds were required (a predeter-mined date). This procedure is required as the ACH network cannot transfer good funds the same day as regular wire transfer systems can. Therefore, some prior planning and knowledge of amounts are necessary. The attrac-tiveness of this form should be its probable lower cost.

All the various types of fund transfers can play important roles in the daily routine of the cash manager. Different ones can be utilized appropri-ately to concentrate funds or fund local bank accounts. However the different types of transfers are used, they are integral parts of the management of the company's cash position.

Cash Position Management

Cash position management is the focal point of cash flow management in that it represents the core function of the company's funding activities. In most companies of any size or diversity, the cash position must be deter-mined daily by accumulating the inflows and outflows throughout the firm's banking and cash management systems. This typically takes the form of a work sheet, although sometimes this sheet may resemble the back of an envelope. The essential aspects of cash position management are shown in Figure 1.17. The preparation of the work sheet is shown as the central focus for the activity, with the prior day's sheet being recycled to start the new day's sheet. The link between the prior one and the actual results is a reconciling procedure; that is, the cash manager must review actual results

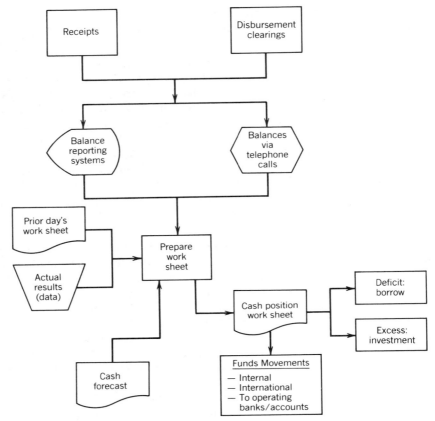

Fig. 1.17 Cash position management.

with the work sheet to determine that everything that was supposed to occur did so. The information from the company's banking network is entered on the new work sheet, as is the current day's cash estimate. The cash position can then be computed, and money market transactions can be initiated to fill deficits or invest excesses. Fund transfers are also triggered by the computation, and appropriate actions are taken. This activity, however mundane it may appear, is a vital and extremely time-sensitive one. Actions must be taken in a short period of time, and the cash position management procedures must be organized in a logical and efficient manner to function smoothly in this dynamic, hectic environment.

NOTES

1. See the Federal Reserve Bank of San Francisco article for further details.
2. See *Business Week* articles, Saltzman, and Wittebort.

3. See Bierce for a good description of J. C. Penney's system.

4. See Hoel and Federal Reserve Bank of Richmond for more about Fed float and check clearing.

5. For yet another type of float, "bureaucratic float," see Krieger and Kramer.

6. See *Cashflow* (Jan–Feb 1982) for newer developments in this area.

7. See *Business Week* (1974 and 1976).

8. For further discussions of controlled disbursements, see Maier (1982) or Ferguson and Maier.

9. See Benton for more on these points.

2 Analyses and Compensation

This chapter deals with the interrelated areas of analyses and bank compensation. These two areas are grouped together because changes in compensation are most often the result of some analytical study, however simple. The various types of studies will be considered, with more detailed emphasis placed on collection and disbursement types. In considering analyses, it is convenient to move on to compensation by concentrating on account analyses, bank service charges, target balance management, and, finally, the elements of a typical bank compensation information system.

One of the major tasks facing the corporate cash manager is the analytical review of existing or potential systems and procedures. It is the major objective of such reviews to improve the overall effectiveness of the firm's cash management system through the use of newer techniques, revised procedures, and elimination of ineffective or unnecessary practices. In the previous chapter the aspects of cash flow and related float management were discussed. In this chapter the application of analytical techniques in that area as well as the bank compensation area will be treated. This section is comprised of a basic discussion of the various types of techniques and tools, general guidelines as to their application, and a detailed description of the most common types of studies, contributed by Ms. Susan Hinko.

SECTION 2.1 TYPES OF ANALYSES

One of the problems in utilizing the various techniques associated with corporate cash management lies in the lack of understanding by the users of the tool or, more importantly, by their supervisors. This is evidenced by the common approach of the latter toward the matter of studying the company's cash management system. Often this activity is viewed quite suspiciously, and the cash manager's request for outside, expert assistance is sometimes viewed rather skeptically or rejected outright. A typical reaction might be, "What do you need a consultant for, that's your job!" The other typical problem that can occur is one in which a senior financial manager (e.g., the treasurer of chief financial officer) "hears about" some new cash management technique. For instance, the cash manager may get ushered into the treasurer's office and asked why the company does not use controlled disbursing or why it does not utilize a new-fangled model that can predict the best location in the entire country for the company's disbursements. In most cases of this sort, the treasurer has previously rejected any such notions or has overlooked the fact that the company is already doing precisely what is being suggested, but he has not understood the changes made to the system. Thus it is vital that the cash manager assure that all members of the treasury staff, both above and below or lateral to the cash manager's position, understand and be aware of the firm's cash management system and the results of all major analytical studies.

Another common problem, or perhaps problematic trait, of analytical techniques is the form of so-called cash management benefits. Hardly any changes are made in a company's cash management systems or procedures unless they provide a substantial financial benefit over current situations. The problem with this lies in the fact that the cash management benefits so estimated are virtually impossible to verify in any real sense. This does not, of course, mean that the results are spurious or even unrepresentative, but because of the nature of most studies, they are, in fact, very difficult to document after the changes have been effected. For example, a lock box study usually takes a sample of one or two months' receipts and simulates what would have happened if those checks had been routed to different combinations of lock box collection points. Obviously, the data are historical, and unless each customer sends similar amounts on similar days of the week and the mail takes the same amount of time, the results will differ. Also, it is impossible to continue to study a collection system in a real-time sense. Thus the lock box model must approximate the opportunity savings of alternate collection systems. This example is not intended to impugn the integrity or veracity of collection studies; it is merely used to point out the nature of the findings. Therefore, the cash manager should bear these considerations in mind before accepting the amounts of potential savings literally. It is recommended that the cash manager apply a great deal of his or her common sense in reviewing any result of a study. If a recommendation does not make sense to the cash manager, based on his or her experience, then it should be questioned seriously before considering implementation. In initially considering alternate lock box collection points for an existing collection system already utilizing lock boxes, a cash manager received a study from his bank consulting team. The study indicated little possible benefit from any changes in the current lock box system, and the cash manager's first inclination was to accept this and go on to other reviews. However, the system had been established many years previously, and the cash manager's experience with the system had given him the impression that the system was not functioning effectively. On further questioning and review, it was discovered that the bank's lock box model contained a fundamental flaw in that it presumed that any lock box in a regional area was comparable to another. On closer inspection, it was also discovered that as many as three or four days of mail and collection float could be reduced through an alternate system. Thus the challenge to the results was quite fruitful in this instance. This type of problem also suggested additional changes to the lock box model to avoid similar problems in the future.

In any case, there are several major types of analytical studies. Collection or lock box studies and disbursement analyses have been the most common by far. These types will be discussed in much finer detail in Ms. Hinko's contribution later in this chapter. Collection studies are intended to determine through quantitative methods optimal collection points for the company's set of data. These points may or may not include any of the current collection points. A normal byproduct of the study is an estimate of the improvement in collections to be obtained from making the optimal changes. Disbursement analyses may take one of two basic forms. The first is essentially a quantitative estimate of current clearing times for corporate checks and may not suggest any major changes in the banking network but may only be used in establishing funding procedures or in developing predictive factors for short-term cash flow scheduling. The other type identifies the optimal location for the company to use in making its disbursements so as to extend the company's disbursement float, or at least that part of the float created by the manner in which the checks are cleared. Collection and disbursement studies can be repeated from time to time, especially if the cash manager has reason to believe that the company's cash flow patterns have changed.

Other studies are more stand-alone in that they tend not to be repeated once completed successfully. Examples of this sort are the overall treasury/organizational reviews or cash management system studies. In these types, the reviews are lengthy, encompassing most aspects of the company's treasury activities, and the recommendations may involve substantial revisions in regular operating procedures and the banking network. Their intent is usually to improve the efficiency of the company's cash management system, and recently they have provided corporate blueprints for major reductions in banking arrangements and for greatly simplifying corporate cash management systems in the process. The major steps in such overall corporate cash management reviews are fairly straightforward:

Review and document current flows, banking arrangements, and responsibilities.

Analyze historical bank balances from major operating banks.

Compare balances maintained with those required for compensation purposes.

Review and compare bank service charges (varies).

Study collections and disbursements in detail (varies).

Devise and recommend alternative system(s) for the company, estimating potential costs and benefits.

These major analytical activities must then be tailored to the company's individual situation and objectives. For instance, the company may wish to evaluate the feasibility of centralizing its cash management functions, instead of continuing with each of the major operating units handling its cash management activities separately. In such a case, the documentation of the current systems is a critical first step and may require a substantial investment of time by the company. In addition, the alternative solutions will have to consider the full impact of organizational changes and the possible reduction of local banking arrangements. Obviously, the enormity of the tasks involved in reviewing the total cash management activities is determined by a number of critical factors.

The most important factors and their primary characteristics are shown in Exhibit 2.1. As outlined in the table, the characteristics define the nature of the review.

The organizational structure of the company can have a direct bearing on how complex and time-consuming a study will be. Often, a major study will be undertaken as part of a major corporate-wide reorganization. Current channels of communication, reporting relationships, and the strength of the financial activity throughout the firm are all important determinants that can affect the study by creating organizational barriers or impeding the effective exchange of information. In addition, the ultimate successful implementation of the study's findings will be dependent on these factors. The cash management awareness of the firm, not just the cash manager or treasury staff, can help or hinder the study as well. If there is little in the way of cash management experience throughout the firm, it may be viewed as a necessary evil by local financial managers who will not be motivated to spend much time on the subject. Thus, a fundamental educational effort must be included within the study itself.

The geographic spread of major locations and the degree of local autonomy are two other major considerations in performing a cash management review. More localized autonomy and decision-making will require more detailed study on-site and the concurrence of local financial managers before any changes can be implemented. On the other hand, the absence of these characteristics may make it easier to perform a cash management review. This is often the case in highly centralized companies or in smaller firms with relatively few locations.

The firm's information systems can provide important support to a cash management review if the treasury area possesses any substantial degree of automation. Lacking this, the regular systems may not be very useful in a review. The review then must be accomplished by using the manual records of the treasury function, thereby creating additional effort for the group conducting the review. In any case, the potential use or availability of in-

EXHIBIT 2.1   CRITICAL FACTORS FOR CASH MANAGEMENT REVIEW

Factors	Primary Characteristics
Organization	Degree of centralization/decentralization, both current and prospective
	Existing communications, formal/informal
	Reporting arrangements
	Strength/importance of finance role to firm (e.g., leading or supporting)
	Cash management experience/proficiency of system participants
Operating locations	Geographic spread, United States and overseas
	Size of each major location, staff, and cash flows
	Business mix, each location and overall
	Levels of local autonomy
	Local control over cash flow initiation
Information systems	Degree of treasury and local automation
	Regular reports available to system participants
	Available data processing resources, systems analysts, hardware, software—internal and external
Cash management services	Current products/services by bank and local operating unit
	Banking relationships, all services
	Level of sophistication for each service

house data processing resources should not be overlooked in conducting the review. The treasury is too often ignored as a user of data processing although it has many a need that can be satisfied by small, in-house applications. It is quite probable that much of the current interest in microcomputers by banks and cash managers alike has come about by the historic indifference of data processing toward the treasury function.

Finally, the scope and effectiveness of current cash management services throughout the firm can greatly influence a review. If there is an absence of any common services such as lock boxes or balance reporting, the review will become more time-consuming and fundamental. If more sophisticated services are already in place, the review will tend to be much simpler, consisting of fine-tuning the existing system by adding other services or modifying procedures as appropriate.

Given the rationale and requirements for a major cash management review, it should not be surprising that most companies must turn to outside experts for assistance. Many of the larger commercial banks, particularly those located in the major money centers, the large public accounting firms, and other independent consulting firms all offer such arrangements for a fee or, in the case of many of the banks, for compensating balances. Most larger corporations faced with the task of selecting a consulting group will usually secure several proposals from one or more of the types of firms mentioned above. The final selection may depend on the firm's demonstrating a solid understanding of the company's problems and a distinguished "track record" of performing such studies. Costs may actually be a secondary consideration, and this is appropriate in that the study will have sufficient importance and impact that a "bargain basement" approach is unwarranted and potentially dangerous. The cash manager or treasurer setting out to conduct such a study cannot afford to engage a group that will cut corners or fail to do a thorough review. The savings from such a study should outweigh the costs substantially, thereby making the direct cost of the study itself a relatively minor consideration. As the study should not have to be repeated if conducted properly in the first place, the selection process should be treated with extreme care.

In the next section, Ms. Susan Hinko will consider in detail typical collection and disbursement studies. Both of these studies represent the majority of analytical effort in cash management to date, and her discussion will show their methodologies and typical findings.

SECTION 2.2   CASH MANAGEMENT CONSULTING*

Structuring and refining an integrated, effective cash management system is one of the major tasks challenging corporate treasury staffs. When cash collection, disbursement, mobilization, investment, and forecasting procedures work efficiently, the firm can realize substantial working capital benefits. However, it is often difficult to gauge the efficiency of an existing system or to determine areas for improvement. Bank cash management consulting departments or specialized treasury consulting services are among the most valuable resources available to assist in the evaluation process.

As corporations have grown more sophisticated in their cash management requirements, commercial banks have been extremely active in developing services and products that facilitate corporate cash management operations. In addition, many management consulting firms now maintain dedicated staff with the necessary technical expertise to provide treasury consulting ser-

---

*This section is written by Ms. Susan Hinko. Ms. Hinko is currently the manager of funds mobilization in the treasurers office at Merrill Lynch Individual Services. She also conducts a cash management course at N.Y.U. School of Continuing Education. She was formerly a cash management consultant with the Chase Manhattan Bank.

vices. These two sources offer various skills at varying costs to help solve the corporate cash manager's problems.

Cash management consultants perform two types of analysis. They can conduct a general audit of the entire cash management function, which usually documents existing systems, discusses the strengths and weaknesses of those systems, and recommends further specific float or technical studies and/or basic structural improvements in the firm's cash management. Or they can perform detailed float analyses of operating cash management systems—collections, disbursements, funds concentration, or information mobilization—and indicate optimal float management decisions within the parameters of existing corporate bank relationships and internal information systems.

Float analyses measure float in terms of days and then translate those days into uncollected balances. The costs associated with supporting those balances is calculated by multiplying the number of float days by the average amount collected or disbursed daily and valuing that amount by the corporation's cost of funds. For example, if a corporation collects $73 million annually and its receipts have an average of four days mail, processing and collection float, the average uncollected balance associated with this float is:

$$\frac{\$73,000,000}{365 \text{ days}} \times 4 \text{ days} = \text{Average daily receipts} \times \text{float} = \$800,000.$$

For a firm with a cost of capital of 12%, the annual cost of receivables/collection float would be $96,000 ($800,000 × 0.12). When float costs for alternative systems are compared, the differences represent the opportunity cost of using one system configuration over another.

The most common float analyses performed are collection and disbursement studies. Actual float study techniques and cases are presented to illustrate the consulting process and its potential benefits. Any dollar savings available from improved float management must always be weighed against the internal administrative costs of modifying an existing system (e.g., printing new invoices, establishing new data processing procedures, etc.). This is especially important in a retail rather than wholesale environment when the receipts or disbursements involve individual consumers rather than other corporations.

Receivables Studies

Objectives.   The primary objective of a receivables study is to define an improved collection system to reduce mail, processing, and collection float associated with converting receipts (checks) into available cash. This is accomplished by:

Quantifying float associated with the current system.
Identifying an optimal lock box network (or networks).

Determining float for alternative networks chosen by the company and comparing these alternatives to the current and optimal systems.

If the current system depends on significant manual office processing of receipts, it is important to quantify the delays resulting from in-house handling of checks. Typical office processing with over-the-counter deposits at a local branch bank will inflate both float and per item processing costs. Some high-volume retailers and insurance companies have established their own dedicated processing facilities operating the same check sorting and encoding equipment as bank lock boxes. When high-volume, low-dollar-amount payments characterize the receipts, an in-house center can be a viable alternative to a bank facility. However, it approximates the automated bank lock box environment and offers the same advantages. Since the relative mail and availability performance of each city would still apply, selecting the location of an in-house facility would follow the same procedure as selecting a bank location.

Study Sample.   A receivables study is based on a typical month's receipts. Photocopies of all checks received during a one-month period and their envelopes provide the necessary data for the study:

   Customer name.
   Date of mailing.
   Date of receipt.
   Zip code source.
   Dollar amount.
   Drawee bank transit routing symbol and ABA number.

Payments from a subsidiary or another corporate division should be excluded, since they can constitute a substantial portion of the receipts and influence the selection of a collection network. They are not considered because any advantage gained from reducing float on these checks is achieved at the expense of another area of the corporation and does not represent a real economic gain. Foreign payments are also excluded, since mail and collection times may not be available for foreign locations. In addition, a dollar cut-off is established for including checks (e.g., $1000, $5000) since 45–50% of the items typically represent 85–95% of the dollars in corporate to corporate payments. A retail payments study would require a more detailed statistical sampling procedure.

It is crucial that the study checks represent one twelfth of the annual corporate receipts or the projected float cost savings will be over- or understated. If necessary, the receipts should be factored up or down to reflect a one-month sample. In addition, a study is only useful when a corporation's customer mix remains fairly stable from one billing cycle to the next. If there is variability in the zip code sources of checks, a lock box network that is optimal for one set of customers may not be appropriate for another. Usually a corporation has the same customers from month to month, but a study should be based on a sample that includes a typical geographic mix of remittance sources and drawee banks. The largest customers should also be represented appropriately; however, if they pay quarterly or semiannually, their payments should be adjusted accordingly so as not to bias the sample.

These preliminary adjustments are important because concentrations of remittance sources or drawee banks among the receipts will affect the dollar-weighted calculations of float for various networks.

Study Procedures.   The ability of an efficiently placed lock box network to minimize the float associated with a particular collection system is contingent on the presence of certain characteristics in the remittances:

Geographic concentration of the check's zip code sources.
Geographic concentration of the check's drawee banks.
Proximity of check source and drawee bank.
Limited use of remotely located banks as drawee locations.

Strong concentrations of drawee banks and remittance sources can facilitate the effectiveness of a small lock box network with locations near those concentrations. The correlation between the two types of concentrations will allow a network to minimize both the mail and collection float simultaneously. For example, if half a corporation's remittances is mailed from New York and the other half is mailed from San Francisco, two lock boxes (one in New York and one in San Francisco) will minimize the float for the system only if the checks mailed from New York are drawn on New York banks and the checks from San Francisco are drawn on San Francisco banks. However, if the checks mailed from San Francisco are drawn on banks in Montana and Texas and the checks mailed from New York are drawn on banks in Georgia and North Carolina, the most effective lock box network may include Chicago, Dallas, Atlanta, and Charlotte. Even these four locations may not be able to minimize mail and collection float completely, since one kind of float may be minimized at the expense of the other. Often a customer will deliberately engage in this type of activity in order to extend disbursement float, and in certain industries (e.g., food supply or retailing) this type of "controlled" disbursement is common practice.

Once the salient characteristics of the receipts are determined, float for the current collection system and alternative systems is computer generated based on a matrix of mail and collection times between cities. Mail float is a function of the geographic location of payee and payor. Mail times are measured by Phoenix–Hecht, Inc. between 106 primary zip code sources and approximately 50 potential lock box sites three times a year and expressed in both the latest times and smoothed average times that capture the trends in performance. The Phoenix–Hecht times are utilized by most banks performing float analyses to form a data base for projection of mail times for current, alternative, and optimal systems.

Some banks will present actual mail float calculations determined from the postmark date and the date of receipt and/or deposit. However, since projections of mail times for all alternative systems are based on Phoenix–Hecht times, this procedure can be misleading. Actual mail times can exceed Phoenix–Hecht times by as much as 1.5 days because of:

Stale meter marks on predated mail.

Illegible postmarks obscuring the date mailed.

Holidays that interrupt normal mail service.

Cancellation date errors in transit.

Skewed percentages of mail in transit over a weekend.

Different measurement procedures (banks usually measure time in days, Phoenix–Hecht measures in tenths of a day).

Thus the Phoenix–Hecht times should be employed in a simulation of the current system and serve as a benchmark against which alternatives can be measured.

Processing float can involve several hours or days in an office processing environment or two or three hours in a lock box processing environment. Usually a lock box simulation model will include processing time when calculating an item's ability to meet an availability schedule cut-off time.

Collection float is calculated for each item based on a matching of the check's receipt time to the availability schedules for the banks on which the check is drawn. Some bank consulting services rely on published Federal Reserve availability schedules to determine float rather than actual bank availability schedules. Given the substantial differences in the ability of banks to clear checks and in the availability that they offer lock box clients, relying on the Federal Reserve schedules is not a precise measure of the relative differences in clearing capabilities among collection locations. Thus many aggressive cash management banks usually bypass the Federal Reserve check clearing system by maintaining direct-send programs with many other banks to clear their checks. By sending checks directly to the banks on which they are drawn, these banks can substantially outperform the published Federal Reserve schedules and should be represented as accurately as possible in a receivables analysis. With the Fed's movement toward pricing its services more competitively, establishing fractional availability calculations, and revising Federal Reserve presentment times throughout the country, direct-send programs may become less attractive for banks and clearing patterns may change. However, it will take some time before the true effect of these policies will be felt.

The mail time and availability data bases generate a float matrix based on the mail arrival patterns in a city. This matrix interacts with the sending locations and drawee banks of the sample to project optimal and alternative solutions. The optimal locations can be determined on the basis of an integer programming algorithm or with an "additive" heuristic approach. The integer programming model finds the optimal locations for each system configuration; the additive approach finds the optimal one-box solution and then adds the next best location as the network expands. This approach ignores the fact that while Chicago may be the single best collection location for a company's receipts, the optimal two-box system would be Dallas and Philadelphia, based on the geographic distribution of the receipts. Alternative solutions are usually "forced" solutions where a client-specified set of cities is assumed as the network, and the float is computed accordingly.

A lock box analysis will determine the optimal system based solely on float considerations, compare it to alternative solutions that include cities where corporate banking relationships already exist, and evaluate the opportunity cost of one system versus another. The model will project float, number of items, and dollar amounts for items routed to each location in these simulated systems. Routing is performed by the model based on the zip code source and the drawee bank of the items. Sometimes substantial benefits can be achieved by simply rerouting customers within the current system, since they may be sending checks to a suboptimal location as a result of haphazard lock box location assignment, a change in corporate accounts payable operations, or a lack of explicit directions by the receiving company.

A receivables study will recommend a final collection system to the corporation based on the float advantages available and the constraints of the corporation's banking network.

A Case Study.   A receivables study was performed for a subsidiary of a major transportation company that had no lock boxes and processed all receipts in local sales offices. The company collected $100 million annually in six sales offices around the country. The actual sample contained 700 items totaling $740 million after exclusion of intracompany payments and foreign receipts. Since the typical month's receipts were slightly higher than those collected during this 31-day sample period, rather than use the month's daily receipts of $238,000, the annualized daily receipts of $249,000 were determined by subtracting 1% of the dollars from $100 million (to represent the typical proportion of foreign and intracompany items) and dividing the result by 365. The company chose 12% as the cost of funds rate.

This particular study was fairly straightforward except for the effect of office processing. Instead of simulating the current system's mail times based on the Phoenix–Hecht figures, the actual time (from mailing date to date of deposit) was calculated for receipts received in each office location. A day was then subtracted from the dollar-weighted totals to achieve normalization with the Phoenix–Hecht numbers for the projected systems. This enabled the company to determine exactly which offices were holding checks for several days before depositing them and to assess the impact of office processing on float. The offices with the smallest volume of checks were delaying deposit of checks until several had been received, rather than depositing them immediately. Since the head office, with the largest dollar/item volume, was fairly efficient in processing the items, the dollar-weighted totals for the current system were projected at 2.66 days mail and processing float and 1.88 days collection float, for a total float of 4.54 days. This translates into $1.1 million in equivalent uncollected balances and $133,000 in float costs.

The remittance sources and drawee banks were heavily concentrated; 75% of the dollar volume was mailed from New York or Illinois and 86% of the dollar volume was drawn on banks in the New York or Chicago Federal Reserve districts. Although 30% of the dollars were drawn on banks located outside the Federal Reserve district from which they were mailed, this was not a particularly serious problem, since two major sources were identified as the basis of the uncorrelated mail source/drawee endpoints:

Two large customers remitting 16% of the dollar volume were drawing checks on controlled disbursement banks.

Various customers (representing 8% of total dollar volume) were drawing checks on New York banks rather than local banks near corporate headquarters.

Nevertheless, since 44% of the dollar volume was drawn on banks outside major Federal Reserve cities, it would not be possible to reduce collection float to less than one day for those items. For example, both Chicago and New York City banks give one-day availability on the checks drawn on upstate New York banks. Thus mail times would influence the selection of a lock box more than availability for those dollars.

The optimal one-city location for the company was Chicago, with 2.73 days projected float (1.58 days mail and 1.15 days collection float), reducing float by 1.81 days, equivalent balances by $442,000, and float costs by $53,000. The optimal two-city location (Chicago and Newark) was projected to generate 2.57 days float (1.49 days mail and 1.08 days collection). This would reduce balances by $481,000 and save $57,000 in float costs. Addition of the third lock box in Houston would only produce a projected incremental float reduction of 0.01 days and save $300 more in float costs over the optimal two-city solution. Figure 2.1 gives a comparison of the various systems and their projected float cost savings. Notice that a substantial portion of the float reduction derives from the decreased mail and processing float despite

Float days   (Current system float days 4.54)

Optimal and alternative
one-box solutions   Float cost savings (in $000)

Chicago	2.73	$53.0
Newark	2.99	$45.4
Philadelphia	3.16	$40.6
Pittsburgh	3.18	$39.8
Detroit	3.46	$31.6

Optimal and alternative
two-box solutions

Chicago-Newark	2.57	$57.7
Chicago-New York	2.71	$53.6
Chicago-Philadelphia	2.72	$52.7

Optimal
three-box solution

| Chicago-Newark-Houston | 2.56 | $58.0 |

Optimal
four-box solution

| Chicago-Newark-Houston-Phila | 2.55 | $58.3 |

Fig. 2.1   Float days and float cost savings.

the collapsing of the system to fewer collection points. This emphasizes the inefficiencies of regional office processing.

Since corporate headquarters were in New York and since a lock box system would be a new experience, the client expressed interest in the opportunity cost of maintaining a single lock box in the metropolitan area. Several New York City banks maintain post office boxes in Newark, since with the special bank pick-up service, Newark mail times are faster than those to Manhattan. Thus single-city solutions in Newark and New York were projected for the receipts and the opportunity cost of collecting all the receivables in Newark rather than the optimal location, Chicago, was only 0.26 days float and $7600 in float costs. Since the customer already maintained significant banking relationships in New York and since the administration of a New York box would be easier than that of a Chicago box (data transmission, balance reporting, time in transit, etc.), the internal control advantages of collecting receipts in Newark outweighed the small additional float costs.

Disbursement Studies

Objectives.   The primary objective of a disbursement study is to identify a disbursement system that will maximize clearing float within the parameters of corporate financial policy and banking relationships. Those parameters will determine whether or not a company will write its checks on a bank in, say, Helena, Montana, or another remote location (usually at a distance from corporate headquarters) where the physical difficulties involved in presenting the checks for payment may extend the company's disbursement float significantly.

In some industries (e.g., food processing and wholesaling) intentional "remote disbursing" is a prevalent and tolerated practice. In some industries (e.g., natural resources) remote disbursing is accepted because the country banks are located near corporate headquarters. However, in many industries, intentional remote disbursing is unacceptable and compromises the corporate image. Furthermore, Federal Reserve regulators have been discouraging small country banks from offering this service, since the dollars flowing through the disbursement accounts can exceed the assets of the bank, thereby endangering its solvency.

In lieu of remote disbursing, "controlled disbursing" has been developing in many areas of the country. A controlled disbursing facility is located in a Federal Reserve regional check processing center (RCPC) that receives only one cash letter a day, early in the morning. This cash letter may include 95% of the checks presented to the bank that day for payment. The early-morning arrival of the cash letter and the large percentage of each day's checks arriving in the letter enable the bank to inform the company of the required funding that day, usually by 11 A.M. This procedure eliminates the need for the company to maintain idle balances in an account to fund checks, since it can transfer funds when notified of the dollar volume of clearing checks. Thus the company can control its cash balances and derive more effective short-term investment of the surplus.

The emergence of controlled disbursing facilities in RCPCs located near major metropolitan areas that are maintained by major metropolitan banks or their holding company affiliates has modified the primary objective of float extension for some companies doing a disbursement analysis.

In order to achieve the objectives established by a corporation for a disbursement study, the group performing the study will:

Quantify the float for the current disbursement system.

Rank potential disbursement locations based on projected float.

Identify the projected float benefits of utilizing multiple disbursement locations.

Study Sample.   A disbursement study is based on a typical month's payments. As in a receivables study, it is crucial that the sample contain one twelfth of the annual corporate disbursements, since potential savings are calculated on the basis of annualized figures. In addition, study recommendations are most effective when the payee composition is consistent from month to month. Intracompany payments, payroll checks, tax payments, dividend checks, and other "nonfloatable" items are excluded from the study. A dollar cut-off is also determined to eliminate the smaller items that are not significant to the decision process.

The data required for a study will vary with the sophistication of the study procedure. A customized study approach will examine the actual disbursement checks to obtain:

Payee name.

Date of issue.

Date of first deposit.

Bank of first deposit transit routing number.

Date paid.

Payee zip code.

A less refined procedure would involve calculating dollar amounts sent to payees in the 106 primary zip codes, assuming that the deposit bank routing code corresponds geographically to the payee zip codes. This is a sound assumption, since a payee will generally not receive a check in one city and deposit it in another. In fact, corporate payees are usually collecting these disbursements in a lock box, which acts as the firm's agent.

Study Procedures.   Projected clearing times for various disbursement location alternatives are usually based on the average times published in the Phoenix–Hecht, Inc. check clearing studies distributed twice a year. These studies determine the current and smoothed average clearing times for $1.00 checks between 113 potential deposit locations and 113 potential drawee locations. Some cash management groups develop a supplemental data base of clearing times based on the clearing times of large dollar deposits, since those checks are often processed more rapidly than smaller checks.

If the data set includes only dollar volumes sent to each deposit point, the study is fairly straightforward. Clearing times for a disbursement account in each of the 113 potential drawee locations are projected based on the configuration of dollar volumes in the current deposit locations for the company's payees. In addition, the best two-location, three-location, and so on, disbursement network will be projected with the disbursement dollar volume for each bank location provided. It is interesting to note that with disbursements there are usually minimal gains available by expanding beyond two locations, and even a two-location network usually provides substantial benefits only to the top Fortune 100 firms.

Once the disbursement locations are ranked on the basis of projected clearing times, the company can choose the location with the longest clearing times that is also compatible with corporate banking relationships and control requirements. The potential gains available from selecting one location over another are expressed in terms of the value of available balances associated with the clearing float. This is calculated as indicated below:

$$
\begin{array}{ccccc}
\text{projected} & & \text{average} & & \text{equivalent} & & \text{corporate} & & \text{value of} \\
\text{clearing} & \times & \text{daily} & = & \text{available} & \times & \text{cost of} & = & \text{available} \\
\text{times} & & \text{disbursement} & & \text{balances} & & \text{funds} & & \text{balances}
\end{array}
$$

A more sophisticated approach utilizes the information available from the actual disbursement checks to generate a profile of the dollars by issue date, payment date, percentage paid each day after issue, and large-dollar customers. Also dollar-weighted actual mail and processing times are calculated for the month's disbursement checks, and the actual clearing time is compared to the projected clearing time for the current drawee location. This identifies any deviations in the actual clearing processes. This level of detail generates an accurate current summary of the corporate disbursement procedures and payee characteristics, offering valuable information beyond the clearing float advantages of various drawee locations.

The core of a disbursement analysis remains, however, the projected clearing float for alternative drawee locations. Disbursement studies assume that the mail and processing float remain constant, since accounts payable functions tend to be centralized and the payee tends to collect and deposit a check in the same place. Nevertheless, it is interesting to note that the payee may subsequently conduct a receivables analysis and change a remittance location for particular disbursement checks. As the process is dynamic, a company should perform receivables and disbursement studies at regular intervals to achieve and maintain optimal float advantages.

A Case Study.   A disbursement study was conducted for a large industrial corporation with more than $1.5 billion in sales, maintaining five disbursement accounts in the United States. Each account cleared a relatively stable percentage of the $0.7 billion annual disbursements from month to month, with the majority of the dollar volume being paid through two separate RCPC accounts at the same location. The corporate accounts payable function was centralized at corporate headquarters on the east coast, where checks were issued. The dollar amounts and percentages for the sample month follow.

Bank Location	Monthly $ Disbursed	% of Total Disbursement
1. Bank A: Utica RCPC	6,883,000	11.4
2. Bank B: Utica RCPC	38,779,000	64.4
3. Chicago City Bank	6,284,000	10.4
4. San Francisco City Bank	2,125,000	3.5
5. Milwaukee RCPC Bank	6,238,000	10.3

The clearing float for each disbursement account was projected and the consolidated weighted-average clearing time for the entire disbursement network was also calculated as follows:

Bank Location	Clearing Float (days)	Equivalent Balances ($)
1	2.88	650,000
2	2.11	2,690,000
3	1.05	216,000
4	1.19	83,000
5	2.07	424,000
Consolidated network	2.05	4,060,000

Alternative systems were subsequently compared to the consolidated system, which served as a benchmark for the current system. The equivalent balances were determined by multiplying the average daily disbursements for each account by the clearing float for that account. The consolidated average daily disbursement was $1.983 million and the annual value of the existing float was $406,000 (equivalent balances of $4.06 million valued at the 10% cost of funds for the company).

Although this company was utilizing a controlled disbursement location for 75.8% of its payments, the concentration of payees on the east coast (58% of the dollar volume being deposited in New York and New Jersey) limited the effectiveness of this disbursement location in terms of clearing float. The ranking of single drawee locations identified several other RCPC locations that offered controlled disbursing facilities with substantial clearing float benefits. Thus Seattle RCPC and Milwaukee RCPC, with 3.04 days and 2.97 days expected clearing float, respectively, appeared as attractive and viable one-site alternatives to the current five-bank system (see Exhibit 2.1A). Either would increase the clearing float and equivalent balances by nearly one day and generate over $3.5 million in available balances.

More remote locations were rejected either because they were inconsistent with corporate policies and existing banking relationships or because the firm wanted to retain the control and information advantages it derived from the controlled disbursing accounts. Note that even centralization of all the disbursements in a Utica RCPC account would be a 0.36-day improvement over the current five-bank system. The west coast and Midwest accounts reduce the total possible clearing float because of aggressive direct-send programs maintained by major banks to metropolitan areas. Thus, moving all disbursements to an RCPC account would generate incremental, if not maximal, benefits.

Because of the volume of disbursement dollars and the network of existing banking relationships, the company was interested in determining the benefits available from a two-location network. The company selected 20 po-

EXHIBIT 2.1A SINGLE-LOCATION DRAWEE ALTERNATIVES

Location	Expected Clearing (days)	Float (Annual) @ Above Rate ($000)
Montana Country	4.33	1 717
El Paso Country	3.63	1 443
Helena	3.29	1 304
Dallas RCPC	3.12	1 239
Charleston RCPC	3.12	1 236
Salt Lake RCPC	3.09	1 227
San Francisco RCPC	3.08	1 220
Seattle RCPC	3.04	1 214
Milwaukee RCPC	2.97	1 178
Little Rock RCPC	2.97	1 177
El Paso	2.96	1 175

tential drawee locations from the initial ranking, and clearing times were projected for combinations of the 20 locations. Exhibit 2.2 presents the strongest two-location rankings. A third location was not considered, since the potential float benefit was only 0.01 days.

The results of this analysis were well received by the firm. A two-location network that would utilize existing banking relationships at controlled dis-

EXHIBIT 2.2 DOUBLE-LOCATION DRAWEE ALTERNATIVES

Alternative	Expected Clearing	Annual Float ($000)
Seattle RCPC & Milwaukee RCPC	3.18	1 262
Seattle RCPC & Louisville RCPC	3.17	1 259
Seattle RCPC & Memphis RCPC	3.17	1 259
Milwaukee RCPC & Utica (NY) RCPC	3.17	1 259
Louisville RCPC & Milwaukee RCPC	3.17	1 257
Memphis RCPC & Milwaukee RCPC	3.17	1 256
Seattle RCPC & Utica (NY) RCPC	3.17	1 256
Portland RCPC & Milwaukee RCPC	3.13	1 242
Seattle RCPC & Nashville RCPC	3.12	1 237
Seattle RCPC & Virginia RCPC	3.11	1 235
Seattle RCPC & Atlanta RCPC	3.11	1 234

bursement facilities in Utica and Milwaukee RCPCs was among the best alternatives (with 3.17 days projected float) and would extend clearing float 0.3 days over the preferred single-location alternative. However, the proportion of dollars disbursed on each bank had to be reversed to achieve these gains. Disbursements from the Milwaukee RCPC Bank would increase to 71.7%, whereas the dollars disbursed on the Utica bank would decrease to 28.3%.

These studies illustrate the insight and assistance, as well as technical expertise, that consultants can provide in the cash management decision-making process. The consultants were able to analyze objectively the current receivables system and structure a new, more efficient yet politically viable system that the corporation could implement. They served the useful purpose of acting as outside catalysts for change. Frequently, the internal resistance to restructuring a system can slow down the process and consultants can facilitate the movement toward innovation by providing an analytical framework for decision making. Proposing a system that was not optimal but that recognized the internal constraints of a company in transition insured that the company would not simply shelve the recommendations but act on them. On the disbursements side, the consultants were able to save the client firm substantial internal administrative costs by reducing the number of disbursing banks while generating additional float and balances. Using consultants for this kind of realignment and refinement of large, sophisticated systems can also yield significant cash flow benefits.

Selecting consultants can be a difficult process but it is worth the time and effort to talk to several groups before selecting them. The best consultant is one who can explain the methodology that will be applied and the rationale for that methodology. In addition, the consultant should be sensitive to the internal constraints of the organization as well as the structure of the corporate banking relationships. The optimal solution for maximizing short-term profits may not be the optimal solution for maximizing the long-term value of the firm if it disrupts existing banking/credit relationships. Developing an ongoing relationship with cash management specialists at several banks will keep the cash manager aware of technological developments in the field as well as educate the banks of trends and concerns in the corporation's treasury policies.

During the study process, it is crucial for the corporate cash manager to stay involved, contributing to the direction of the analysis and guiding the recommendations. This involvement serves to:

Evolve realistic solutions compatible with corporate policies.

Ensure basic data integrity.

Tailor the study procedure to the corporation.

Educate the corporate cash manager in the current cash flow patterns and the implications of alternatives.

A cash management study should produce not only recommendations for improved systems and procedures but a valuable data profile of the corporation's cash flow (e.g., day-of-the-week patterns, geographic patterns, etc.) that can be utilized in other areas of treasury decision making. Working together, the corporate cash manager and the consultants can achieve significant ongoing benefits for the firm.

The analytic aspects are the major areas of focus for academic research in the cash management field as this area seemingly offers fertile ground for the application of many quantitative techniques. However most of the academic work has proven of minimal practical application. This limitation may be caused by unrealistic assumptions such as a high degree of precision in cash flow data, or a lack of understanding of the daily operating procedures for basic cash management functions. The typical cash manager's reaction to the majority of the theoretical models is something like: "That's interesting but that isn't the way it works here." Also, most systems require actions by many diverse parties. To build in too unwieldy a methodology is inviting errors, as many cash managers have learned. It seems that the main role of academic research in the cash management field should be to provoke thought about specific issues while providing useful analytic tools. The tools however, must be developed with more pragmatic features in a language understandable to the typical cash manager. For some other aspects of this topic and some diverse examples of academic studies see Maier and Vander Weide (1982, 1983), Gitman et al., (1979), Stone and Hill (1982), and Kallberg et al., (1982).

SECTION 2.3   BANK SELECTION

A banking acquaintance was always fond of saying, "There's no such thing as a free lunch," usually around the time the waiter was distributing the menus! This statement aptly describes the underlying basis for discussing corporate bank compensation. Put in other words, the corporate cash manager and the treasurer should not expect to get something for nothing from any of the company's banks. The mutual objective of the corporation–bank relationship should be to assure that a reasonable level of compensation is understood and provided for all credit and noncredit services. Attempting to construct a corporate cash management system based on utilizing various banks' "loss leader" services is at best imprudent and at worst doomed to failure. In addition, trading one bank against another in order to secure cut-rate costs for services will only be effective for a short time. Once this tactic has been exhausted, the imprudent cash manager and his corporation will find their tasks far more difficult than if a more rational, reasonable approach had been adopted. Senior financial management, the treasury staff, and other users of bank services should be aware or made aware that bank services have a cost associated with them, no matter how trivial the service. This should come as no surprise and should be considered in the same light as other financial areas. It is the cash manager's responsibility to optimize the firm's banking costs, educating upper management as to the nature and level of these costs and maintaining cordial banking relations concurrently. The key to succeeding in this endeavor lies in the utilization of a reasonable and systematic approach to bank compensation. Bank costs must be identified, quantified, and monitored routinely. This can be effectively accomplished without a large-scale effort.

Historically, bank compensation essentially consisted of a gentleman's understanding between a corporate treasurer and his bankers. Since interest rates were rather low and relatively static in nature, neither side felt the need to determine precisely the amount of compensation required. The system was quite simple—the treasurer and his cash manager knew that they had to maintain 10–15% of the company's credit line in the form of "clear" balances with each of the firm's banks. These balances could be established and maintained by keeping a separate account with the appropriate amount or, even simpler, by funding disbursements at the time checks were sent out. In this manner the disbursement float generated would easily create sufficient balance levels to compensate the banks. These balances could, for instance, come from the float generated by a local or fairly autonomous operating unit, thereby not requiring any "corporate staff" funds. These balances were also usually large enough to compensate the bank for the noncredit bank services it provided, thus creating the notion, especially in the minds of the local financial manager, that the bank services were being provided free of any charge. If the balances were short in any particular month, the company would raise them the next. In any case, their bankers could be counted on to point out any serious deficits and recommend appropriate amounts of compensating balances.

However, interest rates did not remain either low or static in the 1960s and early 1970s, and both bankers and corporate treasurers and cash managers became aware of the levels of compensating balances. Corporations initiated large-scale studies, often utilizing bank cash management consultants, to investigate and analyze the actual levels of and reasons for the balances being maintained throughout the corporation's banking network.[1] In addition, the need for massive credit lines was reassessed. The net result over time was a request for more precise measures of compensation levels, but still in the form of balances. To answer this banks began the preparation and distribution of statements that broke down the compensation levels required of their customers. These *account analysis statements* itemized the corporation's activities with the bank and showed the bank's service charges for each account. By assigning a hypothetical value to the average collected balances maintained by the corporation with the bank and adjusting the balances for regulatory reserve requirements, the "value" of the balances could be compared with the accumulated service charges for the reported period (usually a month). Thus the corporate cash manager could identify any deficits or excesses and make adjustments to the balances maintained with the bank. Balances required for credit lines were not normally shown on these statements, so the cash manager had to add them in as well. Some banks converted the charges to balances to make the comparison simpler. The cash manager also added all deficits and/or excesses to determine the net position for each bank, rather than attempt to balance each account. The underlying assumption was, of course, that if the value of the balances equaled the charges, the bank would not require any other compensation for noncredit services. In recent times the account analyses have become more descriptive and have encouraged companies to compare similar charges among their banks. The account analysis statements have also proved to be extremely informative and educational to cash managers and have assisted them in devising appropriate compensation methods and strategies.

In establishing new banking relationships and in assessing or modifying existing ones, a logical framework of workable criteria is required. There are several general criteria that can assist the cash manager and treasurer in this task:

Role of the bank.
Services needed.
Sophistication and quality of services.
Location.

The *role of the bank* is the overall guide for selecting or modifying the relationship. The cash manager must first decide whether the bank is to play a major role as one or the only concentration bank for the company, thereby fulfilling a substantial portion of the firm's needs. On the other hand, the bank may only be expected to be a regional collector of funds or even a local payroll bank. If the bank is to play a major role, it will have to provide various services to allow the firm to gain control over and effectively mobilize its cash. It will also probably play a major role in the credit requirements of the firm and in general become an important financial resource and advisor for the company. The number of such relationships will usually be dependent on the size of the firm and the nature of its organization and relative internal autonomies. It is obvious that this type of role and banking relationship does not materialize overnight and must be developed in a consistent, logical manner. In addition, it signifies a major commitment from both the corporation and the bank and is not typically changed haphazardly or irrationally. The "lead" bank relationship is something continually sought by most banks, and when established, it is relatively stable. From the company's point of view, it is desirable to have one or a few major relationships in order to concentrate its cash and take advantage of more advanced services and techniques. The attractiveness of a stabilized, effective banking network is also a major factor in establishing major roles for a firm's banks. In the past, there was a tendency on the part of the cash manager and the lead bank to become complacent in that the lead relationship was viewed as sacrosanct. However, in recent years this has not always been the case, and banks and corporations today must continue to work on the lead relationship if it is to be effective and lasting. In any case, though, once a lead relationship has been developed and the bank (or banks) and the company are satisfied that a proper level of compensation has been established, that bank (or banks) will have an advantage over other banks. This is due to the willingness of the company's treasury staff to discuss problems and needs with its major banks first and the ability of a major bank to consider the overall profitability of the firm to the bank in instituting newer services.

If, on the other hand, the bank is expected to play a less major role in the overall corporate network, this should be understood by the treasury staff and the bank at the beginning of any new relationship. This does not mean, of course, that any such bank can never expand its role, but it and the company should not be misled about the role it will be playing. In fulfilling this secondary role the bank should be certain that it will receive the proper level of compensation. This means that the charges for the services should be such that it will not lose money by providing the company with those services. As the bank does not have many different services to be able to "bundle up" its charges, each one it provides should be able to stand on its own. These secondary banks should not be considered lightly by the corporate cash manager, however, as they often provide critical services and serve as key collection points in the corporation's overall cash management system. As such, their selection becomes an extremely important decision in constructing an effective cash management system and supporting bank network.

Finally, banks may be needed at the local level for plant payrolls or small, operating accounts. The selection of these banks is less critical than that of the other types of banks previously discussed, but it does require some attention. Often the local plant personnel will recommend one or two banks because the banks are located conveniently to the plant, have offered personal banking services to local company personnel, or have provided financial assistance to incoming employees or in local financial matters. In states with widespread branching, it may be possible to utilize a local branch of one of the company's major banking relationships, thus keeping that local banking point "in the family."

Implicit in the consideration of a bank's role is the identification by the corporate cash manager of the *type of service needed* with each bank. Obviously, different banks are better suited to offer various types of credit and noncredit services, depending on their size, location, or internal resources. For instance, if a corporation desires substantial lines of credit, it will probably first look at the larger banks, which can offer more credit than the smaller banks. Likewise, if a lock box service is needed, banks located in major cities with more advanced lock box services will offer a more attractive alternative than banks located in more remote cities.

Just as important as the type of service needed is the *degree of sophistication required* for that service. If a company requires an automated lock box service, for example, it must seek out those banks that can provide such a service efficiently and cost-effectively. In considering this aspect of bank selection, the corporate cash manager should expect to be charged more for more sophisticated services than for the regular, "plain vanilla" services. Closely related to the degree of sophistication is the issue of the quality of the service; that is, the relative error rate, efficiency of the service in terms of completion of daily workload on a timely basis or the incorporation of improved productivity measures or work standards in the work flow, or the ability of the bank to provide customized services to various customers economically and efficiently. In order to profile or catalog the differences among the many banks that offer similar services, companies have developed internal questionnaires or lists of criteria to use in investigating new services. One such listing is shown in Exhibit 2.3.

The example shown is for the selection of a lock box location, and it shows the different factors that a cash manager should consider in establishing a new point. Such factors as the availability schedules and methodology of the bank are noted, as are the service charges, operational working guidelines and cutoffs, and some measure of the error rate. These factors, together with reference contacts for representative customers, should enable the cash manager to arrive at an informed, objective decision. The company's own experience with a particular bank could obviously be substituted for one of the references as the case may be.

The last aspect of bank selection is that of the *location of the bank*. Because the U.S. banking system does not permit interstate branching, a corporation doing business in various parts of the country or, more especially, a corporation with one or more plants located in different areas of the country will probably have to establish some sort of local operating relationships. These arrangements may be quite minor or relatively significant, depending on the company and location involved. The more decen-

---

EXHIBIT 2.3 LOCK BOX SELECTION CRITERIA

Criteria for Selecting a Lock Box Bank

Bank's availability schedule.

Benefits of faster collection (direct sends) passed along.

Cost of service (in terms of fees or balances).

Cutoff times.

Number and frequency of daily pickups.

Use of float factor or actual float charged.

Error rate (e.g., expressed as percentage of items processed).

tralized a company's treasury is, the larger the size of local bank relations will be. Thus location can, of its own accord, become a substantial decision criterion in bank selection. If a company's unit is going to make its own treasury decisions but its local banks do not offer many highly sophisticated services, this latter factor may not be very relevant in selecting a bank. However, this should not suggest that a company facing such a situation is helpless. The obvious solution is to determine whether the utilization of a more sophisticated service than the local banks can supply will outweigh the need to maintain local control; that is, perhaps the transfer of certain cash management services to a centralized group, suggested by the lack of local offering of the service, will be of substantial benefit to the overall corporation. This is undoubtedly the manner in which many of the central cash management groups got started in the past and why banks in the major money centers were able to develop and offer sophisticated cash management services before their regional counterparts.

SECTION 2.4   ACCOUNT ANALYSES AND BANK SERVICE CHARGES

The most common reports received by a company from its banks are the bank account analysis statements, usually referred to just as account analyses. An account analysis is a detailed statement prepared by a bank for each corporate account, normally on a monthly basis. The report shows the service charges associated with the activity for each account for the period and computes a theoretical profit that the bank earned on the average balances in the account over the period.

Although the formats for account analyses differ widely from bank to bank, the main elements will usually include the average daily ledger and collected balances (figured on a calendar day basis), an earnings allowance calculated on the collected balance adjusted for the bank's reserve requirements, and the service charges for the individual account, typically itemized by more detailed activity components. Service charges are often converted into collected balances and shown on the account analysis in that form as well. Relatively few banks show only required balances for the service activity. Typically not shown on individual account analyses are such items as required compensation for lines of credit, "intangible" bank services such as employee mortgage assistance, or arrangements for the double counting of operating balances for both service charge activity and lines of credit. These items may be included on an overall company summary or may be detailed in an accompanying cover letter from the bank officer in charge of the company's accounts. It should be noted that the existence of double counting of balances is all but extinct currently. Formerly, banks would allow companies to apply the average collected balances maintained with the bank toward the compensation of service charges and apply the same balances toward compensation for credit lines. Usually, the company did not maintain sufficient operating balances to cover the compensation requirements for lines of credit, normally 10% of the line. Thus the companies had to keep additional balances with the bank. However, double counting was really lowering the effective percentage of compensation, and as these effective rates were offered directly, it was not surprising that double counting should disappear. Intangible services used to encompass many services that were not itemized on the account analysis. However, as most banks have improved their internal reporting and incorporated inputs from individual operating areas of the bank, the number of services that cannot be included on an account analysis has been reduced dramatically. Currently, these types of services tend to be in the mortgage assistance or related area. However, as many companies have their own programs for relocation assistance or even mortgage assistance, the need for additional bank compensation has diminished. For all practical purposes, intangible services currently can be considered as corporate good will balances.

Earnings credit or allowance rates differ from bank to bank in the way the rate is set each month. This practice varies widely, ranging from a mysterious rate with no identification of the underlying bases to various averages (30 days to 3 months; simple and moving) of a money market rate, usually the U.S. Treasury Bill rate. In addition, some banks show a deduction for reserve requirements whereas others adjust the earnings allowance for it.

A simplified sample account analysis is shown in Exhibit 2.4. On the top portion of the statement are shown the balance history for the month and the earnings allowance calculation. The uncollected funds or float represent the average daily amount of funds deposited that have not yet cleared and become good funds to the company. The available or free balance is the average daily balance after the bank has assessed the account for its reserve requirements. In practice, of course, the bank does not do this account by account, but it settles its position in aggregate with the Federal Reserve Bank weekly. This computation represents an apportioning of this overall reserve figure. The next portion of the statement details the service charges for the account and itemizes the activity for the account for the month. This itemization includes the monthly volume, a unit charge for the type of activity, and the total charge for the activity for the month. Also shown in this illustration is the collected balance equivalent for the total service charge for each type of activity. Summing the total service charges shows whether the account created a profit or a loss to the bank for the period. The sum of the collected balance equivalents shows the excess (if a profit) or deficit (if a loss) in terms of average collected balances. This figure, then, represents the amount of extra or insufficient balances that are in this particular account. Most account analyses describe this amount as being available to support other services, since the calculation is a theoretical and historical one. This is due to the fact that the position of just one account cannot determine or

EXHIBIT 2.4   SAMPLE ACCOUNT ANALYSIS

GOTHAM STATE BANK—MONTHLY ACCOUNT ANALYSIS
Customer Acct. No. 141-62-2481   For FEB 83
     Title: General Account
Customer: VIP Company, Inc.
     New York, NY

Average ledger balance	$ 150,000
Average float/uncollected funds	50,000
Average collected balance	100,000
Reserve requirement @ 12.0%	12,000
Average available (free) balance	88,000
Earnings credit allowance @ 10.0% (0.833%/mo)	733

SERVICES & CHARGES

Service	Volume	Unit Charge	Total Charges	Collected Balances Required
Checks Deposited	250	0.10	$ 25	$ 3,409
Deposits	20	0.45	9	1,227
Checks paid	150	0.16	24	3,273
Wire transfers—in	5	10.00	50	6,818
Wire transfers—out	15	8.00	120	16,364
Account maintenance	1	15.00	15	2,045
Grand total			$ 243	$ 33,136

Net profit (loss) on account $ 490

Excess collected balances available for other services $ 54,864

At this earnings credit allowance rate, $1.00 of service charges requires
$ 136.36   in collected balances.

fully reflect the overall position of the company with its bank. Thus this type of computation must be made over all accounts the company maintains with the bank to determine whether, in aggregate, the bank was sufficiently compensated for the services, both credit and noncredit, it provided the firm. This overall computation is often included by the bank in a customer summary, an illustration of which is shown in Exhibit 2.5.

The summary shows the total balances maintained in all accounts, the balances required for noncredit services, and the compensating balances required for credit services. If the balances maintained equal the required, the bank should be adequately compensated for the services it provided to the company. To the extent that excesses exist, the company can treat them

EXHIBIT 2.5   ACCOUNT ANALYSIS—CUSTOMER SUMMARY

GOTHAM STATE BANK—MONTHLY ACCOUNT ANALYSIS
Customer: VIP Company, Inc.
　　　　　　New York, NY
***** CUSTOMER SUMMARY *****　　　　　　　　　　　For FEB 83

Average ledger balance	$ 6,045,300
Average float/uncollected funds	1,103,200
Average collected balance	4,942,100
Reserve requirement @ 12.0%	593,100
Average available (free) balance	4,349,000
Earnings credit allowance @ 10.0% (0.833%/mo)	36,240

SERVICES & CHARGES		
Service	Total Charges	Collected Balances Required
Lock box deposits	$ 120.00	$ 16,400
Checks paid	525.00	71,600
Checks deposited	1945.00	265,200
Deposit tickets	200.00	27,300
Transfers out	850.00	115,900
Transfers in	400.00	54,500
Account reconciliation	2000.00	272,700
Custody/safekeeping	2500.00	340,900
Balance reporting	875.00	119,300
Account maintenance	300.00	40,900
International transfers	225.00	30,700
Grand total/noncredit service	9940.00	1,355,400
Credit lines $25,000,000 @ 10.0%		
Compensating balances required		$ 2,500,000
Total compensating balance requirements		$ 3,855,400
Balances available for other services		$ 493,640
Additional balances required		$ _____

as "good will" balances, or, as is more often the case, deal with this net position on an average basis. Companies may compute a "rolling" average over the most current year, for instance, or they may treat the net position on an average year-to-date basis, resetting to zero at the beginning of each calendar year. In either case, both the bank and the company should be certain that they are both working on the same basis to avoid major misunderstandings over the appropriate levels of compensation.

Note that the collected balance equivalent of one dollar of service charge was shown on the sample account analysis. This conversion is possible by using the monthly earnings credit and reserve requirement rates as follows:

$$ECB = \frac{SC}{EC* (1.0 - RR)}$$

where ECB is the collected balance equivalent, SC is the service charge to be converted, EC is the monthly earnings credit rate (computed by dividing the annual rate shown on the account analysis by 12), and RR is the bank's reserve requirement as shown on the account analysis. In cases in which the reserve requirement has been incorporated into the earnings credit rate, the divisor of the formula simply becomes the monthly earnings credit rate.

This conversion formula is useful in reviewing account analyses that only show service charges. These charges can then be converted to determine the excess or deficit in terms of collected balances. If many such conversions are to be made, computing the collected balance equivalent of $1.00 is helpful in that this answer can then be easily multiplied by the amount of service charges for each account to determine the balances required for each account or activity. The purpose of converting to equivalent collected balances is associated with the cash manager's need to know what amount of balances must be maintained on average with the bank for compensation purposes. This compensation will be accomplished by establishing an overall target balance for the bank and attempting to maintain that target on average over time. (See a later section on target balances for more details.) Therefore the cash manager must find a common denominator for compensating all banks, and collected balances are the usual means. Note that collected balances are used for this purpose, not ledger or free balances. Ledger balances are not used because they also include float and, accordingly, do not reflect good balances to the bank or the firm. On the other hand, free balances are collected balances less reserve requirements, and such balances are not normally reported by banks daily. Thus collected balances represent the most appropriate measure, being good funds and usually reported daily by the bank to its corporate customer.

The methods of charging for noncredit services vary substantially from bank to bank. The trend currently is toward the "unbundling" of service charges, that is, the breaking down of services into smaller units of activity and charging for each portion of the overall service. This is done so that a company is charged for the steps it requires, rather than assessing each customer on an average basis regardless of the extra activities associated with any one customer. This newer approach can make the account analyses quite lengthy and make comparisons between banks for "similar" services all but impossible. Even without this breakdown into subcomponents, comparing service charges between banks is difficult because banks computed their charges in different ways. There are usually two types of major components of service charges: standard charges, which occur fairly commonly on any account analysis, and nonstandard charges, which are usually created by an individual bank for its service charges.

Typical examples of the types of standard and nonstandard components are shown in Exhibit 2.6. A sample of the unbundled approach is shown in Exhibit 2.7. Note that in the latter example, the components of the charge are work-related, rather than just a different method of pricing. In this manner the more work steps the company requires, the more it will have to pay. Also, the unbundled approach differentiates between automated services and those that entail more manual support by the bank. Such services are priced accordingly.

Despite these differences in pricing and approach among banks, it is still possible and useful to compare services across banks. This type of comparison assumes that the services themselves are comparable among the corporation's banks. If this is so, then grouping banks according to their location can provide some interesting insights into the differences in charges for basic bank services. Three basic groupings are appropriate for this purpose: Major Fed City (New York, Chicago, San Francisco/Los Angeles), Other Fed City (Boston, St. Louis, Charlotte, etc.), and Fed Country Points (locations with no Fed branch, such as Indianapolis). Such a comparison is shown in Figure 2.2 for various services in terms of collected balances

EXHIBIT 2.6 MAJOR SERVICE CHARGE COMPONENTS

Standard Charges (relatively common)

Per item charges for checks paid and/or deposited.

Monthly account maintenance.

Wire transfers—outgoing.

Special activities—lock box, account reconciliation, etc.

Nonstandard Charges (peculiar to bank)

FDIC assessment.

Wire transfers—incoming.

Different charges for types of wires (e.g., phone calls, terminal—initiation, repetitive).

Deposit ticket charge (per deposit).

Cash and currency provided.

Check cashing.

Debit/credit memo charges (per ticket).

Encoded check discounts.

Volume rate differentials.

Maintenance charges different for various types of accounts (e.g., controlled disbursements, zero balance accounts, lock boxes).

EXHIBIT 2.7   UNBUNDLED SERVICE CHARGE PRICING

SEABOARD NATIONAL BANK & TRUST—ANALYSIS FOR:
JMP CORPORATION
New York, NY

	For the month of 2/83
Ledger balance (average daily)	$ 250,525
Deposit float (average daily)	124,320
Collected balance (average daily)	126,205

SERVICES

	Volume	Collected Balances Required
Account maintenance	1	$ 1,400
Deposits	45	4,360
Checks deposited	820	12,620
Lock box reporting	FLAT	5,700
Lock box processing	FLAT	2,850
Lock box items handled	800	22,340
Lock box photos made	820	11,500
DTC's paid	20	320
Returned items	10	11,140
Total		$ 72,230
Balances available for other services		$ 53,975
Earnings allowance on collected balances		10.5%

required. Units of 100 items were used for lock box and reconciliation to reflect the differences in bank pricing methods for these services. Also, the effective earnings allowance figures represent the balance equivalent for $1.00 of service charges. Thus for that profile the higher values are less desirable, as it will take more in collected balances than otherwise. In the other profiles shown, the higher values, typically for the Major Fed City averages, represent higher charges for the same service. The orders of magnitude shown in the chart reflect the average charges (or balance equivalents) for a representative number of banks in each type of location.

One of the other types of comparison a cash manager might wish to do is shown in Figure 2.3. This represents the components of the total required balance "pie," broken down by the type of activity and including the average float as well. In other words, the chart represents all balances that must be maintained by the company with its banks for noncredit services in ledger balance terms. In the typical examples shown, float, or uncollected balances, on average was 37% of this total. The next biggest activity was for deposits,

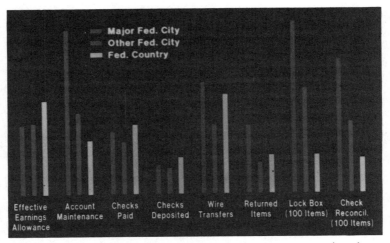

Fig. 2.2 Relative collected balances required to support service charges.

reflecting the relatively higher costs for lock boxes and related concentration services. Note in this case that the company also itemized its intangible services as well. This pie does not include the compensation requirements for credit lines, but the cash manager who prepared the profile showed it as a subscript. The noncredit service charges were 44% of the total required

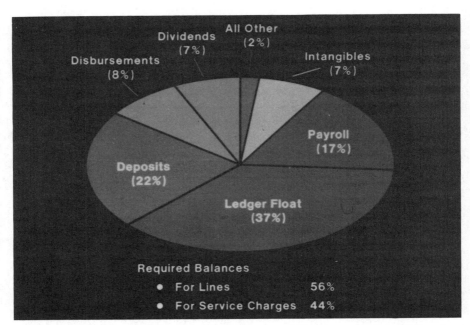

Fig. 2.3 Components of required balances (excluding support of credit lines).

balances, while credit services accounted for the remainder. These percentages were computed in collected balance terms; that is, not reflecting the float figure shown.

Finally, the calculation of a *float factor* for each depository or lock box account is possible by using data from the account analyses for such accounts and internal data. The latter are the total funds deposited in the account for the month. Dividing this monthly deposit figure by the number of calendar days in the month yields the average daily deposit. Then if this average daily deposit figure is divided into the average daily float (either shown directly on the account analysis or computed by subtracting the collected balance from the ledger balance), the answer is the average number of days deposits are taking to clear. Performing this computation for all major depository accounts, whether lock box or local depositories, can provide a simple and effective means of monitoring check clearance float in various corporate banks. A method of comparing and monitoring this type of report is discussed later in this section.

SECTION 2.5   BANK COMPENSATION

Traditionally, bank compensation consisted primarily of balances maintained by the corporation with its many banks. This form of compensation seemed satisfactory to both sides in that it was a relatively easy task to monitor the balance levels and make any necessary adjustments over time. It was also not very precise in that corporations tended to keep excesses more often than deficits. The cost of funds was relatively small, and the banks were a primary source of short-term funds. Recently, however, corporate cash managers have begun to fine-tune their compensation methods and have found balances to be both cumbersome and unattractive in doing so. They are cumbersome because of the time lags in reporting service activity charges (the monthly account analyses) and thereby adjusting target balances properly or at least more responsively. They are unattractive because of the cost of maintaining the balances as compared with alternative corporate uses for the compensating balances. Therefore in recent years more and more companies are changing their methods of compensation from compensating balances to other forms of compensation. These other forms usually are one of two types—non-interest-bearing certificates of deposit (C.D.'s) or fees.

Non-interest-bearing C.D.'s, or in some cases time deposits, are attractive for compensation purposes for two reasons. First, the reserve requirements on this type of account are much lower than those for regular corporate checking accounts, typically being as much as one third the amount assessed on regular accounts. This means that a dollar kept in a non-interest-bearing C.D. will be worth more in terms of the amount of service charges it covers. This can be demonstrated by considering the conversion formula given previously for collected balance equivalents of service charges. The effect of lower reserve requirements is to increase the collected balance equivalent of the same amount of service charge, or, put another way, it will increase the service charge equivalent of the same balance. The other attractive reason for using this form of compensation is that banks will usually use a different earnings credit rate for this form as compared with the rate used on their account analysis. The rate used is usually the bank's own C.D. rate, one that is normally much higher than the money market rate used for account analysis purposes. Again, reflecting on the conversion formula shows that an increased earnings credit rate also increases the amount of service charge that the same balance can cover. The main problem with this sort of compensation method lies in its lack of flexibility. It is inflexible in that the funds must actually be converted into the C.D. form, and this cannot be accomplished simply or for very short periods of time, such as overnight. It is quite probable that the conversion cost of attempting to switch between regular balances and C.D.'s daily would far outweigh the differential in savings. Thus this form of compensation is not used for regular operating charges that are related to collection or disbursement activities. Rather, it is used more often in compensating the bank for special, distinct services provided to the corporation such as consulting–advisory services. In these cases, sufficient funds are segregated in the form of a C.D., which is maintained for an appropriate length of time to provide the proper return to the bank for the service. During the period the corporation does not have use of the funds. This latter feature is often cited by cash managers as the major drawback of this form of compensation.

The other major form of compensation, and one that is increasingly common, is the use of direct fees for services. [2] This increased popularity of fee compensation arrangements for both credit and noncredit services has been the result of a number of factors. The first and most important factor is a simple economic one. For most large corporations with access to the commercial paper market as a short-term source of funds, it will usually be cost effective for the company to pay for its bank services by fees. This is due to the cheaper cost of funds associated with commercial paper (even including the cost of backup lines of credit) as compared with the earnings credit rate, adjusted for reserve requirements. Thus it is more attractive for the corporation to borrow the funds and pay the fees than to leave balances that earn a lower return. To the extent that the effective earnings credit (i.e., reflective of reserves) approximates the cost of borrowing or alternative investments, the corporate cash manager becomes indifferent as to the compensation method. The attractiveness of fees is also enhanced by the fact that most banks simply charge fees at the level shown on the account analyses without taking into account reserve requirements or differences or time lags in the money market rates used in computing earnings credit rates. By failing to do this banks have tended to underprice the fee method of compensation. Several banks have recently begun to offer a different "schedule" of charges on a fee basis than balances. Another major factor increasing the popularity of fees is the ability of a corporation to reduce the amount of its disbursement float present in its bank balances. This is due to the general availability of controlled disbursing services, which allow the corporation to fund its disbursements on the actual day of clearing. This reduces the excess balances that were formerly present and that represented a portion of the disbursement float. Through the use of controlled disbursement accounts, the excess funds can be effectively eliminated. This possibility has also given rise, at least in part, to the last major factor in increasing the popularity of fee compensation—the payment of fees for credit services. Just as the use of fees for noncredit services has increased recently, so has the method of compensation for lines of credit. As more and more banks offer credit lines and even revolving credit agreements (committed lines) on a full fee basis with no compensating balance requirements, there is no alternative use for excess operating balances. Until recently, most U.S. banks would not consider relinquishing the percent compensating balance method. However, the aggressive entry of foreign banks in the U.S. marketplace and the desires or demands of major customers have changed this. Therefore, if a corporation is able to reduce its balances substantially by utilizing controlled disbursing and effective concentration services, it will probably be just as interested in freeing up the balances required for lines of credit. Again, comparing the cost of funds for a large corporation will usually show that it is more cost beneficial to pay for credit lines by fees than by compensating balances. With the foreign banks and major money center banks readily offering credit lines on a fee basis, a corporation wishing to establish this type of compensation arrangement should have no trouble in doing so.

In summary, then, there appears to be a major change and conversion in the method of compensation for both credit and noncredit services taking place. This does not change the basic tools for information requirements of the cash manager appreciably, but it probably heightens the need for timely, accurate bank data. Note that fee compensation virtually requires a streamlined, efficient cash management system, since the ability of the company to remove substantial amounts of its cash balances makes the conversion beneficial and attractive. The inability to do so will cost the firm the full opportunity savings it seeks. By substantially reducing the amount of cash in the cash management pipeline, finer control and a simpler system are required. It is logical to presume and, indeed quite probable, that many corporations will wind up with a mixture of compensation methods, paying for the bulk of its activities at major banks through fees while maintaining a number of secondary relationships on a balance compensation basis. Some companies have also been successful in establishing a fee offset arrangement whereby any collected balances maintained are converted to fee equivalents and subtracted from the total fee due. This conversion is typically done at the bank's earnings credit rate, and this means that the company has lost a small amount in the conversion. This, however, seems to be an appropriate and equitable way to handle excess balances in such arrangements. There is still an impetus for the company to reduce its balances, but if balances do occur, it still has some applicable use for them.

Target Balances

To manage bank balances effectively, the cash manager must establish and maintain an effective target balance system for the overall banking network. This is true no matter what form of compensation is undertaken, because, at worst, the target for any given bank could be zero. For the purposes of this discussion it is assumed that compensation has taken the form of balances. Figure 2.4 illustrates the major aspects of target balance management for the corporate cash manager.

There are two basic activities associated with bank target balance management—setting (and resetting) bank target balances and monitoring daily performance against the target. The target for each bank reflects the overall compensation for all activity with the bank, including credit as well as noncredit services. Credit services are usually set at some percentage of the line of credit, and the required balance only changes when the credit facility changes. Noncredit services, on the other hand, vary with the activity in the account; therefore they are more difficult to measure on an ongoing basis. However, the process of reviewing bank account analyses monthly and reevaluating the overall target for each bank can provide the basis for changes in the targets to reflect any recent changes in activity. Obviously, the review process is dependent on the timely receipt of account analyses and the ability of processing them quickly so that the overall performance in maintaining the bank target can be measured. The longer it takes to receive the analyses and review them to determine past performance, the more difficult it will be in modifying the bank target on a timely basis. The cash manager does not want to deal with data that are two or three months old in deciding what the target balance should be for today.

Note that a basic requirement of any target balance system is the establishment of a target or control account with each major bank that is included in the target balance management system. This is needed in order to be able to alter the balances on any given day. Without this key account the cash manager would not be able to affect the average balances at any bank. This also has implications for the other major activity involved in target balance management, that of using the target in the daily cash position management activity. The control account allows the cash manager to draw down (or add) sufficient balances so that the bank is on target overall. Without this ability the bank's target is a hit or miss proposition. The daily monitoring of the actual bank balances as compared with the planned target can result in short-term changes in the target to incorporate aberrations in the daily position and maintain the target on average. This daily activity is extremely important in that it can smooth out any big swings in the overall balances at the bank and maintain the balances very near the target level. In this manner the monthly evaluation routine will become a "nonevent."

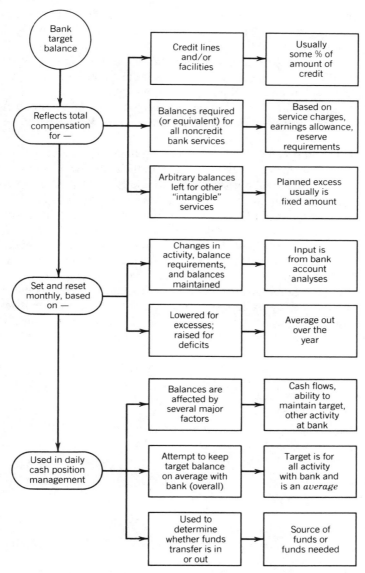

(Note: This assumes compensation is by collected balances, not fees.)

Fig. 2.4 Bank target balances.

Bank Compensation Information System

Unless a corporation has very few banking relationships and fully understands and trusts its major banks implicitly, it will find itself in need of some form of information system regarding its bank compensation. With a relatively small number of banks (e.g., under five) this can be accomplished fairly easily on a manual basis. However, as the number of banks increases, the ability of the cash manager to deal with each relationship on an effective and timely basis diminishes rapidly. It is natural, then, to consider an information system for bank compensation. While there are one or two services available in the marketplace[3] most corporate cash managers will have such individualized requirements that the development of a customized system will be advisable. The costs of doing so have decreased so much recently that it no longer represents a major system development cost to create an in-house system.

The major components for such a system are easily defined. The major ones include descriptive bank data, account-identifying elements, fundamental decision rules, and periodic account and bank data. Descriptive bank data include such items as the bank name, monthly earnings credit, reserve requirements, and overall bank target or the target for credit services. Account-identifying elements include the account number, type of account, operating unit responsible for the account, and method of compensation for the account. Fundamental decision rules lay out guidelines for converting service charges to balances, how to handle bank targets, how to treat different methods of compensation, and how to summarize balances. Periodic account and bank data are inputs from the monthly account analyses. Usually, only the total service charges or required balances are input, together with average balances. Putting all these components together, it is possible

EXHIBIT 2.8 BANK COMPENSATION REPORT

Bank Name	Average Ledger Balance	Average Collected Balance	Average Reqd. Balance	Average Collected O-U Req.	Collected Balances Over/Under Required			
					Nov.	Dec.	Jan.	Feb.
A	604	532	594	(61)	(670)	(46)	399	(143)
B	2525	1369	1183	186	(100)	2225	703	343
C	338	338	77	261	154	311	459	438
D	695	485	369	115	(23)	(31)	228	255
E	507	406	235	171	232	210	269	151
F	746	546	385	161	151	172	282	330
M	1964	1399	1121	178	(223)	246	446	760
N	874	374	218	157	225	323	282	125
O	7603	4825	4690	135	1278	842	1466	1285
R	1024	428	232	196	289	149	(76)	292
S	959	900	517	383	395	712	797	667
T	662	662	348	314	343	143	149	370
Total	92141	70355	66229	4126	6509	5984	8071	9709

EXHIBIT 2.9 NET BANK POSITION—OPERATING DIVISION/SUBSIDIARY

Bank ($000)	Avg. Ldg. Bal.	Avg. Coll. Bal.	Avg. Rqd. Bal.	Avg. Coll. O/U Rqd. Bal.	Collected Balances Over/(Under) Required Balance					
					July	Aug.	Sept.	Oct.	Nov.	Dec.
A	6	6	11	(5)	4	(14)	(8)	(10)	7	(8)
B	44	43	6	36	39	39	36	27	37	35
C	2895	2117	1169	948	1399	1645	341	722	1267	2059
D	958	473	178	295	345	513	497	176	175	2
E	912	707	217	490	467	438	377	635	1099	477
F	908	902	148	753	728	927	707	597	886	771
Total	5734	4256	1732	2522	2983	3551	1951	2148	3477	3343

to create a bank compensation information system to monitor and report on bank activity.

Typical output reports can include an overall bank compensation report (Exhibit 2.8), a similar report for each major operating unit (Exhibit 2.9), and with the input of deposit data, a float factor report (Exhibit 2.10). These reports can provide the cash manager with an in-depth profile of the banking activity for the overall corporation, and the performance in any given period should suggest changes to individual bank targets. For example, the overall bank compensation report can show a trend in excess–deficit-balance positions for the latest six months. This can show the cash manager how well the target balances have been maintained and whether any further changes are warranted. The individual operating unit report can show the cash manager whether each major unit (if somewhat autonomous) has been maintaining its individual target balance effectively. Finally, the float factor can pinpoint problem areas where further review or analysis is suggested. If the computed factors show a marked increase over time, it may indicate a shift in customer remittance habits or the expansion of that particular business into newer geographic areas. In either case, further detailed review is called for and is highlighted in the report.

EXHIBIT 2.10   FLOAT FACTOR REPORT

Bank Compensation System Float Analysis For: Operating Division/Subsidiary, "Float" In Days

Bank	Account Type	Oct.	Nov.	Dec.	Jan.	Feb.
Bank 1	Lock Box	0.80	1.55	1.14	1.35	2.05
Bank 2	Lock Box	1.76	0.92	5.34	1.35	1.10
Bank 3	Lock Box	1.25	2.04	1.55	1.24	3.06
Bank 4	Lock Box	1.08	1.57	1.05	0.85	0.88
Bank 5	Lock Box	0.94	0.88	0.76	0.81	0.76
Bank 6	Lock Box	2.87	1.72	0.90	0.66	0.39
Bank 7	Lock Box	0.31	0.22	0.10	0.23	0.11
Bank 8	Lock Box	0.66	1.26	2.41	4.10	1.38
Bank 9	Lock Box	1.41	2.18	1.22	2.18	1.95
Bank 10	Lock Box	1.09	0.64	0.28	0.58	0.72
Bank 11	Lock Box	1.62	1.06	0.93	0.37	0.41
Bank 12	Lock Box	1.13	0.67	1.18	1.74	1.28
Bank 13	Lock Box	1.40	1.40	1.40	1.86	1.40
Bank 14	Lock Box	0.71	1.17	0.70	0.77	0.75
Bank 15	Lock Box	0.80	0.34	0.74	0.67	0.57

In summary, then, bank compensation is not a simple process and requires a great deal of time and effort on the part of the cash manager. Over time, this area of cash management has taken on a significant role in determining the overall corporation–bank relationship. The selection of banks or the evaluation of existing bank relationships requires a set of logical, rational criteria. Account analyses provide basic data to the corporation and are the building blocks for bank target balances as well as a bank compensation information system. As the bank–corporation relationship drifts more and more toward a fee-based arrangement, the need for an effective information system that can incorporate current data will increase. Thus the bank compensation aspect of cash management will encourage the establishment of more effective control over corporate cash management activities and require a higher degree of information reporting than in previous times.

NOTES

1. Lordan provides an excellent picture of compensation principles from this time period.
2. Harvey has offered one of the first and most thorough treatises on this subject.
3. Chase Manhattan has a product of this sort (ABARS), and Richard Harte & Associates of Columbus, Ohio, offers a product called Convene.

3 Liquidity, Information, and Control

This chapter deals with several other areas of cash management that may not normally be considered when profiling the function. Short-term liquidity management is often looked at as the "plug" for equalizing cash inflows and outflows. Cash scheduling, or short-term cash forecasting, provides the basic roadmap for the cash manager to follow in his or her daily routine. Cash management control is the conceptual design of the overall system such that it works together in a complementary manner. Thus it is appropriate to consider these areas together, covering the breadth of what may be considered supplementary activities for the corporate cash management function. The various areas we will discuss are very conducive to applying many corporate planning and analytical techniques that have been utilized elsewhere in the corporate financial area. These activities also offer an opportunity for the cash manager or other members of the treasury function to establish meaningful planning approaches. This concept has not been applied to the treasury area until recently, a testimony to the evolving maturity of the function.

At either end of the cash management pipeline are the major aspects of short-term liquidity management, providing needed funds from external sources and alternative uses for excess funds. Historically, the management of short-term liquidity was considered to be the essence of cash management. Today it is generally recognized as one of the major functions of cash management, alongside important and related activities such as cash flow or bank relations management. Liquidity management is, of course, heavily interrelated with the other cash management activities, and its effectiveness is largely determined by the efficiency of the corporation's cash position management and short-term forecasting and scheduling of cash flows. When these activities are working properly, the amounts of short-term borrowing can be minimized as internal corporate funds are utilized to their fullest and short-term excesses can be invested in money market instruments, thereby garnering additional interest income that would have been otherwise unavailable to the firm. However, there is a potential danger or pitfall for the cash manager who does not place liquidity management in the proper perspective or context.

That is, the cash manager can lose sight of the role of liquidity management to the firm and within the firm's financial operating systems. The cash manager may, for instance, attempt to utilize this function to compensate for the shortcomings of the firm's cash management system in other areas or be tempted to take excessive risks in choosing investments in trying to increase the return on investments. In certain firms, to be sure, the investment or borrowing of funds is an integral part of the company's business. Consumer and industrial finance companies, for example, must rely very heavily on short-term borrowings as a major source of funds, and accordingly, such firms approach this area far differently from the typical manufacturing company with seasonal working capital needs. Also, many large insurance companies have a relatively permanent investment portfolio and do maintain a full-time professional staff to handle their investment activity (even short term), whereas other firms are usually only interested in relatively short-term, highly liquid investments that represent seasonal excess cash positions. In these cases the investment activity will tend to be much more conservative and need not require the same level of investment experience, expertise, or staffing levels.

In this section we will discuss short-term investing briefly and look in more detail at the different features and options associated with the short-term borrowing activities of corporations. The discussion will consider the typical corporate user, not the specialized users mentioned earlier. Whenever appropriate, however, differences or special considerations will be cited for such firms. In addition, we will discuss fundamental decision criteria, as well as performance and activity reports for these functions.

SECTION 3.1   SHORT-TERM INVESTING

Corporate short-term investing has become an increasingly active aspect of cash management. This is true even in the cases of many firms that have also been active or net borrowers as well. In times when little return could be obtained on investing short-term excess cash, companies tended to be active in only the investing or borrowing markets, but with the current state of volatile, higher interest rates, there has been more pressure and commensurate benefit to the firm if it does both. Also, the effectiveness of cash management techniques in streamlining the banking network for a company and enabling the firm to function efficiently with far less in the way of average bank balances has created an environment in which the company requires ready access to the money markets for both short-term investments and borrowings. In the past a company would maintain a small short-term investment portfolio, for instance, but still have a relatively large cushion of cash throughout its banking network in the form of compensating or operating balances. These cushions could be utilized in the short run to fund needed transactions without borrowing externally. Any shortfalls could be made up at a later time, since the balance compensation level was an *average* figure. However, this situation has changed significantly (especially in the larger firms) as corporations have altered their primary means of compensation from balances to fees and have reduced the overall number of banks used as well. This has created the need for a pool of short-term funds to replace the previous cash cushion. Satisfaction of this need can entail additional short-term borrowing activity on a daily basis as well as the maintenance of a small pool of short-term investments for funding unanticipated cash requirements that cannot be handled any longer from internally generated sources.

The major types of short-term investment instruments available for use by the corporation vary, depending on the objectives of the investor, the amount of funds involved, and the length of time the funds are to be invested.[1] If the cash manager is able to invest relatively large amounts of funds (e.g., $1 million and greater), the choices are rather diverse. On the other hand, for amounts ranging up to $1 million, the choices become much more limited. The major types of instruments include certificates of deposits (C.D.'s) issued by major banks, commercial paper issued by major corporations and bank holding companies, U.S. government securities, and bank time deposits. The major features of these instruments are summarized in Exhibit 3.1. One of the most common methods or arrangements for completing the investment entails the establishment of a *repurchase agreement (repo)* with the bank or broker offering the security. In this manner the seller agrees to buy back the security at the end of the investment period (even if only overnight), thereby assuring the corporate investor that the company's funds are safe. To provide further safeguards, most larger firms with relatively sizable amounts of short-term investments with several or many brokers and/or dealers require that the security be physically delivered to the firm's bank or banks who provide a custody–safekeeping service. Should the seller fail to deliver the appropriate security properly or within the regular time frame, no funds are transferred to the seller by the purchasing firm. In some cases, the corporation may waive this physical delivery and accept a *due bill* instead from the dealer–broker. This is often utilized by companies that are located outside the major money centers or in cases where investment decisions are made too late to accomplish physical delivery effectively. Some companies have reported that their dealers have stated that the acceptance of due bills will result in a marginally better investment rate, sometimes quoting margins of $\frac{1}{4}$ or $\frac{1}{8}$, but others, especially those more active in the marketplace, have maintained that there is no appreciable difference in rates obtained whether actual delivery is made or not. It would appear that, on the whole, the question of due bills or delivery does not appreciably affect the rates; rather, the type of security, amount of funds invested, and the term of the investment are the more substantial influences.

Short-term investment, just as is the case with many of the other aspects of cash management, is a very time-critical activity. Funds available for

EXHIBIT 3.1 MAJOR FEATURES OF SHORT TERM INVESTMENT INSTRUMENTS

Instrument	Features
Treasury Bills	Issued at a discount; noninterest-bearing; redeemed at full face value (par) at maturity; highly liquid; probably considered safest instrument.
Agencies	Farm credit, bank for cooperatives (coops), etc.; usually interest-bearing; issued and redeemed at par (i.e., no discount); highly liquid; safe, but not as safe as Treasury Bills.
Certificates of deposit (C.D.'s)	Sold by banks, either directly to corporations or through dealers; some risk; Eurodollar C.D.'s sold as well by foreign banks and foreign branches of U.S. banks; Euro-C.D.s' offer higher returns due to slightly higher risk.
Commercial paper	Issued/sold by large corporations, finance companies, and bank holding companies; essentially unsecured IOU's; issuers rated by agencies; more risk than other instruments.
Time deposits	Corporate "savings accounts"; often offered on zero-interest basis to compensate bank for services; Euro-time deposits available, offering slightly higher rates than C.D.'s; can be set out for specific dates (Euro-time deposits, that is), which is helpful for fixed maturities, etc.

investment or portions of maturing investments needed for daily funding requirements must be determined as early in the business day as possible, and in any case by the very early afternoon, so that the best rates can be obtained and delivery (if required) can be completed easily. Thus the need for flexible instruments and timely information on bank balances and funding requirements is of great and daily concern to the corporate cash manager. The repos cited earlier help with the need for flexibility when the cash manager is unsure as to the tenure of short-term excesses. If funds are not needed for a definite period, then the cash manager is able to invest more confidently and may not require the flexibility of the repo. However, this is not often the case, and many firms and their dealers have established an "open repo" to accommodate this uncertainty. By using the open repo, either the dealer or the investor can alter the amount invested or the security involved (and, accordingly, the rate obtained) on a daily basis. Although some longer-term return on the investment may be sacrificed in this type of arrangement, the flexibility obtained and the safety of the transaction are attractive features to the short-term investor. Otherwise, unforeseen cash needs would require a premature termination of an investment with possible loss of interest or an increase in short-term borrowing, again costing the firm needlessly.

One of the most important tasks associated with short-term investment activity is the formulation of a policy for the activity. Unless short-term investing is inconsequential or virtually nonexistent, a formal policy should be formulated in order to provide an appropriate framework for short-term investments and guidance and performance benchmarks. The formal policy is also helpful in establishing the limits to which the investor can go in balancing optimal return against the safety of the assets. The policy itself can take many varied forms, usually depending on corporate idiosyncrasies, but it will typically specify the maximum position possible in any institution's securities and acceptance criteria for individual instruments themselves. Often this will take the form of an *approved list,* which identifies those financial institutions or corporations whose securities are eligible for purchase by the investor as well as the maximum amount of investments in dollar terms that can be held for each institution or firm. The list is then utilized in the daily investing activity and can be readily checked during investing discussions with the company's dealers. The maximum position is another safeguard and becomes more relevant when more than one portfolio or investment activity exists within the overall corporation, as is often the case with large, decentralized firms. In such cases, the central cash manager or short-term investor usually bears the responsibility for maintaining a consolidated position for the different activities.

The policy itself should be expressed in understandable operating terms so that it can be easily referred to as necessary. Many companies have also instituted some form of financial review of potential investment sources as part of the policy, and the review must be completed and a positive result found prior to an institution's being added on to the approved list. A negative finding on a potential candidate would, of course, prevent the addition of the candidate to the list. Likewise, a negative result for an existing member on the list would result in that firm's being removed from the list and no longer being acceptable for the investor. This analysis is usually performed on an annual or semiannual basis. There are a few important issues to be considered before establishing this sort of analytical approach:

Value.   There is some question as to the essential value of the exercise itself; that is, top financial management must be genuinely committed to accepting the results of an objective analysis. For instance, one corporate cash manager relates the following experience. After being charged with the responsibility of conducting an exhaustive analysis of potential banks for investment, the manager's staff (his assistant, that is) determined that many of the firm's credit line banks would not qualify for the approved list as stated in the corporate policy. Although many of the major banks were fairly close to the cutoff, one in particular was at the bottom of the list, no matter how it was cut. It also happened that the president of this particular bank was a member of the board of directors of the corporation. When the cash manager presented his findings to the treasurer and chief financial officer, they were appalled to find that not only was the bank taken off the approved list, but it was recommended that the credit line be reduced as well. Both managers remarked that this would never do and that the bank must be restored to its original position in terms of credit lines and the approved list. This obviously brought home the point that the list and some decisions as to which institutions were included on it were less than objectively determined. The "crafty" cash manager was also able to demonstrate to his management that a great deal of effort and exhaustive financial analyses were not worthwhile in his company's case. It should be noted that the company was not a large investor usually, but from time to time had some seasonal excesses to invest. In other words, it may be extremely difficult to establish a consistent and objective approach to bank financial analyses since there are many subjective areas to be considered. Establishing a clear-cut, analytical approach may sound attractive and proper, but it may prove quite illusory for the investment activity of the firm, especially if this activity is not very significant in size. This does not mean, of course, that the financial performance of potential investment sources should be ignored, but by taking a more practical, commonsense approach many companies can avoid needless effort and expense. For example, a simple decision criterion that comprises the top 10 or 20 banks in terms of asset size and any corporate credit line banks can be sufficient for a "small" portfolio of up to $50 million. The latter are included since it makes sense that the banks that would offer credit to the corporation (especially in times when it might need it most) are somehow worthy of reciprocal consideration.

Other Relationships.   Since many of the institutions to be considered are commercial banks, the total bank–company relationship must be considered. This goes beyond the types of considerations cited earlier and looks at the full list of services provided by the bank to the corporation and its operating units. Often by utilizing a bank for basic bank services, a corporation has committed itself as a creditor of the bank (technically by maintaining a demand deposit account it has become one), so this relationship must be considered by the cash manager in reviewing tbe list of possible investment alternatives. It may not be a major determining factor, but all things considered, the manager should be more likely to invest in institutions with which he or she is familiar than not.

Data Accuracy and Comparability.   Establishing and then maintaining a comprehensive data base can be both cumbersome and costly. Several firms and banks offer financial data and varying degrees of analyses. Companies with large, permanent portfolios have developed their own systems, utilizing such services as well as direct data and financial reports from the institutions and banks themselves. However, for the typical short-term investor with a small seasonal portfolio these alternatives can quickly become too costly to be practical. Usually, concerns about financial stability and performance are heightened by bad news from a single incident or institution in trouble, as was the case with the Franklin National Bank failure in the 1970s. Such scares aside, the typical corporate treasury staff does not have the personnel or technical resources to sustain a full-time financial "watchdog" service. Compounding this is the fact that many financial ratios or reports are not really comparable from large banks to smaller ones or for regional banks to money center banks. Finally, the timing and availability of information are also major deficiencies in maintaining a current picture of an institution's performance or status.

An area of short-term investing that is often overlooked in the formal policy is the subject of reporting requirements for the activity. These reporting requirements are usually threefold—normal transaction and operating reports, performance summaries for financial management, and reporting for investment accounting purposes.

Normal transaction and operating reports are important to the investment manager and operating staff who handle the short-term investment activities. Depending on the size of the activity in terms of dollar or transaction volume, a computerized system, whether in-house or timeshare, may be justified. The latter type of automated systems are offered by many major banks and third party vendors for use by the corporate investor. Whatever the case, normal operating reports usually consist of a standard "set" as well as occasional "ad hoc" reports. The standard set typically will include the following types of reports[2]:

Confirmation Letters (Exhibit 3.2).   Confirmation letters are generated or are prepared manually for each investment transaction and document the transaction between the company and its dealer. The letter is signed by an authorized signer (or more than one if required by corporate standards) and is sent to the dealer, the bank providing custody–safekeeping, and corporate accounting. It shows the security purchased, dollar amounts of principal and interest, maturity date, and delivery instructions, all of which have been communicated between the firm and dealer during the completion of the transaction.

Transaction Registers and Summaries (Exhibit 3.3).   Transaction registers and summaries document the transactions in capsulized form and provide summaries of these transactions for normal working periods. Transaction registers provide detailed descriptions of daily activities and can be ex-

EXHIBIT 3.2 INVESTMENT CONFIRMATION LETTER

```
JMP CORPORATION
123 Gotham Avenue
New York, N Y 10101

February 28, 1983


Mega--Brokers
00 Wall Street
New York, N Y 10000

This is to confirm the investment of $ 1,000,000.00
for a period of   3   days at the annual rate of  8.00%.

Total interest due on    March 3.   is $   657.53          .

The security is      Gotham Trust CD's
and is to be delivered for safekeeping to  Metro Trust Bank
1234 Wall Street New York, NY                             .


Sincerely,

    Samuel J. Jones
    Muriel S. Hastings
(Authorized Signers)
```

EXHIBIT 3.3 INVESTMENT ACTIVITY REPORT

JMP Corporation
Daily Transaction Activity Report for 03/15/83

					YIELD	
Security	Broker	Type	Amount	Mat Date	NOM	EFF
Citicorp;	SB	C.D.	10,000,000.	04/15/83	9.0	9.0
Chase/Nassau	CMB	EUROTD	5,000,000.	03/31/83	9.5	9.5

Itemized listing by security by broker (more than one entry would be shown if multiple purchases from same broker).

Subtotals would be shown by broker.

Daily recap also produced; recaps possible for specified period of time (e.g., one week).

Possible breakdown by type of security also available.

EXHIBIT 3.4   SHORT-TERM INVESTMENT—MATURITY SCHEDULE

JMP Corporation

Maturity	Broker	Type	$ Amount	Rate	Inv Date
3/01/83	Sal	CP	3,000	8.68	2/15/83
	G S	CP	4,000	9.25	2/01/83
3/02/83	Sal	CP	10,000	8.40	2/25/83
	AGB	BA	5,000	8.90	2/25/83

tremely useful in reviewing activities or investigating problems. Accordingly, they should provide sufficient detail for each transaction. Summaries by dealer/broker, type of security, or organizational entity should be routinely produced at periodic intervals as well.

Maturity Schedules (Exhibit 3.4).   Maturity schedules provide basic operating information for the investor, informing him or her as to which investments are maturing daily and for what broker. Recaps by week, month, or other periods are also provided. These reports are also important in determining the daily cash position. Often, a simple, manual schedule will be sufficient for the manager's needs. As the volume of investments grows, some form of automated reporting may be helpful, especially for use in future planning and in providing necessary information to the accounting function. This report is also useful in determining the adequacy of future cash flow projections. When used in this manner, it is an effective input to the cash forecasting or projection system.

Portfolio Profiles (Exhibit 3.5).   Portfolio profiles provide an overall presentation of the contents of the firm's portfolio or portfolios. Typically shown are the transaction dates, descriptions of the securities, nominal rates and effective yields, broker/dealer, maturity dates, and interest income. Different, comparative reports by dealer or type of security are often provided as well to help in assessing the performance of different dealers or to obtain a better understanding of the various investment instruments. Such profiles can be incorporated into overall management reporting or performance analysis reports as well. Effective recaps of activities by dealer/broker are useful in developing short-term investment strategies.

The ad hoc reports are often a continuation of one of the preceding types, such as those dealing with the assessment of dealer performance across

EXHIBIT 3.5   INVESTMENT PORTFOLIO/INVENTORY

JMP Corporation
Short-Term Investment Portfolio
02/28/83

Security	Type	Purch Date	Purch Amount ($000)	Mature Date	Mature Amount ($000)	Rate
Gotham Tr	C.D.	013183	10,000	033183	10,200	12.0
Inter-State	EURO	021583	5,000	051583	5,125	10.0
Totals			15,000		15,325	11.3

portfolios or different periods of time, or projecting expected interest income for future periods. A sample performance analysis does not have to be produced in the standard set of reports unless there are several portfolios of any size, the number of brokers or dealers used is relatively large, or some ranking of the brokers/dealers is desired.

Interest income projections are quite useful in preparing short-term cash forecasts. Typical reports are free-form in nature, depending on the period covered or the format of the forecast. By using the investment data base (whether automated or manual) to develop projections of interest income and maturing investment, high degrees of accuracy for short periods (e.g., up to 90 days) can be attained. This type of report can also be useful in developing short-term strategies for investments and determining the effects of expected changes in interest rates, particularly if a computer model is used.

In some form the investment manager should report the results of the short-term investment activity to financial management. This does not necessarily mean that the activity should be viewed as a routine corporate profit center, but some form of managerial responsibility is appropriate, since the activity does involve the control of a corporate asset, excess cash. A sample report of this type is shown in Exhibit 3.6.

As in other areas of cash management, a need exists for the investment transactions and their results (i.e., the receipt of interest income) to be properly accounted for in the firm's financial records. Therefore, a regular report showing sufficient accounting data must be provided on a routine basis. A sample report is shown in Exhibit 3.7. Such reports should be produced periodically (e.g., monthly) in a form useful to the accounting staff. Input from this area in the design of these reports should be sought in order to avoid future problems or misunderstandings.

EXHIBIT 3.6   INVESTMENT MANAGEMENT PERFORMANCE REPORT

JMP Corporation
Short-Term Investments as of 2/28/83

Security Name	Amount Authorized ($000)	Current Balance ($000)	$-Wtd. Ave. Rate (%)
Gotham—C.D.	10,000	5,000	9.67
Seaboard—PAPER	10,000	2,000	9.24
Int'l Trust—EUROC.D.	5,000	3,000	9.42
Metro Guar'y—PAPER	10,000	1,000	8.94
Other unused limits	65,000	—	—
Total	100,000	11,000	9.46%

Interest income for period: $96,000.00
External interest rates/indicators
  GMAC 30-day paper: 9.12%
  U.S. T-Bills (30-day): 8.24%

EXHIBIT 3.7   INTEREST INCOME ACCOUNTING REPORT

JMP Corporation
Interest Income, 2/83

SECURITY NAME	TYPE	PURCH DATE	MATUR DATE	MATUR AMOUNT	INTEREST INCOME	EFFECT YIELD
OUTSTANDING:						
GOTHAM BANK	CD	102082	044083	6,000	354,000	11.80
SEABOARD NATL	CP	012083	032183	10,000	200,000	12.00
MNC FINANCE	CP	122882	032883	15,000	405,000	10.80
TOTAL				31,000	959,000	
SOLD/MATURED:						
INT'L BK & TR	EURO	020483	021483	10,000	26,389	9.50
U.S. GOVT	TB	021883	022283	15,000	15,238	9.27
TOTAL				25,000	41,627	

SECTION 3.2   SHORT-TERM BORROWING

In many ways *short-term borrowing* activities are similar to the short-term investing activities of a company, with one being the mirror image of the other. Large firms, representing the heavy short-term borrowers, aggressively handle borrowing as they do investing. The mechanics and dynamic nature of the money markets require well-planned strategies and effective and frequent interaction with the providers of short-term credit. The short-term debt of a firm can be treated and approached as a portfolio in much the same manner as a firm treats its short-term investments. Many of the reporting and analytical requirements discussed earlier can be applied to this area as well.

The cash manager for most firms is faced with a variety of short-term borrowing alternatives. Some of these options are only available to the largest and more credit-worthy firms (e.g., commercial paper). The major types of borrowing vehicles include short-term bank loans, commercial paper, bankers acceptances, and master notes. The basic features for each are outlined in Exhibit 3.8.

Short-term bank loans have been the most common forms of short-term debt historically. Bank credit lines were the primary source of short-term borrowing for almost every firm until recently. Currently, alternate forms of bank borrowings have been offered and have replaced much of the old-time credit line borrowing by larger firms. These newer forms are either tied to the London InterBank Offered Rate (LIBOR) for fixed periods of one, two, three, or six months or to "money market" or subprime rates for shorter periods of, for instance, up to a week. These new forms have been marketed aggressively by the large U.S. money center banks and the U.S. branches or agencies of foreign banks. Accessing these kinds of loans is quite simple and is usually accomplished over the telephone, with paperwork following the transaction. In the case of LIBOR-related loans, one or more days lead time is normally required since the borrowing must be handled through an off-shore branch of the bank.

Commercial paper has grown substantially in recent years, amounting to more than $160 billion in borrowings. This market is dominated by large industrial companies, major finance companies, and large bank holding companies. The commercial paper market has rebounded from its low point in the early 1970s, when the Penn Central failure disrupted the commercial paper market. At that time, many firms avoided the paper market and moved back to bank borrowings or other forms of credit. For instance, master notes were popular right after this time, and many firms substituted them for commercial paper borrowings. However, the positive side of the failure was the creation of tighter and more widespread use of short-term debt ratings. These ratings, issued by one of the major rating services—Moody's, Standard and Poor's, and Fitch—have become mandatory for any firm wishing to participate in the paper market. Two major ratings are usually required.

EXHIBIT 3.8   BASIC TYPES OF SHORT TERM BORROWING

Type of Borrowing	Basic Features
Short-term bank loans	Under regular line of credit usually at bank's prime rate or prime plus a fraction (e.g., 1%).
	Eurodollar rate option becoming quite common; rates set at *L*ondon *I*nter-*B*ank *O*ffered *R*ate plus a fraction (e.g., $\frac{3}{8}$ or $\frac{1}{2}$%) for 1, 2, 3, or 6 months; interest computed on a 360-day year basis.
	Subprime or "money market" loans for very short periods; may be quoted as spread over Fed funds rate or bank's average cost of funds.
Commercial paper	Dealer placed or issued directly.
	Used primarily to finance working capital needs, up to 270 days maturity.
	Sold at a discount.
	Special type of paper used for noncurrent financing.
	Role of ratings important.
	Relatively few dealers.
Bankers acceptances	Financing foreign trade.
	Backed by company's goods and bank guarantees.
Master notes	Offered by trust areas of major commercial banks.
	Amount and rates can vary daily.
	Rates usually indexed on GMAC rates.
	Used heavily by finance companies as alternate source of funds.
	Only offered to companies with very high credit ratings.

Companies go to great trouble to nurture their ratings, meeting with the services periodically and providing them with appropriate financial and operating data. Indeed, a drop in short-term rating can prove extremely costly to a firm, adding as much as 0.5% to future borrowings or, more seriously, shutting the borrower out of the market altogether. This latter occurrence has decreased in recent times as the market has proved to be quite resilient in providing funds to all would-be borrowers. The commercial paper market's volume has grown immensely and steadily through the 1970s and early 1980s, weathering several financial storms in the meantime. It has clearly established itself as a major source of short-term credit.

Firms borrowing through the commercial paper market do so by selling their own paper directly to investors or by using a commercial paper dealer to sell their paper. There are relatively few dealers in this market—Goldman Sachs, A. G. Becker, First Boston, Lehman Brothers, Salomon Brothers, Merrill Lynch, and Bankers Trust. Bankers Trust is the only commercial bank involved in selling commercial paper, and its participation in the market in that capacity is still being challenged in the courts by the investment banks. In any case, dealers charge a commission for their services, usually 0.125% of the dollar amount of paper sold. Dealers are typically used by firms that do not have sufficient daily volume levels to justify selling paper directly. Dealers represent many different firms and can place larger amounts of paper accordingly. Direct issuers are the largest single group in the commercial paper market. Typical direct issuers are the large finance companies, such as General Motors Acceptance Corporation or CIT. Such firms use the commercial paper markets as the primary source of funds for their financial service businesses. Exhibit 3.9 shows a breakdown of the commercial paper market by different types of issuers.

EXHIBIT 3.9 COMMERCIAL PAPER OUTSTANDING ($BILLIONS)

End of Month	Total Issued	Finance Companies			Nonfinancial Companies
		Total	Direct Issuers	Bank Related	
JAN (1982)	167	112	81	35	40
FEB	167	110	79	34	55
MAR	166	110	78	34	57
APR	172	114	81	37	59
MAY	177	118	83	38	59
JUNE	180	121	85	38	59
JULY	181	117	81	35	57
AUG	174	117	81	35	57
SEPT	172	115	80	34	56
OCT	170	116	80	34	55
NOV	167	116	80	34	51
DEC	163	118	83	33	44
AVERAGE	171	115	81	35	54

Source: Market Reports Division, Federal Reserve Bank of New York.

Maturities for commercial paper can range up to 270 days theoretically, but in recent times the market has generally settled into a 30-day range. This does not mean that longer or shorter maturities are not possible, but only that the most common maturity is 30 days. The interest rates for commercial paper have generally been significantly lower than comparable bank lending rates. In comparing rates, it should be noted that for most users of commercial paper, backup lines of credit are required. Their cost should be added to the commercial paper cost when comparing with other forms of borrowing. Nonetheless, in recent times, commercial paper rates have still been considerably lower than bank rates. If short-term interest rates change rapidly, meaningful comparisons can be difficult. In such instances many borrowers are more concerned about the availability of funds than about the cost. When rates increase rapidly, possible maturities tend to decrease until rates level off somewhat. As rates decrease, the reverse effect occurs. A particular aspect of direct sellers of paper comes into effect when rates drop substantially. This is the *extension privilege* and is offered to the regular purchasers of direct issuers. This allows these investors to extend their maturities up to one week at the same rate initially negotiated. This is considered by many direct issuers as an added incentive to the purchasers of their paper over the dealer-placed paper. However, in times of rapidly falling interest rates, as was the case in the late 1970s, this can create additional and significant rate differentials for the direct issuer.

As the use of the commercial paper market has grown, many firms have reached the point at which they wish to consider more than one dealer for placing their paper. Initially, this prospect was resisted by the majority of dealers, but split programs are fairly commonplace at present, although at least one dealer still steadfastly refuses to participate in such arrangements. The advantages are in additional availability and better rates through competition. Many firms established split programs with two dealers such that each one sold paper on alternating days but seldom did on the same day. However, this diminished any effects of competitive pressures on the firm's rates. Today most effective split program dealers are in the market at the same time, with their business levels determined to some extent by their comparative performance.

Smaller companies that might not be able to access the commercial paper market on their own and other firms that might not be able to obtain satisfactory short-term credit ratings have been using a bank-supported service to obtain short-term funds. In this type of arrangement the firm's borrowings are backed by a bank letter of credit, thereby transferring the credit-worthiness of the borrower to the banking institution rather than the company. The banks charge a fee for this service, typically between 0.25% and 0.5%, but even with this differential included in the overall cost the rates have been attractive.

While the vast majority of commercial paper is sold to finance short-term working capital or trade-related transactions, another form of "commercial paper" exists for noncurrent financing in the short-term markets. For all intents and purposes, short-term notes issued for noncurrent financing look similar to commercial paper notes. However, this type of note bears a legend at the bottom declaring that the note may not be sold. A typical legend would read as follows:

> This note has not been registered under the Securities Act of 1933, and may not be sold, offered for sale or otherwise disposed of in the absence of registration under said Act or an exemption therefrom. Any disposition of this note may only be to or through (dealer's name) or (issuing company), neither of which shall be under any obligation to acquire, pay, or place this Note prior to its maturity.[3]

This form of paper is not sold indiscriminately but must be "offered" to a defined list of so-called sophisticated investors. The dealer must maintain this list and can only include institutions that are experienced or possible investors. The advantages of this form are usually cheaper rates and a method of financing noncurrent transactions such as major construction projects or similar ventures.

Whatever mix of short-term borrowings a firm has, the cash manager will at some point wish to analyze the activity and evaluate the comparative performances of different types and different parts (e.g., dealers or instruments) of each type. This will entail developing a debt analysis system to provide analytical and transaction reports, maintain historical performance data, and supply routine periodic accounting data automatically. It may also be expected to tie into a cash projection system to provide future estimates of maturing debt. The basic requirements of such a system include standard transaction and analytical reports.

Standard transaction reports include regular reports showing daily transactions, maturity schedules, or debt portfolio breakdowns. Examples of these reports are shown in Exhibits 3.10 and 3.11). A *daily transaction report* of commercial paper or other short-term debt serves the same function as its counterpart in short-term investments. It can be used to review the overall activity and to provide an ongoing record of the short-term borrowing activity of the firm. *Maturity schedules* of short-term debt, whether manual or automated, are important inputs to daily cash position management if borrowing is at all significant. They are also integral tools in planning future activities, evaluating projected cash flows, and selecting the optimal mix and maturities of future short-term debt. It is quite effective to have the maturity schedules available during the daily cash management and borrowing activities to be able to select from alternative maturities or amounts for new debt or investments on the spot.

Analytical reports evaluate dealer performance or highlight different aspects of the borrowing activity. For split commercial paper programs, for example, a *Recap by Dealer* (Exhibit 3.12) or a *Common Hit Report* (Exhibit 3.13) is quite useful. These reports tend to be more ad hoc, being customized

EXHIBIT 3.10 SALES ACTIVITY TRANSACTION REPORT—COMMERCIAL PAPER

JMP Corporation
Sales Activity—02/14/83

Maturity	Amount Sold	Days to Maturity	Nominal Rate	Interest Amt	Net Proceeds	Equiv Yield
02/24/83	5,000,000.	10	8.75	12 152.78	4 987 847.22	8.95
03/01/83	5,000,000.	15	8.625	17 722.60	4 982 277.40	8.71
03/16/83	10,000,000.	30	8.500	70 833.33	9 929 166.67	8.56
04/15/83	10,000,000.	60	8.250	137 499.99	9 862 500.01	8.37
Total	30,000,000.			238 208.70	29 761 791.30	

EXHIBIT 3.11   COMMERCIAL PAPER MATURITY REPORT

JMP Corporation
Commercial Paper Maturities, 02/02/83

Maturity Date	Maturity Amount		
02/03/83	6,000,000		
02/04/83	3,000,000		
Week subtotal		9,000,000	
02/10/83	11,000,000		
02/11/83	5,000,000		
Week subtotal		16,000,000	
02/15/83	9,200,000		
02/16/83	5,000,000		
02/17/83	2,100,000		
02/18/83	2,800,000		
Week subtotal		19,100,000	
02/22/83	17,000,000		
Week subtotal		17,000,000	
Month subtotal			61,100,000
03/02/83	3,000,000		
03/12/83	10,000,000		
Month subtotal			13,000,000
Grand total			74,100,000

EXHIBIT 3.12   COMMERCIAL PAPER RECAP

XYZ Company

Month	Program	Broker	Volume	$ Wtd. Averages		Days
				Nominal	Effective	
Jan.	Parent	AGB	105.2	13.26	13.56	57.7
		SB	154.9	13.18	13.42	48.8
	Subsidiary A	LB	69.8	13.08	13.22	27.5
		ML	112.5	13.12	13.23	27.4

EXHIBIT 3.13   COMMON HIT REPORT

This report is issued only if more than one broker or program sells paper on same day for same maturity.

Issue Date	No. of Days	Program	Broker	Amount ($000)	$ Wtd Eff. Rate
11/17/80	15	SUB-A	AGB	4300	14.94*
		PAR	ML	900	14.97
		PAR	SB	4200	15.20
		SUB-B	LB	900	15.06

*Best of the day.

by the individual user. The *Recap of Short-Term Debt* (in Exhibit 3.12, commercial paper is shown) can be used in evaluating dealer performance over time by comparing the weighted average rates. The weighting in these cases is by the dollar amounts of short-term debt. The effective interest rate is often used for comparison between dealers. The weighted average number of days to maturity can also be compared with corporate strategies in order to determine whether the desired lengths of maturity have been attained consistently by the firm's dealers. Some companies may "reward" those dealers doing a consistently superior job with a greater portion of the borrowing activity. It is usually quite difficult to compare dealers in split commercial paper programs. One way is to review the *Common Hit Report*. This report compares rates and volumes for different dealers only when more than one dealer has sold paper for the same number of days on the same business day. A consistent pattern of better rates for significant dollar amounts may indicate better performance by one dealer over another. This type of report is often applicable in larger corporations with multiple programs.

The final end result or application of the system is to evaluate the program and report the available facilities (Exhibit 3.14). The dealer evaluation can be used, for instance, in determining levels of business for each dealer. Alternately, it could show that different dealers have strengths in different maturity ranges or vehicles and should be used in that area more heavily. As such, these reports are essential to the formulation of an effective and responsive short-term debt policy and strategy.

One other major requirement for a debt analysis system is to monitor the available credit for the firm and report its status periodically. An example for bank credit lines in summary form is shown in Exhibit 3.14. The rates shown are either fixed or negotiable ("NEG" on the report), and the lines are either regular lines of credit offered by the firm's banks ("REG" on the report) or part of a revolving credit agreement with a group of banks ("REV" on the report). If any of these lines would have been used as backup for

EXHIBIT 3.14   BANK CREDIT LINE SUMMARY

JMP Corporation 2/28/83

Bank	Type	Credit Line ($000)	Rate	Line Used ($000)	Rate	Balance ($000)
Gotham Tr	REG	10,000	11.0	–0–	–0–	10,000
Metro B & T	REV	15,000	10.5	5,000	10.5	10,000
East State	REV	5,000	10.5	2,000	10.5	3,000
Tri-State	REG	10,000	NEG	10,000	10.0	–0–
N Y Nat'l	REG	5,000	NEG	–0–	–0–	5,000
Yankee Nat'l	REG	5,000	NEG	4,000	10.2	1,000
Total		50,000		21,000		29,000

commercial paper borrowings, this would be shown in a lower portion of
the report. In the case of the example shown, the outstanding paper volume
could not exceed $29 million. The right-hand portion of the report shows
actual usage of the lines with the balances remaining and the actual borrowing
rates as of the report date.

SECTION 3.3   CASH SCHEDULING AND PLANNING

In this section the subject of short-term cash scheduling and overall cash
planning is considered. All too often this part of the overall cash management
process is overlooked or misunderstood. The monthly "forecast" can become "etched in stone" in many cases, with the result that local financial
managers inadvertently create large local pools of unused funds waiting to
be disbursed according to an outdated (but mandatory) projection. In one
such instance, a corporate cash manager was conducting a review with a
local financial manager. The local manager was surprised and somewhat
embarrassed by the size of his bank balances but explained them away by
admitting that his boss would not let him change his monthly forecast, which
called for funds each week. He readily agreed that these estimates were
rough "guess-timates" but felt there was little he could do. His supervisor
had been reprimanded for an erroneous sales and revenue estimate and was
determined to prevent any further situations if at all possible. Another typical
problem is the treasurer's dilemma when he comes into the cash manager's
office with various accounting reports, forecasts, and bank balances and
asks wryly, "Which is the cash we can spend?" These situations demonstrate
many of the ambiguities surrounding this area of cash management.

The first primary distinction that must be made is the one between cash *scheduling* and *forecasting*. The semantic difference between cash scheduling and forecasting is important to note, as the choice of the former term is made deliberately to describe more properly the process itself. In practice, the activity we will treat as cash scheduling is often referred to as short-term forecasting. However, for the purposes of our discussions within this section the distinction will be made. More sophisticated or elaborate statistical forecasting techniques and models are dealt with in the forecasting segment of the text. It is our intention in this section to deal with the short-term projections and estimates of cash flows as applied by the corporate cash manager. Wherever appropriate, we will point out the places that lend themselves to the application of more elaborate techniques. While attempts have been made to incorporate these sophisticated techniques into the corporate cash management "routine," there have not been many noteworthy successes. Thus for this discussion it is more appropriate to deal with the more pragmatic aspects of the scheduling process.

The primary purposes of short-term scheduling are to provide a framework for managing the firm's cash flows and resulting cash position and to enhance the short-term cash planning and liquidity management activities. As such, scheduling serves as an informational interface among most of the other areas of the cash management process. One of the most important aspects of short-term cash scheduling is arriving at a common definition of the term *cash* so that all participants in the scheduling process are dealing with the same thing. In many large companies or in very decentralized firms, the local financial managers providing cash flow estimates are likely to be more familiar with and trained in accounting techniques than treasury. Accordingly, they often tend to consider cash in the balance sheet sense; that is, as a static number somehow related to a regular financial statement, subject to accounting rules and treatment. From the cash manager's point of view, this number may have little relevance as his or her concern is the ready cash, the amount of funds that actually exist throughout the company's collection and payment systems. This possible discrepancy between the initiators of the company's operating cash flows and the central person who is attempting to monitor and control them can create major problems in scheduling and planning in the short term. For longer-term projections, and here the term *forecasting* is applicable, the different interpretations are not as serious because the projection period will tend to be longer (e.g., a month or a quarter); as a result, the variations should not be as significant. Also, the use of longer-term forecasts is more strategic in nature, and as such their impact on daily cash position management and short-term liquidity management decision tends to be minimal.

When faced with establishing or evaluating an existing short-term cash scheduling system, the cash manager must first identify the type of cash flows being projected and take the steps necessary to translate them into a common context. Failure to do so will create a mixture of misleading data and can cause the cash manager to make cash position decisions that are inappropriate. In many companies, however, this translation cannot be easily accomplished because the local financial managers are either unconcerned with or unable to predict actual connections or disbursement clearings. Thus the best that the cash manager can develop will be a rough estimate of possible flows, and he or she will have to develop additional projection techniques or cash management tools. Certainly, bank balance reporting systems and controlled disbursement services have helped immeasurably in this regard. Also, over time the cash manager and local financial managers can gain sufficient experience and knowledge to be able to improve the consistency and mutual understanding to improve the quality and utility of short-term cash flow projections.

This last point is the key to an effective short-term cash scheduling system. The central cash manager and the local managers must be able to interact frequently and knowledgeably. This requires a great deal of mutual education and exchange of information, with the cash manager understanding the problems, concerns, and projecting capabilities of the local managers and the latter understanding the importance, need for accuracy, and use of the projections by the cash manager. The information system cannot be regarded as a necessary evil or a bureaucratic reporting requirement imposed on the local operating units by corporate staff. Continual, two-way feedback is necessary so that major changes can be anticipated or accommodated. The ability to change an estimate must be a staple in any such system in order to avoid the withholding of key data or events for fear of reprimand or corporate "finger pointing." There should not be any "right or wrong" labels attached to the estimates if an effective dialog is to be developed. The central cash manager needs to know what is likely to occur and should not treat the local manager's estimate as perfectly accurate. Obviously, the more sophisticated the company's cash management system becomes, the less need there will be for a high level of accuracy. By utilizing many of the more advanced techniques described in the cash flow management section and putting them together in an effective, controlled system, as will be discussed in a later section, the cash flow estimating process will not be more sensitive than necessary.

Developing a Cash Scheduling System

Given all the preceding semantic differences and organizational caveats, the typical cash manager faces a sensitive task in developing and establishing an effective cash scheduling system for his or her corporation. While individual corporations may exhibit some distinct idiosyncrasies, the fundamental approach to establishing such a system should not vary significantly from case to case. In the guidelines and decision rules that follow, examples demonstrating typical differences will show this point. In any case the cash manager will find it necessary to adopt a rational, systematic approach to this estimating problem.

The first major step in the development process is a definitional stage. That is, before the cash manager can begin to design and receive periodic estimates of the company's cash flows, the basic parameters surrounding the estimation process must be defined. These basic parameters provide the essential framework and heavily influence the operating requirements and procedures of the scheduling system. The basic parameters are as follows:

Description of data items to be estimated.

Identification of the source(s) of estimates.

Frequency of regular estimates.

Time period(s) covered by regular estimates.

Method and format for transmitting estimates.

Procedures for modifying estimates.

Means of gathering actual data.

Level of accuracy required or expected.

Consolidation and reporting procedures.

Expected use of consolidated estimate.

It should appear somewhat elementary to suggest that the data elements need to be defined, but it is often taken for granted by the receiver and providers of data. This can create frequent errors in that all parties are not considering the same level of detail or type of data item. In any case the elements should be set forth. Reviewing the list of elements can be an effective means of determining whether all needed items are included or whether the elements detailed are, in fact, able to be garnered. An example of a data element listing is shown in Exhibit 3.15.

The listing should include all major flows for the corporation and can easily be customized by the cash manager. Whatever the final list looks like, it should encompass all the different uses and sources of funds for the company. The elements should be described in proper form so that the provider of the estimate can understand what is needed. For instance, cash collections may be too broad and may have to be broken down further into lock box and local office deposits for estimating purposes. By breaking the elements down into smaller units the estimates will be more useful, and the identification of variances and the reasons behind the variances will be far easier. Note in the example shown in Exhibit 3.15 the variety of sources throughout the company. These range from individual operating units to other corporate staff departments, including cash management as well. Such a widespread group is typical.

Once the list of data elements has been formulated, it should be a relatively straightforward task to identify the best source for providing regular estimates of each item. The potential sources will, in large part, be dictated by the corporate organization. For instance, in a decentralized company the local financial managers will usually possess a great deal of control over

EXHIBIT 3.15   DATA ELEMENTS FOR CASH FLOW ESTIMATES

Major receipt elements

Lock box collections—derived from estimate from local staff.

Local office deposits—from local staff.

Subsidiary loans to parent—from individual subsidiary.

International/export collections—from international treasury staff.

Corporate tax refunds—from tax affairs staff.

Long-term financing proceeds—from long-term financial planning staff.

Debt proceeds/maturing investments—from cash manager.

Major disbursement elements

Local payables funding—derived from local estimate.

Payroll funding—from payroll processing staff.

Insurance payments—from corporate insurance staff.

Consolidated tax payments—from tax affairs staff.

Corporate payables—from corporate accounting.

Foreign exchange purchases—from international treasury staff.

Corporate dividends—from corporate secretary's staff.

Short-term debt repayment/investments—from cash manager.

---

their individual collections and disbursements. As a result, these managers should be the logical sources of regular estimates, as they are in the best position of knowing the characteristics of their flows. Even in decentralized firms, however, there may also be several centralized activities, such as consolidated tax payments, central pension fund payment processing, corporate insurance payments, or other corporate staff functions. In addition, the treasury area itself may often control various items, such as investments or debt, and should provide the estimates of these variables. At this point of review, it should also be possible to identify any preliminary problems in supplying estimates. For example, the decentralized unit may be unable to provide estimates in a form that the cash manager can readily use. This may often be the case for disbursements that are funded centrally by the cash manager but are prepared and sent out by the local financial manager. In these instances the local manager is not concerned with and usually does not track the clearings in his or her disbursement account. Therefore, the central cash manager must be able to translate the local manager's estimate into terms that are meaningful to the cash manager. This can be done by various methods, the most common one being a disbursement clearing analysis such as the ones discussed in Chapter 2. Historical patterns and percentages are often provided by the company's commercial banks in their full reconciliation program and can be used to update the factors regularly.

However, the company's own internal processing systems must be capable of providing accurate issuance data to the reconciliation program for this tool to have any application at all. If this alternative is not available to the cash manager, he or she must rely on personal experience or construct a rudimentary system. This can be done by receiving daily figures of disbursements mailed and estimating clearings on a proportional basis in a similar fashion to the stagger funding procedure described in Chapter 1. While this procedure may not be extremely accurate, it should at least provide a reasonable approximation of daily clearings, especially if "conservative" percentages are established. In this way the clearings will probably not be as much as anticipated, but overdraft situations can be averted. Also, through the use of controlled disbursement accounts and their ability to be funded on the same day, the cash manager will not be penalized greatly for using conservative estimates.

The next three major parameters—frequency, time periods covered, and method and format for the estimates—can be treated as a related "package" when establishing them. For example, if the frequency is weekly or more often, then the use of the mails may not be timely enough. The time periods covered in such a case will also be affected in that an extremely frequent reporting system will probably not be able to accommodate very lengthy projections. It should be noted as well that the degree of decentralized inputs will have a direct bearing on these parameters. This means that the cash manager should not expect to receive, nor for that matter should he or she attempt to establish, a decentralized system calling for numerous input variables on an extremely frequent basis (e.g., weekly or better). A typical system for cash flow estimates is shown in Figure 3.1. In this illustration local units will provide estimates of their disbursements and collections, and the cash manager will translate them into common terms. Note that the

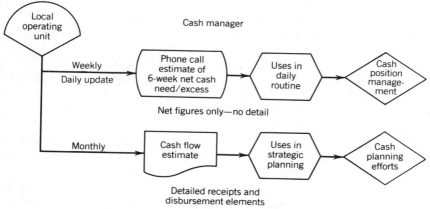

Fig. 3.1 Typical system for cash flow estimates.

system consists of different types of estimates, beginning with a very short-term telephone network for intraweek cash flow projections. On a monthly basis, more detailed items are provided on a standard format. This system should not overburden the local manager while still providing an effective and logical communications interface between the cash manager and the local managers. Note also that the formats and data elements differ for each type of reporting. In a more centralized system, obviously, there would not be the need for this type of arrangement, as the cash manager would be the storehouse for much of the data, tapping centralized accounts receivable and payable systems or possibly other customized projection systems for regular estimates. It should be noted, then, that the more centralized the processing is, the higher the potential for developing more useful projection models.

The telephone network can serve as an effective means of modifying the short-term estimate as well. In a decentralized system, such as the typical one shown earlier, the cash manager will not be in a position to anticipate any major changes in cash flows, since he or she is not initiating payments or receipts. Therefore, the local manager must have a means of communicating this to the cash manager to avoid major deficiencies or unanticipated excesses in the company's cash position. Again, through the use of more sophisticated cash management techniques, the effects of such surprises can be minimized, but the establishment of an effective communications link to report short-term changes will assist the cash manager in planning for cash needs beyond the current day. For changes in the monthly cash flow estimate, the regular written report may be sufficient unless the change is major and occurs shortly after the estimate has been submitted. In such cases the telephone network can be used, or, if practical, a revised estimate can be prepared and sent to the cash manager. Again, the problems are more cumbersome and offer more substantial reporting obstacles in decentralized systems than in centralized ones.

The means of gathering actual cash flow data will be strongly affected by the nature of the company's cash management system. In a system that is characterized by local initiation of cash flow transactions, it is often the case that the central cash manager is responsible for the funding, collection (via lock boxes), and concentration of funds. Thus the local manager will not be able to report those actuals, and the cash manager must establish alternate means. This is usually accomplished by utilizing the detailed reports available through bank balance reporting systems. The local manager can provide the actual amounts of funds disbursed from his or her point of view, and, again, the cash manager can translate this into common terms. This is often treated in the same manner as the modification process discussed earlier. This is another instance in which the decentralization of the cash flow system can create estimating problems for the cash manager. Thus the need for keeping the estimating system quite simple and for establishing a frequent and easy method of transmitting data is quite important and must figure prominently in the establishment of the estimating procedures.

The level of accuracy required or expected is a relevant factor and one that must be understood by all participants in the estimation system. The level does not necessarily have to be expressed in terms of percentage variance of another statistical value, but, rather, it should be established in familiar, operating terms, if possible. This can be relatively simple, such as the estimate should be within a logical dollar range from the actual. The size of this range can obviously differ from company to company, given the differences in company size and diversity. The critical consideration here is the range of sensitivity that the cash manager can accommodate or "live with" in the short term. This level of accuracy will also tend to vary by the length of time periods covered, with the closest periods being expected to be more precise than the ones further out. The size of the range may be affected by the decentralization as well, with a finer estimate expected if the providers are projecting smaller, more discrete flows than for the case of a central projection for the overall corporation.

Finally, the consolidation and reporting of the estimates and the expected use of the consolidated estimates must be considered in conjunction with one another. The primary user of the consolidated estimate will be the cash manager or the member of the corporate treasury staff who manages the daily cash position for the firm. This person needs the estimate expressed in terms of the net effects on the daily cash position, extended out through the normal short-term planning horizon. This latter time period may vary from company to company but must be established in the regular procedures for processing and analyzing the estimates. Summaries of the short-term estimate are typically provided to treasury management, especially in larger firms, where other areas of treasury are responsible for financing or investment transactions. The longer projections, such as the monthly ones shown in the preceding illustration, are often summarized as well and distributed outside the treasury area to other financial areas. The use of these reports will tend to vary from company to company but should be established formally when creating a cash scheduling system.

Once the cash flow estimates are received or prepared regularly, some form of analytical review will be required. This can take the form of simply tracking historical estimates and actuals to more elaborate variance analyses. The purpose of the review is to determine the effectiveness of the system in its ability to provide meaningful estimates within the accuracy guidelines expected for it and to identify operating or communications problems at an early stage. Obviously, the analysis should identify possible sources of the errors, and future reviews should be able to demonstrate the effectiveness of actions taken to resolve the problems identified. Care must be taken, however, not to treat the analysis as a "report card" on the providers of the estimates so as to prevent major organizational and communications problems from being established. Note the example at the beginning of this section and the impact such a situation had on the cash management of the firm. Also, the analyzer must be careful about how the data are treated as far as general quality is concerned. The expected level of accuracy in the estimates must be kept in mind as well as the manner in which variations are treated. That is, there may be logical, reasonable causes of large variations, and overreaction may create different problems for the analyzer. In any case, the analysis process should be kept in the proper perspective: Its objectives are to maintain a sound estimating system and resolve problems as effectively as possible without becoming one itself.

The foregoing discussion was properly concerned with cash scheduling and did not directly deal with the cash planning needs of the corporation. This is where the treasury function of the company plays a leading role, and it is in this area that the short-term scheduling system may not provide enough support. The relatively short time horizons of typical scheduling systems hamper the ability of the company to look further out. This need can be satisfied by some form of longer-term forecasting, and in this context the term *forecasting* is quite appropriate. Now there is indeed a useful application for more sophisticated statistical techniques. Also, with the wider time horizons, the differences between cash flows as shown in financial statements or measured by the actual flows of funds through the firm's banking network are not relevant, because the results of the forecast will not be translated into daily activities. In this larger context, forecasts based on regular financial data will be used in setting broader strategies and financial policy, not participating the disbursement clearings in the company's operating accounts next week.

Many firms have established statistically based forecasting systems and have reported on their successes.[4] Many of the standard techniques of quantitative methods have been applied to this problem but usually on a customized basis. This is logical in that each company must determine what it wishes to know and will tend to tailor the forecast to its own situation. Sources and types of data differ greatly from firm to firm, thereby making any standard method implausible. The end uses for such forecasts typically include long-term financial strategies such as the timing and relative size of long-term debt or equity issues, the establishment of short- and long-term debt "mix," or the impacts financially of acquisitions or divestitures. These forecasts are also used to assess the longer-term impact of changes in short-term and long-term interest rates. These few examples should adequately demonstrate the inherent difference between cash forecasting and cash scheduling and should be kept in mind when dealing with either function.

SECTION 3.4 CONTROL AND INFORMATION MANAGEMENT

For any system to function properly, some form of control must be established over it and, if needed, must be exerted on the system from time to time. Corporate cash management systems are no exception in this regard, but the establishment of control over this function can sometimes prove difficult or illusory. As is the case for many of the corporate functions, the inequality of responsibility with authority can pose substantial barriers in establishing control over cash management. Thus the cash manager may possess a great deal of responsibility for the company's cash management and related financial operations but little in the way of recognized authority. Many experienced cash managers and treasurers can recall their frustrations and difficulties in making even the simplest change in their company's cash management practices. Indeed, many of these people either become diplomats within the firm in order to implement any changes successfully or resigned themselves to a more passive role until organizational revisions or changes allowed more latitude in their roles. The cash managers who took the first path were usually able to accomplish a great deal, maintaining a deferential but innovative posture with the local financial managers throughout the company. This interaction with local personnel is the key to successful implementation, and these relationships can help lay the foundation for the cash manager in establishing control over the company's cash management. One cash manager for a large corporation with many decentralized operating locations was having a great deal of success in modifying his company's cash management systems, setting up strategically located lock box points and funding most operating disbursement accounts efficiently through controlled disbursement accounts, but he was having considerable difficulty with several locations that refused to alter their banking relationships or even to modify the method of compensation from balances to fees. During the course of frequent visits with the local financial managers, the cash manager thought he had arrived at a mutual understanding and agreement only to discover afterward that nothing was changed. This became particularly frustrating after one instance in which one bank had agreed to convert to fees for a large retail lock box service but the local operation kept sufficient excess balances in its disbursement account to offset any fees it was to pay. When questioned about it, the local financial manager freely acknowledged the situation with the comment, "You guys don't understand, do you? In our monthly performance review meetings, I have to explain every lousy charge against my budget, even the bank fees; but no one ever questions my bank balances. Now what do you think I'm going to do?" This "feedback" was instrumental in the cash manager's convincing corporate financial management of the merits of assuming all bank costs and fees centrally under his own budget. Once this change was made, any pressure was removed from the local financial managers and the excess balances disappeared quickly. In addition, the cash manager had then established effective control over bank costs.

In this section we discuss the nature of control in a treasury or cash management sense and consider its logical links with information management. More specifically, our discussion deals with an operational definition of control, the essential elements of control and information, accounting influences and requirements, and a conceptual approach to decision support systems for treasury.

Control Defined

Before considering what *control* means in operational terms, it will be useful to review what *cash* means in a treasury sense. When a treasurer or cash manager looks at or talks about cash, they mean the actual working funds of the corporation, the amounts of funds that are available and/or accessible to the firm through its banking system and related sources of credit (excluding trade-related transactions). This definition of cash, it should be noted, does not consider any accounting aspects of cash and is much more flexible in nature in order to reflect more accurately the pragmatics of the treasury function. Working from this basis, the concept of treasury or cash management *control* can then be defined. Control is, therefore, the ability to establish, identify, monitor, and mobilize flows of funds throughout the entire organization. It entails the cataloging of vast amounts of relevant cash management and banking data, the documentation of financial transactions, and the establishment of effective sources and uses of cash. It is not an imaginary concept but a real, operational "fact of life." It must exist in some way, shape, or form in every corporation, whatever the cash management configuration. During the last few years, the centralization of this control function has become more commonplace, thereby allowing a company to enjoy the economies of scale associated with this form of financial consolidation.

Elements of Control

The essential elements of control are integrally linked with information systems in that bank balance and detail reporting systems, internal corporate projections and financial reporting procedures, and other external sources are fundamental components of an overall control system. The major elements are as follows:

> Flows of funds.
> Flows of data.
> Analytical functions.
> Organizational interactions.

These elements must be brought together in an integrated fashion if an effective control system is to be created.

The *flows of funds*, the first set of these elements, are the basic determinants of the nature of the control system. They affect the scope and complexity of the system and, depending on their size, frequency, and occurrence, will often dictate the level of control necessary or even possible. To integrate the flows of funds into a control system, the cash manager must be able to determine how much of the total flows he or she can effectively incorporate into a central system. For example, if the company's organization is quite decentralized and has been for some time, it will probably be a mammoth undertaking for the cash manager to consider taking over all payment and receipt transactions. On the other hand, an effective control system may be structured to upstream automatically receipts from a network of corporate lock box collection points into a central concentration account and to convert the many major local disbursement accounts to controlled accounts with the corporate concentration bank. In this manner, the cash manager has established control over the funding of disbursements and the concentration of receipts without taking on the detailed initiation of the billing or paying functions.

The *flows of data*, on the other hand, should be handled in a different fashion. To establish an effective control system over the firm's cash management activities, the cash manager will have to construct an accurate, timely, and comprehensive information system that incorporates much of the relevant flows of cash management data. Note the difference between this set of elements and the prior one; data flows should be controlled or incorporated into the control system to a much greater degree than funds flows. This is also the bond between control and information management. The data flows associated with cash management activities are both internal and external to the company. The internal flows encompass many of the types of information described in the cash scheduling and planning section, including estimates of cash flows and cash funding requirements. Other types of data may vary from firm to firm. A typical example of some other types of data would involve the quantitative descriptions of cash management activities for major domestic and foreign subsidiaries that operate autonomously from the parent. Data needed would include the investment and borrowing levels and rates, bank credit line arrangements, and major bank operating relationships. In these instances, the central cash manager would have little control over the subsidiary's activities but should receive and review the data to provide a consolidated analysis and description of the overall company's credit sources and cash management performance. Also, the interchange of data between the cash manager and his or her counterpart at an independent subsidiary can be very educational for both sides. Each side can keep the other informed as to developments in the banking or money markets, and each one can readily compare the terms or details of their financial transactions to determine the feasibility of prospective transactions or the realized benefit of ones already completed. Unencumbered interchange of data is important between such operations without the fear of competition or second-guessing.

External types of data flows usually include current information from the corporation's banks relating to cash flows or bank balances, short-term investing or borrowing transactions, and historical bank balance and service activities normally included in bank account analyses. These types of data are vital portions of the control system. The current balance and cash flow information dictate what funds movements are required and how accurate the cash estimating activities have been. Utilizing these data in cash position management also helps in determining the level of short-term liquidity activity that is necessary daily or in the short run. The account analyses and historical bank balance levels are important in setting or revising bank target balances for the cash position management function and in evaluating different bank services as well. Effective control can be established only when these various types of data are regularly received and incorporated in the routine cash management activities. This usually suggests some form of central review of the data, since receiving the data in many diverse points tends to inhibit the timely review and overall utilization of the information in a manner that will improve the firm's cash management performance.

The most common and effective manner of receiving bank balance and detailed transaction information utilizes bank balance reporting systems. Exhibits 3.16 and 3.17 outline the typical corporate needs, scope, typical problems, and some of the developing trends for these services. The typical needs range from simple balances and detailed debits and credits to more specialized types of data such as incoming wire transfers or summaries of numerous zero balance accounts maintained at the bank. The scope of the systems has continued to expand in recent years, offering transfer initiation capabilities for use in automatically moving funds to more customized services such as investment portfolio and foreign exchange contract reporting. Typical problems relate to the timing and accuracy of the data, as well as to the lack of standardization among different systems. The Tuesday problem cited in the exhibit refers to a common situation on Tuesday mornings in which one or more of the reporting systems is unavailable, or "down," to the user. This occurrence is usually explained by the system providers as related to or caused by the typical overload in check processing in banks on Mondays. It has been decreasing in frequency in recent times, but any cash manager using these systems should not be surprised by such occurrences. Thornier problems are the lack of standardization among systems and the differences in terminology both within systems and across systems. The former poses some problems for the cash manager until familiarity with each system's approach is gained. The latter is also overcome through usage, but it still bothers many cash managers who are used to thinking of their accounts by title or other alphabetic description to find the systems more numeric or abbreviated in their identifying labels. The developing trends in these systems have attempted to overcome the typical problems and expand the scope and usage of the systems by the corporate cash manager. Movements toward common formats and interbank data exchange hold promise for enhanced systems in the relatively near future. The introduction of automation or direct computer linkups are also important developments that can improve treasury control.[5]

Receiving and reviewing the data and controlling some or all of the firm's cash flows are important aspects of control, but they lose much of their impact if not tied together through an analytical function. Analytical func-

EXHIBIT 3.16   BANK BALANCE REPORTING SYSTEMS—NEEDS

Typical Corporate Needs

Account balances.
   Ledger & collected.
   Opening balances/start of day or close of business yesterday.
   Same-day balances.
Detailed debits & credits.
   Accounting use.
   Reconciling purposes.
Lock box deposits.
   Same day clearings.
   Deposit float.
   Major items.
Depository transfer check transactions/registers.
   Available same day (late PM).
   Good funds next day (usually).
   Timing to resolve errors/omissions.
Zero-balance summaries.
Incoming wire transfers (usually over set limit).
   Especially useful for international transfers.
   May offer search capability.
   May offer "you will receive" capability.
Multiple bank/international balance reporting.
   One system for many banks useful when primarily balances are needed;
   more difficult when details are sought. Common carrier(s) evolving; e.g.,
   Banklink, Cash Management Exchange, Interactive Data, ADP.
   Overseas branches & local banks (latter hard to get).

tions can range from the simple to complex, depending on the extent of the company's cash management system. In smaller systems with relatively few operating locations and banking arrangements, these activities can easily be incorporated into the daily cash position and target balance routines and the periodic evaluation of the cash estimates. In more decentralized and larger systems, the analyses will require more effort and supporting tools, such as the bank compensation reporting system discussed in the bank compensation section. As the number and diversity of operating points in the system increase, the need for some automated assistance increases as well. For example, the timing requirements for cash funding decisions in such systems cannot be deferred while laborious manual computations are performed. This

EXHIBIT 3.17   BANK BALANCE REPORTING SYSTEMS—SCOPE, PROBLEMS & TRENDS

Scope of Systems

Balance reporting (details, too).
Transfer initiation capabilities.
   Wire transfers from a timeshare terminal.
   Repetitive transfers.
   Free-form transfers.
   Drawdown transfers.
Other services more specialized.
   Investment/borrowing transaction and portfolio reporting.
   Commercial paper issuance instructions.
   Foreign exchange contracts.
   Money market and foreign exchange rates.
Target balance "routines."

Typical Problems

System down-time—the "Tuesday Problem."
Timing of multiple bank/location reporting.
Quality and accuracy of data.
   Absence of data.
   Error correction capabilities (or lack thereof).
Lack of standardization (yet).
Conceptual problems with terminology, account numbers versus titles, and target balances.
Cost of systems.

Developing Trends

Standardized formats, etc. (BAI).
Use of intelligent terminals/microcomputer interfaces.
Direct computer linkups.
Focus on data security.

emerging role of automation in cash management will be outlined further in a later portion of this section and discussed in more detail in the contribution from Mr. David Spiselman in Chapter 4.

The final set of major elements is that of organizational interactions. Throughout the preceding discussions, there has been a continuing theme of information exchange and intracompany communications. It seems rather obvious that these exchanges and communications are in large part determined by historic and ongoing organizational interactions. In the past the interchange between treasury and the operating locations may not have been well developed and, consequently, has imposed a barrier to establishing any system of control over cash management activities. This barrier may not have been explicitly erected, since both parties may have been unaware of their importance to the other. With large, decentralized organizations, central cash management has been a recent development, if it has been pursued to any degree. Accordingly, central cash management staff and local operating managers have been virtual strangers to each other. This absence of interaction has to be overcome before undertaking the gathering of data or considering the establishment of some form of central control. Otherwise, much misinformation will be transmitted in both directions, and feelings of resentment or failures to provide proper data will create serious internal problems. Both parties must be aware of the other's needs, capabilities, and conflicting activities. For example, cash management activities may be a small part-time chore for the local financial manager while it represents a top priority for the central cash manager. This disparity should be recognized and accommodated in any control system. Also, if the central cash manager and the local financial managers do not have regular contact, the exchange of information between them will not be as effective. These relationships must be nurtured carefully if they are to function properly. One method commonly used by some of the larger corporations is to transfer operating personnel from the local units to central treasury staff to fill various staff positions on a regular basis. Central treasury staff personnel are also transferred to local operating financial positions, and in this manner managers on both sides have gained a better understanding and appreciation of the other's needs and functions.

Accounting Influences and Requirements

Most treasury control systems will be heavily influenced by the corporate accounting function and must have the ability to satisfy accounting reporting and audit requirements. These latter requirements may consist of both internal and external obligations in the sense that the corporate accounting function needs transaction data while internal audit (perhaps) and the firm's independent auditors need to be able to review control points and confirm the financial transactions and bank balances of the company. The accounting function, considered broadly, influences the cash management function in that it normally sets forth its requirements in the form of standard transaction confirmation procedures and documentation, bank statement and reconciliation procedures, official documentation for banking relationship authorization, and necessary details for periodic audit evaluation. Often the cash manager must discuss possible system changes with his or her accounting representatives to ensure that corporate standards are not violated or that the potential service will provide adequate levels of detail.

Standard documentation requirements usually entail both *transactions* and *working agreements* with the corporation's banks. The common types of documents associated with these requirements are shown in Exhibit 3.18. The transaction reporting documents should encompass all types of financial transactions that the treasury function handles or is involved with, even if only partially. Individual confirmation letters or reports can take many forms, including individual letters sent to the firm's banks to document funds movements from corporate accounts or the concentration of funds into a central account. Accounting should receive independent confirmation of these transactions from the banks, and these reports can be individual debit or credit "tickets" or detailed bank balance reporting system outputs, as described earlier. Similarly, short-term investment and borrowing transactions are usually confirmed by letter to the broker/dealer, with the latter independently reconfirming the transaction. In each of these instances the accounting department should have received both internal and independent, external records for each transaction, thereby satisfying the requirements of the corporate "checks and balances." Bank statements and related account reconciliations provide financial data to the accounting function so that it can properly complete its normal account monitoring and check disbursement reconcilement responsibilities. Sometimes the bank account recon-

EXHIBIT 3.18 COMMON TYPES OF DOCUMENTS FOR ACCOUNTING

Transaction Reporting

Confirmation letters or reports of individual funds movements to/from corporate accounts.

Detailed transaction reports/details from company's banks.

Short-term liquidity transactions such as investments and borrowings.

Periodic bank statements (monthly).

Monthly account reconciliation reports (optional as some companies perform their own in-house).

Periodic interest income/expense data and portfolio profiles.

Working Agreements

Account authorization documents, including operating instructions, function(s) of account, and relevant corporate board resolutions.

Credit line agreement letters (from bank) and formal legal agreements for revolving credit arrangements.

Periodic (year-end) audit confirmations of credit facilities and bank balances.

cilement responsibilities have remained in the treasury area, but this is generally viewed as a control weakness in an accounting sense as the initiators of financial funding transactions, for instance, should not be able to handle the reconciling of their bank accounts.

The working agreement documents represent official, written communications between the firm and its bankers or other financial institutions. The accounting function is normally involved in establishing most of the financial arrangements and often must supply financial reports to corporate lenders. Thus the need to provide this information to accounting is self-evident. For example, accounting must understand the details of a revolving credit agreement to supply credit facilities to the firm, since it must know whether to treat the borrowings as short or long term and what periodic financial information must be supplied to the lending institutions. Periodically, the audit confirmations of credit lines and bank balances must be handled by the treasury area for the review of these data by internal or independent auditors. This typically occurs at the beginning of the firm's fiscal year and requires special written communications with each corporate bank to send responses to the audit group independently.

These accounting requirements, then, present another set of considerations for the cash manager in establishing an effective control system. The control system must possess the capabilities of producing all transaction reports routinely on a timely and accurate basis. In addition, the system must provide for a centralized source for all bank documentation so that it can be reviewed easily and modified in an orderly and timely basis due to changes in procedures, policies, or personnel. The requirements may exert influence directly in dictating the form and level of transaction detail needed in the system and indirectly in making it quite costly in terms of manual effort to maintain a substantial number of bank accounts or relationships. Obviously, the latter consideration can be a minor one if the benefits of such a system are significant.

Decision Support Systems for Treasury

Efficient structuring of the firm's payment systems and banking arrangements, in conjunction with the essential elements and influences discussed earlier, suggests the need to consider some form of decision support for the treasury operations involved with the company's cash management. Historically, the treasurer or even the cash manager has had few tools or support in controlling the cash management activities of the company. Conceptually, it is possible to devise a decision support system for essential cash management activities in order to assist the cash manager or treasurer in establishing and maintaining control. The decision support system should tie together the diverse activities of the cash manager and offer him or her the ability both to control the corporate cash management system and to utilize analytical techniques effectively.

There are several major building blocks of the conceptual system, and these blocks establish the framework for the system. They encompass the various cash management activities, and in so doing they offer standard analytical and reporting opportunities. Also, by taking advantage of modern technological advances, they can increase the relative productivity of the cash management function substantially. This should allow the cash management function to extend its control over much of the corporate activities without major increases in central staff resources. The major building blocks can be thought of in terms of individual data bases for each major function:

Bank balance reporting.
Money market operations.
Cash projections.
Bank compensation.

Each of these bases has its own characteristics, the extent of which is defined by each corporate case. However, there are common aspects that will tend to be applicable in most cases. The bases alone will not be very effective without additional analytical capabilities and regular operating reports for the cash manager to use.

The bank balance reporting data base comprises a central repository for bank transaction data, gathering all relevant balance and transaction detail from the company's banking network regularly. While the reporting systems differ in format and content somewhat, the data base offers a uniform medium for this information. The means of gathering numerous bank balance reporting system data is by no means simple. The use of microcomputers to accomplish this task has been increasing recently, and some firms have begun establishing direct computer linkups with their major banks to gather data automatically. (Further discussions of this approach are included in Chapter 4.) Once input into the base, the use of the data for target balance measurement or cash position management is possible. This data base also will support the funds movement activity, as the funds initiation services offered by most bank balance reporting systems can be accessed in conjunction with this data base. Analytical reports can suggest short-term target balance changes and funds movements to accomplish them. Also, when integrated with the other data bases, they can be used to record and effect funds movements for local account funding, cash concentration, and liquidity management activities.

The money market operations data base comprises the short-term liquidity operations for the firm. It records daily investment and/or borrowing transactions and uses these data, together with data from other bases, to project the net cash needs or excesses of the firm. In situations where the money market activity is substantial, involving different sources of short-term borrowings, for instance, this base plays a key role in integrating the cash manager's activities. In such cases, analytical capabilities and comparative reports such as those that were outlined earlier are essential features. The captured data with future maturities also can be of great use in analyzing the company's projected cash position and can help in formulating short-term borrowing or investment strategies as well. Regular operating reports generated by this base should include accounting reports and maturity schedules for the cash manager. At present, most of the data to be input into this base is, unfortunately, not available in machine-readable form and must be input manually. Some bank balance reporting systems are beginning to consider some level of automation in this area. Firms selling their own commercial paper directly, for instance, may possess the ability to spin off essential records for this area, but such firms are few.

The cash projection data base takes the cash estimates and places them in a common format, allowing us to analyze differences and make modifications efficiently. Data can be input manually if they are not too voluminous, or tie-ins to local computer systems can be of help in handling data input. To incorporate the telephone type of system discussed in Section 3.3, manual entry would probably be the method chosen. Again, developments in microcomputer applications may offer some help in the future. The projection data base provides the expected cash flow data to compare with the actual data reported by the bank balance reporting systems. As such, it is an integral part of the cash position management activities. It is also used in analyzing possible future cash positions or anticipated money market transactions and assessing their impact. By linking this base with the others, sophisticated analytical techniques can be incorporated into the cash manager's "toolkit."

The last base is the bank compensation data base, which provides the historical tracking and record of the firm's banking network. Inputs come

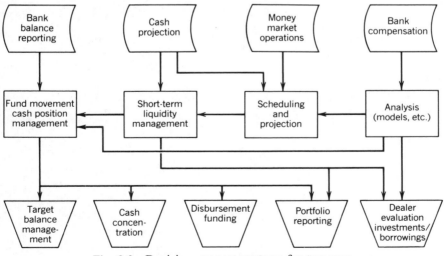

Fig. 3.2   Decision support systems for treasury.

from the monthly account analysis statements and data from the balance reporting data base. This base provides overall analyses of bank compensation performance, producing reports similar to those discussed in Chapter 2. In addition, it computes appropriate bank target balances and compares bank costs for similar services. This data base offers many analytical possibilities, drawing from historical data, and it can be extremely valuable in investigating new services or in resolving problems with the firm's banks. When structured to include the balances from any independent subsidiaries, it also provides a means of monitoring their performance in a manner similar to the rest of the corporation.

These data bases, then, encompass the major areas of cash management that must be included in any control system. The manner in which they fit together and the major analytical capabilities discussed earlier are shown in Figure 3.2. The conceptual decision support system can be considered as a beginning, a blueprint for the cash manager in constructing and maintaining an effective and beneficial system of control for the company's cash management activities.

NOTES

1. Stigum or Meek offers excellent details of major money market instruments for both short-term investing and borrowing.
2. Sample reports shown in these exhibits have been simplified for exemplary purposes.
3. This wording should be reviewed with the firm's legal staff or advisors to suit the individual situation.
4. See, for example, Hodgson on Box-Jenkins.
5. Banklink (from Chemical Bank), the Cash Management Exchange (from National Data Corporation), Interactive Data Corporation, and the Automated Data Processing Corp. offer systems with data interchange capabilities and common input/output standards.

4 Future Directions and Case Studies

Ignoring the dangers of prognostications, it seems appropriate to address some of the newer, more dynamic issues of cash management. As one cash management guru has so eloquently phrased it, "These are exciting times for those who are easily excited!" This comment probably depicts the state of cash management more accurately than anything else at the current time. In this chapter several key developing issues in corporate cash management will be explored, including:

Changes in the banking system structure—in particular, the 1980 Monetary Control Act and the advent of "fee-for-service" banking in the corporate sector.

Electronic funds transfer systems (EFTS)—the fundamental aspects and standard applications for the corporate user; common myths concerning the subject; and counterbalancing forces of EFTS.

The role of automation. This issue will be addressed in a contribution by Mr. David Spiselman.

Direct computer linkups between corporations and banks. This newer development is discussed with an illustration of the concept.

The global cash management environment—the emerging international considerations for corporate cash management, including a brief discussion of the fundamental similarities and differences between domestic and international cash management at the current time. This latter discussion will also look at the extension of cash management techniques and mentalities to overseas locations.

Finally, as a means of review of the cash management function, this chapter will conclude with a series of case studies and exercises. The cases will display the different aspects of cash management by offering relatively simple problems to be solved by the reader.

SECTION 4.1   CHANGES IN BANKING SYSTEM STRUCTURE

For many years the banking system has been a steady factor in corporate cash management, unchanged in any radical sense and slowly evolving over time through the efforts of corporate cash managers and their banking counterparts. However, in 1980 the Monetary Control Act was enacted, and it has created a new environment for cash management. The general intent of the act was to instruct the Federal Reserve to charge for its services on an equitable basis. In doing so, the costs of the Fed's services were to be passed on to the commercial banks, which, in turn, could be expected to pass them on to their corporate customers. This has indeed been the case, as evidenced by the significant growth in bank service charges since 1980. Some reports have put this increase at the 50% level for most major bank noncredit services. This has been a major change in corporation–bank relationships and has been at least a partial cause for reevaluating the number of bank relationships a company maintains. This development, coupled with the general maturity of cash management throughout major corporations, has contributed to a gradual reduction or compression of banking relations. These companies are now tending to use more cash management services with a fewer number of banks. There should be no doubt that the Monetary Control Act was in part responsible for accelerating this decision, and in this sense it has had a beneficial effect. The ultimate effects of the act will not be obvious for some time, but one of the more significant developments will be to force many banks to decide whether they will continue the full complement of cash management services to their corporate customers or not. Already there has been some movement in this area, with Morgan Guaranty Trust announcing in 1982 it was disbanding its corporate lock box services. The implementation of the act has also shown improvement in the Fed's check clearance activities, reducing Fed Float from the $5–6 billion range to a much lower $1.5–2.0 billion level.[1]

All of this activity has created an environment in which the corporate cash manager has been forced to reevaluate the company's method of compensation. This decision has also been encouraged by the volatile conditions in the money markets and the possible scarcity of credit for corporate customers. The compression of bank relationships and related cash management activities has also been a critical factor in causing corporations to consider fee compensation instead of balances. This reorientation has not been ignored by major banks, which have been able to change their approach to assessing the profitability of corporate customers to include fee income as well as or instead of traditional balances maintained. More forward-thinking banks no longer just look at the level of balances a company has maintained but have begun to take all forms of income into consideration. This has important implications for the cash manager in that fee compensation tends to bring a different perspective to bank services. That is, if a cash manager has to pay a direct fee for the various bank services for the company, he or she is more thorough in reviewing the details of the services and becomes more demanding as far as performance is concerned. This change in approach tends to alter the traditional corporation–bank relationship and make it appear more similar to a service provider arrangement. As most cash managers and bankers will admit, balance compensation is somewhat "sloppy" in that the compensating balances are not usually precisely maintained, whereas fee compensation is extremely precise. Thus the corporate cash manager and banker usually assume much tougher postures in assessing the overall profitability of the corporate activity for the current period. This change in approach will have direct influence over the timeliness, accuracy, and level of detail the bank must supply the cash manager in support of the monthly service fees. In addition, if a corporate cash manager has established a fee compensation arrangement with the company's major banks, the need for timely balance reports will be increased as well, as there is no reason for the company to maintain any excess balances with the bank.[2]

SECTION 4.2 ELECTRONIC FUNDS TRANSFER SYSTEMS

In many respects the fundamental concept of electronic funds transfer systems (EFTS) is an appealing one: to replace the current check-based system with an electronic-based one. The relatively slow growth EFTS has exhibited since its basic design in the mid-1970s is not too surprising to most experienced cash managers. The main reason seems to be the perceived loss of significant amounts of float by current issuers of checks, and despite many attempts by well-intentioned champions of the EFTS cause there has not been dramatic acceptance by corporate users. With the recent increased growth in bank charges for paper-based services, improvement by the Fed in its check clearing and reduction of Fed float, and more experience in processing by the automated clearing houses throughout the country, there is an optimistic outlook for EFTS in the near future.

The fundamentals of EFTS are simple and straightforward. The *automated clearinghouses (ACH's)* have the capabilities to interface electronically with each other, thereby linking a member of any clearinghouse with all other members. Transactions can be value-dated, that is, transmitted into the system prior to the day when the funds will be available to the recipient. This should offer attractive options to firms that make routine transfers for similar or predetermined amounts on a regular basis. Through direct deposit of payroll applications, companies can pay their employees around the country electronically without worrying about physically delivering paychecks or setting up special check-cashing arrangements at local banks. The current applications that should be of interest to most corporate cash managers include direct deposit of payroll, electronic depository transfer checks cleared through the ACH network, and funds transfers through the ACH. (These applications are discussed in more detail in Chapter 1.)

In addition, there are some other applications currently under development or utilized by just a few companies. These include preauthorized debit and credit transfers, utilized by some large insurance firms for collection of monthly premium payments (debits) and payments to annuity holders (credits). Several other firms have also begun to use the ACH network for preauthorized credit transfers to local dealers, although not without some problems.[3] Other firms have also begun to use the ACH for payment of periodic dividend payments to shareholders and routine payments to retirement and pension fund recipients, in a similar manner as the U.S. government has done with its social security payments.

There are a few common myths surrounding EFTS, and they may be partially responsible for its slow development. The first one is that corporations are "obsessed" with the generation and elongation of float and will resist anything that works against this process. Although there may be some validity in this, most corporations already are involved in EFTS to the extent that they are frequent users of wire transfers. In addition, many companies routinely depend on electronic transfers for international receipts and payments. Many companies have also converted their cash concentration systems to the ACH network.[4] Another myth involves the costs of EFTS and paper-based functions. Unfortunately, many well-meaning analysts have produced studies showing that EFTS is considerably cheaper than paper with little in the way of actual experience or verification of the cost factors used. This has caused such studies to be received with skepticism or disbelief. Empirical work in this area is necessary to improve the quality and reasonability of approaching EFTS on a cost–benefit basis.[5] One other common myth concerns employee acceptance of any electronic service. Many companies reported early resistance to any such arrangement, citing employee distrust from labor organizations within the firm. However, much of this response seemed to have been created by the natures of the surveys or the general lack of understanding by the employees. Indeed, many companies have successfully implemented direct deposit of payroll, for instance, by replacing costly mailing procedures with electronic transfers. In such cases the employees were rather indifferent to the means of receipt, since they did not personally handle their paychecks anyway.

An illustration of determining the feasibility of using an ACH transfer for paying an employee is shown in Exhibit 4.1. The costs shown are sample ones and should not be taken literally. This type of analysis can be completed by the cash manager with the help of the payroll processing personnel and can put the cost–benefit decision in proper perspective. Additional costs for either alternative can be added as the individual situation warrants. In addition, the computer start-up costs can be expressed as a relatively fixed amount, rather than a per item cost as shown. Again, the individual cash manager should tailor the analysis to suit his or her company's specific case.

In most cases of assessing the feasibility of EFTS for the corporation, the cash manager will encounter several counterbalancing forces. These

EXHIBIT 4.1   COST OF PAYING AN EMPLOYEE

	Check	EFT/ACH
Paid item charge	0.070	0.050
Security cost		
Check signer	0.001	—
Storage	0.014	—
Paper cost	0.028	0.006
Reconciliation		
Bank charges	0.030	—
Accounting dept.	0.016	0.010
Start-up costs	—	0.020
	‾‾‾‾‾	‾‾‾‾‾
Total direct costs	0.159	0.086
Difference*	0.073	

NOTE: These comparisons are based on an "either/or" situation. If only a percentage converted, the potential savings would only be 0.073 times the percentage converting to ACH.

*To the extent that float loss and/or early funding does not exceed $.073 per check, then the EFT/ACH route is cheaper.

forces, shown in Exhibit 4.2, may be either real or perceived (by the cash manager). In either case they will influence any decision regarding EFTS for the corporation. The first one, economic impact, is the natural starting point for consideration. The economics of EFTS are usually the first hurdle, and, as shown on the exhibit, usually are treated in terms of how much of a loss will be experienced. Although this result is not unilateral, the approach may well be. The second force, technology, displays some of the skepticism or mistrust of automation still prevalent in many corporations. Salesmanship and bank relations can become larger forces if not handled effectively and need to be considered seriously. Finally, the auditors' acceptance and understanding, although listed last on the list, can exert much influence over the decision if the audit group does not have a good grasp of EFTS principles

EXHIBIT 4.2   EFTS AND THE CORPORATION

Counterbalancing Forces—Real or Perceived:

Economic impact—what will I lose?

Technology—does it really work as described, or what parts are not "operating" yet?

Salesmanship—will it create another labor problem?

Bank relations—will I have new problems with my local banks?

Audit—will my auditors accept the system?

or the potential application has not been reviewed with them in some detail before final design has been completed.

In summary, EFTS has begun to move from its dormant, slow-growing posture and should be able to develop at a much faster rate in the near future. The impact of rising costs for paper-based systems, improved capabilities, and more efficient clearing options for the ACH network should serve as catalysts in that development. The myths of the past would appear to be diminishing as user acceptance of the field increases.

Recently, this growth in user acceptance has been evidenced by several attempts at establishing corporate-to-corporate EFT payment systems. One major system, PETROCLEAR, has been in existence for some time among major oil companies. Participating companies net each other's obligations monthly with only the net differences being actually transferred, much like most multilateral netting systems used by multinational firms for their internal obligations. The key in this situation was the large dollar amounts of the payments and the fact that the participating firms all dealt with one another quite frequently. Thus, they all perceived a benefit from the netting; that is, the elimination of large amounts of duplicate funds being mailed to each other in check form. Another development has been a pilot system involving several major companies and their vendors. In this pilot a group of firms will attempt to effect vendor payments through the ACH network. The federal government has also announced its intentions to participate in this project, and it is hoped that this will boost the chances of success and general acceptance of the system as was the case in converting many social security payments from check to direct deposit.

SECTION 4.3   THE ROLE OF AUTOMATION

This subject will be discussed in further detail in the accompanying contribution by David Spiselman. In it Mr. Spiselman considers the basic feature of systems development in the treasury area and the cash management function in particular. He provides descriptions of major elements and suggests a conceptual framework for a data base for an automated cash management system.

The second part of this section then deals with the new area of cash management, that of integrating the computer systems of the bank and the corporation.

Automating the Cash Management Function*

Your corporation's computer can actually earn additional income for the firm—and a substantial amount at that. Although most application systems

---

*This section is written by Mr. David Spiselman. Mr. Spiselman is an independent cash management consultant in New York City. He and Susan Hinko conduct a course in cash management at N.Y.U. School of Continuing Education.

are perceived as vehicles to reduce operating expenses or enlarge peak capacity, occasionally a systems development opportunity occurs that may increase net corporate income. The cash management system (CMS) described in this article is such an opportunity.

The past history of financial systems development leaves some problems to be resolved before effective CMS can be routinely developed and implemented in most corporations. The corporate treasurer's office is responsible for controlling the cash balances in the firm's demand deposit accounts by balancing loans due to creditors and investments maturing against receipts from customers and disbursements to suppliers. This set of functions is collectively known as *cash management*, and most corporations currently perform these functions in a labor-intensive manner. Most employees of the typical corporate treasurer's office have not been involved in any large-scale systems development effort. As a result of this lack of contact, treasury officials and systems management often continue to speak different languages and remain unfamiliar with each others' responsibilities. Systems people may be familiar with the language and functions of the controller—who "owns" the data in a typical corporation—but there are significant linguistic and functional differences between the controllership and treasury. The controller's sytems run on a physical month cycle and use accruals, whereas the treasurer depends on a billing statement cycle and needs information reflecting cash receipts and disbursements. This makes it more difficult for a corporate treasury to access and interpret the data that is available in the controller's systems. Accounting systems that might supply data for the treasurer may be distributed geographically, making data access and aggregation very difficult on a cycle other than that of the controller's monthly closing. Note that the treasurer needs more timely information, usually on a daily basis. The volatility of today's business environment creates additional data processing problems—shorter systems life cycle preceding obsolescence, substantial lead times for developing and installing computer systems, increasing speed of technological change, and now, in part as a result of these factors, the increasing incidence of electronic theft of funds—but the changing environment also requires a more thoughtful approach to assisting the corporate treasurer in performing the cash management responsibilities. Specifically, as the cost of funds has increased to record levels and as volatile change in interest rates has become the typical expectation of financial executives, the incentive to control and better use the firm's liquid assets has increased. In some cases the corporate treasurer has already responded by requesting the assistance of the corporate systems group. For an effective CMS to be developed and implemented, the data processing–treasury language barrier must be resolved before or during the early part of the systems development process. Both parties must be sure that they understand each other in order to ensure that the resulting systems product measures up to expectations. Where the firm is decentralized and the accounting systems supplying financial transaction data to the cash management function are organized in a correspondingly distributed pattern, it may be difficult to fulfill the system requirements of timely access to all the firm's financial transaction data if the CMS is to include forecasting models that reflect the receipt and disbursement behavior of the corporation's customers and suppliers and models to perform investment–borrowing analyses.

The contributions that automation can make arise from defining cash management as the "movement of data" (or funds transfers) and the "reporting of data" (or balance reporting) within and across the banking network. Since the flow of funds is heavily influenced by such factors as the variance in the term structure of interest rates across countries, transaction costs and bank fees, and forecasts of profits by line of business and location, the problem of placing funds where they are needed is one that automation can simulate; thus, through forecasting, automation can create a better perspective for the corporate cash manager.

The benefits of automating the cash management function fall into two categories. There are the economic benefits of increasing interest income (or reducing interest expense) through automated forecasting of receipts and disbursements and selectively mismatching sources and uses of funds. Then there are the operating benefits of reducing the possibilities of missed investment opportunities, illiquidity through a data "synchronization" crisis (where the firm's computers and those of its banks report different balance amounts in the corresponding accounts), or lost assets through computer fraud. It may be difficult to quantify the value of the operating benefits of improved data accuracy and security, but the other (economic) benefits can easily be estimated. These economic benefits fall into the following categories.

Interest Income from Reduced Liquidity Buffer.   Improved forecasting can enable the corporate treasury to reduce the firm's cash cushion safely when designed to ensure liquidity in cases of unforeseen requirements or in situations where the firm's banks are paid fees instead of compensating balances. The "reclaimed" funds can be invested or substituted for funds that the firm would have had to borrow or raise in capital markets. Note that as more banks are paid fees instead of compensating balance requirements, these economic benefits will become increasingly attractive.

Interest Income from Closely Matching Domestic Receipt and Disbursement Patterns with Term Structure of Interest Rates for Available Investments and Borrowings.   Improved forecasting may enable the treasurer's office to take advantage of the spread between long-term and short-term interest rates for domestic operations, assuming a single concentration bank account fed by multiple zero-balance accounts. When the yield curve is normal, relatively longer-term investments return higher rates than shorter-term investments. The positive incentive to make longer-term investments instead of shorter-term investments is measured by the difference between these rates, or "spread." The spread for such investments has exceeded 200 basis points (2%) in recent years, averaging about 100 basis points. When the yield curve is inverted and shorter-term investments earn at better rates than longer-term investments, the spreads for borrowings have gone even higher. These spreads can be used to compute the value of accurately forecasting float, and recovering one day's float for use in the short-term investment portfolio, or to reduce the amount of short-term borrowings required. The formula to compute the value of daily cash flow is [(Annual receipts) + (annual disbursements)]/365 days in a year. Multiplying this figure by the interest rate spread between short-term and long-term rates yields the pretax value of recovering one day's productive use of float in the short-term investment portfolio for a whole year. For improvements of more than one day, multiply the answer by the number of days. Note that the same concept works in reverse for borrowing, where there is an economic benefit to be incurred when borrowing for shorter periods at either lower rates or at lower transaction costs. The only problem in applying the concept in a "real-life" environment is the difficulty in hitting and holding equilibrium when interest rates and other factors are ever-changing.

Interest Income from Float on International Receipts and Disbursements.   Improved forecasting may enable the treasurer's office to earn additional interest income on foreign receipts and disbursements where international funds movement makes concentration arrangements unmanageable. This opportunity arises from the large differences among countries between their typical mail and funds clearing times. The realization of the economic benefit may be relatively difficult to achieve, but if the corporation can modify its operating methods to take advantage of country differences in mail and check float, the paybacks can be relatively large.

Current State of the Art.   Most large banks and some systems software vendors provide their corporate clients with off-site cash management system components, which the client can use to select the optimal investment and borrowings mix, given an assumed level of cash and available credit. Corporations attempting to evaluate these systems are in a dilemma regarding just how to interface these systems components with the existing accounting applications software running on their own computers and containing the corporation's raw receipt and disbursement data, and how to develop a system that can provide an effective bank–client financial transaction data interface for reporting and forecasting purposes. A major problem with off-site cash management services is that financial transaction data must be maintained in two locations—the firm's computer, which contains accounting transactions and the forecasting data base, and the off-site timesharing service, which serves to feed the firm's investment–borrowing decision-making function—and both data bases must remain correctly synchronized. This means that both systems must continue to report identical balances on the same account in different computers at the same point in time. If the data bases become unsynchronized, the risks of missed investment opportunities (unused excess cash) and illiquidity (cash shortfalls) arise. Finally, the firm can control data security (authorized access to the firm's bank accounts, which are nothing more than electronic data in computer files at a bank) most effectively when entry to the data is not through a terminal at the firm's site connected by telephone lines to an off-site computer with an open communications link. In consideration of the increasing incidence of electronic theft of funds, the firm should try to keep as much of the cash management function in-house as is possible. The firm can then assume responsibility for physical security of its terminals as well as integrity of its information, since—theoretically, at least—it can better control activities on its own behalf that take place on its own physical premises.

If corporate management is interested in developing a CMS for in-house operation, seminars, university courses in systems and in cash management, and consulting services may help to bridge the language barrier between corporate treasury officials and data processing professionals. Such services are now becoming more commonplace.

System Requirements.   An effectively designed cash management system must achieve seven requirements, regardless of whether the system is partially or entirely automated. These requirements are as follows:

1. Maintaining the CMS data base.
2. Forecasting the net available cash (inclusive of float).
3. Computing the optimal investment–borrowings mix.
4. Posting financial transactions to the general ledger and cash journal.
5. Printing confirmation letters to bankers and brokers.
6. Preparing reports for corporate financial management.
7. Maintaining data accuracy and security.

These requirements are discussed in further detail in subsequent sections.

The CMS would run on-line during the early morning and operate off-line during the later day and at night, as Exhibit 4.3 depicts. Off-line at night, after all new accounting events summarized by journal entries are used to update the corporation's financial transaction data base, the CMS must access the data to forecast the net available cash across the investment–borrowing time horizon and generate the CMS files for on-line use during the early morning. During the early morning, an authorized corporate treasury official examines the net available cash and enters the alternative investment–borrowing set on-line into the computer. The system then computes the optimal investment–borrowing mix and presents it to the corporate treasury official, who can accept it or enter override additions, changes, or deletions prior to acceptance. Later during the day, updates to the CMS data base are made off-line from the accepted investment–borrowing mix, and the CMS generates confirmation letters to the corporation's bankers and brokers. At this time the CMS also posts financial transaction journal entries

XHIBIT 4.3   TYPICAL PROCESSING SCHEDULE

- OFF-LINE AT NIGHT

  PROCESS GENERAL LEDGER ENTRIES
  GENERATE ON-LINE CPMS FILES
  FORECAST NET CASH PORTFOLIO

- ON-LINE DURING EARLY MORNING

  PRESENT THE NET CASH PORTFOLIO
  ACCEPT INVESTMENT SET
  COMPUTE AND PRESENT OPTIMAL INVESTMENT SET
  UPDATE CASH PORTFOLIO DATA BASE

- OFF-LINE LATER IN DAY

  GENERATE CONFIRMATION LETTERS
  CREATE FINANCIAL JOURNAL ENTRIES (FOR LATER BATCH UPDATE)
  PREPARE FINANCIAL REPORTS

and prepares reports for the firm's financial management. These latter functions are done off-line.

Maintaining the CMS Data Base.   Exhibit 4.4 lists some of the more typical data elements that must be keyed by the corporate treasury official to create update transactions to the investments–borrowings mix. The update transactions are keyed on-line during the early morning and are used to update the general ledger cash journal later, off-line at night.

Forecasting the Net Available Cash.   In essence, forecasting of net available cash is the function that is the heart of an effective automated CMS, since it focuses the cash manager's attention on opportunities to control and improve the corporation's cash flow by increasing interest income or reducing interest expense. The state of the art in forecasting makes it possible to

EXHIBIT 4.4   DATA ELEMENTS OF A CMS DATA BASE

1.   TRANSACTION TYPE
2.   TRANSACTION DATE
3.   SETTLEMENT DATE
4.   BANKER / BROKER NAME AND ADDRESS
5.   INVESTMENT / LOAN TYPE
6.   INVESTMENT / LOAN DESCRIPTION
7.   INTEREST RATE OR FEE
8.   INTEREST / FEE TYPE
9.   DAYS TO MATURITY
10. MATURITY DATE
11. PRINCIPAL AMOUNT
12. CURRENCY CODE

select or build dynamic (self-correcting) computer models that automatically and accurately reflect the behavior of "categories" of customer payments and float on the firm's payments made to suppliers. Float itself should be broken down into its components (mail time, internal processing time, and payment clearing time) to improve forecasting precision. The lower the level of detail the CMS can access, the more accurate the forecasts will be, other things held constant. It is not reasonable to assume that enough data will be supplied by manual keying; to make its most significant contribution the CMS must be able to access the firm's computer files (the accounts receivable, accounts payable, expense posting, and cash journal files) without manual intervention. This is so important that it bears repeating: *Short-term forecasting methodologies that work adequately can be developed and implemented*, providing that they:

Have access to the detail financial data transactions of the corporation.

Categorize financial transactions to reflect customer–supplier characteristics accurately.

Contain dynamic models.

Without fulfilling each of these requirements, forecasting is unlikely to be accurate, and relying on inaccurate forecasts can have disastrous results. The key benefits of providing accurate forecasts are as follows:

Improve investment–borrowing mix decisions—liquidate investments prior to maturity or borrow to cover cash shortfalls, and invest or repay existing loans in times of excess cash, based on interest rate spread forecasts.

Modify customer–supplier float characteristics on a gradual and evolving basis, employing forecasts to monitor the effectiveness of the corporation's funding network (lock box network and major banking relations), implementing timely changes to speed receipts and slow disbursements, thereby achieving more productive use of float.

Computing the Optimal Investments–Borrowings Mix.   Taking into account all the corporation's current funding activities, the objective is to mismatch selectively sources and uses of funds to minimize the funding costs over time. Current rates can be accessed in real-time mode through a telecommunications link with outside services such as Telerate. Although both current and future rates are commonly available, an ambitious treasury might forecast future rates and put funds at risk in forward arbitrage. One major corporation does this with a large fraction of its net available cash.

Whatever model the firm purchases or builds to perform this function must permit the treasury to set constraints on the permissible risk characteristics of each element in the acceptable investment set. The borrowings set will also have constraints in the form of credit limits and availability. The CMS maximizes income (minimizes losses) for the firm by optimizing the investments–borrowings mix across the time horizon, subject to constraints. This is a linear programming function. Four events are possible at each point in time, in any combination: Additional funds may be borrowed; investments may mature or be sold prior to maturity; additional investments may be made or rolled over; borrowings may be repaid when due; or some forms of borrowing may be prepaid. The selection of a particular set of tactics will depend on the forecasted low point of the corporation's net cash and the spread between current interest rates and forecasted future rates.

Packaged applications software is available to perform this function, and more will be forthcoming. Alternatively, the corporation's systems management group can undertake a project to custom-build this product.

Posting Financial Transaction Journal Entries.   Exhibit 4.5 displays the activities that require access to the firm's cash journal for posting purposes. At the end of the firm's accounting period these entries will feed the corporate general ledger system. Of course, the entries also constitute an audit trail.

This function cannot be performed by currently existing packages unless they include an integrated general ledger (G/L) system. The situation should improve very shortly since new software packages that perform these functions are now being developed and released at an accelerated rate. This

EXHIBIT 4.5   AUTOMATED POSTING OF GENERAL LEDGER ENTRIES

```
1.  WHEN THE INVESTMENT IS MADE -
    DR - INVESTMENT ASSET
    CR - CASH ASSET

2.  WHEN INVESTMENT MATURES BEFORE END OF PERIOD
    DR - CASH ASSET
    CR - INVESTMENT ASSET
    CR - INTEREST INCOME

3.  WHEN END OF PERIOD OCCURS BEFORE INVESTMENT
    MATURES
    DR - OPEN INVESTMENT ASSET
    CR - INVESTMENT ASSET
    CR - ACCRUED INTEREST INCOME

4.  WHEN INVESTMENT FROM PRIOR PERIOD MATURES
    DR - CASH ASSET
    DR - ACCRUED INTEREST INCOME
    CR - OPEN INVESTMENT ASSET
    CR - INTEREST INCOME

5.  SALE OF INVESTMENT AT LOSS /
    LOAN RESCHEDULING / DEFAULT

6.  DRAW-DOWN OF CREDIT LINE OR
    LOAN

7.  REPAYMENT OR PREPAYMENT OF DEBT
```

interface between the G/L and the CMS is critical to ensure data integrity, data security, and an adequate audit trail.

Printing Confirmation Letters.   A confirmation letter documents the instructions given by the corporation to its broker or banker. It should be printed by the CMS and signed by the corporate treasury officials who authorize the transaction. Keying input records into the system, representing changes to the corporation's net cash, and updating the CMS will automatically trigger the printing of confirmation letters. The letters constitute a physical audit trail.

By prior agreement between the firm and its bankers or brokers, the confirmation letter should have legal standing. Each letter designates the specific service to be performed, subject to the larger contract of the corporate banker–broker relationship. The firm should file a copy of each letter to facilitate the resolution of discrepancies concerning the terms or selection of a particular transaction.

Preparing Reports for Corporate Financial Management.   An effective CMS must produce reports to assist the corporate treasury in performing its function. The CMS must also produce reports for outside parties (auditors and regulatory agencies) and other areas of corporate financial management.

The short-term forecasting subsystem should produce a report summarizing the forecasting errors on a periodic basis to enable financial management to review and adjust the performance of their forecasting models and to control liquidity risk. Of course, forecast reports should also be printed as a backup.

Reporting requirements will vary widely from firm to firm, but the bases from which reports are prepared will always be the financial data transactions and the CMS data base, which yield the net available cash. The system can produce the cash manager's and treasurer's reports daily in batch mode, along with the confirmation letters. Reports for the other parties can be printed in batch mode monthly, with quarterly, semiannual, and annual recaps. Exhibit 4.6 lists some of the typical reports that might constitute the information requirements to support cash management.

Maintaining Data Accuracy and Security.   The CMS data base must have a mechanism that can be used to correct or change data previously entered into the system. Changes and corrections should be keyed by a different person from the one who originally keyed the transaction, especially in larger firms where it might otherwise be difficult to maintain good auditing standards. All data entry activities, especially changes and corrections, should provide a hard-copy audit trail, which should be sent to a third party, such as an internal auditor. Controlling authorized access to the CMS is also an absolute necessity. Where possible, different people should be responsible for moving funds and for investing funds. Finally, when the corporate treas-

EXHIBIT 4.6 REPORTS FOR FINANCIAL MANAGEMENT

1. PERIODIC MONEY MARKET INVESTMENTS INCOME REPORT

2. DAILY PURCHASES REPORT

3. INVESTMENT / CREDIT CONSTRAINTS REPORT

4. MATURED / SOLD / REPAYED
   INVESTMENTS / LOANS REPORT

5. END OF PERIOD OPEN INVESTMENTS REPORT

6. POTENTIAL SWAPS REPORT

7. CASH POSITION FORECAST REPORT

---

ury considers transmitting financial transaction data using terminals that connect through public telephone lines to a computer with an open telecommunications port, the senior management of the firm should understand the lack of laws of evidence in cases of computer fraud and be willing to accept the risk of possible fraud that can arise from this situation. There are two component issues of concern here: data accuracy and data security.

Data Accuracy. On-line data entry of changes to the CMS data base will ensure a low rate of human error and reduce the associated correction and opportunity costs. This is so because on-line review of what is keyed eliminates the need for later return to the terminal to correct the error. All update entries must be authorized by a corporate treasury official, reviewed on-line after keying, and corrections made, if necessary, prior to printing confirmation letters. The reports for financial management and other audit trail reports should ensure data accuracy.

Data Security. There are many effective methods to prevent physical access types of data security problems. Locks can be placed on the CRT, and the CRT can be placed in a locked office. Less-effective methods exist to secure automated access. User passwords and identification codes are insecure at best. Aggravating this problem is the difficulty of securing data communications across voice-grade public telephone lines for data transmitted between the corporate treasurer's terminal located at the corporation and its bankers' and brokers' open telecommunications ports at off-site computers. Two problems can result from such an arrangement.

The first problem revolves around difficulties in synchronizing the firm's financial transaction records with the trustee's off-site cash management system records. Since some of the data elements are maintained at both sites, there is duplication of data, which leaves open the possibility of a data synchronization crisis, causing the two systems to report different balances. Assuming that human error and not computer fraud caused such a crisis, the problem of resynchronization still remains. Left unresolved, the dangers of missed investment opportunities and inadequate liquidity are possible.

The other problem that results from such an arrangement is the difficulty in preventing unauthorized access to the corporation's computer records through the banker–broker's open port. Anyone with access to a computer terminal with an acoustic modem can contact the off-site computer and request investments or divestments, or even transfer cash payments, if he knows or can learn (through trial and error) the telephone number of the computer and its telecommunications protocols. Most of what one needs to know can be learned on the job; no experience is necessary. Check digit routines offer no real security, since, at the very worst, one needs only 10 opportunities to break the code. Finally, since the banker–broker may have thousands of clients, there are many correct combinations of user identification codes and passwords, facilitating successful penetration. Given the current trend in computer fraud of increasing frequency of theft with larger amounts taken, and the legal ambiguities regarding what constitutes evidence, no firm should consider the transmission or receipt of funds over public telephone lines to be without risk. To the greatest extent possible, the firm should use its own computer facility to manage its own cash requirements. Internal automation can minimize the likelihood of "casual" computer fraud. Given that many firms will continue the practice of using telephone networks to report on balances and to move funds, the following precautions may minimize the potential for fraud:

Limit the maximum dollar amount per telephone transaction.

Install leased lines into the open-ported computer.

Use a callback procedure, where the recipient of the instructions calls the sender to confirm their source.

Define, through a legally executed doument, the responsibilities and liabilities of each party in the relationship.

Summary. The benefits of automating the cash management function are as follows:

Increased interest income (or reduced interest expense) through computerized forecasting of receipts and disbursements float, prices of stocks and materials, borrowing and investing interest rates, and foreign exchange rates.

Reduced possibility of missed investment opportunities, illiquidity (through a data synchronization crisis), or lost assets (through a computer fraud).

The economic benefits can easily be estimated prior to commissioning a project. It is likely that an effectively automated cash management system can substantially increase the pretax net income of a firm and yield a surprisingly fast payback of investment. The corporate treasury is the last remaining area of corporate life existing without the benefits of automation and constitutes the greatest challenge to the skills of systems developers.

Bank–Corporation Computer Linkups

Figure 4.1 shows a system layout for a computer linkup between a bank and company. As stated on the chart, it purports to be the next step in cash management information system integration. This can be accomplished by linking the company's major banks in this type of configuration or in a similar one. In this illustration the data reporting is triggered by having the bank dial up the company's computer system directly to transmit balances and details concerning daily activity with the bank. This arrangement can then be repeated by each major bank. The normal time for such transmissions is very early in the morning (usually before 5 or 6 A.M. local time) after the bank's processing has been completed. The bank was chosen as the initiator in this example, as it was the party that knew when the data would be ready for transmission. A practical alternative to this would have the company computer staff be the initiator at a predetermined time or based on an off-line telephone call from the bank's computer personnel. This alternative arrangement has been more popular from the bank's viewpoint to minimize the bank's concerns about data security.

In either case the end result is the receipt of detailed bank balance and transaction data directly into the company's computer system. After this

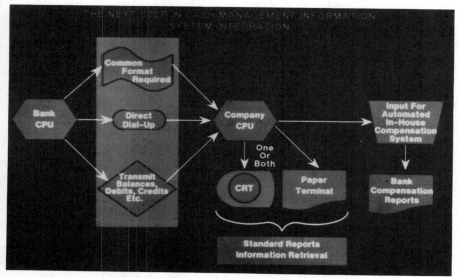

Fig. 4.1 Bank to corporate computer linkup.

the data can be reformatted, analyzed, reported, or transmitted under the company's own control. Reports can be sent to outlying units through the company's internal computer system, for instance, or different areas of corporate treasury and accounting can access individualized reports for their functions. Types of standardized reports that can be obtained include the following:

Cash Management Exception Reports. These reports enable the cash manager to monitor bank balances, react to exceptional situations or surprises in any bank account, and take necessary actions to resolve major problems quickly. Typical reports would include lists of nonreporting banks, balances significantly over or under target (the difference would be set by the user) for corporate accounts as well as for independent operations, total cash available or needed by a major bank for the day, and recommended actions for the cash manager to take that day.

Accounting Transaction Reports. These reports would show detailed debits and credits for corporate accounts in a common format for use by the accounting function. This would replace much of the paperwork currently shipped by treasury to accounting daily and would greatly streamline and integrate the accounting–treasury interface. The common format feature would also be attractive.

Cash Projection Variance Reports. These reports would be produced if the system had been linked to an internal, computerized cash estimate system. Assuming this, periodic variance analyses would be easily accomplished. These reports could also be treated as exception reports, being produced only when the actual cash flows were either substantially higher or lower than the estimate. The determining margin could be set by the cash manager, as well as the level of detail required in the report (e.g., the operating unit involved or the accumulated difference and near-term expected flows). In this manner the cash manager could begin investigating the problem rapidly and possibly resolve it without any major disruption in daily cash management activities.

Statistical Reports. These reports would profile the relevant statistics that could be derived from the daily bank reports. Such items as daily float factor reports, similar in form to those discussed in Chapter 2, but produced on a daily or even weekly basis, would assist in monitoring check clearance from corporate deposit points. It might also be possible to measure the activity volumes in major accounts that are compensated for by collected balances, and by using a predetermined service charge factor compute whether the target for the bank or bank account was sufficient. In this way bank targets could be updated often to reflect changing activity levels. Of course, if compensation is on a fee basis, this would not be applicable. However, this type of data accumulation might be useful in cross-checking monthly account analyses or fee invoices from major banks.

This newer approach to data transmission can offer a wide range of possibilities, as discussed earlier. It can replace many of the manual tasks currently performed in the cash manager's "back office" and eliminate the labyrinthine procedures for obtaining bank balances and transaction data currently in effect. Since these types of transmissions may be less complicated technically from the bank's and company's point of view, cash managers often find that information on their banking activities is available sooner and more reliably than through bank balance reporting systems. Several vendors, companies, and banks have begun to approach this area and utilize microcomputer applications for data transmission and information reporting.[6] This should be of considerable interest to those companies that have not developed any in-house systems or are not large enough to justify doing so. However, most of these companies will have to assess their own internal systems and operations before they can utilize any microcomputer product effectively. Microcomputers are not the direct answer to informational or operating problems. The potential users of such products must become more "computer-literate" before attempting to install these products. If not, there is bound to be a great deal of misunderstanding about these products and a distinct risk that they will become new corporate "toys" and little else.

SECTION 4.4   GLOBAL CASH MANAGEMENT ENVIRONMENT

The last frontier, to paraphrase Captain Kirk of the starship *Enterprise,* is the world (not space). The maturing U.S. cash manager has begun to consider the feasibility of extending cash management philosophies and strategies throughout his or her company's worldwide locations. This area of cash management has been shrouded in as much mystery as its domestic counterpart was some years ago. In the past the U.S. cash manager who attempted to obtain even the slightest information concerning the company's overseas banking arrangements or cash management possibilities had little success. With the emphasis on domestic issues and the volatile costs of funds, most of the cash manager's efforts were logically consumed on the home shore. There were a few brave pioneers who ventured forth with limited success. However, the usual state of international or global cash management could be charitably characterized as "benign neglect" until recent times.

Corporate cash managers who have explored this area have encountered many similarities to the domestic cash management environment of the early to middle 1970s. For instance, many of the problems in initiating cash management overseas have arisen from a general lack of attention or awareness at the local level, as was also true in the United States. In any case there are three common types of problems likely to be encountered by the cash manager as he or she considers international or global cash management. These are internal company-related, cross-border, and banking system problems.

Company-related problems stem from the internal organization itself, and they are probably the first ones that must be overcome in establishing any sort of effective global cash management system. They are primarily educational and political. Educational problems are evidenced by the lack of awareness by overseas personnel, who tend to view cash management as nonexistent and banking as a necessary evil. The basic mechanics of funds movement and the principles of cash position management and effective short-term cash projecting in real terms (not in accounting terms) are typically absent overseas and knowledge of them must be instilled. Political problems derive from the real or perceived loss of autonomy at the local level. These problems are by no means monumental and can be overcome through repeated visits and mutual cooperation.

Cross-border problems also involve internal company problems because there are many interactions between different foreign units of the same firm, and these interactions can create problems in cash management. One method of dealing successfully with this type of problem is offered by netting systems. Essentially, these systems, whether run by the company itself or by one of its banks, legislate the intersubsidiary payment mechanism and set up a common, logical network for funds transfer throughout the corporation.[7] Other types of cross-border problems involve the timely and accurate receipt of export collections from overseas points and international funds transfers in general. Typical problems of this sort are misguided transfers, use of checks instead of some form of electronic means, payment with foreign or "mixed" currencies, and lack of documentation with the transfer. Most of these problems can be easily handled by review and analysis, and then by enforcing effective standards worldwide. The emergence of the SWIFT network has greatly improved international transfers while documentation standards are generally improving in most major banks around the world.[8] The use of foreign currency checks or mixed ones (e.g., a U.S. dollar check drawn on an overseas bank must be cleared back to that bank and back again to the United States before the funds are good) can pose major problems. There are no easy answers for this practice other than to discourage its use or use services offered by one or two banks that accelerate the collection of these items.

Banking system problems arise from the lack of understanding by cash managers of how local systems work and what services are available. One of the most common problems involves the practice of many foreign banks in *value dating* banking transactions. Receipts are delayed before the funds are available to the company, and disbursements are back-valued. Some examples of typical value dating arrangements are shown in Exhibit 4.7. Other banking system problems include the lack of basic bank information locally and a general lack of fundamental cash management services for corporations locally. This situation is improving through the efforts of corporate cash managers, cash management consultants from major money center banks, and the large foreign banks themselves as they begin to dis-

EXHIBIT 4.7   TYPICAL VALUE DATING ARRANGEMENTS (DAYS)

Receipts

Country	Checks		Notes/Drafts	
	Local	Outside	Local	Outside
Italy (Rome)	1	2–3	7–13	10–14
U.K.	1–3	1–3	N/A	N/A
France	1–2	3–5	2–4	4–5
Brazil	0–1	0–1	7	N/A
Malaysia	1	2	N/A	N/A

Disbursements

Country	Checks
France	1–2
U.K.	1–2
Italy	Back-valued to check date
Spain	1–2, or back-valued to check date
Switzerland	1–2
Belgium	1–2
Brazil	0–1

cover cash management locally. Bank balances will be routinely reported in the near future, and other cash management services can be expected to follow shortly.

Problems aside, the extension of basic cash management principles, or what we have referred to as the cash management mentality, to a global setting is indeed a logical step in the evolution of the corporate cash management function. There are, of course, many similarities and differences between global cash management and domestic (U.S.) cash management at the present time. The absence of any real or material establishment of cash management procedures or even basic banking services is no doubt the result of the traditional "mystique" of the international area and the vast geographic locations and their related cultural variations. In addition, the development of cash management in the U.S. corporate environment is, as we have seen, relatively young.

Many aspects of overseas cash management practices and procedures seem strikingly similar to the situation in the United States in the last decade.

The lack of a cash management awareness, the strongly decentralized autonomy, the absence of useful bank statistics or cost comparisons, and the reluctance to report balances are all familiar to most experienced cash managers. Preoccupation with the more peripheral aspects of cash management, such as the short-term liquidity functions, are also typical of past situations in the United States. To be sure, the existence of overdraft checking accounts helps foster a laissez-faire attitude among many local cash managers in overseas locations. This is further evidenced by the absence of meaningful analytical activities, ranging from short-term cash scheduling or planning to the effective structuring of a local banking system.

Although many of the U.S. techniques owe their existence and development to the size of the country and the paper-based payment system, the concepts of cash concentration and cash position management are quite applicable overseas. The daily routine must be tailored to the individual country's banking system and available banking services, but the rewards can be substantial if effective procedures are established. Paying attention to the levels of bank compensation can also prove to be quite beneficial overseas. Particular emphasis on the short-term scheduling of cash flows, just as in the United States, must be an integral part of the cash management activity overseas. This is especially important in instances where the local unit may have short-term excess funds but must invest them for minimum periods such as one month. In these cases a reliable estimate that is expressed in actual cash flow terms (not in accounting terms) is essential if lost opportunities are to be avoided. Thus the similarities strongly suggest that many firms are missing an attractive opportunity overseas.

The differences cannot be ignored or downplayed, however. The foreign exchange area presents many specific problems for the multinational cash manager. Its concerns and influences transcend the cash management function, often affecting the accounting and operating areas of the firm as well. Governmental controls over funds movements can also be troublesome. The controlled practices of overseas banking cartels offer some stiff challenges as well. Nonetheless, the global horizon looms for most cash managers of firms doing business in overseas locations. The opportunities exist, just as they did (and still do) in the United States, and the progressive cash manager must address these challenges and extend the cash management function beyond its current boundaries.

SECTION 4.5   CASE STUDIES AND EXERCISES

The following cases have been designed to provide further work on the principles of corporate cash management. Each one deals with a different aspect of cash management. In most cases the numbers have been simplified somewhat to reduce manual computation time. All numbers and situations are, of course, hypothetical, but the relations between various costs and values, as well as the types of data presented, represent realistic settings. After Chapter 8 a brief discussion of each case study is shown.

CASE 4.1 JMP COMPANY (LOCAL BALANCES). JMP Company, located in New York City, has eight service locations throughout New York state. Although maintaining central control over cash is a major objective of JMP management, each service outlet is expected to exercise autonomy over the issuance and receipt of checks. At present, each office has an imprest account with a local bank for deposit of receipts and disbursements of checks to vendors. Collections are essentially used to offset disbursements, and any excess funds over the imprest level are wire-transferred to JMP's main concentration account in New York City at the end of each week. Shortfalls are extremely rare, and for the purposes of this case they can be ignored. The imprest levels, the minimum balance levels for each bank account, are established to cover the uneven pattern of collections and disbursements and to avoid any accidental overdrafts. The current array of accounts are maintained with eight different, local banks.

JMP's cash manager is reviewing the average, imprest, and required (to cover operating charges) balance levels for each office and wishes to reduce overall balances while still avoiding overdrafts. She has gathered the data shown in the following table (all balances are in thousands):

Location	Average	Imprest	Required
Manhattan	326.0	50.0	25.0
Queens	79.5	30.0	20.0
Brooklyn	67.3	20.0	15.0
White Plains	87.4	15.0	10.0
Utica	95.2	15.0	12.0
Syracuse	99.1	30.0	18.0
Rochester	186.2	40.0	25.0
Buffalo	79.3	20.0	15.0
Totals	1020.0	220.0	140.0

Assume that all bank charges are equivalent, regardless of the bank's location.

Now the cash manager would like to make some changes. Assume a 12% return on any cash freed up by her changes. She wants to consider some modification such that better control over local bank balances can be established. She is willing to consolidate all accounts with the same bank, for example.

What actions should she take?

What are the potential savings?

How would the new system look?

CASE 4.2 BC STORES (CASH CONCENTRATION). BC Stores, an operating division of JMP Company, runs its own cash management system. Its primary business encompasses a chain of wholesale flower and florist supply stores. All sales are in cash or due in 30 days for regular customers. Any customer who becomes past due must settle the delinquency and pay at the time of purchase thereafter. Annual sales are $100 million. There are 10 stores in the chain, located throughout the United States. Central offices are located in Chicago. Each location's receipts consist of checks drawn on local banks. Customers usually drop off their checks when making a purchase. The number of check payments received through the mail is quite small as most customers do not wish to go past due. Each location deposits its receipts at a local bank. For many years the following system has been used:

Deposits are made daily at the end of the workday (approximately 5:00 P.M.).

A copy of each deposit ticket is mailed to the central office treasury staff each day.

All accounts have a minimum, imprest balance level set at $25,000.

Each Monday the cash manager from the central treasury staff is notified by each location as to how much excess cash is available, and that amount is wire-transferred to the central concentration account in Chicago. Excess balances are computed by adding the prior week's check deposits and subtracting the imprest level and any returned checks. This part of the system has only been instituted in recent years; prior to this each location mailed a check for the weekly deposits to the central cash manager.

The cash manager has decided to study the current system and make any necessary changes to improve the concentration of funds centrally. He has two major concerns: how to concentrate funds centrally and how often to do so. Compensation with his main concentration bank in Chicago is in the form of collected balances, so he wants to compare alternatives on that basis. Conversations with his bank officer have provided him with the following cost figures:

Bank service charges

Wire transfers—outgoing	$7.00/transfer
Wire transfers—incoming	5.00/transfer
DTC reporting	0.75/call
DTC processing/preparation	0.50/DTC
DTC—check deposit charge	0.12/DTC
DTC—check paid (clearing)	0.10/DTC
Average earnings credit	10.0%
Reserve requirement	12.0%

(All other charges are the same as current)

Average cash deposits (weekly) for stores (in thousand of dollars)

Store (city)	Week total	Mon	Tues	Wed	Thur	Fri
Chicago	300	100	50	30	40	80
Washington	100	70	10	10	5	5
Denver	200	20	30	40	10	100
Boston	150	60	40	10	20	20
Phoenix	50	10	10	10	10	10
Houston	100	40	10	20	10	20
New York	450	100	100	50	100	100
Atlanta	150	30	30	30	30	30
Los Angeles	300	100	50	50	20	80
St. Louis	200	20	50	30	25	75
Average	200	55	38	28	27	52

What changes should he make to the current system? Assuming a 10% return on any balances freed up, what are the potential savings from the system changes?

CASE 4.3.   MUFFIN MAKES INTERNATIONAL (COLLECTIONS).   Muffin Makers International (MMI) is a producer and seller of pet care products, selling products and supplies to independent wholesale dealers throughout the United States. Annual U.S. sales are approximately $250 million. There are two major plants and distribution centers in Dallas, Texas, and Baltimore, Maryland. MMI's wholesale customers send their remittances to either of these locations as these are the addresses shown on the billing and shipping documents. Customers will remit to one location usually since only the shipping location (whichever one filled the order) address will appear on the documents. The same customers tend to always be handled by the same location; therefore, their remittance patterns are consistent. Average check volumes and dollar amounts of receipts for a typical month are as follows:

Dallas—2500 checks; $9.3 million.
Baltimore—3000 checks; $11.5 million.

All checks are received at the centers, are processed by MMI accounts receivable staff, and are deposited with local banks at the end of each business day. Both banks have suggested lock box services to local personnel, but that decision has been passed on to the corporate cash manager for further study. Both banks are long-standing MMI credit line banks. In addition, MMI corporate headquarters is located near the Baltimore distribution center. MMI's cash manager has asked her major bank (neither the Dallas nor Baltimore bank) to review MMI's collection system, recommend any modifications, and estimate any possible cost savings associated with the recommended changes. Consultants from the bank have visited each distribution center, interviewed local staff, and collected copies of checks and envelopes for a typical month's receipts (the same month was used for each center). The bank consultants then used a computerized analytical model to evaluate alternative collection systems. The results of the computer run showed the following:

Float times—current and prospective collection points

Sending pt.	$ Dep	Curr	Atl	Balt	Chi	Dall	L A	Nwk	St L
				(Balt)					
Boston	1.3	6.8	4.4	4.2	4.4	4.7	4.8	4.2	4.5
New York	2.9	7.8	4.6	4.4	4.3	4.5	4.7	4.0	4.5
Pittsburgh	1.1	4.8	3.9	3.8	3.9	4.0	4.2	4.1	4.0
Philadelphia	0.5	4.5	3.8	3.9	4.1	4.5	4.3	4.0	4.0
Baltimore	0.8	4.5	3.8	2.9	4.0	4.2	4.6	4.1	4.1
Charlotte	0.9	5.3	3.7	4.1	3.9	4.3	4.4	4.1	4.0
Atlanta	1.4	5.4	3.2	4.9	4.2	3.9	4.5	5.0	4.1
Miami	0.6	6.7	3.8	4.0	4.0	3.6	4.3	4.4	4.0
Memphis	0.9	5.7	3.8	4.5	3.9	3.8	4.4	4.5	4.0
Cleveland	0.7	5.5	4.0	4.4	4.1	4.0	4.6	4.4	4.5
				(Dall)					
Minneapolis	0.7	5.3	4.2	4.8	4.2	4.3	4.5	4.5	4.2
Chicago	1.6	5.2	3.6	3.7	3.1	3.9	4.1	4.2	3.9
St. Louis	0.8	4.8	3.9	4.8	3.9	3.7	4.1	4.5	2.9
Kansas City	0.7	5.6	4.0	4.6	4.1	3.5	4.1	4.5	3.9
New Orleans	1.1	5.5	3.8	4.6	4.0	3.7	4.4	4.3	4.0
Dallas	0.9	4.4	4.0	4.1	4.1	2.9	4.1	4.7	4.0
Houston	0.8	4.8	3.8	4.4	3.9	3.5	4.2	4.5	3.9
Denver	0.8	6.7	4.3	5.0	4.1	4.2	4.4	4.8	4.3
Los Angeles	1.1	6.5	4.4	4.9	4.6	4.4	3.1	4.8	4.7
Seattle	0.6	7.1	4.5	4.7	4.5	4.0	4.1	4.7	4.7

Note: Dollar deposit figures are in millions. The first 10 points currently remit to Baltimore and the second group to Dallas. The float figures are in days and include mail, processing, and clearing times for each point.

Assuming that all customers will remit as instructed and that MMI will consider establishing as many as four lock boxes, the cash manager wants to determine what the optimal system should be? In particular, she wants to know which *one* lock box point is best overall, and what the benefits would be if lock boxes were established in the two current distribution center cities. In computing the alternative costs and benefits for various arrangements, some or all of the following data may be relevant:

Average lock box charges (collected balances required/item)

Atlanta	50	Dallas	45
Baltimore	40	St. Louis	38
Newark	55	Los Angeles	50
Chicago	60		

Check volumes (items/month)

Boston	340	Minneapolis	180
New York	770	Chicago	420
Pittsburgh	290	St. Louis	210
Philadelphia	130	Kansas City	180
Baltimore	200	New Orleans	290
Charlotte	230	Dallas	240
Atlanta	340	Houston	210
Miami	150	Denver	210
Memphis	230	Los Angeles	280
Cleveland	160	Seattle	160

Company's rate of return on funds saved   10% annual

Bank concentration charges

Wire transfers from lock box bank(s) (coll. bals. per transfer)

Atlanta	650	Dallas	640
Baltimore	630	St. Louis	660
Newark	680	Los Angeles	720
Chicago	750		

Wire transfers to major concentration bank   600

DTC charges:

Phone call and preparation	100 (coll. bals. per DTC)
DTC deposit and clearing	50 (per DTC)*

*Assume DTC per item paid charges are equal for any potential lock box bank and are included in the above figure.

In considering alternative systems, are there any nonquantitative factors that may influence the cash manager's decision?

CASE 4.4 DAISY MANUFACTURING (DISBURSEMENTS). Daisy Manufacturing is a producer of fertilizer, located in suburban New Jersey. The firm's average monthly disbursements to its suppliers consist of 4000 checks for a total of $10 million. Checks are mailed out weekly on Thursdays (Wednesdays if Thursday is a holiday) to suppliers heavily concentrated in the Northeast and Southeast. Checks are drawn on a large New York City bank, and the account is funded on the day the checks are mailed out by wire transfer from the main corporate concentration account at a large New Jersey bank in the amount of the total disbursements.

Daisy's cash manager has noted that substantial balances have built up in the New York City account, far beyond what is required to support the credit line with that bank ($500,000). Daisy's cash manager and treasurer have recently attended a conference and heard about a new service called controlled disbursing. They would like to know whether this service is applicable to their situation and what the potential savings are (if any) should they choose to use the service. The cash manager has gathered the following data relating to Daisy's disbursements for a typical month:

Average monthly disbursements—10 major vendors (in thousands of dollars)

Vendor*	Location	Clearing times (est.) Curr	New	Average monthly disbursements ($000)
United Rendering	Boston	5.0	6.0	1500
Northern Chemical	Syracuse	3.0	3.0	1000
New England Industries	Hartford	3.2	3.5	1250
New Jersey Utilities	Newark	2.5	3.0	250
Mid-Atlantic Solvents	Phila.	4.5	5.0	500
Georgia Supply	Atlanta	5.0	6.0	1000
Dixie Organics	Raleigh	4.5	5.5	800
Semi-Natural Chemicals	Roanoke	5.0	7.0	500
Inorganic International	Wheeling	4.0	6.5	1400
Sun-Belt Agri-Chem	Tampa	6.0	7.5	600

Average bank balance	1250 ($000)
Check volume	4000
Current wire transfers	Five per month
Cost of wires	$5.50/transfer

Average monthly disbursements (*Continued*)

New costs
Controlled disbursement account flat fee $50.00/mo.
Extra charge per check paid $0.04/item
(All other costs same)
Assume bank will accept fees for compensation of controlled disbursing service.

*These vendors account for 88% of average monthly volume.

As a cash management consultant to Daisy, what (if any) changes would you recommend in the handling of Daisy's disbursements? What are the potential savings associated with your recommendations if balances freed up can be invested at 10%?

CASE 4.5   JBK LTD. (CASH SCHEDULING).   Each Friday JBK's cash manager establishes the expected cash flow and net daily cash position for the following week. During the week, actual results from the previous day's activity are made to the cash schedule.

The cash schedule for the current week is shown in the following table:

Flows	Mon	Tues	Wed	Thur	Fri
Incoming					
Lock box collections	10,000	2,000	1,000	500	1,500
Local deposits	250	500	100	50	100
Subsidiary transfers	1,000	2,000	4,000	500	5,000
Maturing investments	5,000	1,000	2,000	0	5,000
Total incoming	16,250	5,500	7,100	1,050	11,600
Outgoing					
Payables	100	2,000	3,500	5,000	5,000
Payroll	500	1,000	250	2,000	5,000
Subsidiary funding	3,500	5,000	500	1,000	2,000
Maturing loans	2,000	5,000	1,000	5,000	5,200
Total outgoing	6,100	13,000	5,250	13,000	17,200
Net flow	10,150	− 7,500	1,850	− 11,950	− 5,600
Bank balance					
Beginning	2,000	12,150	4,650	6,500	− 5,450
Ending	12,150	4,650	6,500	− 5,450	− 11,050

On Wednesday morning (beginning of the day) the following actual flows have occurred (no actions were taken either day besides rolling over the ending balances in overnight investments; these figures were not entered on the estimate):

Actual cash flows	Monday	Tuesday
Incoming		
Lock box collections	7,500	1,000
Local deposits	500	250
Subsidiary transfers	2,000	2,500
Maturing investments	5,000	1,000
Total incoming	15,000	4,750
Outgoing		
Payables	5,000	500
Payroll	1,500	250
Subsidiary transfers	5,500	500
Maturing loans	2,000	5,000
Total outgoing	14,000	6,250
Net flow	1,000	− 1,500
Bank balance		
Beginning	2,000	3,000
Ending	3,000	1,500

Any variances are handled by the following rules.

Collections: any differences are added/subtracted to next day's estimate.
Disbursements: payables differences are apportioned 50% over each of the next two days (plus or minus); payroll all goes into next day.
Subsidiary transfers: inflow differences split 50/50 over next two days; outflows go into next day.

You are substituting for the cash manager as of Wednesday morning. Your tasks are as follows:

Make all necessary adjustments and compute a new cash flow estimate for the rest of the week.

Determine whether any new borrowing or investment decisions must be made. Assume all are overnight.

Incorporate any of the preceding decisions in your revised estimate.

Compute the starting position for the following Monday.

Do any of the assumptions need to be changed? If so, what impact will the change(s) have on the estimate?

Assuming that the relative daily estimates of operating flows do not change for next week (i.e., the same percentage of total weekly flows can be expected on each day), compute an estimate for the next week using the percentage changes in total weekly flows shown below. Investment and borrowing decisions and related flows should be derived from computed differences in estimated daily flows. Also, you may invest or borrow up to Friday of next week.

Cash flow changes, next week

Lock box collections	Increase 50%
Local deposits	Increase 10%
Subsidiary transfers (in)	Increase 50%
Subsidiary transfers (out)	No change
Payables and payroll	Increase 20%

CASE 4.6   PUFF DISTRIBUTORS (BANK SERVICE CHARGES).   Puff Distributors, a large manufacturer and distributor of video games, is in the process of updating its cash management systems. At present, it is faced with the difficult task of comparing bank service charges for similar services. The cash manager has selected four basic services to be profiled: lock box, concentration, payroll disbursements, and payable disbursements.

In each case the company has already established ongoing relationships with each of its five major banks. Also, for the most part the cash manager has determined that potential float improvements are comparable from bank to bank (unless otherwise noted below). The cash manager is willing to deal with any or all five banks for any combination of the services.

Average monthly volumes for each service are as follows:

Lock box: 5000 checks.

Concentration: 20 transfers/depository (daily transfers).

Payroll: 10,000 checks.

Payables: 4000 checks.

The cash manager has compiled the following information from each major bank in attempting to decide what to do:

Service and charges	Metro Trust	Gotham Guar'y	Yankee State	Midwest Bk & Tr	Eastern Nat'l
Lock Box					
Maintenance	7.50	5.00	12.00	10.00	6.00
Processing/flat	0.00	20.00	10.00	25.00	0.00
Processing/item	0.33	0.25	0.35	0.22	0.30
Deposit tickets	0.30	0.00	0.25	0.22	0.00
Deposit/item	0.12	0.12	0.00	0.11	0.11
Wires out	6.50	7.00	5.00	5.50	7.00
DTC/check paid	0.16	0.15	0.11	0.12	0.13
Concentration					
Maintenance	7.50	5.00	12.00	10.00	6.00
Wires in	3.00	5.00	3.50	5.50	4.00
DTC prep.	0.67	0.75	0.60	0.55	0.80
DTC/item dep.	0.12	0.12	0.10	0.11	0.11
ZBA maint	0.00	15.00	10.00	0.00	25.00
ZBA/each acct.	0.00	5.00	2.50	7.50	10.00
Payroll					
Maintenance	7.50	5.00	12.00	10.00	6.00
Checks pd./item	0.16	0.15	0.11	0.12	0.13
Acct. rec./flat	40.00	25.00	0.00	45.00	30.00
Acct. rec./item	0.06	0.07	0.10	0.05	0.06
Wires in	3.00	5.00	3.50	5.50	4.00
Payables					
Maintenance	7.50	5.00	12.00	10.00	6.00
Checks pd./item	0.16	0.15	0.11	0.12	0.13
Acct. rec./flat	25.00	0.00	0.00	30.00	30.00
Acct. rec./item	0.07	0.11	0.15	0.06	0.06
Wires in	3.00	5.00	3.50	5.50	4.00
Ctlld. disb./maint.	100.00	50.00	25.00	75.00	30.00
Miscellaneous					
Balance rept./flat	25.00	22.00	30.00	100.00	20.00
Bal. reptg./each acc.	15.00	15.00	10.00	5.00	10.00
Earnings credit	10.35	10.00	10.75	10.15	9.50
Reserve rqmt.	12.75	12.00	12.50	12.25	12.00

The cash manager now wishes to analyze this mountain of data. There are two plant locations and the home office, all of whom have payroll and payables disbursing activities. Collections are centralized, and the cash manager will establish only *one* lock box arrangement. However, there will be concentration activities from that lock box, each plant location, and the home office (assume none of the five banks are near the home office).
The following questions must be answered:

Which one bank is most economical for each type of service, assuming all float benefits are comparable?

Which one bank is the best choice if the cash manager wishes to deal with just one bank?

As an advisor to the cash manager, what do you recommend? Are there any nonquantitative factors to be considered? If so, which ones?

CASE 4.7   TRIUMPH PRODUCTS (SHORT-TERM FUNDING).   The cash manager at Triumph Products, a major manufacturer of transportation products, is responsible for funding the company's short-term funding needs. She receives a cash flow projection from each operating unit for the next six weeks and computes the estimated net cash flow on a consolidated basis. The current projection shows:

Week	Net flow ($000) in/(out)
1	(20,000)
2	(10,000)
3	5,000
4	15,000
5	(5,000)
6	(15,000)

The following unused facilities are available:

Facility available	Maximum amt. ($000)	Estimated rates
Commercial paper	25,000	8.75
Bank lines	100,000	11.00
Subprime loans	10,000	10.25

Other possible information that may be important for the cash manager to consider in deciding her course of action:

Bank lines of credit must be used to back up paper issuance. Lines cost $\frac{1}{2}$% to maintain. This is charged for backup lines but not for usage.

Subprime loans are offered without any required compensating charges, but their maximum term is two weeks.

Commercial paper can be sold in weekly maturities with a minimum amount of $5 million. Maximum maturity cannot exceed six weeks.

The net cash flow estimate is usually accurate to plus or minus $1 million for any one week.

Short-term investment rates are 9% for one-week maximum periods. This rate holds for overnight also.

The cash manager has asked you for counsel on what she should do. Assuming the accuracy range mentioned above, what is the most economical plan for Triumph?

What noneconomic considerations should you point out to her as she makes her decisions?

She would also like some guidelines for making sound decisions in case you are not around for advice. In particular, she wants to know at what rates for each type should she first choose a particular facility; that is, what should the *differences* in rates be to make their effective rates equivalent? If her net cash outflow worsens, at what point would you recommend that she increase her facilities? What types should she change first?

CASE 4.8   JEFF-PARK, INC. (DIRECT DEPOSIT OF PAYROLL).   At one of its major office and plant locations, Jeff-Park, Inc., offers a special service to salaried employees by mailing semimonthly paychecks to individual bank accounts. All accounts are with local banks. Lately this has become a problem for the payroll processing staff because of the unpredictable nature of mail delivery and time delays for payroll preparation. After some detailed review, the cash manager wants to determine the feasibility of converting to an automated form of payroll deposit, using one of his major bank's direct deposit of payroll service through the ACH network. The current method of funding the payroll generates three days of float each time the payroll is paid. Other data are as follows:

Average payroll for salaried employees is $1.5 million.

250 employees are involved.

All local banks are ACH members.

Mail costs are $0.75 per check.

Bank costs are $0.15 per check and $0.05 per ACH credit.

All other costs are the same.

Now the cash manager wants to know:

Is the conversion feasible on a cost–benefit basis, assuming all employees can be converted? Is there a "breakeven" percentage for enrolled employees above which the electronic system is better?

If the payroll increased to $3.0 million, what would you recommend? At what level of payroll dollars does the float generated equal the costs of the automated transfer system with 100% participation?

CASE 4.9   MALDWYN INTERNATIONAL (TARGET BALANCES).   The cash manager at Maldwyn International, a major record company, has four major banks. Compensation with each bank is on a collected-balance basis. The cash manager has decided to evaluate his target balance management performance at these key banks. In doing so, he has gathered the following data, which he feels should enable him to evaluate overall performance and determine whether any changes are necessary:

Data	Gotham Trust	Midwest Nat'l	Dixie Bank	Seaboard State
Collected balances				
Average past year ($000)	2,500	1,500	500	3,050
Average past month ($000)	3,125	500	3,500	4,100
Current target ($000)	1,500	500	5,000	6,000
Other information				
Credit lines ($000)	10,000	5,000	5,000	10,000
% compens. balances	0.05	0.075	0.05	0.05
Average service charge (mo.) ($)	7,500	500	5,000	6,000
Average earnings credit	0.104	0.107	0.114	0.101
Reserve requirements	0.12	0	0.125	0.125

Now he needs help. He wishes to answer the following:

Which banks are over, under, or on target for the past year? For the past month?

What should his new targets be so that each bank will be on target (maintained = required) in *three* months? Can they all be brought on target within this period?

Assuming he is willing and able to reduce or increase balances in any time period, how quickly can he bring all banks on target? He does not want to go beyond six months.

In your analysis, assume you cannot reduce balances below $25,000 in any one account.

CASE 4.10 HILL-MILLS (FEES VERSUS BALANCES). Hill-Mills, a diversified manufacturer of consumer products, has six lead banking relationships. The cash manager for H-M, after attending a cash management seminar, wishes to determine whether any or all of her banks should be compensated on some other basis than the current method of collected balances. The first thing she did was to gather the following data on current levels:

Bank name	Required balances ($000)	Service charges ($000)	Earnings credit (%)	Reserve requirements (%)
Last National	2500	21.88	0.105	-0-
Gotham Trust	3000	24.94	0.114	0.125
Southern Guaranty	4240	37.33	0.121	0.1275
Metro Bank & Trust	5210	46.89	0.108	-0-
Desert State	2200	19.04	0.118	0.12
City State	1500	9.95	0.091	0.14

H-M is a net borrower of funds, and the cash manager notes that the company's effective borrowing rate (short-term) is currently 9.75%.

Assuming that all banks will accept fees in the amount of their average monthly service charges shown above, how should the cash manager compensate *each* bank?

There are also some other considerations:

Assuming that H-M cannot remove all its balances effectively from its banks, what percentage at each bank must it be able to remove to break even between fees and balances? This assumes that the cash manager compensates banks only one way (i.e., fees or balances only). If all of the banks were to offer a balance offset for any excess balances maintained, but at their own earnings credit adjusted for reserves, what would the breakeven percentages then become?

Metro Bank & Trust suggests the use of a non-interest-bearing time deposit for compensation. The net effective earnings credit rate after reserves would be 14%. Is this a better alternative than fees or not? By how much?

The company currently maintains credit lines with its banks in amounts of $20 million per bank with a 5% level of compensating balances (not included in preceding figures). With the same cost of funds as indicated above, at what fee rate ($\frac{1}{4}, \frac{3}{8}, \frac{1}{2}, \frac{5}{8}, \frac{3}{4}$) would it be more economical or equal to pay fees instead of balances?

NOTES

1. For an interesting review of the Fed's implementation of the act, see the Comptroller General's Report (May 1982).
2. Carfang presents some good insights for the corporate treasurer and cash manager.
3. See Orr for an interesting example.
4. See Morris for the U.S. Postal Service's experience with EFTS.
5. White (December 1979) provides a discussion of key factors and future implications.
6. See Goodman or Gage for developments.
7. For more details on netting, see Parkinson (August–September 1981) or Grandinetti.
8. Reuterskiold or Simpson give more detailed descriptions of SWIFT and international payment systems in general.

5 Management of Accounts Receivable

*Lady Stutfield: How very, very charming those gold-tipped ciga-
rettes of yours are, Lord Alfred.*

*Lord Alfred: They are awfully expensive. I can only afford them
when I'm in debt.*

L.S.:   It must be terribly, terribly distressing to be in debt.

*L.A.:   One must have some occupation nowadays. If I hadn't my
debts I shouldn't have anything to think about. All the chaps
I know are in debt.*

*L.S.:   But don't the people to whom you owe the money give you
a great, great deal of annoyance?*

L.A.:   Oh no! they write; I don't.

L.S.:   How very, very strange.

A WOMAN OF NO IMPORTANCE
OSCAR WILDE

This chapter describes the fundamentals of accounts receivable management.
The basic emphasis is on the evaluation of the costs and benefits of alternative
strategies within the following areas:

Initial granting of credit (the question of whether or not to grant an applicant credit and the closely related question of how much credit to grant).

Control of credit (accounting and other measures of receivables performance and strategies for evaluating the liquidity of a portfolio of accounts
receivable; collection strategies are relevant as are methods for forecasting
cash flows from accounts receivable).

Trade credit (the effects of offering a discount for early payment).

Accounts receivable financing [the use of receivables as collateral for
borrowing or factoring (the sale of receivables)].

Credit agreements common in the United States contain two basic types
of information. The first defines the account category; there are three basic
ones:

Open book credit. (Here goods are sold without a contract evidencing the transaction. Most types of trade credit are in this category; the invoice provides an informal statement of the transaction.)

Installment credit. (Here repayment is made by a series of regular "installments." Most of these arrangements are for a one-time purchase of an expensive item, for example, an automobile.)

Revolving credit. [Revolving credit is essentially a hybrid of the first two; the usual retail credit card is of the type. Here the debt is classified as current as long as a minimum payment (a fraction of the outstanding balance) is met each month.]

The second part of the credit agreement stipulates the terms. In many industries there are established norms, often relating to the perishability or turnover of the items. These are usually stated as "net t" or "d/t_1 net t_2". The first example specifies that payment is due within t days from a given date (typically from receipt of goods). The second allows a discount of $d\%$ if payment is made by t_1 days. For example, 2/10 net 30 specifies that if payment is made within 10 days, 2% may be discounted from the stated price; otherwise payment is due within 30 days. One of the most subjective areas of accounts receivable management relates to the degree of enforcement of stated terms.

Exercise. Viewing the credit terms as a loan from the seller to the buyer, what is the implicit interest rate in a 2/10 net 30 agreement? Verify that for d/t_1 net t_2 terms the implicit interest rate (assuming nominal rather than continuous compounding) is

$$\left(\frac{d}{1-d}\right)\left(\frac{365}{t_2-t_1}\right).$$

This trade credit example suggests some of the relationships between credit decisions and interest rates or price changes. These issues will be treated within this chapter.

SECTION 5.1 COSTS AND BENEFITS OF OFFERING CREDIT

This section is concerned with the cost–benefit tradeoffs for a firm maintaining its own ("in-house") credit operations. Section 5.6 will treat the case of a firm offering credit but (through factoring, third-party credit, and so on) transferring the receivables to an outside agency.

The major costs can be grouped into three general categories: (1) financing costs, (2) bad debt costs, and (3) collection expenses and overhead. Financing costs of receivables are exactly analogous to financing costs of inventory (see Section 5.6). These costs can be determined either explicitly as the cost of financing the assets or indirectly as the opportunity cost of capital tied up in the assets. For a firm with a significant portfolio of outstanding receivables, these can be substantial and volatile. For the credit operations at Sears, Roebuck, and Company: "we estimate that each increase in the interest rate of one percentage point will increase our annual operating costs by $20 million" (Spurlock, 1980, p. 68).

In extending credit the seller is taking the role of a lender and thus is subject to related risks. A major part of this risk is the possibility of "unsatisfactory" payment behavior—ranging from delinquent payments to outright default. Altman (1981) provides a methodology for estimating the latter in the context of bank loan charge-offs. For a sample of large banks he finds that the average recovery (percentage of charged-off balance collected) on loans that have been written off is 30%, depending on the bank and the loan type. Meanwhile, in 1982 commercial collection agencies were reporting a recovery rate of about 60%.

Even prompt accounts incur expenses in the initial application stage and in the processing of payments. (Aspects of the latter situation have been discussed in Chapter 2.) For delinquent accounts these expenses may also include the costs of further correspondence, telephone calls, personal visits, and legal fees. The overhead attached to credit operations includes the costs of personnel, space, and so on.

Larson (1982) reports the situation for the 1600 VISA card-issuing members for the quarter ending June 30, 1981 (data are an annualized percentage of outstandings): Operations costs were 7%; charge-offs for credit and fraud were 2.8%; cost of funds was 13.6%. The net result is a negative 1.9% return on assets.

In addition, the credit grantor must be aware of the complex regulatory structure surrounding credit operations. To illustrate, Exhibit 5.1 summa-

EXHIBIT 5.1 A SAMPLING OF U.S. RETAIL CREDIT LEGISLATION

Truth in Lending Act (July 1969): to require meaningful disclosure of credit terms (notably dollar amount of finance charges and annual percentage rate).

Credit Card Issuance Act (October 1970): to prohibit unsolicited credit card issuance.

Fair Credit Reporting Act (April 1971): to require justification of rejected credit applications.

Fair Credit Billing Act (October 1975): to control inaccurate billing.

Equal Credit Opportunity Act (October 1975 and June 1976): to prevent discrimination on the basis of sex, marital status, race, color, religion, national origin, age, receipt of income from public assistance, exercise of rights under the Consumer Credit Protection Act.

Fair Debt Collection Practices Act (March 1978): to protect against improper (harassing, deceptive, etc.) collection practices.

Note: In parentheses is the effective date of the legislation. All of these entries are titles of the Consumer Credit Protection Act except for the Fair Credit Billing Act, which is an amendment to the Truth in Lending Act. For descriptions see Cole (1980).

rizes some of the relevant U.S. federal laws on consumer credit. This increasing tangle of federal and state credit legislation has driven many small credit grantors out of the business.

Measured by accounting data, most (nonfinancial) firms that offer trade and consumer credit do not attain a positive rate of return. For example, the interest rates issuers of retail credit charge their customers must be kept reasonably near market rates to avoid customers borrowing elsewhere to finance their purchases. Furthermore, in some states, usury ceilings still constrain the rates on credit card financing. Finally, there is a period of float (typically the time from purchase until the date when interest is calculated) during which the buyer is receiving an interest-free loan. In some cases credit card fees and the like can also supplement these revenues. Johnson (1963, p. 50) summarizes the retailers' situation:

> It seems apparent that the average department store could enhance its profits by eliminating the credit function—if it could maintain the same sales volume. Not only could it make a greater profit, but it could be doing so on a much smaller investment, since discontinuing credit operations would also eliminate the need for investing capital in accounts receivable.

Thus it is necessary to evaluate credit as a merchandising and promotional tool. In any given situation the credit grantor would need to determine the significance of the diverse reasons for the use of credit by its customers. These would include:

Convenience: the buyer need not have the required cash for each purchase.

Price discrimination: because of the float generated in a retail credit card transaction, for example, it is often said that cash customers are subsidizing credit buyers. (This has led to two-tiered pricing—one price for cash and another for credit—in a number of situations.)

Credit rationing: there is likely to be a demand for consumer credit above that available from other sources. (A recent case would be the Federal Reserve Credit Controls of 1980, which affected the usage of bank credit cards.)

The credit grantor must also consider the value of the information obtained by examining credit purchases; this information can be used to target mail promotions for example. This base of credit card customers has also been used as a springboard for further offerings of financial services. The following example illustrates one firm's strategy in the credit-granting question.

Example 5.1 On April 15, 1982, the Atlantic Richfield Company (ARCO), the eighth largest gasoline retailer in the United States, stopped honoring credit cards (its own, of which there were about three million, and all others) for retail gasoline purchases and simultaneously lowered its prices by about 3 cents per gallon. This came at a time of nationwide surpluses in gasoline supplies and an increasing market share by independent ("discount") retailers. "ARCO spent about $73 million last year maintaining the credit card system—a bill that included everything from the postage to mail monthly statements to the salaries paid 150 employees at ARCO's computer center in Atlanta" (*Newsweek,* March 15, 1982, p. 56). Other sources estimated gasoline retailers' cost of credit operations to be 6–9 cents per gallon. (*Business Week,* May 10, 1982, p. 111) The cost savings from eliminating credit operations could enable ARCO to offer a lower retail price, which would presumably increase sales and profitability. It would also avoid the increasing problems other retailers had been having with bad debts and lost and stolen cards.

Because of the convenience of credit cards, many ARCO credit customers were expected to buy elsewhere, a move that was encouraged by ARCO's competitors. A number of them began accepting ARCO cards while issuing the holder one of their own label; SUNOCO even gave ARCO cardholders a $2.50 rebate on a SUNOCO card (*New York Times,* April 14, 1982, p. D14).

By August of 1982, most observers felt that the ARCO move had been successful. ARCO reported that sales at their service stations had increased by about 50%. A number of major competitors maintained their own credit operations and introduced a two-tiered pricing scheme with discounts of about 4 cents per gallon for cash sales. However, the Service Station Dealers of America filed a complaint with the Federal Trade Commission alleging that the companies had first raised their prices and then offered the cash discount. This violation of truth in lending was denied by the companies involved. The competition has also reacted in a number of other ways. Shell installed computer terminals for credit verification at all of their gas stations to cut down on bad debt losses. Gulf, in conjunction with Mellon Bank, is arranging to have customers pay by on-site electronic funds transfer. Finally, AMOCO is intending to broaden the scope of its credit cards to allow purchases at restaurants, car rental agencies, etc.

The apparent success of ARCO in curtailing its credit operations holds a number of lessons for other retailers. First, it emphasizes the cost of credit operations and the components of this cost. It shows how price elastic consumers are when it comes to a product like gasoline for which there is very little brand loyalty. Lastly, it has shown how powerful the marketing aspects of credit and pricing are.

SECTION 5.2   CREDIT GRANTING

All credit analysis, whether performed subjectively by loan officers or statistically by credit-scoring systems, is rooted in the principle that past credit experience can be used as a guide in predicting future credit performance. That is, past and future creditworthy borrowers will share certain attributes and will tend to resemble each other more closely than noncreditworthy applicants, and these attributes can be reliable indicators of creditworthiness. [Eisenbeis, 1980, p. 727].

The basic goal of the credit-granting process is to evaluate credit applicants with the objective of determining the "appropriate" risk–return tradeoff. The problem can be viewed as a forecasting question: Given the credit applicant's characteristics, what will future payment behavior be? As such, many of the issues to be raised in Chapter 7 are relevant here particularly the costs of errors in prediction, the relevant characteristics for prediction, and the complexity of the forecasting method, relative to the anticipated benefits.

The basic qualitative principles of credit granting are often referred to as the four C's of credit: character, capacity, capital, and conditions. The first concerns the willingness to pay and the others measure the ability to pay. In this context, character is usually inferred from past payment performance, personal references, and verification of statements made in the credit application. Capacity is usually related to the financial and managerial ability to generate earnings. Capital measures the financial resources (including collateral) of the applicant. Conditions refer to the pertinent economic environment in which the credit applicant and credit grantor operate. The generality of these four characteristics cannot be easily translated into workable policies; they do however suggest a framework for credit investigation.

Credit Information

Just as in forecasting, more information does not necessarily mean a better forecast. A crucial issue is the marginal value of the information versus the cost of acquiring it.

> Unless the information is used and useful, it is not worth what it costs in either time or money. When the extensive investigation develops a mass of factual data, the very mass of the evidence may interfere with the analysis and decision. The sheer extent of the evidence may result in its not being correctly weighed or interpreted [Cole, 1980, p. 251].

In a credit investigation, the relevant information includes the following:

Payment record: important both as a proxy for character and as a predictor of future payment behavior. A number of agencies collect data on consumer and corporate payment behavior and these reports are routinely utilized in the credit evaluation process.

Income: for consumer credit, a verification of the applicant's stated earnings is desirable. For corporate credit, financial statement analysis is an integral part of credit investigation. This includes the type of ratio analysis discussed in the preface.

Collateral: determine if there is an asset offered as security and establish its market value. (This is a particularly important point when dealing with inventory financing, as often the book figures for inventory include obsolete and unmarketable items.)

Total assets: evaluate the capacity to service the commitment in case of a fall in earnings.

While the type of data most important to the credit granting process must vary according to circumstance, ratio analysis has proven a powerful tool. We next summarize the most important ratios used in credit granting (and in current asset management). Refer to Exhibit P.1 for definitions.

Liquidity ratios measure the ability of current assets to meet current liabilities. Each industry and each country has its own norms for these ratios. The usual rule in the U.S. for the current ratio is 2. Since current assets may contain obsolete or slow-moving inventory, the quick ratio measures the ability to meet current liabilities from cash and receivables. A quick ratio of 1 is often considered adequate.

The turnover ratios and days outstanding figures both measure the rate at which current assets are being utilized. For example, the inventory turnover ratio for American auto makers is about 8; for Japanese auto makers this figure is closer to 80 (see Section 6.5 for some reasons for this discrepancy). Receivables days outstanding are also used to evaluate payment performance. For example, if credit terms are net 30 (all debts are due within 30 days of receipt of invoice) but the receivables days sales outstanding is 49, we may infer that the stated terms are not being enforced effectively.

The conversion cycle is based on the working capital cycle (inventory to accounts receivable to cash to inventory . . .) and is intended to measure the overall performance of (and investment in) current assets. Ceteris paribus, the smaller the conversion cycle, the more efficient is the utilization of current assets.

As the quote by Cole indicates, these and other relevant data are not costlessly acquired. Even if some information is obtained from credit applications, there remains the costs of verification and processing. Because of this, many credit grantors utilize a prescreen for processing credit applicants. An example taken from Showers and Chakrin (1981) is given below.

Example 5.2   This example concerns reducing the bad debt losses on residential telephone customers for the Bell System; in 1979 their net residential bad debt was $256 million. Bell sought a more effective way of screening high risks. Those so classified would be required to place a deposit prior to installation of a telephone. Regulatory agencies would not permit Bell to demand a deposit from all applicants.

The first stage of the procedure they implemented applied to applicants with prior telephone service of over a year's duration. The applicant was required to pay a deposit only if previous service ended with an amount still outstanding. (A credit-scoring scheme was used on applicants without prior telephone service; see Section 5.3.) This simple check allowed an inexpensive prescreen and saved on acquiring further information that would be of little help in classifying the applicant.

This type of simple credit screening can be very useful. A somewhat more elaborate way to perform discrimination is discussed in the next section. Naturally these types of techniques are not intended to replace a full credit investigation. They can however often provide a cost-effective, systematic approach to utilizing available data in the credit-granting decision.

SECTION 5.3   CREDIT SCORING

Herman said he was desperate for the money. "Not a chance," I said.
"Something tells me you're a deadbeat, Herman. Something electronic."
                                                  SO THIS IS DEPRAVITY
                                                  RUSSELL BAKER

A credit-scoring model is a procedure for weighting characteristics (deemed relevant to payment behavior) to obtain a numerical score that can then be used to determine whether or not credit should be granted. Churchill et al. (1977) note that 16 of the 20 largest consumer finance companies utilize credit scoring.

The structure of a credit-scoring model is precisely that of a linear regression model (see Section 7.4): There is a set of variables $x_1, \ldots, x_n$ used to determine the creditworthiness of a given applicant. These variables may measure (for consumer credit) annual income, years at current address, and so on. Corresponding to each x_i is a weight a_i that determines how much each variable contributes to the total score Z:

$$Z = a_1 x_1 + \cdots + a_n x_n.$$

Generally the higher the score the more credit worthy is the applicant. Churchill et al. (1977, p. 6) cite five benefits to a firm from using a credit-scoring model: "(1) gains in management control; (2) benefits in training new personnel; (3) a reduction in loan applicant processing costs; (4) a more legally defensible system for denying credit; and (5) increased input to the firm's management information system." The first benefit arises from the ability to quantify objectives; more stringent credit can be interpreted as raising the cutoff score (i.e., assuming that a higher Z value means more creditworthiness; this means raising the minimum Z score required to obtain credit). Based on historical information the impact of this can be assessed. The second benefit comes from summarizing the credit grantor's past experience and highlighting in the credit-scoring model those characteristics that have proved most significant in discriminating between good and bad credit accounts. After the initial development stage, a successful credit-scoring system is clearly simpler, cheaper, and faster than having a credit analyst interpret the financial statements. As previously mentioned, U.S. credit legislation requires informing rejected credit applicants of the reasons for credit denial. A credit-scoring scheme simplifies this procedure.

In developing a credit-scoring model, essentially we want to weight heavily a characteristic that discriminates well between good and bad accounts. We can relate our past experience with customers of varying scores to determine a "cutoff score"; that is, applicants with a score less than the cutoff score will be classified as a bad risk (rejected for credit) and others will be classified as a good risk (accepted for credit).[1] There are two types of errors generated by choosing a particular cutoff score:

Type 1: accepting a bad risk (bad debt loss).

Type 2: rejecting a good risk (lost revenue, an opportunity cost usually).

As the cutoff score increases, we decrease the probability of type 1 error and increase the probability of type 2 error. The expected costs of the two types of misclassification are depicted in Figure 5.3 for Example 5.4.

Credit scoring using subjective weights is often used. However, in 1941 David Durand suggested the use of discriminant analysis as a statistical method for obtaining the weights. [As will be noted in Chapter 7, this approach has been successful in the prediction of bankruptcies as well as in a number of other financial contexts; see Altman et al. (1981)].

Discriminant Analysis

Discriminant analysis is a quantitative method for assessing the importance of various factors in a classification problem. It gives a consistent and unambiguous rule for classifying each observation into one of a variety of possible categories. We illustrate the technique for determining whether or not a given applicant is likely to be a good credit risk based on a number of characteristics belonging to a sample of good and bad credit risk. It is hypothesized that these characteristics are systematically related to payment behavior. Discriminant analysis allows us to determine the significant characteristics and to assign to them the appropriate weights in order to obtain an index (discriminant score).

For the credit-granting example, the sequence of steps may proceed as follows:

1. *Determination of the significant factors.* For firms, we may choose factors like liquidity, working capital position, profitability, size, leverage,

etc. The factors under consideration should be quantifiable and justifiable on economic grounds.

2. *Selection of the sample.* The sample should be large enough to give approximate normality of each population factor (see the discussion in Appendix A). It should also be unbiased in that the sample from which we estimate the model is statistically equivalent to the sample to which we will apply the model. This is important for our example. Typically there is a great deal of preselection in that we have payment data only on the subpopulation to which we have granted credit, a population that is likely to have rather different characteristics than the general population of applicants.

3. *Construction of the index.* Here we determine the relative weights on each of the significant factors. We next give a simple example of using discriminant analysis. The technique illustrated is described in detail in Altman et al., (1981) and in most texts on multivariate statistics. Example 5.3 merely applies these formulas to the two-dimensional case.

Example 5.3 Suppose that we believe the following two variables are related to an individual's payment behavior:

$$x = \text{past year's income (in thousands)}$$
$$y = \text{number of years at current job.}$$

(Of course, in practice we would use many more variables and more data.) We want to determine the weights a_1 and a_2 for the discriminant index:

$$z = a_1 x + a_2 y.$$

Suppose we have the following credit risks from which we will estimate a_1 and a_2:

Customer	x	y
1	25 (-12)	1.0 (-3.8)
2	20 (-17)	2.5 (-2.3)
3	30 (-7)	3.0 (-1.8)
4	35 (-2)	6.0 (1.2)
5	55 (18)	20.0 (15.2)
6	40 (3)	6.0 (1.2)
7	40 (3)	2.5 (-2.3)
8	30 (-7)	1.0 (-3.8)
9	35 (-2)	4.0 ($-.8$)
10	60 (23)	2.0 (-2.8)
	$\bar{x} = 37$	$\bar{y} = 4.8$

(The values in parentheses are the centered values of each characteristic obtained by subtracting the respective means.)

Over the span of one year, we are able to segregate this sample into two subpopulations:

Subpopulation 1: those with "satisfactory" payment behavior.
Subpopulation 2: those with "unsatisfactory" payment behavior.

$$\text{pop. } 1 = (3, 5, 6, 9, 10)$$
$$\text{pop. } 2 = (1, 2, 4, 7, 8).$$

To determine a_1 and a_2 we first compute the average x and y within each subpopulation.

$$\bar{x}_1 = 0.2(30 + 55 + 40 + 35 + 60) = 44,$$

the average value of x within the satisfactory payment group. Continuing,

$$\bar{x}_2 = 0.2(25 + 20 + 35 + 40 + 30) = 30$$
$$\bar{y}_1 = 0.2(3 + 20 + 6 + 4 + 2) = 7$$
$$\bar{y}_2 = 0.2(1 + 2.5 + 6 + 2.5 + 1) = 2.6$$

Thus the difference between the means is in each case:

$$d_x = 44 - 30 = 14$$
$$d_y = 7 - 2.6 = 4.4$$

Intuitively we want to weight heavily any characteristic for which there is a significant difference between the two groups. Significance naturally involves the average differences, d_x and d_y, but must also consider the variability of the characteristics. We now determine the variance and covariance:[2]

$$s_{xx} = \tfrac{1}{9}[(-12)^2 + (-17)^2 + \cdots + 23^2]$$
$$= 157 \text{ (variance of } x)$$
$$s_{yy} = \tfrac{1}{9}[(-3.8)^2 + (-2.3)^2 + \cdots + (-2.8)^2]$$
$$= 31.7 \text{ (variance of } y)$$
$$s_{xy} = \tfrac{1}{8}[(-12)(-3.8) + (-17)(-2.3) + \cdots + (23)(-2.8)]$$
$$= 41.1 \text{ (covariance between } x \text{ and } y).$$

To determine a_1 and a_2 we solve the equations:

$$s_{xx}a_1 + s_{xy}a_2 = d_x$$
$$s_{xy}a_1 + s_{yy}a_2 = d_y,$$

that is,

$$157a_1 + 41.1a_2 = 14 \qquad\qquad (5.1)$$
$$41.1a_1 + 31.7a_2 = 4.4. \qquad\qquad (5.2)$$

From (5.1)

$$a_2 = \frac{1}{41.1}(14 - 157a_1) = 0.341 - 3.82a_1,$$

and substituting into (5.2)

$$41.1a_1 + 31.7(0.341 - 3.82a_1) = 4.4.$$

Thus

$$a_1 = 0.080 \qquad \text{and} \qquad a_2 = 0.035.$$

Our discriminant function is then

$$z = 0.08x + 0.035y$$

and the discriminant line is computed by

$$\bar{z} = 0.08 \left(\frac{\bar{x}_1 + \bar{x}_2}{2}\right) + 0.035 \left(\frac{\bar{y}_1 + \bar{y}_2}{2}\right) = 3.128.$$

The normalized discriminant function is obtained by subtracting $\bar{z}$ from z

$$Z_1 = -3.128 + 0.08x + 0.035y.$$

Thus an individual will be classified into subpopulation 1 if the discriminant score (Z_1 value) is at least 0, and into subpopulation 2 if the discriminant score is less than 0. Returning to the original sample, using Z_1, we would classify observations with a negative Z_1 value as bad risks and observations with a nonnegative Z_1 value as good risks.

Customer	Discriminant Score	Decision	Correct	Outcome	
				Type 1 Error	Type 2 Error
1	−1.093	Reject	*		
2	−1.440	Reject	*		
3	−0.623	Reject			*
4	−0.118	Reject	*		
5	1.972	Accept	*		
6	0.282	Accept	*		
7	0.160	Accept		*	
8	−0.693	Reject	*		
9	−0.188	Reject			*
10	1.742	Accept	*		

(Here if customer is classified into pop. 2, the application is rejected.)

Figure 5.1 illustrates this example. The discriminant line bisects the sample. In fact, what we have constructed is the best linear boundary between the two subpopulations. The further from the "border" a given observation is, the stronger is its association to the particular group. In practice, we would probably generate lines like D_1 and D_2 and use additional information to classify observations that lie in this marginal area.

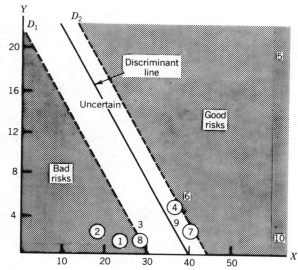

Fig. 5.1   Example 5.3 discriminant boundary.

Note that the simplest formulation we have illustrated above assumes that the prior probability of each subpopulation is the same, as is the cost of each type of error. More generally, we would develop a cutoff score such that the sum of the expected error costs is minimized.[3]

Another point that is often missed in applications of discriminant analysis is that the covariance matrices of each characteristic in each subpopulation are the same. If this is not the case (but we still have approximate normality of the characteristics), then we need to use quadratic discriminant analysis. Similarly, if the characteristics are not normally distributed, we should use some more general form of discriminant analysis.[4]

Exercise. Explain how regression could be used to determine a_1 and a_2? Can you see any potential problems?

Bankruptcy

> I am always amused at a meeting like this when the credit community, always desperate to get its facilities into as many hands as possible, whines like a bunch of stuck pigs because here and there it got stuck. They remind me of the insurance companies, who want the large premiums but do not want any risk. As I listen at meetings like this, it occurs to me that you persist in throwing your credit cards out in the mail—and then you scream because you got stuck by people you never really checked out [Judge Roy Babbit, 1981].

The changing aspects of business and personal bankruptcies are clearly pertinent to our discussion of credit granting and monitoring. Focusing for the moment on personal bankruptcies, events have moved rather far from the Draconian Code of Athens (ca. 600 B.C.) where default was punishable by death. In the United States, the revision of the bankruptcy laws in 1978 has made it easier to individuals to opt for Chapter 7 (liquidation), by allowing for more generous exemptions for property and benefits, and for Chapter 13 (the "wage-earner" plan), which creates a three to five year schedule for repayment of (an often miniscule fraction of) debts. The Credit Research Institute at Purdue in a 1981 study showed that of the surveyed petitioners for bankruptcy under Chapter 7, 52.1% could not have repaid any of their outstanding debts, while 31.3% could have repaid more than 50% of their debts (within three years). Of those surveyed, 62.6% said they expected to lose nothing (no assets) as a result of bankruptcy (see Sullivan, 1981). However, credit grantors are seemingly losing a considerable amount. Sears, Roebuck and Co. estimated that it lost $51.9 million in 1981 because of personal bankruptcies. Also, those utilizing credit-scoring techniques have found them rather ineffective at predicting this type of behavior, thus highlighting the inability of these quantitative techniques to estimate "character."

Business bankruptcies have also been prominent. Firms liquidating file under Chapter 7, and those attempting protection from debtors while reorganizing file under Chapter 11 in most cases. This is a voluntary procedure where the management of the firm often retains control while a plan is developed for the disposition of debts. The assets of the firm remain in court custody. An interesting recent case is Manville Corporation, which, supposedly, filed to escape a large number of lawsuits related to its asbestos operations and in the meanwhile remains rather profitable.

Example 5.4   This example applies discriminant analysis to a credit-granting problem. Initially we are given 78 observations from a collection of past corporate credit customers. From their payment behavior we are able to group each observation into those with "good" payment records (denoted group 1) and those with "bad" payment records (denoted group 2). We have available for each of the 78 customers the following ratios:

x_1 = current ratio.
x_2 = quick ratio.
x_3 = earnings before interest and taxes (EBIT)/total assets.
x_4 = EBIT/total sales.
x_5 = total liabilities/total assets.
x_6 = interest coverage.

Exhibit 5.2 displays the mean and standard deviation of each ratio within each group.

EXHIBIT 5.2   EXAMPLE 5.4: MEAN AND STANDARD DEVIATION OF EACH RATIO WITHIN EACH GROUP

		x_1	x_2	x_3	x_4	x_5	x_6
Group 1	Mean	2.797	0.399	0.129	0.081	0.491	7.874
	Standard deviation	1.411	0.567	0.082	0.047	0.179	24.424
Group 2	Mean	1.430	0.069	-0.092	-0.060	0.807	-1.302
	Standard deviation	0.586	0.066	0.144	0.114	0.142	3.562

Exhibit 5.2 suggests which ratios should discriminate best. However (see the discussion of the t-statistic in Chapter 7), the mere difference in group means signifies little. This difference should be divided by the appropriate standard deviation to obtain a t-statistic that tests whether or not there is a significant difference between the two group means. If we find that the difference is insignificant, then that ratio will not be useful in discriminating between good and bad payers. We proceed with stepwise discriminant analysis. This technique builds a series of models from a set of explanatory variables by selecting the best additional variable at each iteration. In the

first step it chooses the single variable, say x_1, with the highest explanatory power. In the second step, from the remaining variables, it chooses the one that, together with x_1, has the highest explanatory power, and so on. In the present context, explanatory power refers to the model's ability to discriminate the sample into the two categories.

Initially we seek the single variable (ratio) that will discriminate best between the two groups. As in regression the F-statistic provides a ranking of explanatory power. For these data x_5 (total liabilities/total assets) turns out to be the best. The normalized model is

$$Z_1 = -4.02 + 6.19x_5. \qquad (5.3)$$

This model has been normalized so that a negative Z_1 value would lead to classification into group 2 (bad payers). This model correctly classifies 82.05%, making eight type 1 errors and six type 2 errors. Figure 5.2 is a histogram of x_5 within each group. Observe that while there is some overlap, generally bad risks have a higher value of x_5. Figure 5.3 plots the two types of errors created by varying the cutoff level Z_1.

In stepwise discriminant analysis (as in stepwise regression) we select the next variable to enter on the basis of the maximum F-statistic. Here we obtain the normalized model

$$Z_2 = -2.399 + 3.834x_5 - 4.853x_3. \qquad (5.4)$$

Thus the next variable to enter is EBIT/total assets. Again, a negative Z_2 would lead to classification into group 2. The model (5.4) correctly classifies

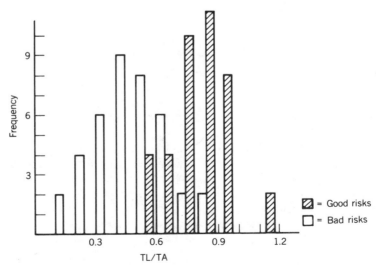

Fig. 5.2 Example 5.4 total liabilities/total assets within each group.

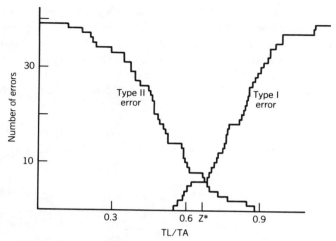

Fig. 5.3 Example 5.4 type 1 and type 2 errors with univariate classification.

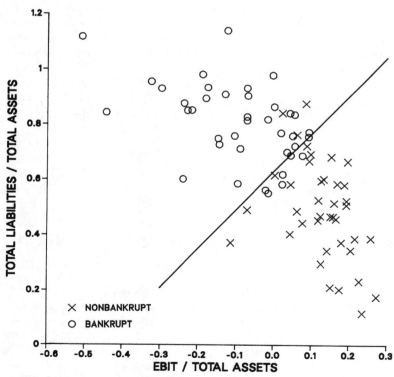

Fig. 5.4 Example 5.4 linear discriminant analysis by two criteria.

89.74% of the sample. Figure 5.4 plots x_5 and x_3 for the sample together with the discriminant model boundary from (5.4).

We could continue the stepwise technique to include a third explanatory variable but for these data very little would be gained. This example points out that discriminant analysis can be effective in generating a simple model that can extract the essential information embedded in a large data set.

SECTION 5.4 MONITORING ACCOUNTS RECEIVABLE

Once the question of credit granting has been settled, the next phase of accounts receivable management is the monitoring of the outstanding receivables. The goals are to detect changes in payment behavior, to assess the liquidity of the receivables portfolio, and to generate forecasts of cash flows from a given collection of receivables. We begin by surveying some of the most important measures of receivables performance.

Stone (1976) includes a survey of the primary forecasting and control techniques utilized by 150 large U.S. firms. The most important control method was the aging schedule (76% of respondents) while the forecasting technique stated as most utilized was ratio projection (including day's sales outstanding projections) (70% of respondents). In the following discussion we describe these and a number of other important methods for forecasting and control of accounts receivable. The following example will be used to illustrate these approaches.

Example 5.5 For a firm with an average annual sales of $30 million and trade credit terms of net 30, assume that we have the following data:

Month (end of)	Total AR Balance (in $M)	Aging (in $M)				Addition to Bad Debts
		0	1	2	3	
January	3.5	2.2	0.4	0.3	0.3	0.3
February	4.0	2.8	0.6	0.3	0.2	0.1
March	4.1	2.7	0.8	0.4	0.1	0.1
April	4.6	3.1	0.7	0.5	0.2	0.1

Here the aging categories refer to a classification of current accounts receivable into current debts and into three categories of overdue debts (1, 2, and 3 months overdue). Assume any debt more than three months overdue is classified as a bad debt.

The Aging Schedule. Determine the percentage (or amount as above) of accounts receivable in each of a number of age classes (usually divided monthly). The percentages are called the aging fractions. For this example we get

Month	Current (%)	Overdue 1 Month (%)	Overdue 2 Months (%)	Overdue 3 Months (%)
January	63	11	9	9
February	70	15	7.5	5
March	66	20	10	2
April	67	15	11	4

Note that one problem is the difficulty in separating the effects of changes in sales from changes in payment behavior. For example, in Feburary we observe a smaller percentage of overdue accounts than in January. This may be due to an improvement in the payment behavior of our customers or may merely reflect the fact that there were fewer credit sales in January, i.e., a smaller amount in the current account. Realizing this, many firms use various methods of seasonally adjusting aging figures.

Day's Sales Outstanding (DSO).   This is computed as the ratio of receivables to (a forecast of) average daily sales.[5] For our example we get

$$\text{DSO (Jan.)} = 43 \, [= 3.5/(30/365)],$$
$$\text{DSO (Feb.)} = 49,$$
$$\text{DSO (Mar.)} = 50,$$
$$\text{DSO (Apr.)} = 56.$$

The first figure shows that there are 43 days of sales outstanding in January.
   These figures seem to suggest an increasing investment in receivables, the cause of which is uncertain. A related ratio is average annual credit sales divided by average outstanding receivables (the receivables turnover ratio).

Ratio-Based Projections.   Such projections assume that receivables are proportional to (a forecast of) sales; for example, in the simplest case we may assume that receivables in month t are some fraction r of sales in month t. For our example, if we take $r = 1.4$ and our sales forecast for January is 2.2 million, then the forecast receivables in January are $1.4(2.2) = 3.08$. More generally, we would relate receivables to more than just the current month's sales. This is developed in Study 5.1.

Percentage of Balance.   This method assumes that payments in a given month are some constant multiple of the start of the month's receivables.[6] For our example, if we assume that we collect one-half of the past month's receivables in the current month, our estimate for May's payments is $\frac{1}{2}(4.6) = 2.3$.

The basic problem of separating payment patterns from sales patterns exists for all of the preceding methods. One way around this weakness is to use what Stone calls the payment pattern approach, which is actually a very simple application of Markov chains, a fundamental tool in operations research.[7] The following discussion is most applicable to installment credit.

Following our example [and simplifying the approach of Corcoran (1979)], a given sale in a given month can be classified into one of a number of possible categories (states). For instance, we may have the possible categories (the "state space") given by the aging categories:

$$P = \text{paid},$$
$$B = \text{bad debt},$$
$$0 = \text{current (terms are net 30)},$$
$$1 = \text{one month past due},$$
$$2 = \text{two months past due},$$
$$3 = \text{three months past due}.$$

If we fix one month as the length of one period, any given sale will change states during the period (except for the states P and B which are termed *absorbing* states; once a sale enters state P or B it is no longer relevant for our cash forecasting purposes). The possible transitions can be described by Figure 5.5. The possible transitions can also be represented by a (probability transition) matrix, whose rows represent the possible starting states and whose columns represent the possible ending states for a one-period transition. For our example, letting P_{ij} be the probability of an account moving from state i to state j in one period, we have

		Ending State					
		P	B	0	1	2	3
	P	1	0	0	0	0	0
	B	0	1	0	0	0	0
Beginning	0	P_{0p}	0	0	P_{01}	0	0
State	1	P_{1p}	0	0	0	P_{12}	0
	2	P_{2p}	0	0	0	0	P_{23}
	3	P_{3p}	P_{3B}	0	0	0	0

Note that all rows sum to 1 and all entries are nonnegative. To illustrate, a zero in the third row and fifth column implies that the transition $(0 \rightarrow 2)$ is impossible.

Exercise.   Why should the transition $(0 \rightarrow 2)$ be impossible?

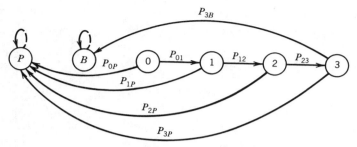

Fig. 5.5 Transition probabilities for the accounts receivable model.

We may use the January and February data from our example to estimate Π. The 2.2 that was current in January is divided into 0.6, which became one month past due, and 1.6, which was paid in February. Hence $P_{0P} = 1.6/2.2$ and $P_{01} = 0.6/2.2$. Similarly, we construct the rest of Π.

$$\Pi = \begin{bmatrix} 1 & 0 & 0 & 0 & 0 & 0 \\ 0 & 1 & 0 & 0 & 0 & 0 \\ 0.73 & 0 & 0 & 0.27 & 0 & 0 \\ 0.25 & 0 & 0 & 0 & 0.75 & 0 \\ 0.33 & 0 & 0 & 0 & 0 & 0.67 \\ 0.67 & 0.33 & 0 & 0 & 0 & 0 \end{bmatrix}.$$

Of course, this is the most trivial way to estimate Π; more generally, we would use exponential smoothing[8] or some other way of incorporating seasonal and other elements into the forecast. Corcoran (1979) gives examples of how much superior this method is to more conventional methods. To demonstrate Corcoran's exponential smoothing technique, first we generate the transition matrix from the February–March data.

$$\Pi_1 = \begin{bmatrix} 1 & 0 & 0 & 0 & 0 & 0 \\ 0 & 1 & 0 & 0 & 0 & 0 \\ 0.71 & 0 & 0 & 0.29 & 0 & 0 \\ 0.33 & 0 & 0 & 0 & 0.67 & 0 \\ 0.67 & 0 & 0 & 0 & 0 & 0.33 \\ 0.50 & 0.50 & 0 & 0 & 0 & 0 \end{bmatrix}.$$

Exercise. Verify the computation of Π_1.

Taking an exponential smoothing formula with, say $\alpha = \frac{1}{2}$, and letting $\Pi = S_1$, we would generate our transition matrix for March–April by the natural generalization of (7.3):

$$\Pi_t = \alpha\Pi_{t-1} + (1 - \alpha)S_{t-1}$$

where Π_{t-1} is the transition matrix estimated from the period $n - 1$ and S_{t-1} is the forecast transition matrix for period $n - 1$. Thus

$$
\Pi_2 = \begin{bmatrix}
1 & 0 & 0 & 0 & 0 & 0 \\
0 & 1 & 0 & 0 & 0 & 0 \\
0.72 & 0 & 0 & 0.28 & 0 & 0 \\
0.29 & 0 & 0 & 0 & 0.71 & 0 \\
0.50 & 0 & 0 & 0 & 0 & 0.50 \\
0.59 & 0.41 & 0 & 0 & 0 & 0
\end{bmatrix}.
$$

Of course, we may use a variety of methods to determine these matrices, adjusting for trend, seasonality, etc.

We can illustrate how one can use Π to (among other things)[9] generate a forecast of cash flows for the next period. Suppose that we have data for February summarized as

$$(0, 0, 2.8, 0.6, 0.3, 0.2)$$

representing the amount in states $P, B, \ldots, 3$, respectively (assuming, for simplicity, zero in states P and B). The states that communicate with state P (i.e., from which we can move to state P) are P, 0, 1, 2, and 3 with probabilities 1, 0.73, 0.25, 0.33, and 0.67, respectively. Thus the expected amount of cash that will be received in the next period is

$$0.73(2.8) + 0.25(0.6) + 0.33(0.3) + 0.67(0.2) = 2.427.$$

We can do this for any state and it is easy to see that all we are doing is multiplying the initial data by the transition matrix to get the estimated final data. In this case the final distribution would be

$$(2.427, 0.066, 0, 0.756, 0.45, 0.201).$$

Exercise. Show that by using Π, and the February data we can estimate new bad debts for March of 0.066.

SECTION 5.5 TRADE CREDIT

Trade credit is the most common form of credit transaction between two firms and is arguably the most important source of short-term financing for U.S. firms. This section treats the questions of why trade credit exists and what constitutes an "optimal" trade credit policy.

The first question is partially answered by the discussion in Section 5.1

of why credit should be granted. Schwartz and Whitcomb (1979, p. 259) go further to argue that there exist three motives for a trade credit offer:

> The transaction motive reflects the fact that buyers' transaction costs are reduced if invoices are allowed to accumulate for periodic payment. . . . The financing motive exists if firms can profitably link financial intermediation to the sale of a product due to capital market inperfections. The pricing motive exists if product market imperfections make trade credit an effective means for disguised price reductions or discriminatory pricing.

The strength of these motives needs to be considered in determining the optimal trade credit policy.

Evaluation of the explicit costs of credit policy changes can be placed within a capital budgeting framework. Here we develop only the simplest case [from Hill and Riener (1979)] but many variants and extensions exist: Weston and Tuan (1980), Sartoris and Hill (1981, 1983) and Kallberg (1983). Lieber and Orgler (1975) remains perhaps the most comprehensive, allowing variable cash discounts, variable length of discount and credit period, penalty charges for late payment, collection expenditures, and duration of past due collection effort. Each of these generalizations in the cited papers uses a framework analogous to the one we shall develop.

Assume the following:

The firm's initial credit policy has no discount.

Cash payments totaling $S arrive on day N (i.e., we equate the actual payments distributed over a number of dates to a single amount received on day N).

The firm is considering a credit policy with a discount of $d\%$ for early payment. Because of this discount, it is estimated that some fraction p of $S will now be paid on day M (to take the discount) and the remainder will pay on day N'.

The discount d should be offered if the net present value of revenues under the new credit policy is greater than the net present value of revenues under the old credit policy. The net present value of the new credit policy is

$$\frac{p(1 - d)S}{(1 + i)^M} + \frac{(1 - p)S}{(1 + i)^{N'}},\tag{5.5}$$

where i is the relevant daily interest rate. The net present value of the initial credit policy is

$$\frac{S}{(1 + i)^N}\tag{5.6}$$

The decision rule says adopt discount d if $(5.5) > (5.6)$. Simplifying this yields

$$d < 1 - (1 + i)^{M-N'} \left[\frac{p - (1 - (1 + i)^{N'-N})}{p} \right]. \qquad (5.7)$$

Example 5.6 Suppose that the firm currently has daily sales of \$1 million ($S = 1$) with an average daily collection time of 40 days ($N = 40$). It is considering a credit policy with a cash discount that will result in 80% of daily sales being received on day 10 ($p = 0.8$; $M = 10$) and the remainder on day 50 ($N' = 50$). Assuming a daily interest rate of 0.035% ($i = 0.00035$), (5.7) yields

$$d < 1 - (1.00035)^{-40} \left[\frac{.8 - (1 - (1.00035)^{10})}{.8} \right] = 0.0096.$$

Hence the firm would not benefit from offering a discount above 0.0096.

Exercise. Why is S irrelevant in this calculation?

Exercise. Suppose now that the current average collection time is 50 days and that 50% of the sales would be paid early if a cash discount was offered (and all other data are unchanged). Verify that the new break-even discount is 1.39%

Recall that (5.7) presents only the most simple case. The worst flaw is that S and d are not interconnected in this model, so that no matter how large the discount offered, average sales do not change. This and many other generalizations can be found in the references given above.

While this capital budgeting analysis describes the cash flow evaluations under each alternative, there are other important effects of changes in credit policy. Some of these are discussed in the following section.

SECTION 5.6 ACCOUNTS RECEIVABLE FINANCING

The use of current assets either as security for a loan or for outright sale has become an increasingly important source of financing. In particular, funding for working capital needs is often acquired in this manner. The practice is termed *asset-based* financing and it covers what traditionally was called commercial financing and factoring, respectively. Although formerly these practices were confined to certain industries (e.g., textiles or rubber) or to firms without other sources of financing, their usage has spread and the dire connotations associated with "resorting" to this type of financing have diminished. Asset-based financing is still most commonly used by firms without sufficient access to lower-cost debt but this also is changing.

In this section we focus on receivables financing. Here the firm transfers the receivables to the factor and receives at a negotiated date some percentage of the face value. (This discounting is similar to the merchant's discount on third-party credit card sales which is the percentage of the sale taken by the credit card issuer.) The discount reflects the risk of the receivables and possibly a financing charge for payment in advance of the collection date. This factoring can be done on a recourse or nonrecourse basis. In the latter case the factor assumes all risk of collections. This type of financing is generally more expensive than other sources of capital and the firm loses some degree of control over the credit process, particularly the collection aspect. The advantages though are important:

More flexible cash flows, since timing of the payments from the factor can be negotiated.

Less dependence on other sources of financing.

Protection against bad debt losses.

Reduced credit and collections expense.

In addition, the balance sheet effects can be very important. This idea is developed in the following example.

Example 5.7   Suppose that a retailer has entered into an agreement to sell 50% of its receivables to a factor and will use the funds to retire short-term debt. To facilitate the comparison, assume that the interest income on receivables equals the interest cost of short-term debt. The balance sheet and income statement before and after the sale together with selected ratio changes are given in Exhibit 5.3.

In this example the current ratio has improved, leverage has decreased, and return on assets has risen; all of these are desirable outcomes.

A number of points complicate the comparison. There are tax effects. Aside from tax effects arising from interest payments, for retailers there is a tax deferral on revolving credit until the receivables are collected. This deferral, which can be very substantial, is diminished through the sale. Also, some analysts consider these financial statement changes to be merely cosmetic, and financial markets cannot always be expected to react to this type of manipulation.

At this point the linkages between credit policy and cash management should become clear. Here the decision to sell converts one current asset

EXHIBIT 5.3   FINANCIAL STATEMENT IMPACT FOR EXAMPLE 5.7

	Before Sale	After Sale		Before Sale	After Sale
Cash	50	50	Short-term debt	400	150
Receivables	500	250	Other payables	100	100
Inventory	400	400	Current liabilities	500	250
Current assets	950	700	Long-term debt	300	300
Net plant	300	300	Equity	450	450
Total assets	1250	1000	Total liabilities and equity	1250	1000

	Before Sale	After Sale
Income Statement Changes		
Sales	1000	1000
Earnings before interest and taxes	200	170
Interest (@ 12%)	96	66
Before tax profit	104	104
After tax profit	52	52
Selected Ratio Changes		
Current ratio	1.90	2.80
Total debt/equity	1.56	1.00
After-tax return/total assets	4.16%	5.20%

to another: receivables to cash. Similarly, shortening the credit period in a trade credit policy will speed up collection of receivables.

SECTION 5.7   STUDY 5.1 ANALYSIS OF RETAIL CREDIT DATA

This study is based on retail credit data from a large East Coast department store. The data consist of monthly records from a random sample of 200 revolving credit accounts. For each account and each month the following data were recorded:

Opening balance.
Purchases during the month.
Payment received.
Minimum required payment (based on the opening balance and the classification of the account into current, one month overdue, etc.).

The goal of this study is to use these data for cash flow forecasting and to apply the Markov chain approach to study payment behavior. (For the reader who may be uncomfortable with some of the statistical methodology, it may be advisable to read Chapter 7 before this study.)

Forecasting of Cash Flows by Regression

This analysis is similar to Shim (1981); see also Section 7.6. Using the data described previously, we compare models for forecasting the cash flows in a given month from information on credit sales in past months. In month t, C_t is the cash flow from credit sales and S_t is the current credit sales. The four models estimated are given below. (Note that unlike Shim, we allow a nonzero constant term. This allows cash flows from credit sales in months not included in the independent variables to be nonzero.)

$$C_t = 7136.7 + 0.326S_{t-1} \qquad (5.8)$$
$$(6.423) \qquad (3.231)$$

$R^2 = 0.3805$; $\sigma_u = 1157.8$; $D.W. = 1.54$;   degrees of freedom $= 17$.

$$C_t = 5650.0 + 0.277S_{t-1} + 0.191S_{t-2} \qquad (5.9)$$
$$(4.232) \qquad (2.679) \qquad (1.848)$$

$R^2 = 0.4917$; $\sigma_u = 1111.1$; $D.W. = 1.72$;   degrees of freedom $= 15$.

$$C_t = 4156.5 + 0.317S_{t-1} + 0.123S_{t-2} + 0.168S_{t-3} \qquad (5.10)$$
$$(2.514) \qquad (3.010) \qquad (1.094) \qquad (1.570)$$

$R^2 = 0.5598$; $\sigma_u = 1093.4$; $D.W. = 1.91$;   degrees of freedom $= 13$.

$$C_t = 3372.7 + 0.285S_{t-1} + 0.159S_{t-2} + 0.128S_{t-3} + 0.110S_{t-4} \quad (5.11)$$
$$(1.778) \qquad (2.292) \qquad (1.283) \qquad (0.989) \qquad (0.891)$$

$R^2 = 0.5875$; $\sigma_u = 1137.4$; $D.W. = 2.15$;   degrees of freedom $= 11$.

As usual, t-statistics are given in brackets below the estimate and DW is the Durbin–Watson statistic. See Chapter 7 for details.

   For each of the models a Box–Jenkins identification (see Section 7.5) of residuals was attempted. Surprisingly, none of the models had any significant residual autocorrelation (the largest autocorrelation was 0.381, which compared to a standard error of 0.22, was not significant).

Note that for models (5.10) and (5.11), all estimates other than the constant term and the coefficient on S_{t-1} are not significant at the 0.10 level. With (5.11), while the R^2 is the best of the four models, σ_u is higher than in (5.9) or (5.10).

This type of model is commonly used for this purpose. Values of R^2 about 0.60 seem to be quite typical.

Markov Chain Analysis of Payment Behavior

As previously noted in this chapter, the Markov chain model allows payment behavior to be analyzed relatively independently of fluctuations in sales patterns. Its application to cash flow forecasting and bad debt losses has also been mentioned. Here, rather than forecasting cash flows, we investigate the payment patterns utilizing a different state space definition.

The first model is related to the classification of accounts in an aging schedule. We assume that a given credit account, at the start of month t, can be classified into exactly one of five states. P denotes the "paid-up" state [the account has no outstanding balance]; 0 denotes a current account [the account has a positive balance and the payment in period $(t - 1)$ was at least the minimum required payment]; 1 denotes the one-month overdue state [the payment in period $(t - 1)$ was less than the minimum required, but the payment in period $(t - 2)$, if any, was at least the minimum]; 2 denotes the two-month overdue state; 3 denotes the bad debt state (the account is at least three months overdue). We let p_{ij} denote the proportion of accounts that began the month in state i and ended in state j. The estimated transition matrix of the p_{ij} over the entire sample and time period is given in Exhibit 5.4.

EXHIBIT 5.4   ESTIMATED TRANSITION MATRIX: BASIC STATE DEFINITION

| | | Ending State | | | | |
		P	0	1	2	3
	P	0.793	0.207	0.000	0.000	0.000
	0	0.091	0.732	0.177	0.000	0.000
Beginning	1	0.087	0.509	0.000	0.404	0.000
State	2	0.070	0.383	0.000	0.000	0.547
	3	0.065	0.315	0.000	0.000	0.620

We can easily interpret a number of the figures given in Exhibit 5.4:

> The probability of a current account becoming one-month overdue (in the span of one month) is 17.7% (p_{01}).
>
> The probability of a one-month overdue account missing the next payment is 40.4% (p_{12}).
>
> The probability of a two-month overdue account missing the next payment is 54.7% (p_{23}).

This suggests that the more overdue accounts are harder to collect. If we were dealing with net 30 rather than revolving credit, we could use this matrix to estimate the probability of a current account becoming overdue from $p_{01} \cdot p_{12} \cdot p_{23} = 0.039$.

This state definition overaggregates the current state. We would expect different payment behavior if a current account had a large or a small outstanding balance. This leads to the second state definition. Here we retain the original definitions of states P, 1, 2, and 3 but we subdivide state 0 as follows:

> $0a$: current account with an opening balance less than $50.
>
> $0b$: current account with an opening balance between $50 and $100.
>
> $0c$: current account with an opening balance between $100 and $200.
>
> $0d$: current account with an opening balance between $200 and $400.
>
> $0e$: current account with an opening balance in excess of $400.

The transition matrix obtained for this state space definition is given in Exhibit 5.5.

One interesting observation can be made from Exhibit 5.5 from observing the state 1 column. Note that from all the current states the probability of ending up in state 1 is approximately the same. This means that the probability of a current account missing a payment is independent of its opening balance, a result some might find surprising.

Exhibits 5.4 and 5.5 are part of a larger study that attempts to test the reactions of consumers to changes in credit pricing (due to lifting of usury ceilings) and seasonality. It was found (for these data at least) that retail customers are relatively insensitive to changes in finance charges and that there is no significant seasonality in their payment behavior.[10] It goes on to show that the Markov chain approach generates superior forecasts of cash flows from accounts receivable.

EXHIBIT 5.5 ESTIMATED TRANSITION MATRIX: EXPANDED CURRENT STATE

					Ending State					
		P	0a	0b	0c	0d	0e	1	2	3
	P	0.793	0.085	0.046	0.040	0.028	0.008	0.000	0.000	0.000
	0a	0.295	0.283	0.121	0.067	0.051	0.010	0.175	0.000	0.000
	0b	0.108	0.165	0.365	0.150	0.034	0.003	0.176	0.000	0.000
	0c	0.043	0.041	0.151	0.413	0.145	0.023	0.184	0.000	0.000
Beginning	0d	0.025	0.010	0.023	0.155	0.544	0.078	0.165	0.000	0.000
State	0e	0.025	0.020	0.015	0.012	0.229	0.498	0.194	0.000	0.000
	1	0.087	0.084	0.108	0.147	0.090	0.081	0.000	0.404	0.000
	2	0.070	0.047	0.086	0.117	0.078	0.055	0.000	0.000	0.547
	3	0.065	0.050	0.080	0.100	0.060	0.025	0.000	0.000	0.620

NOTES

1. It is also possible to allow a third type of classification, an area of uncertainty as exemplified earlier.
2. See Appendix A for further details on this type of estimation.
3. That is, if p_i represents the prior probability of group i, and c_i represents the type i error cost ($i = 1,2$), then we would minimize $(p_1c_1 + p_2c_2)$.
4. See Altman et al. (1981).
5. Another way of determining day's sales outstanding is given in Problem 5.
6. See Section 5.7 for an extension of this approach.
7. See Ross (1974) or a similar text for details.
8. See Chapter 7.
9. See Cyert et al. (1964) for a more complete analysis of this aspect of the problem. Karson and Wrobleski (1976) have shown how to construct confidence intervals for bad debt estimates determined in this way. See also Frydman, et al. (1983) for discussion of a variety of related statistical concepts.
10. See Kallberg and Saunders (1983).

CASE 5.1   ABC BANK.   ABC is a medium-sized bank which has been incurring losses on its loans to small and medium-sized corporations. In order to improve this function ABC hired the MBA Consulting Agency (MBACA) to analyze past performance and to make recommendations on a superior loan granting procedure.

MBACA being replete with statistical expertise decided to use discriminant analysis to automate the loan granting process. MBACA examined the last 100 accepted loans. Thirty of the loans were classified as unacceptable because of poor payment behavior (either due to having missed one or more payments or being in default of principle). The other 70 were classified as acceptable. Using available accounting information MBACA developed the linear discriminant model

$$Z = -100 + 40x_1 + 87x_2 + 21x_3$$

where x_1 = quick ratio.

x_2 = net working capital/total assets.

x_3 = net sales/total assets.

The model was normalized so that a negative score would lead to rejection of the loan applicant and a nonnegative score would lead to acceptance of the loan application.

Questions

1. Given the data for XYZ Corporation (see Exhibit 5.6), determine whether or not its loan application should be granted.

EXHIBIT 5.6 XYZ   SELECTED FINANCIAL INFORMATION

	Dec. 31, 1981	Dec. 31, 1982
Cash	132	102
Inventory	706	603
Accounts Receivable	300	375
Other Current Assets	12	8
Total Current Assets	1150	1088
Other Assets	2300	2200
Total Assets	3450	3288
Current Liabilities	640	770
Net Sales	12,306	11,202

2. Comment on the suitability of this technique (linear discriminant analysis and credit scoring) for this application.

CASE 5.2   NATIONAL P.B. CORPORATION.   Exhibits 5.7 and 5.8 present the income statement and balance sheet for this firm (a small publicly traded manufacturing firm). What can you conclude about the working capital position of the National P.B. Corporation?

EXHIBIT 5.7   NATIONAL P.B. CORPORATION INCOME STATEMENT YEAR END 1982 ($000)

Net sales*	$9,000
Cost of goods sold	4,000
Gross profit	5,000
Selling expenses	3,000
Administrative expenses	500
Earnings before interest and taxes	1,500
Taxes payable†	600
After tax earnings	900
Dividends‡	500
Additions to retained earnings	400

*On net 30 terms.
†Computed at 40%.
‡On 100,000 shares.

EXHIBIT 5.8 NATIONAL P.B. CORPORATION BALANCE SHEET YEAR END 1982 ($000)

Assets		Liabilities	
Cash	$ 240	Accounts payable	$1300
Accounts receivable	1450	Other payables	100
Other receivables	50	Total current liabilities	1400
Inventories	900	Long-term debt	3000
Other current assets	40	Common stock and	
Total current assets	2680	paid-in surplus*	950
Net plant	4500	Retained earnings	1830
Total assets	7180	Total liabilities and equity	7180

*Market value of equity equals 4000.

PROBLEMS

1. The annual sales rate divided by the total amount outstanding in accounts receivable is the receivables turnover ratio. An optimal accounts receivable control policy would maximize this ratio. (True or false?)

2. Consider the following perishable inventory problem. We currently stock an item with a shelf life of four months. As it ages its probability of being sold decreases. In the first month the probability is 0.6, after one month the probability is 0.4, after two months the probability is 0.3, after three months the probability is 0.2, finally after four months the item is discarded.

   a. Model this process as a Markov chain (see the accounts receivable example in this chapter).

   b. If the item sells for $10, what is its expected net present value? (Assume an interest rate of 12% per annum.)

   c. If discounting the sales price to $9 will change the first probability from 0.6 to $(0.6 + p)$, what is the minimum p that would make the discount profitable (using the criterion of part b)?

3. Suppose we have observed the following credit risks and have divided them into two populations (good and bad risks) on the basis of three characteristics (deemed relevant to the credit-granting decision)

Customer No.	x_1	x_2	x_3	
1	3	1	3	
2	3	0	3	
Good Risks 3	2	2	3	Population One
4	6	1	4	
5	5	1	7	
6	4	6	2	
7	3	2	4	
Bad Risks 8	2	2	2	Population Two
9	1	4	2	
10	0	1	2	

a. If the discriminant model is $z = x_1 - 2x_2 + 3x_3$, determine the usual cutoff score (assuming unweighted errors).

b. If the rejection of a good risk has expected cost $10 and each acceptance of a bad risk has expected cost $25, sketch a graph of total expected cost versus cutoff score. From this graph determine the optimal cutoff score.

c. With the cutoff scores generated in parts a and b, determine the probability of a type 1 and of a type 2 error.

4. Firm A has a policy where all credit customers pay on net 30 terms. Accounts receivable are classified as current (less than 30 days from billing date), overdue (31–60 days from billing date), and bad debts (more than 60 days from billing date). All bad debts are sold to a collection agency for an immediate cash payment of one-half of the face value. Currently, 80% of the accounts receivable are paid within the 30-day period and 10% end up as bad debts.

a. Using one month as the length of a period, estimate the Markov transition matrix (the set of probabilities of moving from one state to another in one period) for the preceding process.

b. If the annual interest rate is 12% and monthly credit sales average $100,000, what is the expected net present value of a month's credit sales?

5. Another way of estimating day's sales outstanding can be illustrated using Example 5.5. Here the March receivables balance is 4.1. Since February's credit sales were 2.8 (the current figure) and January's credit sales were 2.2, this 4.1 can be viewed as being composed of February's sales plus (1.3/2.2) of January's sales. This is roughly 46 days [28 + (1.3/2.2)31].

a. Compute day's sales outstanding for April using this method.

b. Explain when this approach might be preferable to the method given in Section 5.4.

6. Suppose we have observed the following credit risks over a fixed period and have classified them as good and bad risks as follows:

	Good Risks	Bad Risks
Applicant #	1 2 3 4 5 6 7	8 9 10 11 12 13 14
x_1 = Credit outstanding in thousands $	.4 .8 1.3 1.0 1.6 2.0 1.9	4.0 2.2 3.0 1.0 6.0 1.4 4.8

Part I.

a. Use regression to develop a credit scoring model of the form $Z = a_0 + a_1 x_1$, to be used in forecasting the payment behavior of credit applicants.

b. What might make you doubt the applicability of your results?

c. By varying the cutoff score (i.e., the level Z^* such that applicants with a score $(a_0 + a_1 x)$ less than Z^* are classified as *good* risks), graph the possible combinations of the two types of classification errors. Explain how this can solve some of the problems you have mentioned in b.

Part II.

a. Assume now that we also have information on the annual income of each of the applicants:

	Good Risks	Bad Risks
Applicant #	1 2 3 4 5 6 7	8 9 10 11 12 13 14
x_2 = Annual income in thousands $	30. 24. 60. 50. 40. 35. 30.	28. 48. 18. 20. 14. 11. 32.

Use regression (or discriminant analysis) to develop a credit scoring model of the form $Z = a_0 + a_1 x_1 + a_2 x_2$, to be used in forecasting the payment behavior of credit applicants.

b. Do as in part c. for this bivariate model.

7. Verify that the National P. B. Corporation (data given in Exhibits 5.7 and 5.8) would be classified as a bad risk using model (5.4).

8. Describe how you think a credit department's performance should be evaluated.

6 Inventory Management

The basic questions addressed in this chapter are:

> When to place an order for an item (determination of the reorder point).
> How much to order (determination of the order size).

These questions are important because of the magnitude of the inventory investment of most firms (in the United States, inventory investment is estimated to be 16% of the gross national product[1]) and because of the intricacy of the interactions in inventory decisions. By the latter we mean that inventory decisions require a complex balancing of quantitative and qualitative aspects. By holding high inventory levels we maintain "availability" (however measured) at the cost of high inventory carrying costs. The standard cliché is, "I may get chewed out for carrying excess inventories but I'll get fired for running out."

We begin our analysis under the assumption that we have in fact decided to stock the items in question.[2] The degree of complexity with which we choose to model the problem should be addressed next. This decision will be based on the perceived benefits of control, the quality of data available for estimating model parameters, and the operating environment. The framework developed in this chapter is built around the following questions:

> What are the relevant costs?
> (1) ordering costs, (2) carrying costs, (3) shortage costs, and (4) inventory "policy costs."
>
> What is the demand pattern?
> (1) constant, (2) varying but deterministic, and (3) following a known distribution.
>
> What item characteristics are important?
> (1) perishability/obsolescence, (2) interaction with other items, (3) price changes, and (4) lead times.

The preceding questions do not attempt to address all the relevant issues. The reader interested in pursuing these issues further has a number of good references available; these include, Starr and Miller (1962), Love (1979), Peterson and Silver (1979) and Jannis, et al. (1980).

A reasonable working definition of inventory management is "the determination of optimal procedures for maintaining stocks of items (tangible or intangible) to meet anticipated demand."[3] *Optimal* is taken to mean the procedure that best balances the benefits of carrying inventory with the explicit and implicit costs involved.

Basically, there are three classes of inventory:

Raw materials inventory (factors of production, presumably to be used in a later stage of production or assembly).

Work-in-progress inventory (partially assembled or completed products).

Finished goods inventory (items ready for distribution or sale).

To reduce firm and industry-dependent discussion, our focus will be on finished goods inventory. Most of what we develop is relevant for the other two classes of inventory as well; however, they present a number of specific problems that will not be treated here. [See, for example, Plossl and Wight (1967) and other texts dealing with production or operations management.] Furthermore, for simplicity, we will utilize the language of a firm purchasing goods for resale rather than that of a firm producing these goods.

It is useful to subdivide these stocks further into three types:

Economic order quantity (EOQ) inventories (inventories maintained whenever a firm buys or produces more of an item than it can immediately utilize in order to synchronize supply and demand).

Safety stocks [inventories maintained because of the uncertainty in future demand, which is usually dependent upon demand variability during the lead-time period (the lag between placement of an order and its delivery)].

Anticipation stocks [inventories maintained in anticipation of price changes or fluctuations in demand patterns (e.g., because of seasonality), including reduction of inventory to reduce inventory taxes levied by some states, or increase in inventory to reduce taxable income].

We may summarize the preceding in the following way:

Inventory level = EOQ stock + safety stock + anticipation stock.

For most of this chapter we consider these stocks separately, postponing aggregate decisions until the last section.

The two basic types of inventory systems we consider are fixed-order systems, where an order of size Q is placed whenever the (continuously monitored) inventory level reaches a predetermined level (the reorder point R), and fixed-period systems, where inventory levels are monitored at regular intervals, triggering an order that will bring the inventory level to a pre-specified amount. (See Figure 6.1.)

Exercise. Why is the distinction between a fixed-order system and a fixed-period system irrelevant if demand is constant?

SECTION 6.1 INVENTORY COSTS

The only costs that are relevant inventory costs are those that change as the inventory policies change. Thus costs related to routinely filling a customer's order will not be discussed. The most important cost components fall into four categories:

1. Procurement (replenishment) costs (fixed and variable costs resulting from the placement and processing of an order). These include the actual

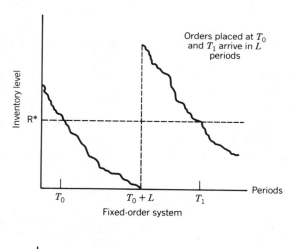

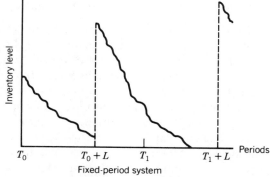

Fig. 6.1 Fixed-period system and fixed-order system.

cost of the item and may include freight charges. In theory these costs are generally assumed to be proportional to the number of orders placed.

2.   Carrying costs (out-of-pocket and indirect expenses), including some or all of the following. These costs are usually assumed to be proportional to the average inventory. Adjustments for the riskiness of the inventory may enter in either a. or c.

a.   Cost of capital invested in inventory (viewed either as an opportunity cost or as an explicit cost of financing).

b.   Storage cost (the cost of the space and equipment required to store the item, including property taxes, electricity, depreciation, etc.).

c.   Deterioration cost (cost of actual physical deterioration as well as obsolescence or pilferage).

d.   Insurance cost.

e.   Overstocking cost (the cost of items remaining after the demand has terminated).

f.   Handling cost.

Carrying costs are often split into financing costs (a.) and holding costs (b.–f.).

3.   Shortage costs. Here the characterization depends on the action taken. This cost is usually assumed to be proportional to the number of units short per period.

a.   Lost sale. This cost assumes that the demand for the quantity ordered is lost (e.g., the customer buys at another store).

b.   Backorder. Here the order is backlogged and delivery is usually delayed until supply is available.

c.   Substitution. Here the demand for the item can be satisfied by other sources or other items.

4.   Policy costs [the costs of data gathering (monitoring inventory levels, inspecting stock, obtaining cost data, etc.) and operating procedures that depend on the particular inventory control system utilized].

To illustrate, consider the costs associated with maintaining an inventory of cash (discussed in Section 7.7, currency demand at one branch of a credit union). Here replenishment costs are the cost of transferring cash from the main branch (the cost of an armored car delivery, about $30 at the time) plus a small amount for paperwork and handling. For carrying costs, the only factor of significance is the opportunity cost of capital invested. A reasonable figure might be the credit union's short-term investment rate. Note that although storage costs are not zero, the marginal cost is negligible. Shortage costs are awkward to quantify. In this case they were implicitly determined by specifying a probability of shortage. Policy costs appear implicitly through management restricting the feasible operating policies.

It is important to emphasize the difficulty in estimating cost parameters in an inventory problem. From Bock (1974, p. 59): "the effectiveness of any inventory control system depends not only on selecting the right models but also on estimating the cost parameters used in the models. . . . The richness of the models presently exceeds the sophistication of the cost information." Most of the models discussed in this section require specification of the marginal costs associated with a given inventory policy. For example, for replenishment costs we would need to determine the incremental costs of the personnel, paperwork, telephone calls, and so on, associated with the placement and processing of the order. For storage costs, this would mean specifying lighting, heating, insurance, taxes, and so on, as incremental costs. Another difficult point is the determination of the financing costs. Bock argues that these are inherently before-tax costs (since they reduce taxable income) and, furthermore, that some degree of risk adjustment is necessary. Because of obsolescence, demand uncertainty, or other factors, some inventories have a higher risk than others, and this can be handled by differing financing costs. As will become apparent, other types of risk can also be incorporated within the structure of many inventory models.

The cost of a stockout is usually computed as a loss of good will, and there are a number of ways to estimate this. It is most often taken to be the cost of a lost sale (namely, the profit margin associated with the sale). Starr and Miller (1962) note that this is inaccurate for a number of reasons; it is a confusion of opportunity costs and explicit costs and it ignores the probability that a customer experiencing a stockout may be less likely to return to that seller in the future. A related approach is to estimate the percentage of customers who will buy elsewhere if the desired item is unavailable. This multiplied by the gross margin will give the expected percentage of gross margin loss per unit out of stock. Herron (1979) discusses the expected percentage of gross margin loss among supermarket product lines. This figure "ranges over a factor of ten—from 1.9% for canned peaches and peanut butter to 17% for deodorants. Many companies structure their ordering policies to keep all products on the shelf for the same percentage of time; yet obviously such policies make little sense if the profit consequences of stockouts vary so widely from one product line to another" (Herron, 1979, pp. 123–124).

This profit penalty is only one aspect of the cost. As noted earlier, we must also consider what else results from the stockout: backorder, product substitution, permanent loss of a customer, and so on. Herron (1979) gives an example of estimating these outcomes in generating a matrix giving the estimated profit penalty from a stockout.

Another and radically different approach to incorporating shortages was developed by Schwartz (1970) and extended by Hill (1976). The main point of their "perturbed demand" models is:

The effect of a stockout is not to impose a cost ("penalty cost") against the firm at the time of incidence, but rather to modify the demand pattern in the future from that which otherwise would have occurred. This is a manifestation of loss of good will, in which the customer alters his future course of action due to meeting a stockout, rather than causing the firm some immediate, vaguely defined, loss [Schwartz, 1970, p. B-509].

The key characterization in this approach is the demand rate D:

$$D = \frac{D_0}{1 + \lambda I}$$

where D_0 is the demand rate that would occur if there were no stockouts, λ is the percentage of shortages, and I is a constant index of customer responsiveness. Schwartz presents some loose guidelines for the estimation of these parameters. It turns out (in a formal sense) that the perturbed demand approach is not equivalent to the usual approach incorporating a unit shortage cost.

Note that policy costs [Starr and Miller (1962) call them "systemic costs"] are important in the applications of inventory theory but are seldom explicit in the theory itself. Often there are a number of inventory control systems applicable to a given problem. The systems may vary in the frequency of monitoring of inventory levels, the data required, and the degree of human intervention. These points will be clarified in the discussion of ABC analysis.

To summarize, the measurement of inventory costs is difficult. Accounting data at best give average rather than marginal costs, but more likely inventory costs cannot even be disaggregated from other costs.[4] Nonetheless, many firms seem to arrive at aggregate figures: "One dollar of inventory costs 25¢ to carry, estimates Robert B. Stone, vice president, materials management, GM. That's 15 or 16¢ for the interest rate, plus 9 or 10¢ for the costs of ordering, shipping, receiving, and storing inventory . . . Ford estimates of the carrying cost of inventory are lower: 20¢ per dollar" (Berry, 1982, p. 61).

Even with these difficulties, inventory models like the ones developed in this chapter appear to work well in practice. One reason will be demonstrated in Section 6.2, the robustness of the basic model. Furthermore, Section 6.4 suggests an approach that is applicable in cases where cost data are not available or are not considered reliable.

SECTION 6.2   DETERMINING ORDER SIZES

This section deals with quantitative approaches to determining optimal order sizes, assuming that future demand and lead time are certain. The standard model is the economic order quantity model, also known as the EOQ model or the Wilson model. The more obvious and important assumptions are the following:

Constant demand of D per period.

No lead time.

Instant replenishment rate.

Need for demand always to be met.

Constant price of C per item.

No upper bound on the number of units ordered (Q).

The cost of replenishment is fixed (F) (independent of Q).

Each item in the inventory system is handled independently.

Inventory carrying costs are separated into holding costs (h per item period) and financing costs (C at $i\%$ per item period).

Here item refers to stock-keeping units; for example, an inventory of chewing gum with five different flavors would mean five items, irrespective of the quantities of each flavor.

To summarize the most crucial restrictions, there is a constant continuous demand for the item. Whenever an order is placed, the entire amount ordered is instantly available. The total cost is composed of replenishment costs (proportional to the number of orders placed) and carrying costs (proportional to the average inventory). A number of these assumptions will be relaxed in the rest of this chapter. Now the average total per period cost (TC) is

$$TC = (h + iC)\frac{Q}{2} + F\left(\frac{D}{Q}\right) + CD. \qquad (6.1)$$

The first summand is the per period holding and financing costs; $(h + iC)$ gives the cost of holding one item in inventory for one period and $Q/2$ is the average inventory (because of the constant demand rate). (Note that because of the constant demand rate and instant replenishment, we would never order until the inventory level hits zero; that is, the reorder point is 0.) The second summand is the fixed cost of ordering times the number of orders placed in a period. The final summand is the total cost of supplying demand. Taking the derivative of TC with respect to Q and setting this expression to zero, one obtains a version of the classical EOQ formula:

$$Q^* = \sqrt{(2FD)/(h + iC)}. \qquad (6.2)$$

This formula can also be expressed in terms of the optimal time between orders, t^*. Since $t^* = Q^*/D$, we have

$$t^* = \sqrt{2F/(h + iC)D}. \qquad (6.3)$$

An important fact is that at Q^*

$$\frac{(h + iC)Q}{2} = \frac{FD}{Q},$$

so that the holding and financing costs equal the ordering costs. This stems from the particular form of (6.1) and provides some intuitive justification for (6.2).

Exercise. Verify that the minimal total cost is

$$TC^* = \sqrt{2FD(h + iC)} + CD. \tag{6.4}$$

The following example will be utilized throughout the chapter.

Example 6.1. Assume:

Cost of item $= C = 4$,
Per period interest rate $= i = 0.05$,
Fixed cost of ordering $= F = 125$,
Fixed holding costs per unit period $= h = 0.2$,
Per period demand $= D = 14,400$.

Now

$$Q^* = \sqrt{(2 \cdot 125 \cdot 14,400)/(0.2 + 0.05 \cdot 4)} = 3000.$$

Carrying cost (as a function of Q) is

$$\frac{(h + iC)Q}{2} = 0.2Q,$$

which is a line with slope 0.2.

The order cost (as a function of Q) is

$$F\left(\frac{D}{Q}\right) = \frac{1,800,000}{Q},$$

which is a hyperbola. Figure 6.2 sketches these two components together with their sum: the total variable cost function. As mentioned, Q^* is at the point of intersection of the two variable cost curves. A graph of the total cost would simply add 56,000 to each point on the variable cost curve.

Exercise. Verify that the optimal time between orders is 0.2083 periods and that the minimum variable cost is 1200.

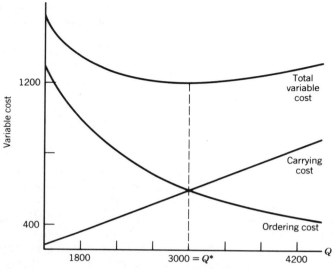

Fig. 6.2   Example 6.1 total cost curve.

A number of other results stem from (6.2). First, if the demand rate doubles, Q^* increases by only a factor of $\sqrt{2}$, ceteris paribus. Thus if sales of the item increase (and all other relevant factors remain unchanged), the inventory/sales ratio should fall if we use (6.2) to determine the ordering quantity.

Second, note in Figure 6.2 that the total variable cost curve is very flat near Q^*. This has often been noted [see, for example, Snyder (1964)] and has been used as a justification for employing the EOQ model even when the required data are very inaccurate. As long as the figures are reasonable, the EOQ seems to give a good answer.

Exercise.   Given the data of Example 6.1, verify that any Q^* in the range of 1925 to 4675 will generate a total (variable, per period) cost within 10% of the minimum. (This can be done either graphically or algebraically.)

Third, the EOQ gives a way of obtaining imputed cost parameters from observing an existing inventory policy. If a firm typically orders 200 each month and claims to be using an annual carrying cost $(h + iC)$ of \$3, then (if the EOQ assumptions hold reasonably well) we can infer a value of F from (6.2)

$$100 = \sqrt{2F(200 \cdot 12)/3}$$

so that $F = \$6.25$. This figure's plausibility then can be evaluated.

Fourth, in many applications the term $2F/(h + iC)$ can be taken to be approximately constant over a large class of items. For this class, (6.2) can be written

$$Q^* = K\sqrt{D},$$

where

$$K = \sqrt{2F/(h + iC)}$$

is assumed fixed. Now the order quantity depends only on (a forecast of) the demand. This is a very practical heuristic in many multi-item systems.

Last, in many applications there are restrictions on Q due to storage limitations, maximum inventory investment, shelf life, or otherwise. These are easy to represent in terms of Figure 6.2; the constraints merely specify that certain parts of the cost curve (i.e., certain values of Q) are not feasible. We are then restricted to choosing the best feasible Q, which in general will not coincide with the (unconstrained) EOQ. With multiple items the problem becomes less trivial. Instead of an unconstrained optimization of (6.1), we need to represent the constraint in the optimization explicitly, typically by using Lagrangian multipliers (discussed in any intermediate level calculus text).

Extensions of the EOQ Model

We now develop some of the more important extensions of the basic EOQ model. Extensions incorporating uncertainty are discussed in Section 6.3. It is important to note that despite the thoroughly artificial assumptions of the basic model, it remains rather robust to generalizations. It is also a simple bench mark when evaluating more complex systems.

Fixed Lead Times

One of the most artificial assumptions of the basic model is that of no lead time, that is, that there is no lag between the placement of an order and its delivery. Here assume that there is a fixed lead time of L periods. (See Example 6.4 for an example of the important complications that arise with a variable lead time.) It is clear that with perfectly predictable demand the existence of a lead time creates no problem: Merely order when the stock on hand is just sufficient to supply the lead time demand. Thus the reorder point is $L \cdot D$ rather than zero. Since (6.1) is unchanged, Q^* is still given by (6.2). In Example 6.1, with a lead time of 0.01 periods, the reorder point is 144.

Shortages

Assume that demand that cannot be immediately supplied is not lost but is backordered at an extra cost of u per unit period. For example, u might represent the incremental cost of expediting delivery or of utilizing another (more expensive) source of supply. The average per period cost changes in two ways: the average inventory will change (because there will be periods with effectively zero inventory and Q will increase) and the shortage costs need to be added. To develop the appropriate form of (6.2) it is convenient to decompose each order cycle (the time between orders $= Q/D$) into two phases. The first is of length S/D when there are positive inventory levels; here S represents the maximum inventory level ($S < Q$). The second phase is of duration $(Q - S)/D$ when shortages are incurred. The average inventory during the first phase is $S/2$. So, per order cycle, the inventory cost is

$$\left(\frac{S}{2}\right) \left(\frac{S}{D}\right) (h + iC) = \frac{S^2(h + iC)}{2D}. \tag{6.5}$$

Similarly, the average amount short during phase 2 is $(Q - S)/2$. Per order cycle, the shortage cost is

$$\left(\frac{Q - S}{2}\right) \left(\frac{Q - S}{D}\right) u = \frac{(Q - S)^2 u}{2D}. \tag{6.6}$$

To convert to per period costs, multiply (6.5) and (6.6) by the number of orders in one period, D/Q. The total per period cost equation is then the fixed cost of ordering (FD/Q, as before), plus the holding cost (6.5), plus the shortage cost (6.6), plus the item cost (CD):

$$T = \frac{FD}{Q} + \frac{S^2(h + iC)}{2Q} + \frac{(Q - S)^2 u}{2Q} + CD. \tag{6.7}$$

Differentiating (6.7) with respect to S and with respect to Q and setting these two expressions to zero, the optimal S and Q are

$$S^* = \sqrt{(2FD)/(h + iC)} \cdot \sqrt{u/(u + h + iC)}. \tag{6.8}$$

$$Q^* = \sqrt{(2FD)/(h + iC)} \cdot \sqrt{(u + h + iC)/u}. \tag{6.9}$$

Observe that (6.2) is a special case of (6.9) with $u = \infty$, recalling that the basic EOQ is a special case where shortages are not permitted.

In Example 6.1, setting $u = \$5$,

$$S^* = 3000\sqrt{5/5.4} = 2887.$$

$$Q^* = 3000\sqrt{5.4/5} = 3118.$$

See Figure 6.3.

Exercise. In Example 6.1 (with $u = 5$), what is the "fill rate" (i.e., what percentage of orders are not backordered)?

As the preceding exercise suggests, specifying a shortage cost is equivalent to fixing a "service level," here measured in terms of the orders filled out of available stock. Note that the fill rate is S^*/Q^*, which from (6.8) and (6.9) can be written as $u/(u + h + iC)$.

The following example shows that the arguments used to derive (6.2) can be easily adapted to conform to other assumptions on the cost or demand structure.

Carrying Costs Proportional to Maximum Inventory. There are a number of cases where carrying costs are more accurately represented as proportional to maximum inventory (Q) rather than average inventory ($Q/2$) as has been previously assumed. We discuss two cases: (1) warehouse space must be allocated for maximum inventory [see Fetter and Dalleck (1961)]; (2) inventory is financed by a loan that is repaid at the end of the order cycle.[5] [See Beranek (1967) for this and a number of other financing and repayment

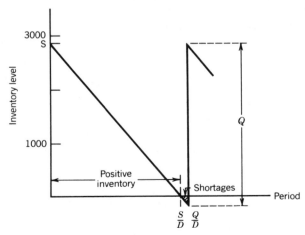

Fig. 6.3   Example 6.1 shortages.

strategies. A related work is Haley and Higgins (1973), which discusses the interaction between trade credit and inventory policy.] Assuming all the other EOQ assumptions hold, in the first case the average per period cost equation is

$$TC = F\left(\frac{D}{Q}\right) + iC\left(\frac{Q}{2}\right) + hQ + CD. \tag{6.10}$$

The usual calculus yields

$$Q^* = \sqrt{2FD/(iC + 2h)}. \tag{6.11}$$

Exercise.   Verify (6.11). For the data of Example 6.1, verify that $Q^* = 2449$ and that the average per period variable cost has increased by 18%.

For the second example assume that all the usual EOQ assumptions hold, except that financing costs are proportional to CQ rather than $CQ/2$. Now

$$Q^* = \sqrt{2FD/(h + 2iC)}. \tag{6.12}$$

Exercise.   Verify (6.12) and show that (coincidentally) for Example 6.1, we obtain the same Q^* and variable cost increase as in the previous exercise.

Price Changes

Some of the most practical extensions of the basic model concern changes in the assumptions of the cost of the item. Here we outline three possibilities. Although the second "extension" is not directly related to the EOQ, it is included for completeness.

Quantity Discounts

It is often the case that by ordering greater quantities one can obtain a lower unit price. This is easily incorporated into our framework. We illustrate the technique by the following example. In Example 6.1 the unit price is $4. Suppose that a price of $3.90 is offered on the purchase of 5000 or more units. There are now three possible optimal order quantities:

Q^*: the original (without discount) EOQ (here 3000).
Q_1: the lowest quantity that will obtain the discount (here 5000).
Q_2^*: the EOQ determined from (6.2) using $C = \$3.9$ if this quantity > 5000.

Clearly, the optimal Q is the one that minimizes the total cost (6.1). Thus

$$TC(3000) = 0.5 \cdot 3000 \cdot 0.4 + 125\left(\frac{14,400}{3000}\right) + 4 \cdot 14,400 = 58,800.$$

$$TC(5000) = 0.5 \cdot 5000 \cdot 0.395 + 125\left(\frac{14,400}{5000}\right) + 3.9 \cdot 14,400 = 57,508.$$

$$Q_2^* = \sqrt{(2 \cdot 125 \cdot 14,400)/(0.2 + (0.05)(3.9))} = 3019.$$

Since $Q_2^* < 5000$, we need only compare $TC(3000)$ and $TC(5000)$. Thus $Q^* = 5000$. See Figure 6.4 for the total cost curve. The reader should be able to generalize this example to arbitrary step price changes.

Discounting Slow-Moving Stock.   One of the most important features of any inventory system is the ability to identify items that are moving more slowly than anticipated. This is simplified in automated inventory systems that give inventory levels in terms of months of supply where this figure is based on a forecast of demand. (Occasionally, users find that they have 50 years of supply on hand, which suggests that some action should be taken.) One reaction to this declining demand is to offer price reductions.[6] This is a well-established practice in soft goods. Here we give a simple approach to determining the optimal discount price.

Assume the firm has an average turnover (sales/average inventory) of A per year and an average markup (gross profit/sales) of μ. Suppose that we have a slow-moving item in stock. We estimate that our current inventory of this item (at the current sales price of $\$P$) will last B periods. The question is, "If by offering a discount price of $\$D$ we could sell all the units immediately, what is the break-even D?" (Assume that the funds from the sales

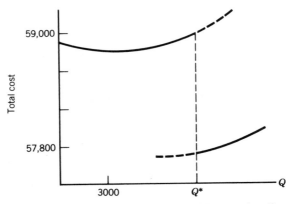

Fig. 6.4 Example 6.1 total cost curve with quantity discounts.

will be invested in regular inventory.) The solution [given in George (1982)]
is

$$D = \frac{P}{(1 + \mu)^T}, \tag{6.13}$$

where $T = \frac{1}{2}AB$ represents the ratio of the turnover of the average item to
the slow item. In terms of a proportional discount,

$$d = \frac{P - D}{P} = 1 - (1 + \mu)^{-AB/2}, \tag{6.14}$$

Figure 6.5 [adapted from George (1982, p. 54)] shows the break-even values
of d for representative values of T and μ.

Exercise.   A firm reports annual sales of $5 million and an average in-
ventory of $1 million. It has estimated that the current supply of Brand X
will last one year at its current price of $100. If the firm could sell Brand X
to another retailer, getting rid of their entire supply immediately, show that
the break-even discount price is $36.29 if $\mu = 0.5$.

The third example of price changes involves the (too common) situation
of rising purchase prices for an item. In particular, it is assumed that as of

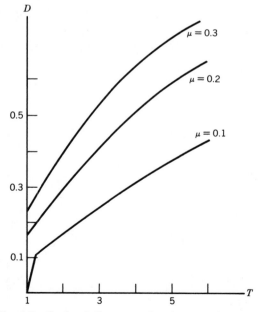

Fig. 6.5   Optimal discounts for slow-moving stock.

a fixed future date the price of an item we inventory will rise. Should we order an additional amount or place a special order to take advantage of the current lower price? In other words, what should our anticipation stock be?

Assume at time t_0 we receive notification that after time t' ($t' > t_0$) the unit cost of an item will increase from C to C'. This price change will quite possibly affect our ordering decisions after time t', but at time t_0, the question is whether or not it is advantageous to depart from our current ordering policies to place a special order of size Q^* at a time t^* ($t^* \leq t'$). Under certainty, it suffices to consider only two possible dates for t^*: either $t^* = t'$ (case 1: place the special order at the last possible date to obtain the lower price) or $t^* = t_1$ (case 2: where t_1 denotes the last usual reorder point before t'). It is clear that other dates will cause excessive inventory to be held. For the following derivation we retain all the assumptions of the basic EOQ model. An example of this situation is depicted in Figure 6.6.

Exercise. Assuming that the order quantity is obtained from (6.2), under the preceding conditions would the order quantity rise or fall after t'?

In this situation we trade off savings from two sources, the cheaper unit cost and the cost of operating the old system against the cost of operating the new system. Over the time the special order will last, the unit cost saving is given by $(C' - C) \cdot Q^*$. The per period variable cost of the old system is $\sqrt{2FD(h + iC')}$ (obtained from (6.4), assuming that the order quantity is given by (6.2)) times the number of periods this saving is available, Q^*/D. We let $y(t)$ denote the inventory level at time t. The cost of the alternative system is the unit holding cost ($h + iC$) times the average inventory ($y(t^*) + \frac{1}{2}Q^*$) times the number of periods the special order lasts Q^*/D (temporarily ignoring the ordering cost of the new system). The expression for the total savings is thus

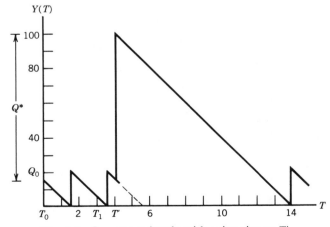

Fig. 6.6 Inventory levels with price rise at T'.

$$T(Q^*) = (C' - C) Q^* + \left(\frac{Q^*}{D}\right)\left[\sqrt{2FD(h + iC')}\right.$$

$$\left. - (h + iC) (y(t^*) + \tfrac{1}{2} Q^*)\right] \quad (6.15)$$

Differentiating with respect to Q^* and setting the resulting expression to zero yields

$$Q^* = \frac{(C' - C) D}{h + iC} + \sqrt{(2FD/(h + iC'))}$$

$$\cdot [(h + iC')/(h + iC)] - y(t^*) \quad (6.16)$$

Exercise: Derive (6.16).

As Love (1979) notes, a heuristic described in Myers et al. (1972) can be obtained by ignoring the last two terms, assuming that h is insignificant and that the special order is placed at time t'. Then

$$Q^\dagger = \frac{(C' - C)D}{iC}. \quad (6.17)$$

This can be rationalized as another form of the balancing of inventory costs; here the time covered by the special order $Q^\dagger/D$ is the ratio of $(C' - C)/C$ (the proportional increase) to i (the financing cost). We illustrate the technique on the following simple example.

Example 6.2   The following data are given. The demand rate is 10 per month ($D = 10$). The fixed cost of placing an order is \$5 ($F = 5$). The unit storage costs are \$0.17 per month ($h = 0.17$). Financing charges are 1% per month ($i = 0.01$). At time t_0 we have an inventory of 15 units, $y(0) = 15$, and it is announced that in four months the unit price will increase from \$8 ($C = 8) to \$10 ($C' = 10$)($t' = 4$). How should we react to this announcement? [Assume that the EOQ (6.2) is used for determining order quantities before t^*.]

Solution.   Prior to t' the order size is

$$Q_0 = \sqrt{2FD/(h + iC)} = 20,$$

which implies that an order lasts two months. Since $y(0)$ will last until $t = 1.5$, this means that $t_1 = 3.5$.

CASE 1.   If we order at t', $y(4) = 15$ and

$$Q^* = 86.$$
$$T(86) = 102.74.$$

CASE 2.   If we order at t_1, from (6.16) we obtain

$$Q^* = 101.$$

From (6.15) we obtain

$$T(101) = 126.97.$$

For case 1 we also subtract the fixed cost of placing the order ($5) to obtain a net saving in this case of 97.74. Finally, the policy of ordering 101 at time t_1 is the best policy, resulting in a saving of $126.97 over the 10.1 months that the special order lasts. Applying the heuristic (6.17), we obtain

$$Q^\dagger = 250.$$

This special order will last for 25 months and will result in a saving of -245.10 [from (6.15) minus 5 for the ordering cost]. This heuristic yields a solution very much worse than the status quo because h is significant. The application of Myers et al. (1972) is that of purchasing prescription drugs, and here h will be much less significant. Figure 6.6 depicts the situation assuming case 1 applies.

Varying Demand Rates.   We conclude this section with one final version of the EOQ. It relaxes the assumption that the demand rate is constant and assumes instead that over the next n periods we have forecasts of the demand rates $D_1, \ldots, D_n$. The rest of the EOQ framework is unchanged. The exact solution of this problem is difficult [see Hadley and Whitin (1967)], but Silver and Meal (1969) have developed the heuristic described below, which works well in practice and is very tractable.

To motivate the heuristic we manipulate the basic (fixed demand rate of D) case. If we let $K = 2F/(h + iC)$, then (6.3) can be rewritten

$$t^* = \left(\frac{K}{D}\right)^{1/2}$$

or

$$K = D(t^*)^2$$

for the optimal t^*. The Silver–Meal heuristic works by seeking a D_t that satisfies this condition. The procedure has the following steps:

1. Let $t = 1$.
2. Let $M = t^2 D_t$. If $M \geq K$, then go to step 4.
3. $t = t + 1$. Go to step 2.
4. $T^* = (K/D_t)^{1/2}$ and the corresponding optimal order size is the number of units required to supply demand up to time T^*.

Example 6.3   A firm has estimated that its per month carrying cost is 2% ($= h + iC$). It considers the cost of placing an order to be \$5. The forecast demand for the next six months is 20, 60, 100, 100, 50, and 25. If the current inventory level is zero, what is the optimal (at least approximately) order size?

Solution.   Here $K = 2 \cdot 5/0.02 = 500$. Going stepwise through the procedure:

$$t = 1.$$
$$M = 1 \cdot 20 < 500, \text{ so } t = 2,$$
$$M = 2^2 \cdot 60 < 500, \text{ so } t = 3,$$
$$M = 3^2 \cdot 100 > 500.$$

Now $T^* = \sqrt{500/100} = 2.24$, so that the order should last 2.24 months. This implies $Q^* = 20 + 60 + 0.24 \cdot 100 = 104$.

Exercise.   If the fixed cost of placing an order is changed to \$10, verify that the new optimal order size is 196.

Here we assumed that we can place an order at any time. Versions of this heuristic exist for the case of ordering only at the start of a period; see Woolsey and Swanson (1974).

SECTION 6.3   DETERMINING SAFETY STOCKS

The previous section focused on determining order quantities assuming that it was acceptable to treat demand as known. In reality, the demand rate is the mean of the distribution of demand. In this section we consider how the variability of demand should affect our inventory decisions. In particular, we assume that the per period demand follows a known distribution and that we maintain a safety stock: a buffer in case actual demand exceeds expected demand. This safety stock is the difference between the expected demand during the lead time and the stock expected to be available to meet this demand. The system we are describing is often referred to as the "two-bin" model. Inventory is kept in each bin and items are initially drawn from the first bin. When this bin is empty it signals a reorder and the second bin's supply is utilized until the order arrives. When the order arrives, the second bin is replenished and the remainder goes into the first bin. This has been a very traditional way of handling inventories of parts in an assembly process, and variants of it are still common.

The size of the safety stock depends on a variety of factors. Some of the most important follow:

Service levels (by raising the safety stock fewer stockouts will occur).

Carrying costs (since the safety stock adds to average inventory, we need to consider its contribution to total carrying costs).

Lead time (the larger the lead time, the larger the safety stock required to maintain the same service levels; further complications arise if the lead time is random).

Demand variability (as pointed out in Section 6.2, if demand is constant then there is no need for a safety stock; the size of the safety stock rises with our inability to forecast demand).

Order size (a larger order means that the reorder point will be reached less often, so that a smaller safety stock is needed to maintain the same rate of availability).

Temporarily we assume that the determination of Q^* is separate from the determination of the safety stock. Thus the ordering decision is independent of the service level decision. Note that in a fixed-order system the lead time is as previously defined (the time between placement of an order and its delivery), but in a fixed-period system, the "lead time" must also include the time between inventory reviews. (See case 6.1 for example.) In the latter system the interaction between Q^* and R^* is more crucial. We also assume that the lead time is less than the order cycle. The other case is similar except that more than one order is outstanding at a given time, and this creates some unnecessary notational complexity.

Exercise. Explain why the continuous monitoring of stock in a fixed-order system can lead to a smaller safety stock required than in a similar fixed-period system.

Demand and Lead Time Distributions

To determine the reorder point under uncertain demand requires a specification of the distribution of demand and of the lead time. The basic approaches use past data either to determine an empirical distribution or to estimate the parameters of a particular "theoretical" distribution. Although a priori we cannot assume any particular form for the distribution, here we focus on those that have been most utilized: the Poisson and the normal. A proper statistical analysis of the "goodness of fit" of data to a given probability distribution is not given here [see, for example, Snedecor and Cochran (1967)]; rather we illustrate the basics through the following example. See Appendix A for basic properties of the Poisson and normal distributions.

Example 6.4   Suppose we have observed 200 typical days of sales (no stockouts, no promotions, etc.) for an item with no seasonality or trend in demand. We wish to use these data as a basis for a specification of the daily demand for the item. The (rather contrived) data are given in Exhibit 6.1.

(Note that we needed to assume stationarity of demand to make the estimation of the empirical demand distribution valid. If the demand is not stationary, then we use the techniques described in Chapter 7.) Also we require that the number of possible outcomes be small enough that reasonable estimates of each possible outcome are available. Finally, since we simply average all the available observations, we are assuming more recent data do not contain more information than older data.

Suppose now that the lead time is two days. To determine the effects of different reorder points, we can compute the joint (two-day) distribution in a number of ways.[7] A straightforward way is to enumerate all the possible combinations (assuming that the relative frequency of an outcome is its probability). This calculation is given in Exhibit 6.2. It is clear that for a longer lead time this calculation would become rather tedious.

Although this approach is usable for the preceding situations, it is often simpler to try to fit a theoretical distribution to the data. Here instead of using the data to obtain relative frequencies of each outcome, we use them

EXHIBIT 6.1   OBSERVED DATA FOR EXAMPLE 6.4

Demand	Number of Days with This Demand	Relative Frequency
0	78	0.39
1	66	0.33
2	40	0.20
3	10	0.05
4	6	0.03

Mean daily demand = 1.00
Variance of daily demand = 1.06.

EXHIBIT 6.2 EXAMPLE 6.4. DETERMINING THE LEAD TIME DISTRIBUTION

Day 2 Demand	Probability	Day 1 Demand				
		Demand: 0 Probability: 0.39	1 0.33	2 0.20	3 0.05	4 0.03
0	0.39	0 (0.1521)	1 (0.1287)	2 (0.0780)	3 (0.0200)	4 (0.0120)
1	0.33	1 (0.1287)	2 (0.1089)	3 (0.0660)	4 (0.0165)	5 (0.0099)
2	0.20	2 (0.0780)	3 (0.0660)	4 (0.0400)	5 (0.0100)	6 (0.0060)
3	0.05	3 (0.0200)	4 (0.0165)	5 (0.0100)	6 (0.0025)	7 (0.0015)
4	0.03	4 (0.0120)	5 (0.0099)	6 (0.0060)	7 (0.0015)	8 (0.0009)

Here the entries in the table are the total demand and the probability (in parentheses). Hence

i	P (demand $= i$)	P (demand $\leq i$)
0	0.1521	0.1521
1	0.2574	0.4095
2	0.2649	0.6744
3	0.1720	0.8464
4	0.0970	0.9434
5	0.0398	0.9832
6	0.0145	0.9977
7	0.0009	0.9986

(Because of rounding the probabilities do not sum precisely to 1.)

to find the "best" values of the parameters of a chosen distribution. Here we discuss a model that is applicable for slow-moving items (the Poisson distribution) and a model for faster-moving items (the normal distribution). As will be seen, these two are very natural choices for demand distributions on both theoretical and empirical grounds.

A similar methodology can be used in characterizing lead time distributions. In practice this is a very important problem but is made rather difficult by the typically small number of observations, the variability of these observations, and the fact that lead times are often dependent on order size. (As the last point makes things very difficult, we treat only the case where the distributions of demand and lead time are independent.) As before, we are trying to determine the demand during the lead time. We illustrate the simplest approach: determination of the joint probabilities. The analogies with Example 6.3 should be clear.

Recall Example 6.4. It turns out that we should expect the Poisson distribution to be a good fit to these data. Since the mean is 1, the logical choice for the Poisson parameter (λ) is 1. Since the variance of the series is very near 1, we have some faith in the accuracy of the Poisson fit. This is furthered by an informal comparison of the histogram of the relative frequency with the predicted values of a Poisson distribution with $\lambda = 1$. This is given in Figure 6.7.

From the properties of the Poisson distribution, we know that the two-day demand is Poisson with $\lambda = 2$ (since we have assumed that daily demands

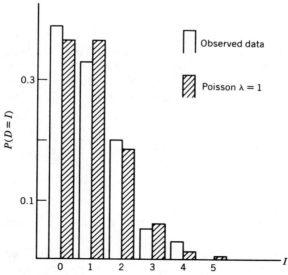

Fig. 6.7 Example 6.4 observed data and Poisson approximation.

are independent). This is a simpler way to compute the individual lead time probabilities than that given in Exhibit 6.2. If the lead time were 20 days, this theoretical approach would offer a substantial computational advantage. As λ gets large, the Poisson is well approximated by the normal distribution with mean $= \lambda =$ variance. This has a number of implications that will be discussed in Section 6.5.

Determining Safety Stocks with Discrete Demand Distributions

The key to determining a safety stock (or equivalently, a reorder point) is first a characterization of the "tail" of the demand distribution—the probability of obtaining very high demands during the lead time—and second, a statement of the service level required. In Section 6.2 we used a unit shortage charge to relate to a service level in terms of a fill rate; here we will treat only the case where service levels are characterized by the probability of a stockout occurring in a given time period. Note that here the interaction between the reorder point (R^*) and the order size (Q^*) becomes important. We illustrate this with the following example.

Example 6.5 Suppose that weekly demand for the product is given by a Poisson distribution with mean 4. Lead time is assumed to be half a week. If we allow an expected stockout once per year, what is the reorder point if

1. $Q^* = 8$?
2. $Q^* = 30$?

Solution. Since the expected weekly demand is 4, assuming independent demands, the expected annual demand is 208. If $Q^* = 8$, this means that 26 orders are placed per year. Since we allow only one (on average) to result in a stockout, this implies a stockout probability of 1/26. Thus we need to specify a R^* such that

$$\text{Prob(lead time demand} > R^*) \leq \frac{1}{26} = 0.0385.$$

Equivalently,

$$\text{Prob(lead time demand} \leq R^*) > 1 - 0.0385 = 0.9615.$$

Since the lead time distribution is Poisson with a mean of 2, we can compute the probability of a lead time demand of i (see appendix A):

i	Prob (Lead Time Demand $= i$)	Prob (Lead Time Demand $\leq i$)
0	0.1353	0.1353
1	0.2707	0.4060
2	0.2707	0.6767
3	0.1804	0.8571
4	0.0902	0.9473
5	0.0361	0.9834
6	0.0120	0.9954

Thus if $Q^* = 8$, $R^* = 5$.

Exercise. Verify that if $Q^* = 30$, then $R^* = 3$.

In terms of safety stocks, in the first case the safety stock is 3, in the second case the safety stock is 1.

The next example shows a simple case of random lead time demand. The basic idea is to compute the joint probabilities, that is, the combinations of the two random events.

Example 6.6 Variable Lead Times. We currently stock an item with a price of $1000. We have estimated that the only other significant inventory costs for the item are the $20 it costs us to replenish our supply and the financing cost, which we calculate to be 10% per year. As described in Example 6.4, we have observed 200 days of demand for this item and these results are tabulated in Exhibit 6.1. We have also recorded the following lead times from our supplier over the last 20 orders:

Lead Time (Business Days)	Number of Orders with This Lead Time	Relative Frequency
1	10	0.50
2	7	0.35
3	3	0.15

Since the item is crucial to the production process, we cannot allow more than one stockout every two years. What order size and reorder point should be set?

Solution. Assuming that we can use (6.2) to compute the order size, we find

$$Q^* = \sqrt{(2 \cdot 20 \cdot 1 \cdot 250)/(0.1 \cdot 1000)} = 10.$$

For the per period demand (D) we take 250, which is the expected daily demand times 250 business days per year. This means that 50 orders are placed in two years and thus that, on average, we can allow one of the 50 orders to result in a stockout: a 0.02 stockout probability per order cycle.

We now need to specify a reorder point R^* such that the probability of a lead time demand greater than R^* is less than 0.02.

The variable lead time complicates the calculation of the lead time demand. We first consider the three possible cases: a lead time of 1, 2, or 3 days. As shown earlier (assuming daily demands are independent and that the demand patterns are adequately approximated by a Poisson distribution): for a one-day lead time:

$$\text{Prob(demand} = i) = \frac{e^{-1}1^i}{i!}; \tag{6.18}$$

for a two-day lead time

$$\text{Prob(demand} = i) = \frac{e^{-2}2^i}{i!}; \tag{6.19}$$

for a three-day lead time

$$\text{Prob(demand} = i) = \frac{e^{-3}3^i}{i!}. \tag{6.20}$$

If the lead time distribution and demand distribution are independent of each other, then the distribution of lead time demand is given by weighting each of (6.18), (6.19), and (6.20) by its likelihood of occurrence. Thus

Prob(lead time demand $= i$)

$$= 0.5 \left(\frac{e^{-1}}{i!}\right) + 0.35 \left(\frac{e^{-2}2^i}{i!}\right) + 0.15 \left(\frac{e^{-3}3^i}{i!}\right). \tag{6.21}$$

Using (6.21) yields

i	Prob (Lead Time Demand $= i$)	Prob (Lead Time Demand $\leq i$)
0	0.2388	0.2388
1	0.3012	0.5400

i	Prob (Lead Time Demand $= i$)	Prob (Lead Time Demand $\leq i$)
2	0.2205	0.7605
3	0.1276	0.8881
4	0.0646	0.9527
5	0.0294	0.9821
6	0.0121	0.9942
7	0.0045	0.9987

Hence a reorder point of 5 (corresponding to a stockout probability of $1 - 0.9821 = 0.0179$ per order cycle) is required. Problem 4 discussed the computation of R^* if we ignore the fact that the lead time is random and assume that the problem features a fixed lead time of 1.65 days (where 1.65 is the average lead time).

Computing Safety Stocks with Continuous Demand Distributions

With continuous distributions we can no longer explicitly enumerate all possible outcomes; rather, we characterize the tail of the distribution through some statistical measure of its dispersion, usually the variance. We confine our attention to the normal distribution largely because of its importance as a model for demand of fast-moving items and because of its tractability. (Also, as shown in Chapter 7, if we use a forecasting method like regression or Box–Jenkins, the forecast itself is normally distributed under the usual assumptions on the distribution of the random term.) In this case the mean is given by the forecast and the variance by (at least approximately) σ_u^2.

Assume now that per period demand can be approximated adequately by a normal distribution with mean $\bar{D}$ and variance σ_D^2. If the lead time is L periods, then (as shown in Appendix A) the mean lead time demand is $L \cdot \bar{D}$ and the standard deviation of lead time demand is $\sigma_D \sqrt{L}$. By using Table A, Appendix C, we can make the correspondence between a safety stock (here proportional to $\sigma_D \sqrt{L}$) and a service level defined in terms of α: the stockout probability per order cycle. If N_α is the entry in Table A corresponding to a service level of α, we have

$$R^* = L\,\bar{D} + N_\alpha \sigma_D \sqrt{L}. \tag{6.22}$$

Example 6.1 (continued)   Recall $Q^* = 3000$. Now suppose that the per month demand is normally distributed with a mean of 2400 and a variance of 90,000. The lead time is assumed fixed at two months. If we specify that there be no more than one stockout expected per year, since there are 9.6 orders placed per year (on average), this translates to a 10.4% probability of a stockout per order cycle. (Observe that here we are not specifying the number of units short, merely the chance of there being some shortage.) From Table A, Appendix C, $N_\alpha = 1.26$. Using (6.22),

$$R^* = 4800 + 1.26(300)\sqrt{2} = 5335.$$

The safety stock is 535, from 5335 minus 4800.

Exercise. If we specify that no more than two stockouts per year are permitted, verify that the safety stock is now 233.

SECTION 6.4   MULTI-ITEM SYSTEMS

Previously, we assumed that each item is managed without regard to its interaction with other items in the inventory system. With the possible exception of cash management, there exist very few practical circumstances where this is rational. Some of the reasons for this are as follows:

Demand interaction (the effects of a particular item's demand on the demand for other items; for example, substitution and complementarity of items).

Joint replenishment (where multiple items can be ordered simultaneously from one supplier).

Constraints on maximum investment or storage (or any other scenario where the items must share scarce resources).

Demand Interaction

The most important type of demand interaction is substitutability, when the demand for one item can be satisfied by the supply of another item. This can be treated by methods related to our analysis of shortage penalties; for example, by adjusting the profit consequences of a stockout to account for demand interaction. Intuitively, an item with a high degree of substitutability would be given a lower cost of stockout and lower safety stock than a similar item with no demand interaction. A formal treatment of demand transference in a fixed-period system is presented in McGillivray and Silver (1976).

Joint Replenishment

It is common practice to allow a number of small orders to accumulate before an order is actually placed. This may be because of economies of scale in handling and ordering, minimum order size, or other factors. It is also a natural procedure in a fixed-period system. Here we discuss an effective heuristic for grouping items into an order. This development is adapted from Love (1979); alternatives are given in Woolsey and Swanson (1974) or

Peterson and Silver (1979). We assume that there are n items that can be grouped into one order. For each item j ($j = 1, \ldots, n$) we adopt the usual restrictions on the EOQ model as given in Section 6.2: a fixed cost of ordering (F_j), a per period demand (D_j), a unit item cost (C_j), a per unit period cost of handling (h_j), and a per period percentage financing cost (i_j). Finally, we assume that the cost of placing the total order is F. (This cost structure can be illustrated by viewing F_j and F as fixed costs of a production run for one product manufactured in n different sizes. Here F would be the basic (major) setup cost and each F_j would be the cost of adjusting to a different size.) For notational ease let

$$H_j = (h_j + i_j C_j).$$

Let t_j be the time between orders for item j. These times will be chosen so that each is a multiple of the shortest replenishment time; otherwise we incur excessive ordering costs. Ignoring F, the relative replenishment times are obtained from (6.3):

$$\tau_j = \sqrt{2F_j/H_j D_j}.$$

Determine the smallest τ_j and denote it τ^*. Let

$$\alpha_j = \frac{\tau_j}{\tau^*}.$$

As noted, in the final policy, the t_j must be integers. Thus set

$$t_j = [\alpha_j]\,\tau^*$$

where $[\alpha]$ denotes the integer nearest α. (Thus $[1.2] = 1$; $[2.7] = 3$, etc.) The first replenishment time t^* is chosen to minimize the total per period cost

$$TC = \frac{F}{t^*} + \sum_{j=1}^{n} \frac{F_j}{t_j} + \frac{1}{2} \sum_{j=1}^{n} H_j \cdot D_j \cdot t_j \qquad (6.23)$$

Therefore the optimal time to the first replenishment (t^*) is the minimum of (6.23):

$$t^* = \sqrt{\frac{2\left(F + \sum_{j=1}^{n} F_j/[\alpha_j]\right)}{\sum_{j=1}^{n} H_j \cdot D_j \cdot [\alpha_j]}}. \qquad (6.24)$$

Example 6.7   Assume that the overall cost of placing an order (F) is 20. We are given the following data on the four items that can be grouped together into one order and then compute τ_j and α_j:

j	F_j	H_j	D_j	τ_j	α_j
1	5	0.7	500	0.169	1
2	50	0.2	200	1.581	9
3	20	0.2	300	0.816	5
4	10	0.3	400	0.408	2
5	20	0.5	100	0.894	5

Hence we determine t^*:

$$t^* = \sqrt{\frac{2\,[20 + (5/1 + \cdots + 20/5)]}{[(.7 \cdot 500 \cdot 1) + \cdots + (.5 \cdot 100 \cdot 5)]}} = 0.241,$$

which generates a total per period cost of

$$TC = \frac{43.556}{0.241} + \frac{0.241(1500)}{2} = 361.48.$$

To compare this solution to one where all the items are ordered simultaneously (i.e., $\alpha_j = 1$ for each j), we compute the new t^*:

$$t^* = \sqrt{\frac{2\,[20 + (5 + \cdots + 20)]}{0.7 \cdot 500 + \cdots + .5 \cdot 100)}} = 0.635.$$

Here the total per period cost is

$$TC = \left(\frac{1}{0.635}\right)(125)\,(2) = 393.7. \tag{6.25}$$

Thus we have generated an 8.9% savings by ordering jointly and optimally. Naturally, the cost of ordering each item optimally [using (6.24)] but independently of the others will be much greater than that for either of these two choices.

Exercise.   Why was (6.25) a legitimate way to compute the minimum cost?

ABC Classification

The value of this tool [ABC classification] lies in the way it illustrates that the greatest benefits may be possible if inventory analysis and control are directed toward the top items [Morgan, 1963, p. 103].

In a multi-item setting relatively few items will require a high degree of control, so it is important to manage each item with a level of complexity appropriate to the cost–benefit tradeoff. A standard approach to determine the priorities of items within an inventory system is called ABC classification. Here items are categorized into three groups, A, B, and C (or a finer partition if desired). A items have the highest priority; they are items whose control is most vital and/or profitable. C items have the lowest priority; B items are intermediate between the other two.

Classification is generally from ranking items by decreasing annual dollar sales. Illustrative guidelines might be:

A items are 20% of all items but 70% of dollar sales.

B items are 30% of all items but 20% of dollar sales.

C items are 50% of all items but only 10% of dollar sales.

Obviously, these numbers will vary according to the particular problem. Clearly, different management approaches would be taken within each category. For example, A items would be treated individually in terms of ordering policy, forecasting methods, and cost estimation; B items would probably be grouped for joint replenishment strategies and forecasts (see Section 7.6); C items may be managed using very simple rules (e.g., keep one month of supply on hand). For further discussion see Peterson and Silver (1979) or Love (1979).

Two standard examples of this technique are Flowers and O'Neill (1978) and Canen and Galvao (1980). The first deals with spare parts inventories;

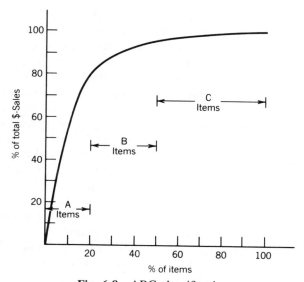

Fig. 6.8   ABC classification.

they determined that 363 of 1337 items were placed on perpetual inventory cards and traveling requisitions were created for them.

> Preparing traveling requisitions for these items means that complete and accurate information concerning the item is immediately available for ordering purposes. This information includes the past history of the item, its specification, primary and secondary vendors and lead times. Departmental purchase approval . . . is required only once a year rather than every time the item is purchased. [Flowers and O'Neill, 1980, p. 77].

Canen and Galvao (1980) deal with controlling an inventory containing imported materials. Management of this is more complex because of longer lead times, import restrictions, and so on. They determined that 36 of 436 items constituting 75% of annual dollar usage were A items. They then focused on those items within the A class that were imported and dedicated their inventory control system largely toward these.

SECTION 6.5 IMPLEMENTING INVENTORY SYSTEMS

In this section we attempt to piece together the previous sections of this chapter and to offer alternatives to the quantitative models previously discussed. As we have noted, although inventory decisions must be done on the "micro" level (individual items and individual locations), it is difficult to measure inventory costs (and to an extent, performance) except on a "macro" level. A number of methods have emerged to treat inventory management on a more aggregated level.

One important alternative is the policy surface (or exchange curve, policy curve, etc.) concept [see Starr and Miller (1962), Gardner and Dannenbring (1979), and Peterson and Silver (1979)]. Here rather than explicitly attaching costs, one determines the "attainable surface," for example, those combinations of shortage probabilities, number of orders, average inventory, and so on that are attainable by alternative inventory policies. These criteria create three dimensions for the suface—service levels, workload, and investment—that cannot easily be related in dollar terms. By looking at this type of curve we can see how, for example, inventory investment and the number of orders placed interact. As stated by Starr and Miller (1962, pp. 103–104): "It provides the means for the executive to utilize his knowledge and experience under circumstances where this knowledge and experience cannot be boiled down into the form of cost estimates. The executive, with his intimate knowledge of the circumstances of the company, can often quickly converge on the optimal point on the curve for the company without having had to convert his knowledge into the form of carrying and inventory costs—something which can often be done only badly if at all." We illustrate this idea in a context somewhat different from that of Starr and Miller.

Example 6.1   (continued)   Suppose that we have no reliable estimate of the fixed cost of replenishment. However, by varying Q we can generate different combinations of carrying costs (20% of average inventory as before) and number of orders placed. This is given in Figure 6.9, which shows how these two cost components interact. The inventory manager would choose a Q on this curve because of particular criteria desired. If, for example, it is determined that $F = \$125$, then we are at point Q^* as before.

Just-in-Time Versus Just-in-Case

An important reason for holding inventory is because of the inability of the firm to synchronize delivery with demand. Thus the typical (North American) inventory system is of the "just-in-case" type; large safety stocks are maintained to cover the uncertainty of demand during the usually long and variable lead time. Although the majority of inventory management revolves around what to do because of this lead time, other approaches work toward eliminating the lead time. The classic example is the Kanban ("just-in-time") system developed at Toyota Motor Company Ltd. in the 1950s. Although this system is of most relevance for inventory management in a production setting, some discussion of it is warranted.

As the *just-in-time* adjective implies, the essence of the Kanban system is to coordinate the production processes so that items are delivered and available precisely when required. Lot sizes may indeed be as low as 10% of a day's usage. Clearly, for this type of system to work, a special envi-

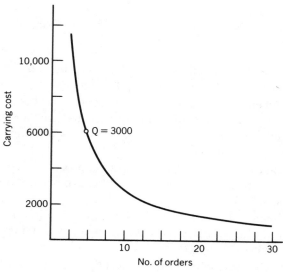

Fig. 6.9   Example 6.1 policy curve.

ronment is required. Hoeffe (1982) gives "eight commandments for effective just-in-time":

1. Short distances between buyer and supplier.
2. Dependable quality.
3. Small supplier network.
4. Dependable transportation.
5. Manufacturing flexibility.
6. Small lot sizes.
7. Effective receiving and materials-handling facilities.
8. Strong management commitment.

This type of inventory management has proved highly effective in Japan and a number of U.S. firms (notably auto makers) are attempting to adapt it to the U.S. environment. This is requiring radical changes in relationships with suppliers and in materials-handling facilities. But the savings in terms of inventory carrying costs, space utilization, and so on, seem to make this an attractive alternative to existing systems: "Indeed, simply taking delivery of material only as it's immediately needed—at least daily, ideally every few hours—U.S. automakers not only would unshackle the cash typically trapped in stock but also save outright the tremendous yearly expense of holding it" (Bush and Smith, 1982, p. 24).

Implementation

Here the general strategy can be viewed as five steps prior to the final implementation.

1. Analysis of the current system. (What are the current performance levels? What are the current system's defects?)
2. Establishment of a data base. [What demand and lead time data are available? What are the operating constraints (shelf life, storage space, investment, personnel, . . .)? What cost data are relevant? How are service levels measured?]
3. Classification of items. (Can an ABC approach be developed to determine the most important items? What groups of items can be controlled jointly?)
4. Determination of control policies. [According to the preceding steps, what are the appropriate forecasting techniques and ordering policies for each (class of) item(s)?]
5. Testing. (On a subset of the items, test the chosen operating strategies: Do they perform as predicted? Is this performance adequate? If not, return to step 4.)

To illustrate these points we give two examples of large-scale inventory implementations. The first was developed for a U.S. firm with a large inventory of spare parts. Because of the number of items and stocking locations, former inventory policies were simple: Orders were determined as a number of months of supply, and inventory levels were reviewed at most once per week. Cost data were nonexistent but service levels were considered very important. The system was being reevaluated because of excessively high inventory levels and because of the inability of the system to react to seasonal and fluctuating demands.

After an analysis of the system, recommendations were made to separate the items into two groups according to their importance: A items (for which detailed cost data would be obtained) and B items (for which only service levels would be considered). These two groups were further subdivided into slow- and fast-moving items. The former were modeled by a Poisson distribution and the latter by a normal distribution. (As previously mentioned, for large values of the mean demand, the Poisson and normal distributions are nearly identical. Thus by using these two distributions we have a degree of consistency; if we calculate a reorder point based on either assumption, the answer is likely to be very similar.) EOQ ordering policies were instituted taking shelf life and storage constraints into consideration. The implementation of this system generated a reduction in inventory of 20% with no change in service levels.

The second example is taken from Austin (1977). It describes part of the USAF system for maintaining inventories of weapon spare parts. The existing system had 250,000 items and incurred annual procurement costs of $350–400 million. Demand forecasts were eight-month simple autoregressive models.[9] The annual holding charge ($h + iC$) was calculated as 32% for all items. This was composed of 10% for financing, 1% for storage, and 21% for obsolescence. Safety stock was fixed at one month of demand. The ordering costs were estimated to be $142 for orders of value less than $2500 and $424 for larger orders. Another administrative constraint was that all orders must cover a three-month to a three-year supply.

The preceding system is a natural one for the application of ABC analysis. Austin's group recommended that A items be those where the order quantity was less than a six-month supply. (This turned out to be 4% of all items and 67% of dollar value.) The forecasting methods were also changed. Exponential smoothing with a smoothing coefficient of 0.1 worked well and for the 250 highest dollar demand items, regression forecasts were developed. The obsolescence estimates were also modified to range from 0 to 28%.

These two examples point out a number of important factors in large-scale implementations. First, that because of the extreme complexity of running the system, relatively simple procedures must be utilized for the vast majority of the items. The inventory control system should be geared to those A items whose control will yield the best cost–benefit tradeoff. As indicated in Chapter 7 and Section 6.4, strategies for grouping items either in the forecasting method or in the ordering policy should be utilized.

NOTES

1. See Zanakis et al. (1980).
2. The stocking–no-stocking decision is discussed in Peterson and Silver (1979).
3. This paraphrases the definition of Starr and Miller (1962).
4. See Gardner (1980).
5. This is the case for gasoline retailers who pay "load-to-load." When a load of gasoline arrives they are required to pay for the previous one.
6. An interesting case of this for a spare parts inventory is given in Phillips (1978).
7. For example, a more elegant and much more general approach would be to use the moment-generating function of the distribution; see Starr and Miller (1962).
8. See Ray (1982).
9. See Chapter 7 for the relevant material on forecasting.

CASE 6.1 The Management of Blood Supplies.   Maintaining inventories of blood involve a number of complexities; these include:

Perishability. Human blood has a lifetime of 35 days, after which it cannot be transfused.

Diversity. There exist four main groups of human blood: O, A, B, and AB, with two types: those with the Rh plus factor (Rh +) and those without the Rh minus factor (Rh −). The most frequently occurring type is 0+ (39% of the population) while the rarest is AB − (0.5% of the population).

Uncertainty in demand and supply.

High operating costs.

The inability to quantify costs, especially wastage and shortage costs.

We are, as is typical in inventory problems, faced with the conflicting objectives of maximizing availability (to satisfy emergency needs, to avoid postponement of operations, etc.) and of minimizing wastage. Currently about 20% of all units supplied are never transfused. In a very simplified manner this case deals with one possible approach to inventory problems of this type.

We assume that the hospital has a simple fixed period inventory system. At the beginning of each week the inventory of each type of blood is determined. If the level is below the reorder level (R), an order is placed to bring the level to R; if the current level is at least R, no action is taken. Initially we assume that there is no lead time between placement of an order and its delivery.

Since the costs are difficult to quantify, it is reasonable to adopt the policy surface approach. The basic tradeoff is here between availability and wastage. The former is measured by S, the weekly shortage probability. The latter unfortunately is very difficult to assess without knowledge of the hospital's blood issuing policies (often FIFO) and crossmatching (preassigning units to compatible patients) policies. As a proxy for wastage we utilize A, the expected number of units that will age another week. Here

$$A = (R - \text{average weekly demand})/R.$$

For example, suppose the weekly demand was normally distributed (see Appendix A and Table A) with a mean of 100 and a standard deviation of 20. A reorder point of 120 would result in $S = 1 - 0.841 = .159$ (using Table A to look up the entry for 1, for 1 standard deviation above the mean); $A = (120 - 100)/120 = .167$. Similarly with $R = 130$, $S = .067$ and $A = .231$. Continuing in this manner we can build up a curve representing the attainable tradeoffs between S and A.

Questions

1. Suppose that the following 20 weeks of demand for O+ blood given in Exhibit 6.3 have been observed. Assume that the weekly demands are independent of each other. Estimate the mean and the standard deviation of weekly demand.

2. Assuming weekly reorder points between 120 and 200, graph the policy curve representing the tradeoffs between S and A. Using this curve determine the minimal reorder point that corresponds to $S \leq .05$.

3. If we now assume that there is a one week lead time between an order placement and its delivery, what reorder point is needed to attain $S \leq .05$?

PROBLEMS

1. One of the important aspects of inventory management is the evaluation of the cost of goods sold. The IRS allows firms to adopt an assumption on goods flows for tax purposes. FIFO assumes that goods are used on a first-in-first-out basis. LIFO assumes that goods are used on a last-in-first-out basis.
    a. In the present climate of rapidly rising prices, discuss the impact of these two assumptions with respect to the following factors: tax liability, total earnings, accurate inventory valuation, and any other criteria you believe relevant.
    b. Assuming we are trying to maximize after-tax profits and supposing that all other factors are held constant, discuss the effect a higher tax rate would have on optimal average inventory levels under FIFO and LIFO.

**EXHIBIT 6.3
OBSERVED
WEEKLY DEMANDS**

Week	Demand
1	130
2	85
3	171
4	120
5	102
6	71
7	133
8	112
9	153
10	128
11	100
12	191
13	108
14	109
15	72
16	150
17	65
18	102
19	160
20	138

2. Show that in the basic EOQ model, if we changed the cost of placing an order from F (a fixed cost) to $F + aQ$ (the fixed cost plus a proportion of the amount ordered), we would not change the optimal order quantity.

3. Suppose we currently order our product from the producer. We pay $50 to place an order and the lead time is one month. Our handling and financing costs are 20% per annum and our average monthly sales are constant at 150. We currently pay $10 for the item.

    a. Using the EOQ formula, determine how many orders we will place in a year (on average).

    b. Suppose a local wholesaler offers to supply the item for $10.50. This option will eliminate our need to maintain an inventory, since all items can be delivered to the customer by the wholesaler with no lead time and no ordering cost. Is this option better than the status quo?

    c. Can you think of a (clever) way of combining the two options?

4. Assume the data of Example 6.6 except that now the lead time is fixed at 1.65 days. Show that to obtain a service level of no more than one stockout every two years, we now need only a reorder point of four.

5. Does the joint replenishment formula (6.24) guarantee that at the optimum ordering costs equal holding costs?

6. In a fixed order inventory model assume that the lead time distribution of demand is Poisson with a mean of 10. If the lead time demand distribution becomes Poisson with a mean of 20, by how much should the safety stock increase to maintain the same stockout probability? (Assume that the amount ordered does not change.)

7. Comment on the validity of the following statements:

   Theoretical models for inventory management are useless because they are based on data that cannot be accurately estimated.

   Simple inventory models do not allow us to incorporate the perishability of inventory.

8. Consider a two currency cash management problem with constant per-period demand of units D_A units of currency A and D_B units of currency B. One unit of currency A equals A dollars; one unit of currency B equals B dollars. These outflows are funded by transfers in dollars of a fixed amount Q. The opportunity cost of these funds is i per period. The transfer cost (which includes the cost of converting dollars into the 2 currencies) is F dollars, independent of the amount transferred. Determine the formula for the optimal Q. (Hint: this is another version of the EOQ.)

9. Assume the following data: constant demand of 100 per month; unit cost of $5.00; fixed cost of ordering of $50.; annual handling cost of $.50 per item; financing cost of 10% per annum; annual unit shortage cost of $3.00.

   a. Verify that any order quantity between 292 and 548 yields a variable annual cost within 5% of the minimum.

   b. Show that a unit shortage cost of $99.00 corresponds to a fill rate of 99%.

10. Explain how a firm may reduce its investment in inventory by inducing its suppliers and customers to hold more. What are the limitations of these policies?

7 Forecasting

All foreseen by fate and seers, of course, and all to be forgotten. If God will have prognostications made, why, let God himself prognosticate.

OEDIPUS THE KING
SOPHOCLES

It would be foolish to oversell the ability of science, as yet, to forecast complex events accurately. Yet the danger today is not that we will overestimate our ability; the real danger is that we will under-utilize it. For even when our still-primitive attempts at scientific forecasting turn out to be grossly in error, the very effort helps us identify key variables in change, it helps clarify goals, and it forces more careful evaluation of policy alternatives.

FUTURE SHOCK
ALVIN TOFFLER

This chapter describes the basic short-term forecasting techniques that have proven useful in current asset management. The objective is to give a foundation for determining the suitability of a given forecasting technique in a given situation. Toward this end, for each of the methods discussed in this chapter we emphasize the underlying assumptions, the optimality criteria, and the applications. For further reference consult, for example, Draper and Smith (1966) (for regression), Box and Jenkins (1970) (for time series), Nelson (1973) (for time series), or Granger (1980) (for many of the topics in this chapter). Also, a review of some of the statistical concepts used in this book is given in Appendix A.

The techniques we discuss can be broken into two major groups, qualitative and quantitative, and each group can be further divided into causal and extrapolative models. Causal models attempt to explain the entity being forecast by a set of external, observable factors. Extrapolative models try to find a pattern in the past data that will be replicated in the future. We will discuss each of the four types, but our treatment of quantitative extrapolative (time series) models will be more complete than for the others because of the importance of this technique in current asset management. See Figure 7.1 for an overview of this classification and some examples of the techniques and applications to be discussed in this chapter.

Chambers et al. (1971) suggest that the following questions be answered when approaching a forecasting problem:

1. What is the purpose of the forecast?
2. What are the dynamics of the system for which a forecast is being made?
3. How important is the past in estimating the future?

The first question addresses the importance of the forecast. The techniques we discuss have differing degrees of complexity (in terms of data requirements, effort in model estimation, etc.) so that detailing the purpose of the forecast will improve the chances of obtaining a forecast with characteristics appropriate to the application. The second and third questions deal with the structure of the forecast. Can the model be extrapolative? How should a causal model be constructed? A final caveat before plunging into the techniques: ''Reducing forecast errors requires increasing expenditures on forecasting techniques, and there is a point of diminishing return in forecast

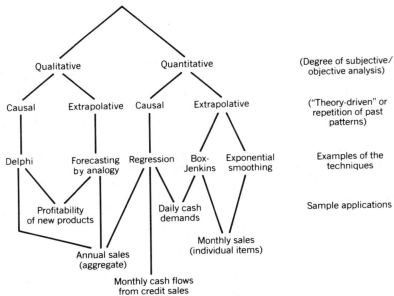

Fig. 7.1 An overview of short-term forecasting.

accuracy. Spending large amounts of money on improved forecasting technique will not produce a perfect forecast'' (Plossl and Wight, 1967, pp. 30–31).

SECTION 7.1   QUALITATIVE FORECASTING

In many business situations it is difficult, even misleading, to attempt prediction purely on the basis of quantitative data. Often a systematic but subjective analysis is a more acceptable substitute for statistically oriented methods. An example of this situation might be forecasting sales for a new product; here there is often little relevant data on which to base a quantitative forecast. Forecasting methods applicable in these contexts usually depend on "expert" judgments, sometimes involving only one expert but more commonly a group consensus. Little need be said about the first case, but a number of approaches have been suggested to obtain a prediction from a group of experts.

One example is the "jury of executive opinion." This may range from an informal consensus of a panel of executives from various concerned departments, to more formal methods. One of the most well-known methods is the Delphi technique. Developed in the mid-1960s by the RAND Corporation, its basic purpose is to generate a forecast by combining the opinions of a panel of experts. It attempts to avoid the problems of personal interaction, corporate hierarchy, or group dynamics. As most of us have observed, the loudest and most persistent member of a panel is seldom the most informative. The technique is also applicable when an actual forecast is not required, merely a spread of opinion.

The technique is structured so that those participants with relatively extreme opinions are forced to defend them or move their forecast closer to the median. The Delphi procedure goes roughly as follows:

1. Identify a panel of experts (kept physically separate).

2. Compose a questionnaire on the topic.

3. Distribute the questionnaire to each member of the panel. (Again observe that they do not collectively discuss any aspect of the questions.)

4. Analyze the responses. If there is too great a divergence of opinion, use the responses to formulate a new, narrower questionnaire. Return to step 3.

While this and other qualitative techniques are more common to longer-range planning, they also have found application in the area of working capital management. One example is due to Ang et al., (1979). This study concerns the forecasting of cash flows from a newly developed chemical product. For this and related problems,

> Capital budgeting decisions may have long time horizons or may involve new projects. In the first case, time series and econometric analyses may have little value because the original relationships that govern cash flows cannot be expected to persist. In the second case, data are not even available for constructing these models. In such situations, there seems to be no alternative but to rely on the best judgements of experts [Ang et al., 1979, p. 64].

Their study used 15 experts. A question in the first round was the following: What is the most important source of uncertainty concerning cash flows or profitability? The second round featured multiple-choice questions, for example: Which of the following sources of uncertainty affecting cash flows or profitability do you think is the most important? In this application the technique was judged successful and yielded estimates that differed considerably from (unspecified) "textbook" solutions.

There remain a number of problems with the Delphi method. All experts are not actually equal; some may have convincing arguments that do not surface during the Delphi rounds. Panelists may not take the procedure seriously enough and rapidly become bored. Questions are often difficult to determine and responses may be awkward to utilize objectively in further rounds. The problems of validation and "robustness" of the solution are also relevant.[1] Dory and Lord (1970) (discussing a related class of techniques: technological forecasts) point out that the Delphi method is expensive, depends on the skill of the experts and administrator, and on the climate under which it is administered.[2]

One final important qualitative technique is forecasting by analogy. It deals with attempting to find a paradigm that can be used to describe the phenomenon being investigated. An example is technical analysis in the capital and commodities market. Chartists, using various mechanical rules based on past prices and/or trading volume (or other market data such as short interest), try to predict future prices. Chartists

> . . . all assume that the past behavior of a security's price is rich in information concerning its future behavior. History repeats itself in that "patterns" of past price behavior will tend to recur in the future. Thus, if through careful analysis of price charts one develops an understanding of these "patterns," this can be used to predict the future behavior of prices and in this way increase expected gains [Fama, 1965, p. 34].

This technique is of importance in inferring future behavior of sales and similar matters from an analysis of related past products' performance.[3]

Naturally, these and other qualitative methods (scenario planning, morphological analysis, etc.) must be judged against the available alternatives. In a 1975 survey of forecasting techniques of large U.S. corporations, Wheelwright and Clarke (1976) suggest that these methods are most applicable to a firm just initiating its forecasting efforts. Some references for this topic include Dory and Lord (1970) or Martino (1980) and references therein.

SECTION 7.2 BASIC TIME SERIES TECHNIQUES

A time series is a sequence of observations $x_1, x_2, \ldots, x_t$ taken at times 1, 2, . . . , t. Examples discussed in this chapter include x_t representing sales in quarter t, cash receipts from accounts receivable in month t, and net cash flows on day t. Generally we assume that the observations are equally spaced in time but as the last example may indicate, this is not always the case. In this section we introduce the easiest methods for generating forecasts of x_{t+h} for $h \geq 1$, using only the past values of x_t and past forecasts of x_t, denoted S_t. As is the case throughout this chapter, our focus is on short-term applications and methods. To keep our discussion and notation relatively uncluttered, we emphasize the one-step forecast: $h = 1$. Thus, unless otherwise stated, we are able to use all of the past data to generate a forecast of the next period's value. We begin with two very basic techniques: simple autoregressive forecasts and exponential smoothing.

Simple autoregressive forecasts are averages of the past n observations. (These are also called moving averages but we will shun this terminology for reasons that will become evident.) A simple (one-step) autoregressive forecast with lag n is SAR(n):

$$S_{t+1} = \left(\frac{1}{n}\right) \sum_{i=0}^{n-1} x_{t-i} = \left(\frac{1}{n}\right)(x_t + x_{t-1} + \cdots + x_{t-n+1}). \quad (7.1)$$

The term *autoregressive* means that the current value of x_t can be determined from weighting its past values. Simple means that each of the n past observations is equally important in determining the forecast. In general, the greater the lag n, the greater is the smoothing of the irregularities in the series. Often a reasonable value for n is the length of the season of the data, if one exists. Thus with quarterly data $n = 4$ would mitigate the seasonal bias. While the SAR forecast is trivial to generate, in most circumstances it is plausible that the more recent observations contain more information and hence deserve more weight, but in a SAR(n) forecast, each of the n past observations is equally weighted. Note that if we were trying to predict daily rates of return for a publicly traded security, the random walk hypothesis [see, for example, Fama (1965)] would imply that a SAR(1) model is optimal (i.e., the best forecast of the current rate of return is the last observed rate of return). This would mean that there is no additional information to be garnered by looking at previous rates of return (other than the last); see our earlier discussion of technical analysis.

In exponential smoothing more weight is given to more recent observations and less to each successively older observation. To retain the desirable characteristic of an average (the weights summing to 1), this technique uses geometrically declining coefficients. Thus a (simple) exponential smoothing forecast with smoothing parameter α, $0 \leq \alpha \leq 1$, is EXP(α),

$$S_{t+1} = \alpha x_t + \alpha(1 - \alpha)x_{t-1} + \alpha(1 - \alpha)^2 x_{t-2} + \cdots. \qquad (7.2)$$

Here the forecast depends on all past observations.[4] The larger α is, the greater is the emphasis on the more recent observations. It is easy to show that (7.2) can be rewritten

$$S_{t+1} = \alpha x_t + (1 - \alpha)S_t. \qquad (7.3)$$

This gives an easy mechanism for generating forecasts. Note that we need a value of the previous forecast to utilize (7.3); the following examples will demonstrate some possible initializations. Another way to express (7.3) is

$$S_{t+1} = S_t + \alpha(x_t - S_t),$$

so that the new forecast is the old forecast plus a correction (feedback) of α times the most recent forecasting error.

Example 7.1 The following time series will be analyzed throughout this chapter. It is quarterly sales data in millions from a major U.S. fast food retailer over the period 1974 to 1980. See Exhibit 7.1 and Figure 7.2. It is clear that the series exhibits an upward trend and a quarterly seasonal pattern. We first demonstrate the application of simple autoregressive and exponential smoothing models to these data assuming that we wish to generate one-step "forecasts" for each quarter 1979 to 1980, in our notation, x_{21} to x_{28}.

EXHIBIT 7.1   QUARTERLY SALES DATA (IN MILLIONS)

Year	Quarter 1	Quarter 2	Quarter 3	Quarter 4
1974	$x_1 = 162$	190	197	198
1975	204	241	270	257
1976	251	298	311	297
1977	291	351	378	364
1978	354	423	446	421
1979	410	484	513	504
1980	483	553	582	$565 = x_{28}$

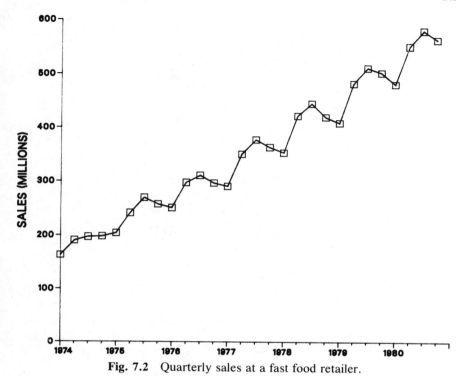

Fig. 7.2   Quarterly sales at a fast food retailer.

The four models used are as follows:

$$SAR(2): \quad S_{t+1} = 0.5(x_t + x_{t-1})$$
$$SAR(4): \quad S_{t+1} = 0.25(x_t + x_{t-1} + x_{t-2} + x_{t-3})$$
$$EXP(0.3): \quad S_{t+1} = 0.3x_t + 0.7S_t$$
$$EXP(0.7): \quad S_{t+1} = 0.7x_t + 0.3S_t.$$

As noted earlier, exponential smoothing models require the initialization of one S_t. Here we take a simple choice, setting S_{20} to be the mean of the previous four observations, 411. Exhibit 7.2 gives x_t, S_t, and the forecasting error ("residual")

$$u_t = x_t - S_t$$

for each method. We will postpone till the next section discussion of which method generates the "best" forecast, but one can note that most of the residuals are positive and that they follow a quarterly pattern. It is natural to assume that a forecasting method that can exploit these patterns would be more efficient than any of these four methods.

EXHIBIT 7.2 EXAMPLE 7.1: FORECASTS AND ERRORS*

t	x_t	SAR(2)	SAR(4)	EXP(0.3)	EXP(0.7)
21	410	433.5 (−23.5)	411.0 (−1.0)	414.0 (−4.0)	418.0 (−8.0)
22	484	415.5 (68.5)	425.0 (59.0)	412.8 (71.2)	412.4 (71.6)
23	513	447.0 (66.0)	440.3 (72.7)	434.2 (78.8)	462.5 (50.5)
24	504	498.5 (5.5)	457.0 (47.0)	457.8 (46.2)	497.9 (6.1)
25	483	508.5 (−25.5)	477.8 (5.2)	471.7 (11.3)	502.2 (−19.2)
26	553	493.5 (59.5)	496.0 (57.0)	475.1 (77.9)	488.7 (64.3)
27	582	518.0 (64.0)	513.3 (68.7)	498.4 (83.6)	533.7 (48.3)
28	565	567.5 (−2.5)	530.5 (34.5)	523.5 (41.5)	567.5 (−2.5)

*Forecasting errors are given in parentheses.

Exponential Smoothing Adapted for Trend and Seasonality

As Example 7.1 indicated, the simplest types of time series forecasting essentially ignore the seasonality and trend in the series. However, exponential smoothing can be adapted to include these components of a time series pattern. The basic technique described here is due to Winters (1960). A number of other modifications of exponential smoothing exist that are able to handle these components, but in practice it seems to make little difference which extension is used.

The basic idea is to smooth the level, the (additive) trend, and the (multiplicative) seasonal components of the series. At time t the one-step forecast is

$$S_{t+1} = (\bar{x}_t + G_t)F_{t+1-s}, \tag{7.4}$$

where

$$
\begin{aligned}
\bar{x}_t &= \text{level of the series at time t,} \\
G_t &= \text{trend at time t,} \\
F_{t+1-s} &= \text{seasonal factor at time } (t+1-s), \\
s &= \text{number of periods in a season,} \\
\alpha, \beta, \text{ and } \gamma &= \text{smoothing constants for the level,} \\
&\quad \text{seasonality, and trend, respectively; } 0 \le \alpha, \beta, \gamma \le 1.
\end{aligned}
$$

An h-step forecast at time t is

$$S_{t+h} = (\bar{x}_t + hG_t)F_{t+h-s}. \tag{7.5}$$

At the end of period t (i.e., when x_t becomes known), the estimates of the three components of the time series are updated as follows. The analogies with (7.3) should be clear.

1. Update the level:

$$\bar{x}_t = \alpha\left(\frac{x_t}{F_{t-s}}\right) + (1 - \alpha)(\bar{x}_{t-1} + G_{t-1}). \tag{7.6}$$

2. Update the seasonality:

$$F_t = \beta\left(\frac{x_t}{\bar{x}_t}\right) + (1 - \beta)F_{t-s}. \tag{7.7}$$

3. Update the trend:

$$G_t = \gamma(\bar{x}_t - \bar{x}_{t-1}) + (1 - \gamma)G_{t-1}. \tag{7.8}$$

Initialization is more complex than before. We next describe a method that assumes only $(s + 1)$ periods of past data: $x_{t-s}, \ldots, x_t$. For other, more complex approaches, see, for example, Groff (1973) or Peterson and Silver (1979). Of course, given a sufficiently long series of data, one way to reduce the effects of the initialization is to begin forecasting and updating a number of periods prior to time t, thereby washing out the effects before the actual prediction begins.

Let M be the average over the past s periods,

$$M = \left(\frac{1}{s}\right) \sum_{j=t-s+1}^{t} x_j. \tag{7.9}$$

Seasonality is initialized by

$$F_{j-s} = \frac{x_{j-s}}{M,} \qquad j = t, \ldots, (t + s). \tag{7.10}$$

For example, $F_j > 1$ suggests that the corresponding season is "higher" than average. The trend is initialized by

$$G_t = \left(\frac{1}{s}\right) (x_t - x_{t-s}), \tag{7.11}$$

which is an estimate of the per period growth over the past 5 observations. The level is initialized by

$$\bar{x}_t = M. \tag{7.12}$$

Example 7.1 (continued) As before, we are determining the one-step forecasts $S_{21}, \ldots, S_{28}$. To perform the initialization, assume $x_{16}, \ldots, x_{20}$ are known. Since there is quarterly seasonality, $s = 4$. From (7.9)

$$M = \tfrac{1}{4}(354 + 423 + 446 + 421) = 411.$$

Thus the initial seasonality terms are given by (7.10)

$$F_{17} = \frac{354}{411} = 0.861$$

$$F_{18} = \frac{423}{411} = 1.029$$

$$F_{19} = \frac{446}{411} = 1.085$$

$$F_{20} = \frac{421}{411} = 1.024.$$

The initial growth estimate is from (7.11)

$$G_{20} = \tfrac{1}{4}(421 - 364) = 14.25.$$

Finally, by (7.12), the initialized level is

$$\bar{x}_{20} = 411.$$

Somewhat arbitrarily we take the smoothing coefficients to be

$$\alpha = 0.3, \qquad \beta = 0.5, \qquad \text{and } \gamma = 0.5.$$

Using these initializations and (7.4),

$$S_{21} = (411 + 14.25)(0.861) = 366.14.$$

Assuming knowledge of x_{21} we can update the components.

$$\bar{x}_{21} = 0.3\left(\frac{410}{.861}\right) + 0.7(411 + 14.25) = 440.523$$

$$F_{21} = 0.5\left(\frac{410}{440.523}\right) + 0.5(0.861) = 0.896$$

$$G_{21} = 0.5(440.532 - 411) + 0.5(14.25) = 21.891.$$

Thus

$$S_{22} = (440.532 + 21.891)(1.029) = 475.833.$$

Continuing, we may summarize the forecasts and residuals:

$$
\begin{aligned}
S_{21} &= 366.140 & u_{21} &= 43.860 \\
S_{22} &= 475.833 & u_{22} &= 8.167 \\
S_{23} &= 529.536 & u_{23} &= -16.356 \\
S_{24} &= 516.285 & u_{24} &= -12.285 \\
S_{25} &= 465.571 & u_{25} &= 17.429 \\
S_{26} &= 566.547 & u_{26} &= -13.547 \\
S_{27} &= 604.573 & u_{27} &= -22.573 \\
S_{28} &= 582.754 & u_{28} &= -17.754.
\end{aligned}
$$

SECTION 7.3   EVALUATING FORECASTS

The techniques described in the previous section all generate forecasts with a minimal amount of effort (if sufficient data are available). However, there is no generally accepted way to determine the averaging interval (n) in a simple autoregressive model or the smoothing constants in an exponential smoothing model so that the forecasts generated are "optimal." This makes choice among these alternatives somewhat ad hoc. Here we outline some of the more important measures of forecasting accuracy, assuming that a sequence of n residuals $u_1, \ldots, u_n$ is known. Given a particular forecasting application, it is then important to choose the appropriate criteria in evaluating alternative forecasting methods. A proper evaluation requires that the residuals be "out of sample," that is, not part of the data used to estimate the forecasting model.

The ordinary least squares criterion (OLS) states that the best forecast is the one that minimizes the sum of the squared forecasting errors,

$$S = \sum_{i=1}^{n} u_i^2.$$

This criterion is closely related to the standard error of the forecast[5]

$$\sigma_u = \sqrt{\frac{S}{n}}$$

and forms the basis of regression analysis. It penalizes positive and negative errors equally and, because of squaring u_i, large errors are penalized heavily. It is not trivial to think of a business application where this would accurately reflect the cost of forecasting errors. Nonetheless, it remains a very important forecasting criterion because of its tractability.

The maximum absolute deviation (MAX) is the absolute value of the maximum residual,

$$\text{MAX} = \max_{1 \leq i \leq n} |u_i|.$$

This and related criteria are useful when one is concerned with the extreme values of a forecast error. For example, if predicting the demand for blood at a hospital, we would want to avoid large residuals.

The mean absolute deviation (MAD)[6] is the average absolute value of the residuals,

$$\text{MAD} = \left(\frac{1}{n}\right) \sum_{i=1}^{n} |u_i|.$$

A closely related measure is the mean percentage deviation (MPD),

$$MPD = \left(\frac{1}{n}\right) \sum_{i=1}^{n} \left|\frac{u_i}{x_i}\right|.$$

The previous 3 measures assume that positive and negative residuals are equally significant, but unlike ordinary least squares, errors are penalized linearly.

A final measure we will utilize is the mean deviation,

$$\bar{u} = \left(\frac{1}{n}\right) \sum_{i=1}^{n} u_i.$$

This measures the bias in the forecast. It is usually desirable that a forecast be unbiased: $\bar{u} = 0$. If, for example, $\bar{u} > 0$, then the forecast tends to underestimate the true values of the series; it would be reasonable to correct this forecast by adding an appropriate constant, namely, $\bar{u}$.

In Exhibit 7.3 we evaluate the five forecasting methods applied to Example 7.1 on the preceding six criteria. It is readily apparent that the deck was stacked against the first four methods; the Winters smoothing method, by incorporating the trend and seasonality does better on all of the criteria. Of the first four methods, EXP(0.7) seems to be the best.

Exercise. How does the naïve forecast : SAR(1) $S_{t+1} = x_t$ compare against these five alternatives on Example 7.1?

It is interesting to note that $\bar{u} > 0$ for all the methods used, especially the first four. This is typical for smoothing and averaging methods, as they tend to lag the general movements of the series. Here, because of the increasing trend, the forecasts systematically lie below the actual values of the series.

More generally, when evaluating forecasts, one attempts to mimimize some function of the residuals that may not be of the preceding forms.[7] For

EXHIBIT 7.3 EXAMPLE 7.1: EVALUATING THE FORECASTS

		Method				
		SAR(2)	SAR(4)	EXP(0.3)	EXP(0.7)	Winters Smoothing
	S	17898	20160	28322	14586	4004
	σ_u	47.3	50.2	59.5	42.7	22.4
Criterion	MAX	68.5	72.7	83.6	71.6	43.9
	MAD	39.4	43.1	51.8	33.8	19.8
	MPD	0.077	0.082	0.098	0.065	0.040
	$\bar{u}$	26.5	42.9	50.8	26.4	2.5

example, consider the problem of forecasting the demand for a product that we hold in inventory. Underestimating the demand incurs a unit shortage cost; overestimating the demand incurs unit holding costs, which may include perishability, financing costs, storage costs, etc. These two costs are unlikely to be equal, so that here the forecasting criterion is asymmetric. Finally, in many applications we are interested in determining the turning points of a time series. These situations have seen limited exposure in the literature; see for example Wecker (1979).

In summary, the methods outlined in this section lack some of the characteristic that are important in practice: most importantly, a measure of the reliability of the forecast, and an objective way of determining the best parameters for a given model. To return to the inventory example, having a forecast that says next month's demand is expected to be x is not as useful as knowing that with a given probability the demand will lie within a given (confidence) interval, say, $x \pm 20$ with 95% probability. To make this type of statement requires a more formal statistical setting for our forecasting models. This is developed in the following sections.

SECTION 7.4 FORECASTING BY REGRESSION

In this section we outline the fundamentals of (linear) regression. For exposition, the results are given in more detail for the case of one explanatory variable (defined below). Readers wishing more detail are referred to the sources listed in the introduction to this chapter.

We distinguish between two types of variable: independent (regressor or explanatory) variables, the levels of which affect the dependent (response) variable. In the previous section the SAR(n) model is a special case of a regression model. Here x_{t+1}, the dependent variable (S_{t+1} is a proxy for x_{t+1}), is expressed as an equally weighted sum of $x_t, \ldots, x_{t-n+1}$, the independent variables. In this section we describe a methodology that could be used to determine "optimal" weights on $x_t, \ldots, x_{t-n+1}$. In Example 7.1, the dependent variable is x_t sales in quarter t; one plausible independent variable is t, time. In general, we focus on how changes in the independent variables will induce a change in the dependent variable. We assume a linear relationship and hope the approximation will be adequate within the relevant range. We begin by discussing the case of one independent variable.

Regression with a Single Independent Variable

We assume that there are n observations of x and y: $(x_1, y_1), \ldots, (x_n, y_n)$. We are considering the linear model

$$x_i = a_0 + a_1 y_i + u_i \tag{7.13}$$

where a_0 and a_1 = coefficients to be determined from the data,
  $x_1, \ldots, x_n$ = observations of the dependent variable,
  $y_1, \ldots, y_n$ = observations of the independent variable,
  $u_1, \ldots, u_n$ = (unobservable) "random disturbances."

Thus there is assumed to be a linear relationship between x and y that is perturbed by u. Then we estimate u_i by the deviation of x_i from the prediction $(a_0 + a_1 y_i)$, which we denote $\hat{x}_i$. As before,

$$\hat{u}_i = x_i - \hat{x}_i.$$

Note the difference between u_i (the "theoretical" error) and $\hat{u}_i$ (the realized error). Equation (7.13) says that changes in y cause changes in x but the relationship is not perfect; there is a random component that we denote by u. In engineering parlance, $(a_0 + a_1 y)$ is the "signal" and u is the "noise." Henceforth " $\hat{}$ " will denote an estimated value.

The most common method for determining a_0 and a_1 is the principle of ordinary least squares. Thus the optimal a_0 and a_1 are those for which the sum of the squared residuals is minimized. If we denote this sum by S,

$$S = \sum_{i=1}^{n} \hat{u}_i^2 = \sum (x_i - \hat{x}_i)^2 = \sum (x_i - a_0 - a_1 y_i)^2. \qquad (7.14)$$

Using standard calculus techniques to minimize S, we take the derivative of S with respect to a_0 and with respect to a_1 and set these two expressions to zero. After some simplification, we obtain the expressions

$$\hat{a}_1 = \frac{\sum_{i=1}^{n} (y_i - \bar{y})(x_i - \bar{x})}{\sum_{i=1}^{n} (y_i - \bar{y})^2} \qquad (7.15)$$

and

$$\hat{a}_0 = \bar{x} - a_1 \bar{y} \qquad (7.16)$$

where $\bar{x}$ and $\bar{y}$ are the sample means

$$\bar{y} = \frac{\sum_{i=1}^{n} y_i}{n}, \qquad \bar{x} = \frac{\sum_{i=1}^{n} x_i}{n}.$$

One may observe that $\hat{a}_1$ is the covariance between x and y divided by the variance of y.

We will use the following (oversimplified, but pleasant) example to illustrate a number of points.

Example 7.2 Suppose that we are interested in predicting future sales of some product. We assume that sales in month i (x_i) are affected by time ($y_i = i$) and that we have the model (7.13). We have observed the last seven monthly sales figures, $(x_1, \ldots, x_7) = (2.5, 2, 3, 3.4, 3.3, 3.2, 3.6)$. The relevant computations are given in Exhibit 7.4.

Having obtained the regression estimates we next investigate the strength of this relationship, first by measuring the variance of the residual series. If this is small relative to the total variance of the dependent variable, then a major part of the dependent variable's fluctuations has been explained by

EXHIBIT 7.4   COMPUTATIONS FOR EXAMPLE 7.2

Month $y_i = i$	Sales x_i	Centered Observations $(x_i - \bar{x})$	$(y_i - \bar{y})$	Prediction $\hat{x}_i$	Residual $\hat{u}_i$
1	2.5	−.5	−3.0	2.358	0.142
2	2.0	−1.0	−2.0	2.572	−0.572
3	3.0	0.0	−1.0	2.786	0.214
4	3.4	0.4	0.0	3.000	0.400
5	3.3	0.3	1.0	3.214	0.086
6	3.2	0.2	2.0	3.428	−0.228
7	3.6	0.6	3.0	3.642	−0.042

$$\bar{x} = \frac{2.5 + \cdots + 3.6}{7} = 3$$

$$\bar{y} = \frac{1 + \cdots + 7}{7} = 4$$

$$\Sigma(y_i - \bar{y})(x_i - \bar{x}) = 6$$

$$\Sigma(y_i - \bar{y})^2 = 28.$$

So that

$$\hat{a}_1 = \frac{6}{28} = 0.214,$$

$$\hat{a}_0 = 3 - 0.214(4) = 2.144.$$

The forecasts are generated from

$$\hat{x} = 2.144 + 0.214y.$$

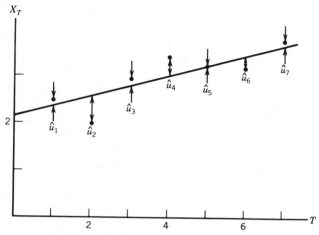

Fig. 7.3   Example 7.2 linear regression and residuals.

the regression. This relative measure of residual variability (squared multiple correlation coefficient or coefficient of determination) is denoted R^2 ;[8]

$$R^2 = \frac{\text{variance due to the regression}}{\text{total variance}}$$

$$= \frac{\displaystyle\sum_{i=1}^{n} (x_i - \bar{x})^2 - \sum_{i=1}^{n} \hat{u}_i^2}{\displaystyle\sum_{i=1}^{n} (x_i - \bar{x})^2}. \tag{7.17}$$

Exercise.   Show that in Example 7.2, $R^2 = 0.677$.

An R^2 of 0.677 can be loosely interpreted to mean that 67.7% of the variation in x can be explained by changes in y. Note that $0 < R^2 \le 1$ and $R^2 = 1$ if and only if $\Sigma \hat{u}_i^2 = 0$ (which means that there is no error in the regression).

In addition to R^2, it is important to test whether or not the estimates of a_0 and a_1 are statistically significant or merely a "random outcome." This test involves the t-statistic, defined as

$$t = \frac{\text{estimate}}{\text{standard error of the estimate}}.$$

Observe that while $\hat{a}_0$ and $\hat{a}_1$ are uniquely determined by (7.15) and (7.16), they are random variables since they depend on the particular realization of the u_i (the random disturbances).

To interpret the *t*-statistic requires some assumptions about the random disturbances; henceforth we will assume that the u_i are independently, normally distributed with mean zero and variance σ_u^2. Table B, Appendix C, gives the *t*-distribution. The degrees of freedom in our case (testing the significance of $\hat{a}_0$ and $\hat{a}_1$) are $(n - 2)$. More generally, the degrees of freedom are $(n - m)$, where n is the number of observations and m is the number of parameters estimated from these data. Observe that as the degrees of freedom become greater, the *t*-distribution more closely resembles the normal distribution. See Appendix B for formulas and calculations for Example 7.2.

The *t*-distribution is here used to test the hypothesis that a regression estimate is zero, but since an estimate is random, there exists a positive probability (with normally distributed u_i) that any *t*-statistic could arise from a "true" parameter of zero. Thus we need to specify some tolerance α such that we accept a probability of $(1 - 2\alpha)$ that the estimated coefficient is indeed zero. (We need 2α because we can infer that the estimate is not zero by obtaining a value that is very large or very small. Table B, Appendix C, gives only a one-sided probability so (using the symmetry of the *t*-distribution) we are required to double α). For example, with 20 degrees of freedom and $\alpha = 0.05$, the *t*-statistic (see Table B, Appendix C) is 1.7247. If we compute from our data a *t*-statistic greater than 1.7247, the estimate is said to be significant at the 0.10 level. That is, there exists no more than a 10% chance that the true value of the parameter is zero. A common rule of thumb is that a *t*-statistic is significant if $|t| > 2$. Note that since the *t*-statistic is symmetric around its mean, here the sign of the *t*-statistic is irrelevant.

Exercise. If the *t*-statistic with 100 degrees of freedom is 2.413, at what level is it significant? What is the level of significance if the statistic were normally distributed?

Example 7.3 Beardsley and Mansfield (1978) took data from a firm that had recorded forecast and actual discounted profits on all major new products and processes over an extensive time period. They used regression to try to evaluate the accuracy of the forecasts. Letting A_i represent the actual discounted profit and F_i the forecast profit, they obtained the two regressions:
For new products:

$$F_i = 0.71 + 0.24A_i$$
$$(3.78)\ (2.41), \qquad R^2 = 0.14.$$

For new processes:

$$F_i = 1.38 + 0.46A_i$$
$$(2.08)\ (10.44), \qquad R^2 = 0.87.$$

Here and subsequently t-statistics are shown in brackets under the estimated coefficient.

Exercise.   With 100 degrees of freedom verify that all four coefficients are significant at the 0.05 level.

The fact that the R^2 of the regression for new processes is much higher than the regression for new products confirms our intuition about which is easier to predict. Finally, observe that the constant coefficient in both regressions is (significantly) positive, indicating that, as expected, profitability forecasts tend to be biased upward.

Another phase in the statistical evaluation of a regression forecast is the analysis of the residuals. While this topic will be discussed further in this chapter, we first focus on one statistic, the Durbin–Watson (d), which tests the correlation between adjacent residuals. Recall that we have assumed that the u_i are independently distributed. If we find however that there is a predictable pattern ("autocorrelation") in the residuals, then not only is one of the basic assumptions underlying regression analysis not true, but, perhaps more importantly, a forecast that could exploit this pattern would be more efficient.

As shown in Appendix B, if the adjacent u_i are not correlated, the Durbin–Watson statistic d, should be "near" 2. If $d < 2$ then adjacent forecasting errors tend to be overestimates or underestimates together; if $d > 2$, then adjacent forecasting errors tend to be of opposite sign. The former case is more common in forecasting. Evaluating the d-statistic is only part of the analysis of the residuals, which is a necessary part of determining how good a regression is. This will be developed through the examples in the rest of this chapter and in Section 7.7.

Another measure of the accuracy of a regression forecast is the standard error of estimate. What should be clear from the preceding analysis is that a forecast is merely an estimate of the mean value of the dependent variable given the value(s) of the independent variable(s); the standard error allows us to compute the variability of this estimate. The t-statistic is again applicable (in the one independent variable case) with $(n - 2)$ degrees of freedom. To construct a 95% confidence interval around the forecast at $y = 8$, using the fact that the standard error in Example 7.2 is 0.459 (see Appendix B for the relevant calculation), we obtain

$$2.144 + 0.214(8) \pm 2.5706(0.459) = 3.856 \pm 1.18.$$

The figure 2.5706 corresponds to the t-value with $\alpha = 0.025$ (again, recall that the entries in Table B, Appendix C, give only one-sided probabilities) and five degrees of freedom. What we have shown is that the "response" to $y = 8$ will lie in the interval from 2.676 to 5.036 with a probability of 95%. That this interval is rather large is due to the significant uncertainty attached to our forecast. In practice we usually estimate the standard error by σ_u, the standard deviation of the residual series.

Exercise. Construct a 98% interval around Example 7.2's forecast for month eight sales.

Example 7.1 (continued) Recalling Figure 7.2, it is clear that the simple regression

$$x_t = a_0 + a_1 t + u_t,$$

which expresses sales as a linear function of time, will generate a good fit to the past data. Performing this estimation gives

$$x_t = 140.35 + 14.914t \qquad (7.18)$$
$$\quad (1.710) \quad (29.662)$$

$$R^2 = 0.9702, \quad \sigma_u = 22.655, \quad \text{Durbin–Watson} = 1.78,$$
$$\text{degrees of freedom} = 26.$$

The time variable is significant at all levels but the constant is only significant at the 0.10 level. The R^2 indicates a very good fit; about 97% of the variability in sales has been accounted for by time. Using σ_u we can construct a 95% confidence interval around the next sales forecast ($t = 29$). (Using the more accurate formula (A.4) we compute the standard error of the forecast for $t = 29$ to be 23.144. Note that this is very close to σ_u.) Hence the confidence interval is

$$140.35 + 14.914(29) \pm 2.055(22.655) = 572.9 \pm 46.6.$$

(The 2.055 figure comes from Table A.)

That is, there is only a 5% chance that the next sales Figure will lie outside the range 526.3 to 619.5. Although the Durbin–Watson statistic is near 2, before concluding that we have developed a good model for forecasting sales, it is instructive to plot the residual. This is given in Figure 7.4 and it suggests that the errors are not random. There is a definite quarterly pattern (which cannot be detected by the Durbin–Watson statistic because it can only detect the correlation between adjacent residuals.) One way to exploit this pattern is to include further independent variables in the forecast; that is the topic of the next section.

Regression with Several Independent Variables

Here we extend the number of explanatory variables that are used to predict the values of the dependent variable. Since practical-sized problems are

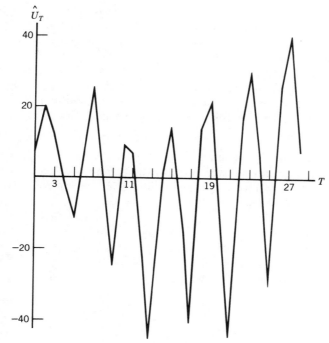

Fig. 7.4   Example 7.1 residuals from the univariate regression.

invariably solved by computer, we will omit any computational formulas; these may be found in the references previously cited.

We are considering the model

$$x_j = a_0 + a_1 y_{1j} + a_2 y_{2j} + \cdots + a_m y_{mj} + u_j \qquad (7.19)$$

where $a_0, a_1, \ldots, a_m$ = coefficients to be estimated from the data,

$x_1, \ldots, x_n$ = observations of the dependent variable,

$y_{i1}, \ldots, y_{in}$ = observations of the ith independent variable,

$u_1, \ldots, u_n$ = random disturbances.

As before, the a_i are chosen to minimize the sum of the squared residuals:

$$S = \sum_{j=1}^{n} (x_j - a_0 - a_1 y_{1j} - \cdots - a_m y_{mj})^2.$$

Setting the $(m + 1)$ partial derivatives of S with respect to $a_0, \ldots, a_m$, to zero, we obtain $(m + 1)$ linear equations in $(m + 1)$ variables (the normal equations), which are solved to yield the optimal a_i.

The t-statistics, R^2, and Durbin–Watson statistic retain the interpretation given them in the previous section. For the t-statistic, however, (A.1) and (A.2) are no longer valid and the degrees of freedom are now $(n - m - 1)$. The standard error of the regression no longer follows the t-distribution, rather it has an F-distribution with m and $(n - m - 1)$ degrees of freedom. As before, the standard error of the regression measures the significance of R^2, that is, whether or not there is a linear relationship between x and the y_i. Table C, Appendix C gives representative values of the F-distribution.

Example 7.1 (continued)   The residuals from the regression (7.18) indicated what could have been expected a priori, that there is a seasonal pattern in the residuals. This pattern is weaker than the increasing trend and is more evident when the trend has been "filtered" out by (7.18). We can incorporate this pattern into the forecast by dummy variables to indicate the season of the observation or forecast. Thus we define d_1, d_2, and d_3 by $d_i = 1$ if the observation occurs in quarter i and is zero otherwise. (Note that a fourth dummy variable is not necessary. An observation in the fourth quarter is identified by $d_1 = d_2 = d_3 = 0$.) We now estimate (by computer) the equation

$$x_t = 114.471 + 38.7C1d_1 + 45.871d_2 + 18.287d_3 + 14.985t$$
$$\quad\;\; (5.409) \qquad (5.655) \qquad\;\; (6.708) \qquad (2.672) \qquad (50.942)$$

$$R^2 = 0.991, \quad \sigma_u = 13.212, \quad \text{Durbin–Watson} = 1.70,$$
$$\text{degrees of freedom} = 23.$$

All estimates are significant at the 0.01 level except for d_3, which is significant at the 0.02 level. Note that the R^2 and σ_u have improved from the previous regression. Whether or not this improvement is important enough to offset the increased complexity of the forecasting model is not clear. As in more general forecasting contexts, there is a tradeoff between increased accuracy and increased complexity.

Exercise.   If the F statistic for this regression was 26.813, verify that it is significant at the 0.01 level.

SECTION 7.5   FORMAL TIME SERIES TECHNIQUES

The common thread uniting all such models (time series) is that they shun economic theory and rely instead on numbers alone. The user manipulates vast series of data going back in history to spew forth a picture of the future ["Why Bother with Theory," *The New York Times,* September 12, 1982].

In this section we discuss the fundamentals of a more structured approach to forecasting time series that uses the correlations between the observations to construct an appropriate forecasting model. This methodology is described more completely in Box and Jenkins (1970) and Nelson (1973).

The reader unfamiliar with statistical concepts may find this section difficult. It is included here because, as Sections 7.6 and 7.7 clarify, it is an approach that has had much application in short-term forecasting. Despite its purely numerical methodology, it provides a viable alternative to more elaborate models. See Armstrong (1978).

The Box–Jenkins approach consists of three stages:

1. Identification of a time series.
2. Parameter estimation.
3. Diagnostic checking.

The first stage attempts to find a (class of) models that can be used to forecast the given time series. It is important to note that this methodology does not assume that a particular model will be used, but rather lets the data suggest the type of model that can be applied through an analysis of the statistics (autocorrelations and partial autocorrelations) that define the "pattern" of the time series.

The chosen models' parameters will be estimated in stage 2. These models are then used to forecast the time series, and stage 3 evaluates the performance. Often stages 2 and 3 are repeated until an adequate model is found or until it can be determined that none is likely to exist. In this section we emphasise the first stage of the Box–Jenkins methodology and illustrate the other two stages through examples.

Identification of a Time Series

As elaborated in Appendix A, the covariance between two random variables U and V measures their tendency to move together. Negative covariance means that "high" values of U tend to coincide with "low" values of V and vice versa; positive covariance would suggest that U and V are high or low together. For example, the rates of return on two securities in the same industry would be likely to have positive covariance, while the rates of return on a call and a put option on the same security would have negative covariance. Here high and low is measured in relation to the respective averages. The correlation coefficient (ρ) standardizes the covariance to a measure between -1 and 1. A $\rho = -1$, 0, or 1 corresponds to perfect negative correlation, (approximate) independence, or perfect positive correlation. If we were using U to infer values of V, clearly the closer $|\rho|$ was to 1, the more information U contains about V. Analogously, if we find that the past values of a time series contain significant information about the value to be forecast, then a time series model will be useful. An analysis of the correlations of past values with the value to be forecast will suggest particular forecasting models.

Thus we define ρ_i (the autocorrelation at lag i) to be the correlation between observations (of the time series $\{x_t\}$) i periods apart; see Appendix A for formal definition. Estimation of ρ_i parallels the usual approach to determining correlations. First, γ_i, the covariance between observations i periods apart, is estimated from

$$\hat{\gamma}_i = \left(\frac{1}{n}\right) \sum_{t=1}^{n-i} (x_t - \bar{x})(x_{t+i} - \bar{x}), \qquad (7.20)$$

as before

$$\bar{x} = \left(\frac{1}{n}\right) \sum_{t=1}^{n} x_t.$$

Observe that $\hat{\gamma}_0$ is the usual estimate of the variance of $\{x_t\}$. Now the autocorrelation at lag i is

$$\hat{\rho}_i = \frac{\hat{\gamma}_i}{\hat{\gamma}_0}. \qquad (7.21)$$

The graph of $\hat{\rho}_i$ versus i is called the (sample) correlogram. It indicates the "length" and "strength" of the memory of the series. As a histogram uses the relative frequencies of occurrences of outcomes to infer particular distributional forms of the outcomes (normal, uniform, or otherwise), here the shape of the correlogram helps identify a process that could have generated the observed data.

Example 7.4 The data are as follows:

t	1	2	3	4	5	6	7	8	9	10	11	12	13	14	15
x_t	5	4	0	3	2	0	-4	-5	-6	-1	-2	2	3	2	-3.

The graph of $\{x_t\}$ is given in Figure 7.5.

$$\bar{x} = \left(\frac{1}{15}\right) [5 + 4 + \cdots + (-3)] = 0,$$

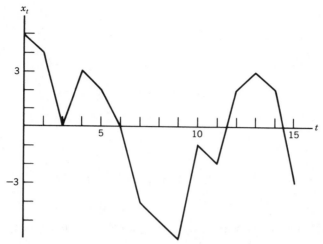

Fig. 7.5   Example 7.4.

which makes determining $\hat{\gamma}_i$ much simpler.

$$\hat{\gamma}_0 = \left(\frac{1}{15}\right) [5^2 + 4^2 + \cdots + (-3)^2] = 10.800$$

$$\hat{\gamma}_1 = \left(\frac{1}{15}\right) [5 \cdot 4 + 4 \cdot 0 + \cdots + 2(-3)] = 5.733$$

$$\hat{\gamma}_2 = \left(\frac{1}{15}\right) [5 \cdot 0 + 4 \cdot 3 + \cdots + 3(-3)] = 2.133$$

$$\hat{\gamma}_3 = \left(\frac{1}{15}\right) [5 \cdot 3 + 4 \cdot 2 + \cdots + 2(-3)] = -0.677.$$

So that

$$\hat{\rho}_1 = 0.531, \quad \hat{\rho}_2 = 0.198, \quad \hat{\rho}_3 = -0.062.$$

The sample correlogram is given in Figure 7.6.

   Exercise.   Verify that $\hat{\rho}_4 = -0.204$, $\hat{\rho}_5 = -0.420$, $\hat{\rho}_6 = -0.315$.

Time Series Models

The previous section has shown how to develop statistics (autocorrelations) that characterize the "pattern" within a time series. We now describe a class of theoretical models that can approximate the same pattern as the data. The matching of the autocorrelations (theoretical and sample) is one

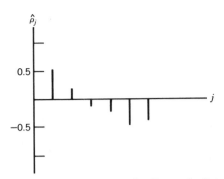

Fig. 7.6   Correlogram for Example 7.4.

of the foundations of the Box–Jenkins approach to time series forecasting: the identification of a model.

We assume a linear relationship between x_t and its past values (x_{t-1}, x_{t-2}, . . .) and/or its past random disturbances (u_{t-1}, u_{t-2}, . . .). Recall that we estimate u_t by ($x_t - S_t$), the difference between the observation at time t and the forecast for time t. The forecasting models are linear with fixed coefficients representing a time-invariant structure. For brevity we focus on the autoregressive model, which assumes that x_t is is a linear combination of its past values. We briefly describe the moving average (MA) models, which express x_t as a linear combination of the past random disturbances and mixtures of the moving average and autoregressive (ARMA) models. For the remainder of this section we assume that we have subtracted the mean of the series from each of the observations so that $\bar{x} = 0$.

The autoregressive model, AR(p), assumes the current observation x_t is a linear combination of the past p observations plus a random disturbance:

$$x_t = \phi_1 x_{t-1} + \phi_2 x_{t-2} + \cdots + \phi_p x_{t-p} + u_t \qquad (7.22)$$

where ϕ_1, ϕ_2, $\cdots$, ϕ_p = coefficients to be estimated from the data,

x_{t-1}, $\cdots$, x_{t-p} = p observations of the time series,

u_t = a random disturbance.

Note that (7.22) is actually a regression model explaining x_t by its past p values. The Box–Jenkins methodology allows us to determine the structure of the model (7.22) from the data.

As in regression, to allow an effective statistical analysis we assume that each u_t is independently (i.e., independent of past x_s and u_s) normally distributed with mean zero and variance σ_u^2.

We describe the primary model AR(1) in some detail and are more brief for the more complex models. The reader is again referred to the listed sources for elaboration on these and any other cryptic points within this section. The AR(1) model is

$$x_t = \phi_1 x_{t-1} + u_t. \tag{7.23}$$

Problem 13 shows that the ("theoretical") autocorrelations are

$$\rho_i = \phi_1^i. \tag{7.24}$$

Hence, the AR(1) process has an infinite memory with exponentially declining weights and x_t depends on all past observations. Note that if $|\phi_1| \geq 1$, it is clear that the series will eventually diverge from its mean value. Of course, this restriction $|\phi_1| < 1$ is also required for (7.24) to be sensible. It is very important to note that although $\rho_j > 0$ for $j \geq 1$, all the relevant information about x_t is captured in x_{t-1}.[9]

Example 7.5   For the AR(1) model

$$x_t = 0.6x_{t-1} + u_t$$

the correlogram is given in Figure 7.8. A realization of this process is given in Figure 7.7. (This realization is generated by finding a random starting point and then drawing a series of random numbers from a normal distribution with zero mean and variance (σ_u^2) of 0.25.) In this example ρ_1 and ρ_2 indicate significant positive autocorrelation. This is reflected in Figure 7.7; observations one or two periods apart tend to lie on the same side of the (zero) mean.

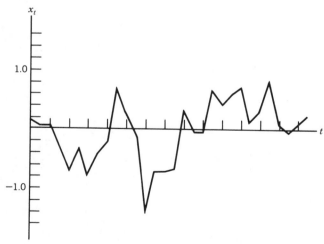

Fig. 7.7   A realization of an AR(1) process.

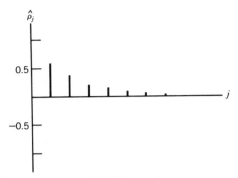

Fig. 7.8 AR(1) correlogram.

Exercise. Sketch the correlogram for the model

$$x_t = -0.7x_{t-1} + u_t.$$

Of course, the AR(1) model can only fit a tiny subset of all the possible patterns that a time series could have. It turns out that AR(p) models can, however, generate almost all the "reasonable" patterns by selecting a p sufficiently large. As p becomes larger, the model has more flexibility to capture the relevant autocorrelations in the data.

The AR(2) model is

$$x_t = \phi_1 x_{t-1} + \phi_2 x_{t-2} + u_t. \tag{7.25}$$

Problem 13 shows that for the AR(2) model

$$\rho_1 = \frac{\phi_1}{1 - \phi_2} \tag{7.26}$$

$$\rho_2 = \phi_2 + \frac{\phi_1^2}{1 - \phi_2} \tag{7.27}$$

and for $j > 2$,

$$\rho_i = \phi_1 \rho_{i-1} + \phi_2 \rho_{i-2}. \tag{7.28}$$

Alternatively, we can write (7.26) and (7.27) as

$$\phi_2 = \frac{\rho_2 - \rho_1^2}{1 - \rho_1^2} \tag{7.29}$$

$$\phi_1 = \rho_1(1 - \phi_2). \tag{7.30}$$

Equations (7.29) and (7.30) are a special case of the Yule–Walker equations, which show how to link ρ_i with ϕ_i for general AR(p) models.

Example 7.6 Consider the AR(2) model

$$x_t = -0.6x_{t-1} + 0.3x_{t-2} + u_t.$$

The correlogram is given in Figure 7.10. This correlogram resembles two exponentially declining patterns intertwined. Figure 7.9 gives a realization of this process (generated as in Example 7.5). Observe that $\rho_2 > 0$ suggests that observations two periods apart lie on the same side of the mean (zero) while $\rho_1 > 0$ suggests that adjacent observations tend to cross the mean.

One of the standard examples of an AR(p) process is the (additive) random walk

$$x_t = x_{t-1} + u_t,$$

[cf. SAR(1)]. This process has gained much currency as a model for properly anticipated prices in the commodity, equity, or other markets. Another example (from Granger, 1980, p. 54) is a naïve model for unemployment: x_t is the number of unemployed in a given city in month t. Suppose $(1 - \phi_1)$ of last month's unemployed get jobs within the month and u_t (a random disturbance) enter the ranks of the unemployed in month t. Then

$$x_t = \phi_1 x_{t-1} + u_t.$$

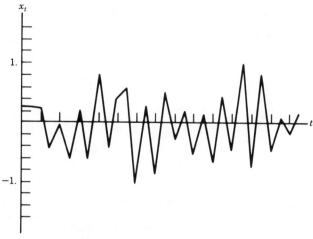

Fig. 7.9 A realization of an AR(2) process.

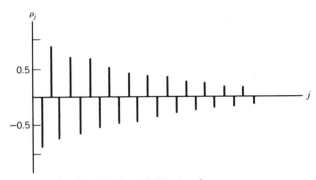

Fig. 7.10   AR(2) correlogram.

A third example is in Meyer and Kim (1975). This paper utilizes an auto-regressive forecast [AR(1)] of changes in the monthly average spot sugar prices and is a straightforward example of the Box–Jenkins methodology.

Moving Average Models

The model MA(q) represents the current observation as a linear combination of the past q random disturbances plus a (current) random disturbance:

$$x_t = -\theta_1 u_{t-1} - \theta_2 u_{t-2} - \cdots - \theta_q u_{t-q} + u_t, \tag{7.31}$$

where $\theta_1, \ldots, \theta_q$ = coefficients to be estimated from the data,
$u_t, \ldots, u_{t-q}$ = random disturbances (defined as before).

The MA(1) model is

$$x_t = -\theta_1 u_{t-1} + u_t. \tag{7.32}$$

It can be shown that

$$\rho_j = \begin{cases} -\theta_1/(1 + \theta_1^2), & \text{if } j = 1 \\ 0, & \text{otherwise.} \end{cases} \tag{7.33}$$

Thus the memory of an MA(1) process is of length 1. Observations further apart are uncorrelated. As always, the parameter θ_1 must be restricted. Using the intuitive argument outlined for AR(1). We require

$$|\theta_1| < 1. \tag{7.34}$$

Although there are generally two solutions to (7.33), only one will satisfy (7.34); see Problem 10.

Exercise. Show that for an MA(1), $|\rho_1| \leq 0.5$.

Example 7.7 Consider the MA(1) model

$$x_t = -0.8u_{t-1} + u_t.$$

The correlogram (given in Figure 7.12) consists of $\rho_1 = -0.488$ and $\rho_2 = \rho_3 = \ldots = 0$. A realization of the process is given in Figure 7.11.
Generally, for MA(q)

$$\rho_j = \begin{cases} \dfrac{(-\theta_j + \theta_1\theta_{j+1} + \cdots + \theta_{q-j}\theta_q)}{(1 + \theta_1^2 + \cdots + \theta_q^2)} & \text{for } j = 1, \cdots, q \\ 0 & \text{otherwise.} \end{cases} \qquad (7.35)$$

Example 7.8 Given the MA(2) model

$$x_t = 0.5u_{t-1} - 0.5u_{t-2} + u_t$$

we can determine $\rho_1 = 0.2$ and $\rho_2 = -0.4$; $\rho_3 = \rho_4 = \ldots = 0$.

Exercise. Sketch the correlogram for the model

$$x_t = -0.6u_{t-1} + 0.8u_{t-2} - 0.3u_{t-3} + u_t.$$

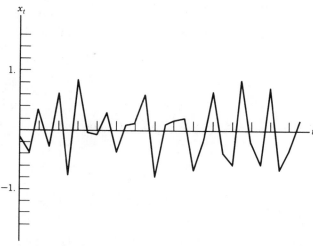

Fig. 7.11 A realization of an MA(1) process.

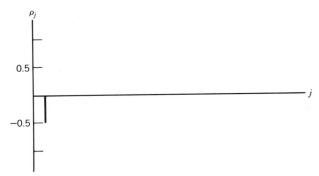

Fig. 7.12 MA(1) correlogram.

Granger (1980, p. 49) suggests the following example of an MA process. Let ϵ_t be the number of new patients at a maternity hospital arriving on day t. Assume ϵ_t is independent of ϵ_s for $t \neq s$. Suppose that an average of 10% stay just one day, 50% two days, 30% three days, and 10% four days. If x_t represents the number of patients leaving the hospital on day t it can be modeled as the MA(4) process

$$x_t = 0.1\epsilon_{t-1} + 0.5\epsilon_{t-2} + 0.3\epsilon_{t-3} + 0.1\epsilon_{t-4} + u_t$$

with u_t a random disturbance. Thus it is possible to predict the number of patients leaving within one, two, three, or four days time. Forecasting over a longer horizon is not possible with this model.

Autoregressive Moving Average Models

The natural combination of an AR and an MA model is the ARMA(p,q) model:

$$x_t = \phi_1 x_{t-1} + \phi_2 x_{t-2} + \cdots + \phi_p x_{t-p}$$
$$- \theta_1 u_{t-1} - \cdots - \theta_q u_{t-q} + u_t, \quad (7.36)$$

where each of the terms has been previously defined. For the ARMA(1,1) case:

$$x_t = \phi_1 x_{t-1} - \theta_1 u_{t-1} + u_t. \quad (7.37)$$

One can verify that

$$\rho_j = \begin{cases} \{(1 - \theta_1\phi_1)(\phi_1 - \theta_1)\}/\{(1 + \theta_1^2 - 2\phi_1\theta_1)\}, & \text{if } j = 1 \\ \phi_1\rho_{j-1} & \text{for } j > 1. \end{cases} \quad (7.38)$$

Example 7.9　Consider the ARMA(1,1) model

$$x_t = 0.8x_{t-1} - 0.4u_{t-1} + u_t.$$

A realization of this process is given in Figure 7.13 and the correlogram is given in Figure 7.14. Note that the correlogram for $j > 1$ is identical to the correlogram for the AR(1) model $x_t = 0.8x_{t-1} + u_t$; the presence of the MA term allows us to modify ρ_1.

ARMA processes are very important in practice. They provide parsimonious (in terms of the number of parameters to be estimated) models for fitting data. In addition, sums of AR processes and mixtures of AR and MA processes generate ARMA models.

Box–Jenkins Models

The previous sections have shown how to use the (sample) autocorrelations to characterize the pattern in a time series and have presented a number of models and their corresponding (theoretical) autocorrelations. Now we attempt to link the two concepts.

Fitting a Box–Jenkins Model begins with finding a model whose theoretical autocorrelations prove a good match to the data's sample autocorrelations. Before this can be done, it is often necessary to manipulate the time series until it is "stationary." Stationarity ("statistical equilibrium") is a very important concept in time series. Essentially it means that the distribution of any observation x_t does not depend on t; that is, we obtain no information about the observation by knowing that it occurred in, say, the third quarter of 1980. Note that this rules out a time series with trend or

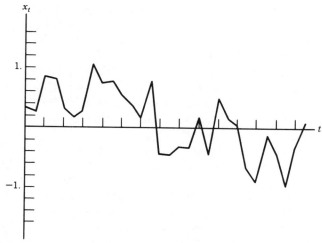

Fig. 7.13　A realization of an ARMA(1,1) process.

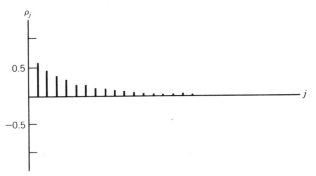

Fig. 7.14 ARMA(1,1) correlogram.

seasonality, since in both cases the expected value of x_t depends on t. The data of Example 7.1 are not stationary, since the series has both trend and seasonality.

Since trend and seasonality are common to most series we are likely to encounter, it is fortunate that there exists a simple technique that usually filters out these nonstationarities. The concept is that of differencing. If a series[10] $\{x_t\}$ has a trend, it is replaced by the series of its first differences $\{w_t\}$, where $w_t = x_t - x_{t-1}$. If the trend in $\{x_t\}$ is linear, then $\{w_t\}$ will have no trend. Similarly, if $\{x_t\}$ has a season of length s, it would be replaced by the series of sth differences: $\{z_t\}$, where $z_t = x_t - x_{t-s}$. The basic idea is that we get rid of the obvious patterns that can swamp the correlogram.

If we found that the series of first differences $\{w_t\}$ was stationary, we would then apply our theory to obtain a forecasting model for $\{w_t\}$. Then to obtain the (one-step) forecast of, say, x_{t+1} (which is what we originally wanted), we "integrate" the $\{w_t\}$ series, that is, undo the differencing. Thus the forecast of w_{t+1} is added to x_t to obtain a forecast of x_{t+1}.

This differencing and integrating of the original time series introduces one more layer of notation; d, which indicates the level of differencing. Thus the general Box–Jenkins model is denoted ARIMA (p,d,q) (autoregressive-integrated-moving average), where p indicates the order of the autoregressive part, d indicates the level of differencing, and q indicates the order of the moving average part. In the literature, Box–Jenkins models are often called ARIMA models.

Now assume that the data are stationary and that we have determined the correlogram. How do we find a good Box–Jenkins model? The key is given by the characteristics of the correlograms of the autoregressive and moving average processes. As the previous examples have shown, the correlogram of an autoregressive process declines exponentially, while the correlogram of a moving average process cuts off (has no significant values after) abruptly. This gives us some clues as to the correct model.

Another powerful tool in determining the proper model is the partial autocorrelation. This concept can be explained as follows: Assume the data can be approximated by an AR(1) model and that ϕ_1 is estimated by (7.24). Thus

$$\phi_1 = \hat{\rho}_1.$$

If ϕ_1 is not "near" zero, it suggests that the order of the autoregressive part (p) is at least 1. Similarly, estimating ϕ_2 for an AR(2) model from (7.29) yields

$$\phi_2 = \frac{\rho_2 - \rho_1^2}{1 - \rho_1^2}.$$

If ϕ_2 is not "near" zero, it suggests that p is at least 2. If we estimate ϕ_1, ϕ_2, . . . in this way, we obtain the partial correlogram; ϕ_n is called the nth partial autocorrelation. If the partial correlogram cuts off after p values, it suggests that the order of the autoregressive part of the process is p. (Note the symmetry: If the correlogram cuts off, it suggests a moving average process; if the partial correlogram cuts off, it suggests an autoregressive process.)

Stationarity can be investigated by studying the graph of $\{x_t\}$ and it can also be inferred from the correlogram and partial correlogram. A stationary series should not have significant autocorrelations or partial autocorrelations at "long" lags. Intuitively, why should a very old observation contain much significant information about the current level? The usual (but rough) rule of thumb is that the standard error of the autocorrelation or partial autocorrelation is approximately $\sqrt{1/T}$, where T is the number of observations.

Exercise.   Explain why with 100 observations, one might conclude that an autocorrelation of -0.23 was significant.

This rule indicates why Box–Jenkins models require a large amount of data to obtain accurate estimates of $\hat{\rho}_j$. Reliable models can seldom be obtained with less than 30 data points. Even with this notion of significance: "the practitioner must be on the lookout for general characteristics which are recognizable in the sample correlogram and not attach significance to every detail. Thus sample autocorrelations produced by a first-order autoregression will decline approximately, although not precisely in an exponential fashion" (Nelson, 1973, p. 72).

Thus it is something of an art to determine from the correlogram and partial correlogram what models could be utilized. Since the data are not likely to conform exactly to any particular model, the user must rely on some subjective analysis in model selection.

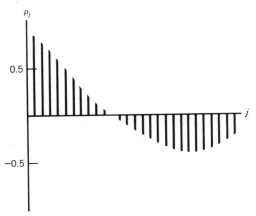

Fig. 7.15 Example 7.1 correlogram.

For the chosen models, initial parameter estimates are usually generated by matching the theoretical and sample autocorrelations [using (7.24) for an AR(1), (7.33) for a MA(1), etc.]. Optimal parameters are then obtained by minimizing the sum of squared errors, using these estimates as a starting point. Because of the complexity of this calculation, optimal parameters are invariably obtained by utilizing one of the many available software packages for this application. We illustrate the Box–Jenkins methodology on the following two examples. Other aspects are treated in Section 7.7.

Example 7.1 (continued) Figure 7.15 is the correlogram generated from the data of Example 7.1. The fact that the autocorrelations at long lags do not vanish suggests that the series is not stationary. This is due to the strong trend evident from the high positive autocorrelations at the early lags (and

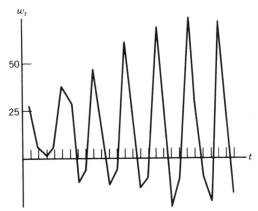

Fig. 7.16 Example 7.1 the series of first differences.

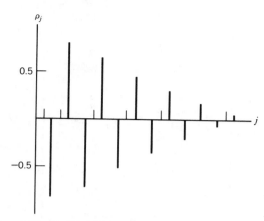

Fig. 7.17   First-difference correlogram.

more directly from Figure 7.2). A linear trend can be removed by replacing the original series $\{x_t\}$ with the series of first differences $w_t = x_t - x_{t-1}$ for $t \geq 2$. This series is plotted in Figure 7.16 and its correlogram is given in Figure 7.17. Again the fact that there are significant autocorrelations at long lags suggests that $\{w_t\}$ is nonstationary. The high positive autocorrelations at lags 4, 8, 12, and 16 are indicative of a season of length 4. To eliminate this seasonality, we replace $\{w_t\}$ by its fourth differences $z_t = w_t - w_{t-4}$ for $t \geq 6$. This series is graphed in Figure 7.18 and its correlogram is given in Figure 7.19.

Figure 7.18 now shows a series with no readily exploitable pattern. The partial autocorrelations given in Figure 7.20 confirm this and suggest that

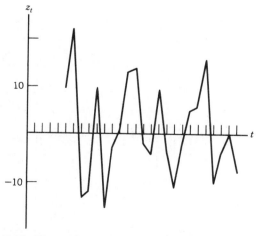

Fig. 7.18   Example 7.1 the series of fourth differences.

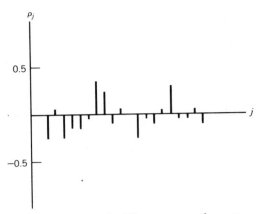

Fig. 7.19 Fourth-difference correlogram.

no autoregressive model is likely to fit $\{z_t\}$. From this series of correlograms we may conclude that $\{x_t\}$, the original sales data, is basically a random component superimposed on the trend and quarterly seasonality.

Example 7.10 The data are given below and are graphed in Figure 7.21

t	1	2	3	4	5	6	7	8	9	10	11	12	13	14	15
x_t	-2	1	-1	2	0	2	-1	2	-2	-1	1	-3	2	-2	2.

The mean of the series is 0.0 and its standard deviation is 1.813. We assume that $\{x_t\}$ is stationary. (This is plausible since it has no apparent trend or

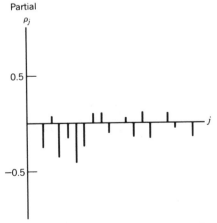

Fig. 7.20 Fourth-difference partial correlogram.

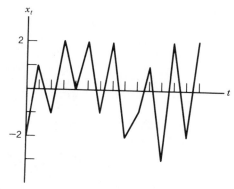

Fig. 7.21   Example 7.10.

seasonality.) The correlogram is presented in Figure 7.22 and the partial autocorrelations in Figure 7.23. Figures 7.22 and 7.23 suggest that an autoregressive model is plausible. Below we try to fit an AR(1), AR(2), and AR(3) model to $\{x_t\}$.

The AR(1) estimated is

$$x_t = -0.774x_{t-1} + u_t$$
$$(-7.068)$$

with $\sigma_u = 1.306$; degrees of freedom $= 14$. The forecast errors and correlogram are given in Figures 7.24 and 7.25. For further illustration, Figure 7.26 plots the sum of squared errors for the various values of ϕ_1. Observe that setting $\phi_1 = \hat{\rho}_1 = -0.63$ generates a sum of squared errors close to the minimum; that is, the usual guess for ϕ_1 turns out to be reasonably good here.

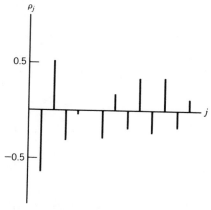

Fig. 7.22   Example 7.10 correlogram.

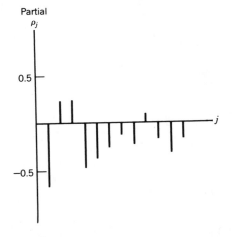

Fig. 7.23 Example 7.10 partial correlogram.

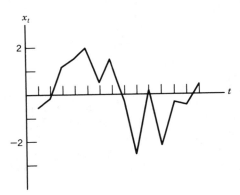

Fig. 7.24 Example 7.10 AR(1) forecast errors.

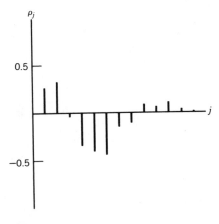

Fig. 7.25 AR(1) forecast error correlogram.

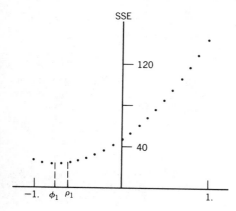

Fig. 7.26   Example 7.10 sum of squared errors versus ϕ_1.

Although the AR(1) model is reasonable (in terms of significant t-statistic, reduction in σ_u, etc.), we compare its performance with an AR(2) and AR(3) model. The estimated models are as follows:

$$\text{AR(2): } x_t = \underset{(-2.222)}{-0.5374x_{t-1}} + \underset{(1.607)}{0.3861x_{t-2}} + u_t$$

with $\sigma_u = 1.270$; degrees of freedom $= 13$.

$$\text{AR(3): } x_t = \underset{(-2.413)}{-0.612x_{t-1}} + \underset{(1.720)}{0.498x_{t-2}} + \underset{(1.017)}{0.262x_{t-3}} + u_t$$

with $\sigma_u = 1.290$; degrees of freedom $= 12$.

The preceding results confirm what the partial autocorrelations indicated: that an AR(1) model is adequate. Although the AR(2) yields a slightly lower σ_u, the t-statistic on ϕ_2 is not significant at the 0.05 level. The AR(3) yields a higher value of σ_u. Because of the shape (exponentially declining) of the correlogram of $\{x_t\}$, moving average models are not explicitly discussed here. However, an MA(3) model is plausible but generates a σ_u higher than that of the AR(1) model.

SECTION 7.6   FORECASTING APPLICATIONS IN CURRENT ASSET MANAGEMENT

. . . the forecasting and operational planning functions are so closely interrelated that it is sometimes difficult to determine where one ends and the other one starts. In effect, every operational plan is based on a forecast of some type. Sometimes the forecast is a sophisticated analysis and prediction of future conditions; in other cases, the forecast is based on the intuitive judgment of the individuals preparing the plan, and is often not recognized as a forecast per se [Jannis, et al., 1980, p. 38].

This section attempts to link the forecasting methodology previously described in this chapter to current asset management as developed in the remainder of this work. We present applications of the techniques and raise some issues which have been discussed in the relevant chapters. We begin with a few comments on current forecasting practice.

Wheelwright and Clarke (1977) surveyed 127 firms in an attempt to determine their commitment to and success with forecasting. For example, they found that for respondant firms with annual sales greater than $500 million, 59.2% had annual forecasting budgets over $100,000. Wheelwright and Clarke listed eight forecasting methods and found that 7 of the 8 were used by more than half of the firms. In approximately decreasing order of usage these seven methods were as follows:

Jury of executive opinion.
Regression analysis.
Time series smoothing.
Sales force composite.
Index numbers.
Econometric models.
Customer expectations.

Since this survey dealt with forecasting in its most general sense, it is not surprising that there would be an emphasis on qualitative methods. The only method not stated as used by a majority was Box–Jenkins; 39% of the respondants were unfamiliar with the method.

The past decade has witnessed an increase in the degree of sophistication in forecasting methodology and perhaps a greater awareness of the advantages of combining forecasts. A greater degree of computerization has simultaneously created superior data bases for forecasting and the capability of examining a variety of alternative forecasting techniques.

When evaluating a forecasting methodology, the following questions are pertinent:

1. Efficiency. How does the cost of generating forecasts compare with the benefits?
2. Accuracy. Under the appropriate criteria, how reliable will the forecast be?
3. Timeliness. Are the forecasts available when required?
4. Flexibility. Can the methodology adapt to "abnormal" events? Can it easily be updated?

5.   **Complexity.** Can the methodology be understood by the user? Can the user conveniently override the system?

In the remainder of this section we discuss forecasting methods for inventory, accounts receivable and cash management.

Inventory Management

As discussed in Chapter 6, different inventory items necessitate different management approaches, but generally, short-term forecasting applications are based on time series. This is largely due to the automated nature of many inventory systems and a cost–benefit tradeoff that usually makes more sophisticated modeling inappropriate. Most recent texts on inventory management [e.g., Peterson and Silver (1979) or Love (1979)] focus largely on exponential smoothing techniques. As Section 7.1 indicates, there exist a great many variants on the basic technique that can be adapted to the particular application.

It is important to note that while inventory control systems require forecasts of demand, most forecasting systems are built on past sales or usage data. This presents a number of problems because in the presence of stockouts or related events, these are poor proxies for actual demand.

An extensive empirical study was conducted by Groff (1973). He compared a variety of exponentially smoothed, harmonic, and Box–Jenkins models on 63 monthly sales series (72 observations each of monthly factory shipments of auto parts and drug items). The forecasting criterion was mean absolute error for forecasting horizons of one and six months. Groff concluded that single-parameter seasonal exponential smoothing models performed the best. An observation of relevance for inventory forecasting is the following:

> . . . A single "general purpose" seasonal model might be suitable for most items in an inventory control system. The use of a single computationally efficient general purpose model eliminates the need to search for and select a forecasting model and allows standard routines to be used for initialization, operation, and control of the forecasting system [Groff, 1973, p. 30].

While Groff's general findings have been corroborated elsewhere [e.g., Gardner (1979)], his findings are slightly tainted:

> . . . these results are explained by the fact that, over a number of series, Groff was evaluating the performance of various individual members of the ARIMA class. . . . Thus the performance of the Box–Jenkins methodology was not really being evaluated since, for any specific series, the data was not used to select, and verify the accuracy of, a particular model from the general class [Newbold, 1979, p. 62].

Steece and White (1979) present an interesting methodology for predicting demand within a multi-item system. Rather than forecasting the demand for each item separately, they develop a model of the aggregate demand for a general class of items and then a second model to determine what fraction of the aggregate demand each item will represent. They illustrate this technique on a hospital pharmacy problem of forecasting the demand for three types of antihistamines. A fractional demand series is forecast by means of exponential smoothing and then aggregate demand is forecast by a Box–Jenkins model. This approach presents an elegant compromise between accuracy and complexity.

Accounts Receivable Management

This section describes a methodology for forecasting cash collections from past credit sales. Shim (1981) describes and applies a simple regression model to this problem. Using 33 monthly observations of seasonally adjusted sales and collections, he estimates

$$C_t = 0.583 S_{t-1} + 0.209 S_{t-2} + 0.144 S_{t-3}$$
$$\quad (6.34) \qquad\quad (2.30) \qquad\quad (2.12)$$

$$R^2 = 0.63; \quad \text{Durbin–Watson} = 2.24; \quad \sigma_u = 82.64.$$

Here C_t is cash collections in period t and S_t is credit sales in period t; as usual, t-statistics are given in parentheses under the estimate.

Exercise. Verify that all the regression coefficients are significant at the 0.05 level.

Note that the interpretation of the constant term (a_0) would be collections in month t given no credit sales in the past three months. Shim has chosen to constrain the model to have $a_0 = 0$.

Another accounts receivable management problem is credit granting. Here on the basis of available data we attempt to classify credit applicants as "good" or "bad" risks. This problem is often approached through linear discriminant analysis, a concept closely related to regression. Perhaps the most well-known application of linear discriminant analysis in finance is the bankruptcy prediction model of Altman (1968). (It should be clear that credit granting and bankruptcy prediction can involve very similar analyses.) The Altman (Z-score) model is

$$Z = 1.2(\text{WCTA}) + 1.4(\text{RETA}) + 3.3(\text{EBIT})$$
$$+ 0.6(\text{MEBD}) + 1.0(\text{SLTA}), \quad (7.39)$$

where

$$
\begin{aligned}
Z &= \text{firm's bankruptcy score,} \\
\text{WCTA} &= \text{working capital/total assets,} \\
\text{RETA} &= \text{retained earnings/total assets,} \\
\text{EBIT} &= \text{earnings before interest and taxes/total assets,} \\
\text{MEBD} &= \text{market value of equity/book value of total debt,} \\
\text{SLTA} &= \text{sales/total assets.}
\end{aligned}
$$

Altman estimated that 2.675 is the cutoff score; a firm is thus assigned to the bankrupt group if its Z-score is less than 2.675; otherwise it is assigned to the nonbankrupt group. Models like (7.39) can be estimated by regression as well as by linear discriminant analysis. Note that t-statistics are not interpretable as in a regression, however; see Section 5.3 for further discussion.

Cash Forecasting

Cash forecasting here is defined to be the short-term prediction of net cash flows, usually on a daily basis. (The relationship with cash budgeting and cash scheduling is described in Chapter 2.) Here we illustrate two diverse approaches.

Stone and Wood (1977) present a dummy variable regression model to forecast daily cash flows from data contained in the monthly cash budget. The model essentially is

$$
C_t = \sum_{i=1}^{M} a_i m_i + \sum_{w=1}^{4} b_w d_w
$$

where

$$
\begin{aligned}
C_t &= \text{daily forecast cash flow,} \\
1, \dots, M &= \text{workdays in a month,} \\
a_1, \dots, a_M &= \text{coefficients to be estimated (representing the monthly} \\
& \quad \text{pattern of cash flows),} \\
m_1, \dots, m_M &= \text{dummy variables for day of the month,} \\
b_1, \dots, b_4 &= \text{coefficients to be estimated (representing the weekly} \\
& \quad \text{pattern of cash flows),} \\
d_1, \dots, d_4 &= \text{dummy variables for the days of the week.}
\end{aligned}
$$

From past data the a_i and b_w are estimated. And from the monthly budgeted cash flows, the model estimates how these will be distributed over the month. (A model very similar to this is described in Section 7.7.)

In the implementation they describe, the average daily error ranges from 12% to 20% in each of the three components: transfer deposits (deposits from collecting banks), other deposits, and disbursements. They judged the approach adequate for three- to four-day forecast horizons.

Exercise. Can you explain why Stone and Wood obtained a negative autocorrelation (at lag one) for the daily forecast errors in their implementation?

Hodgson (1979) describes the well-structured and effective short-term cash forecasting system used by Standard Oil Company of Indiana. Here we very briefly describe the techniques adopted for eight major components of the cash flow. Two Box–Jenkins models were built for each component. The first is a model of daily cash flows and the second is a model of monthly cash flows. The principle of this decomposition is similar to that used by Stone and Wood. The monthly model forecasts the level of cash flows and the daily model forecasts the pattern of these flows. (The similarity with the Steece and Wood approach described earlier should also be evident.) Combining these forecasts and qualitative predictions of the other components of net cash flow resulted in an average error (of the one month ahead net cash flow forecast) within 5% (here $31 million).

SECTION 7.7 STUDY 7.1. FORECASTING CASH FLOWS OF A CREDIT UNION BY REGRESSION AND TIME SERIES FORECASTING*

This study describes two approaches to the forecasting of cash flows at one branch of a credit union. The data are three years of daily observations of net cash flows. These data have a complex pattern (an increasing trend with weekly, monthly, and yearly seasonality) and the first forecasting method utilized, Box–Jenkins, is a natural choice. However, since cash flows are affected by observable, exogenous (calendar day) events, forecasting by regression is also applied. This study treats many of the ideas developed in this chapter and is a good example of the implementation and estimation of models that have become important in many related business contexts.

The purpose of the study is to forecast daily and weekly cash flows. Since almost all of the flows are negative, in reality this is a demand for cash (currency) model. The context is common to many inventory problems in that the credit union is concerned with balancing the cost of cash shortages with the cost of holding idle funds. By forecasting more accurately it should be possible to reduce cash on hand without incurring significantly greater shortage probabilities.

---

*This section is written by Professor Gordon Sick of the University of Alberta.

The Data

Data on cash balances and cash orders for the credit union branch were analyzed for a three-year period. Closing till cash balances were obtained for the 768 days from general ledger accounts and information on cash deliveries was obtained from delivery invoices. This allowed the computation of net daily cash flows. In addition, in one month several deposits were solicited from a local merchant to cover shortages. These were treated as regular cash deliveries for the calculation of daily flows. All but 36 of 768 flows were negative (outflows), primarily because the branch dealt with consumer rather than commercial accounts.

Collection of data was complicated because maintenance of the general ledger was oriented toward ensuring correct end-of-month figures. Three types of discrepancies were observed in the accounts, only some of which could be corrected. The first type of discrepancy arose when two tellers exchanged cash between themselves and offsetting credits and debits to the general ledger were not made on the same day. Frequently there was enough detail to infer the correct adjustment. The second type of discrepancy arose when a journal entry was posted to the wrong account and was not corrected the same day; little could be done to account for this type of error. A third error type resulted from cash delivery invoices being filed incorrectly.

Forecasting Cash Demand as a Time Series

In a time series model the only independent variables are lagged values of the dependent variable, x_t. Many classical forecasting models such as simple autoregressive forecasts and exponential smoothing have this form. These models are adaptive in the sense that if there is an increase or decrease in the mean of the time series, the forecasts increase or decrease accordingly and eventually converge to the new level. Thus absolute forecast errors decrease in an adaptive manner (unless the level of the series changes again). Classical theory says little about selecting optimal values for the time period of a simple autoregressive model or the weight for an exponentially smoothed model. Also, these techniques fail to provide any description of the distribution of the random error term, u_t.

For this application some description of the error term is valuable in assessing the risk of a cash shortage. In addition, cash flows fluctuate significantly from day to day, week to week, and month to month because of (partially) forecastable variations in demand. The need for quantification of forecasting errors and a sophisticated weighting scheme suggests the use of Box–Jenkins (ARIMA) techniques, which are described here.

The parsimony concept requires selection of a model with as few parameters as possible. This represents a potential problem for the application of Box–Jenkins techniques to forecast cash demand, for one would expect information in high-order autocorrelations. For daily cash demands there should be high positive autocorrelations at five-day lags because of the correspondence of the business days of the week. There should also be significant autocorrelation at 260-day lags because there are approximately 260 working days per year. Since the number of days in a month is not constant, the lags corresponding to semimonthly paydays will vary in a cyclic fashion with a very long period, creating an important autocorrelation at that lag. Moreover, some weeks have only four business days, and this will upset the basic autocorrelation structure at five-day lags. All this suggests it will be difficult to fit a parsimonious model to daily data.

These problems are mitigated somewhat by considering weekly cash flows. A 260-day lag now becomes a more plausible 52-week lag. The problem of holidays reducing the workweek does not affect weekly lag structures as seriously as it does daily lag structures. Figure 7.27 depicts the weekly cash demands and Figure 7.28 gives the corresponding correlogram. Since cash flows apparently increase over time, first differences are required; Figure 7.29 depicts the first differenced series and Figure 7.30 gives the corresponding correlogram. The evident nonstationarity of the first differenced series suggests a seasonal pattern and fourth differences were taken. Figure 7.31 shows the fourth differenced series and Figure 7.32 presents the corresponding correlogram.

Note that the fourth differenced series $(z_t = x_t - x_{t-4})$ corresponds roughly to observations one month apart. Figures 7.31 and 7.32 suggest that

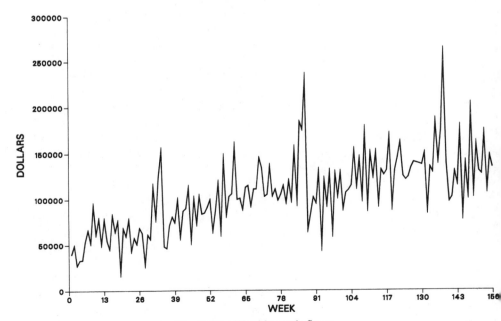

Fig. 7.27 Weekly cash flows.

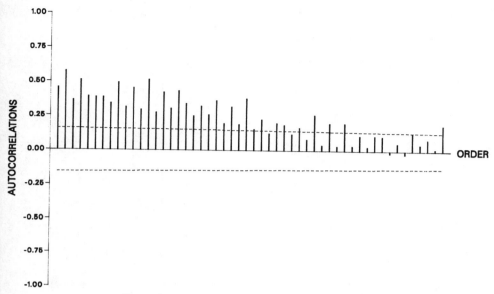

Fig. 7.28 Correlogram of weekly cash flows.

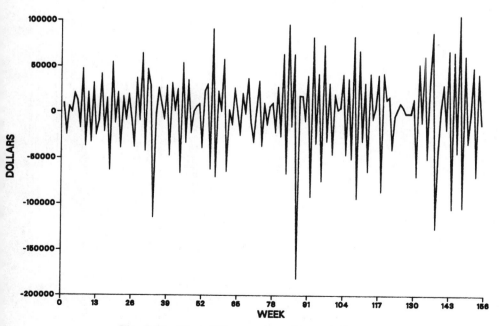

Fig. 7.29 First-differenced weekly cash flows.

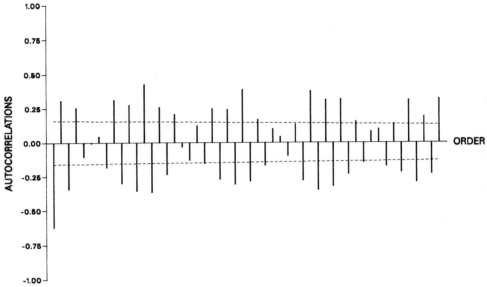

Fig. 7.30 Correlogram of first-differenced weekly cash flows.

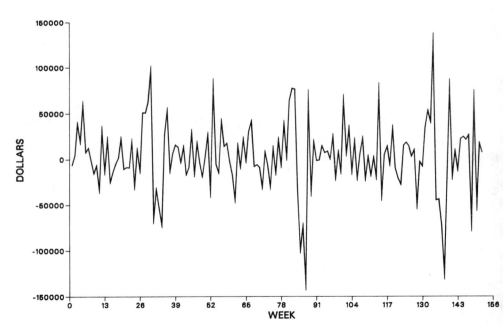

Fig. 7.31 Fourth-differenced weekly cash flows.

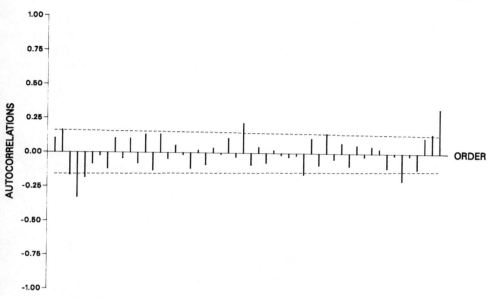

Fig. 7.32 Correlogram of fourth-differenced weekly cash flows.

this series is stationary and that the process $\{z_t\}$ is a fourth or fifth order moving average. An MA(4) model was estimated by minimizing the sum of squared residuals iteratively by the Marquardt algorithm [see Marquardt (1963)]. Under the hypothesis that the u_t are independent and normally distributed with zero mean and constant variance σ_u^2, this procedure yields estimates with desirable statistical properties. The MA(4) model is

$$z_t = 2479 + 0.117u_{t-1} + 0.250u_{t-2} - 0.266u_{t-3} - 0.698u_{t-4} + u_t$$
$$\quad\;\;(5.05)\quad(1.84)\qquad\;(4.25)\qquad\;\;(-4.65)\qquad(5.22)$$

where the t-statistics with 147 degrees of freedom are given in parentheses.

The model appears to be plausible in that all coefficients but θ_1 are significantly different from zero; the $R^2 = 0.382$. However, when checking the invertibility[11] of the process, one finds that the MA(4) forecasts will be unstable. When other feasible models are fitted overdifferencing is still apparent, even though differencing is required to achieve stationarity. Thus, from a Box–Jenkins point of view, there is not enough information in the autocorrelations of weekly cash flows to overcome the "noise" and the time series is not estimable. One might conjecture that if the trend was eliminated from cash demand, as in the following trend model, a major source of the random error is eliminated and the remaining series may be fitted. Since the real requirement was to develop a model for daily rather than weekly cash flows, this last hypothesis was not tested for weekly flows but for daily flows deflated by the trend. For all combinations of first-order and seasonal differencing, the series of autocorrelations failed to die out at large lags, indicating that there is still too much information at long lags to allow the fitting of a parsimonious Box–Jenkins model.

Forecasting Demand by Regression

Earlier it was argued that time series forecasting may be inappropriate for this application. An alternative, causal model, is the following linear regression model.

$$x_t = a_0 + a_1 y_{1t} + \cdots + a_n y_{nt} + u_t \qquad (7.40)$$

where x_t = the dependent variable in period t,

$\quad y_t$ = an n-vector of independent (explanatory) variables in period t,

$\quad u_t$ = a random error in period t, $[E(u_t) = 0; \text{var}(u_t) = \sigma_u^2]$ and

$\quad a$ = a $(n + 1)$-vector of regression coefficients.

Explanatory variables may include dummy variables, these take on the value 1 for various days of the week, months of the year, paydays, and holidays, otherwise they are 0. Another component that must be considered for y_t is the level of interest rates. There are several problems with introducing interest rates into the model: First, over the three-year period of available data interest rates are highly collinear with time, so that it would be difficult to distinguish growth effects from interest rate effects; second, it is unclear which is the correct interest rate to use; third, if some macroeconomic model were available to express the demand for money in terms of interest rates, such a model would be oriented toward money in the form of demand deposits and other forms of cash, rather than currency. Thus interest rates are excluded from the model.

The model must also explain the historical growth in cash demand. One possibility is to have an explanatory variable that increases with time (such as t). However, this would only model an additive growth effect, and not any increase in the effects of the dummy variables over time. To model the growth, consider also a related problem—heteroscedasticity.[12] Preliminary regression models indicated that the variance of u_t increases with time, and indeed is proportional to d_t^2, where d_t is the general level of weekly demand at time t. This suggests using a multiplicative growth model to model growth and eliminate heteroscedasticity simultaneously. In the model (7.40) we replace x_t by $w_t = x_t/d_t$; now w_t is the cash flow at time t expressed as a proportion of the general trend level of weekly cash demand, so one can think of w_t as being normalized cash demand. The d_t provide for growth of x_t and eliminate heteroscedasticity.

The estimated nonlinear trend of 156 weekly cash flows d_t is

$$d_t = 170,000 - 28,900,000/(t + 240), \qquad (7.41)$$
$$(26.32) \quad (-9.00) \quad R^2 = 0.345$$

where t is the number of business days from the start of the period, and t-statistics are given in parentheses. The ultimate capacity level of real weekly cash demand that is forecast by (7.41) is \$170,000 (expressed in January 1976 dollars). Substituting $t = 767$ yields an estimated trend level (current year) of \$141,000, or 83% of the ultimate level of cash demand. This figure is thought to be reasonable in light of the actual remaining potential for growth at the branch. Note that since precisely three years of data were used to estimate the trend, no bias was introduced as a result of seasonal fluctuations in demand.

The trend estimates (multiplied by the consumer price index) were then used as weights d_t in the estimation of fluctuations of cash demand about the trend line. The independent variables were dummy variables indicating the incidence of days of the week, months of the year, semimonthly and monthly paydays, and holidays. The final form of the demand equation with $k = 28$ explanatory variables is presented in Exhibit 7.5. To avoid multicollinearity the regression was run with no dummy variable for January. Since November and February had coefficients insignificantly different from zero, they were dropped from the model and hence equated with January. The coefficients for Tuesday and Wednesday midmonth and month-end paydays were essentially equal, so they were included as one dummy variable.

Recall that the equation is for daily cash demand expressed as a proportion of the general weekly trend level of cash flow and that the explanatory variables are 0 or 1. Thus the ith regression coefficient indicates the estimated increase in cash demand (expressed as a proportion of the weekly trend level) that is caused by the incidence of the event that the ith explanatory variables indicates. For example, a Tuesday in January that is not on or prior to a payday will have an estimated increase in demand of 5.32% of the general weekly trend level. From the first five coefficients one can see that the demand for cash rises through the week, peaking on Saturday (even though Saturday has shorter hours of operation than other days).

The Durbin–Watson statistic shows no significant autocorrelation of the residuals. Furthermore, a Box–Jenkins identification of the residuals was performed and, with only one exception, all the autocorrelations out to 60-day lags were within a 95% confidence interval about zero. In particular, for the five-day (one-week) lag, the autocorrelation was 0.01 and the partial autocorrelation was 0.00. At the 10-day (two-week) lag the autocorrelation and partial autocorrelation were both -0.02. This indicates that there is no observable effect on cash demand from weekly pay periods (as opposed to the semimonthly pay periods used in the regression). Furthermore, the lack of any significant autocorrelation structure indicates that the first two types

EXHIBIT 7.5 ESTIMATED REGRESSION COEFFICIENTS FOR DAILY DEMAND

i	Estimate	Standard Error	Dummy Variable Indicator for:
1	0.0532	0.0120†	Tuesday
2	0.0844	0.0144†	Wednesday
3	0.1139	0.0123†	Thursday
4	0.2358	0.0123†	Friday
5	0.2848	0.0121†	Saturday
6	0.0178	0.0138†	March
7	0.0375	0.0144†	April
8	0.0233	0.0139†	May
9	0.0349	0.0140†	June
10	0.0530	0.0139†	July
11	0.0193	0.0136†	August
12	0.0210	0.0140†	September
13	0.0291	0.0137†	October
14	0.1249	0.0148†	December
15	0.0931	0.0198†	Tuesday or Wednesday and payday
16	0.1285	0.0440†	Thursday and midmonth payday
17	0.1817	0.0439†	Thursday and month-end payday
18	0.0707	0.0261†	Friday and midmonth payday
19	0.1345	0.0263†	Friday and month-end payday
20	0.0936	0.0260†	Saturday and midmonth payday
21	0.0820	0.0254†	Saturday and month-end payday
22	−0.0207	0.0212	Thursday and payday earlier in week
23	−0.0505	0.0194†	Friday and payday earlier in week
24	−0.0377	0.0190*	Saturday and payday earlier in week
25	0.0481	0.0165†	Tuesday and payday later in week
26	0.0630	0.0171†	Wednesday and payday later in week
27	0.0546	0.0197†	Thursday and payday later in week
28	0.1336	0.0260†	Holiday occurs next day (May, June, July, August, September, and December only).

$R^2 = 0.5468$, 759 observations, Durbin–Watson statistic = 2.08.
*Significant at the 0.10 level.
†Significant at the 0.01 level.

of data discrepancies are either insignificant or occur at random lags. There was no evidence of heteroscedasticity, except for an increased variance of the residuals around Christmas.

Conclusions

This study provides an example of some of the limitations of Box–Jenkins (ARIMA) models. The cash flows exhibited cyclical variations, as one would expect, which can often be forecast successfully with ARIMA models. However, the cyclical structure was induced by the incidence of days of the week, paydays, and other observable variables that in fact can be used to construct the regression model. Thus the weekly data exhibit strong autocorrelations at four-week lags because monthly paydays occur about once every four weeks, and not because a high cash demand in one week tends to cause a high cash demand four weeks later. Since it is possible to identify a priori the exogenous variables that cause the autocorrelations, it is more sensible to use them directly in a regression model rather than make indirect inferences about their effect in an ARIMA model.

To illustrate this, examine Figure 7.31, which shows the fourth-order differences of weekly cash flows. There are three large peaks immediately followed by troughs, spread at 52-week intervals; these correspond to high cash demands just prior to Christmas. The low points result because January cash demands are smaller than December flows, and not so much because January flows are inherently small. In an ARIMA model one might be tempted to account for this with a 52nd order MA term, in effect hoping to use 52-week lagged cash flows to forecast what week of the year it is. It is much more efficient to model this effect directly with a dummy variable for December (or Christmas), rather than indirectly (and with error) by looking at 52-week lagged cash flows.

To make this point somewhat differently, note that the 52-week autocorrelation relationship from December to December is stronger than that from March to March. Similarly, the cash flow relationships at four-week lags have a different structure from December to January than from May to June. However, ARIMA models implicitly assume that there are no such distinctions, since they are stationary. Hence, a 52-week MA term in an ARIMA model would impose the same lagged correlations between successive Decembers as between successive Mays, understating the former and overstating the latter. Also, an ARIMA model with fourth-order differences to pickup monthly payday effects will be imposing the same relationship between mid-December and mid-January as occurs between a May payday week and the June payday week. Again, the result is to overstate the former effect and understate the latter. When dummy variables for calendar time effects are introduced in a regression model, these nonstationarities that foil ARIMA models are explicitly exploited in forecasting cash flows.[13]

Finally, to test the forecasting ability of the regression model, the first two years of data were used to re-estimate the coefficients of the model, using the same methods as discussed. This model was used to forecast cash flows in the third year. On the basis of Theil's inequality proportions one can conclude that the model's performance could not have been improved without further explanatory variables, and in general, the model performed well in tests of predictive ability.[14]

CASE 7.1   EASTERN ELECTRONICS COMPONENTS SYSTEMS (EECS). EECS is currently investigating a problem it has had with its forecasting of monthly revenues. EECS needs a forecasting model that will be useful for financial planning over horizons of three and six months (i.e., by the first of each month there should be available a forecast of revenues for the next three and the next six months). Its current system generates percentage errors of about 10% over the shorter horizon and 15% over the longer horizon. The three month forecast is used for the short-term management of each of the six divisions' working capital position. (This horizon is based on their typical maximum 90 day cycle of delivery to payment date.) The six month forecast will be used in planning EECS's borrowing and investment strategies.

In this case, part of the difficulty in generating accurate forecasts stems from the lack of easily available data. Also, because of the rapid expansion of EECS's western operations, data from before 1981 are not considered usable for prediction. The monthly revenue figures for EECS over the last 28 months (January, 1981 to April, 1983) are given in Exhibit 7.6.

Some preliminary statistical calculations have come up with the following regression equation, explaining revenues in month t, R_t, as a function of time, t.

$$R_t = 970.8 + 45.6t$$
$$\quad\;\;(23.82) \quad (18.57)$$

$$R^2 = .930; \text{D.W.} = 1.252; \sigma_u = 105.0$$

(As usual, the t statistics for each estimated coefficient are given in brackets underneath the estimated value.) Exhibit 7.7 gives a table of the actual values, forecast values, residuals, and percentage error for the available data period.

A second set of calculations is the correlations between R_t and a number of observable factors thought by management to be related to revenues. The most significant of these correlations are given in Exhibit 7.8. For example, from this table we can read that the correlation between this month's revenue and this month's accounts receivable is .877.

EXHIBIT 7.6 MONTHLY REVENUES AT EECS

Observation	Date	Monthly Revenue
1	1/81	1187.6
2	2/81	1075.5
3	3/81	1145.5
4	4/81	1247.0
5	5/81	1207.9
6	6/81	1275.5
7	7/81	1310.9
8	8/81	1274.5
9	9/81	1117.7
10	10/81	1242.3
11	11/81	1370.5
12	12/81	1386.0
13	1/82	1698.2
14	2/82	1751.4
15	3/82	1725.8
16	4/82	1671.0
17	5/82	1687.0
18	6/82	1818.8
19	7/82	1865.0
20	8/82	1831.4
21	9/82	1929.6
22	10/82	1838.2
23	11/82	2106.7
24	12/82	2071.4
25	1/83	2131.7
26	2/83	2135.0
27	3/83	2376.6
28	4/83	2218.1

EXHIBIT 7.7 REGRESSION RESULTS FOR EECS

Observation	Actual	Forecast	Residual	Percentage Error
1	1187.6	1016.4	171.2	16.85
2	1075.5	1062.0	13.5	1.27
3	1145.5	1107.6	37.9	3.42
4	1247.0	1153.2	93.8	8.14
5	1207.9	1198.8	9.1	0.76
6	1275.5	1244.4	31.1	2.50
7	1310.9	1290.0	20.9	1.62
8	1274.5	1335.6	−61.1	−4.57
9	1117.7	1381.2	−263.5	−19.08
10	1242.3	1426.8	−184.5	−12.93
11	1370.5	1472.4	−101.9	−6.92
12	1386.0	1518.0	−132.0	−8.70
13	1698.2	1562.6	134.6	8.61
14	1751.4	1609.2	142.2	8.83
15	1725.8	1654.8	71.0	4.29
16	1671.0	1700.4	−29.4	−1.73
17	1687.0	1746.0	−59.0	−3.38
18	1818.8	1791.6	27.2	1.52
19	1865.0	1837.3	27.7	1.51
20	1831.4	1882.9	−51.5	−2.73
21	1929.6	1928.5	1.1	0.06
22	1838.2	1974.0	−135.9	−6.88
23	2106.7	2019.7	87.0	4.31
24	2071.4	2065.3	6.1	0.30
25	2131.7	2110.9	20.8	0.99
26	2135.0	2156.5	−21.5	−1.00
27	2376.6	2202.1	174.5	7.92
28	2218.1	2247.7	−29.6	−1.32

EXHIBIT 7.8   CORRELATIONS WITH MONTHLY REVENUES FOR EECS

Variable	Correlation with R_t
Accounts Receivable:	
in month t	.877
in month $t-1$	.833
in month $t-2$	.712
in month $t-3$	.749
Accounts Payable:	
in month t	.495
in month $t-1$	.580
in month $t-2$	.289
in month $t-3$	.481
Inventory:	
in month t	.742
in month $t-1$	.721
in month $t-2$	.762
in month $t-3$	.713
Capital Expenditures:	
in month t	.881
in month $t-1$	.239
in month $t-2$	.265
in month $t-3$	.630.

Questions

1. What can you conclude from the results of the regression?
2. Given the preceding data, describe how you would approach constructing the required forecasting models, assuming that EECS wants a minimal 50% improvement over their current ad hoc forecasting results. (Describe what techniques you think would be useful, what other data you would consider acquiring, etc.)
3. Suppose the actual revenue figures for May 1983 to September 1983 were 2202.2, 2141.0, 2491.2, 2288.6, and 2210.1 respectively. What do these figures suggest about your answer to 1.?
4. After some questioning you discover that from August, 1981 to December, 1981, revenues were affected by extensive rennovations at a western production facility. How could you use this information to revise your answers to 1. and 2.?

NOTES

1. Helmer (1979) cites a survey showing that the Delphi method has generated very accurate forecasts.
2. Another interesting application of the Delphi method is Basu and Schroeder (1977), which deals with sales forecasting at American Hoist and Derrick. They were able to reduce absolute error to less than 1% in its first year of operation.
3. Chambers et al. (1971) provide an interesting example, using the historical pattern of black and white television growth to predict the sales potential of color television.
4. The smoothing coefficient can be related to the length of averaging in simple autoregressive model by the formula

$$\alpha = \frac{2}{n + 1}.$$

   This equates the average age of the data used in the two methods. See Plossl and Wight (1967).
5. The divisor is taken to be n for consistency with the rest of this chapter. If the mean is estimated, it is more common to divide by $(n - 1)$.
6. A rule of thumb relating the standard deviation to the mean absolute deviation is

$$\sigma_u = 1.25\text{MAD}.$$

   This is very useful in practice; see Plossl and Wight (1967).
7. Another criterion would be judging how well the forecast anticipates turning points. Wecker (1980) is one of the few attempts to formalize this approach.
8. When n is small, a better measure to use is the corrected R^2 given by

$$\bar{R}^2 = 1 - \frac{(1 - R^2)(n - 1)}{n - m}$$

   where m is the number of independent variables and n is the number of data points. This formula gives a penalty weight for the number of independent variables.
9. As will be clarified later, this means that the "partial autocorrelations" after the first are zero.
10. Here $\{x_t\}$ denotes $x_1, x_2, \ldots, x_T$.
11. For MA processes invertibility plays the same role that stationarity plays for AR processes.
12. Heteroscedasticity means that the variance of the residual series is not constant.
13. There have been a number of attempts to model calendar day effects within the Box–Jenkins methodology; see Liu (1980).
14. Boyd and Mabert (1977) present a model similar in structure for the forecasting of daily check volumes.

PROBLEMS

1. How can qualitative techniques (like the Delphi) be validated?

2. Give some common examples of forecasting by analogy.

3. Regression without the constant term.

   In many applications we know that the regression line must pass through the origin. For example, if we were regressing output (y) on total expenditure (x), we'd expect that zero expenditure leads to zero output.

   a. Develop the ordinary least squares estimator of a in the regression

   $$y = ax + u$$

   b. Does this regression line pass through $(\bar{x}, \bar{y})$?

4. Suppose we are given the following forecasting models:

   $$\text{Model A: } S_t^A = 0.6x_{t-1} - 0.4x_{t-2}$$
   $$\text{Model B: } S_t^B = 0.8x_{t-1} + 0.2S_{t-1} \ (S_1 = 2)$$

   Where the data for the 10 periods in question are:

t:	1	2	3	4	5	6	7	8	9	10
x_t:	2	−1	−1	0	2	3	3	2	1	0

   a. Rate the two models using four separate criteria.
   b. For each of the criteria given earlier, find a "business example" where this criterion would be appropriate.

5. Suppose we are given the following time series:

t:	1	2	3	4	5	6	7	8	9	10	11	12
y_t:	−3	1	1	4	−2	−1	0	4	−4	−1	1	4

   a. Use linear regression to estimate the coefficients a and b in the model

   $$y = a + bt.$$

   b. Determine the t-statistic for the slope coefficient. Is it significant at the 0.01 level?
   c. Does your answer to part b imply that the series is stationary? Explain.

6. If we are examining the residuals from a regression forecast and find that the Durbin–Watson statistic (d) is approximately 2, we may conclude that there is no significant autocorrelation in the residual series. (True or false?)

7. a. Explain why the Box–Jenkins (ARMA) models usually lead to better forecasts than the traditional approaches (e.g., exponential smoothing).

    b.   Stationary time series are more the exception than the rule in most business situations. Explain why this is true. Give examples from the "business" environment of stationary and nonstationary time series.

    c.   A time series can be nonstationary by having constantly increasing variance. Can you think of a transformation that may be able to get rid of this type of nonstationary?

8.   We have the following (stationary, zero mean) time series

$$x_1 = -2, \quad x_2 = 0, \quad x_3 = -1, \quad x_4 = 3, \quad x_5 = -6, \quad x_6 = 4, \quad x_7 = 2.$$

    Suppose we are testing the model (AR(2)) $x_t = x_{t-1}/2 + x_{t-2}/3$.

    a.   Calculate the $\hat{\rho}_1$, and $\hat{\rho}_2$ from the data and the ρ_1 and ρ_2 from the model.

    b.   Does your answer to part a suggest that the model is likely to fit well?

    c.   Generate $S_3, \ldots, S_7$ and compute σ_u for the series of residuals.

    d.   What is the connection between your answers to parts a and c?

9.   For the AR(1) model

$$x_t = \phi_1 x_{t-1} + u_t$$

    Estimates of ϕ_1 can be obtained through matching ρ_1 and $\hat{\rho}_1$ (viz., $\phi_1 = \hat{\rho}_1$) or through viewing this as a regression equation. Explain how these two estimates are related.

10. Show that (7.33) for $|\rho_1| < \frac{1}{2}$ has two solutions: one with absolute value greater than 1 and one with absolute value less than 1.

11. Restating slightly the random walk hypothesis (described in Section 7.2), we would say that the daily difference in security prices is white noise. If this hypothesis were true, what would a correlogram obtained from a time series of daily price changes look like? If there was a systematic effect due to the day of the week, what would this correlogram look like?

12. Verify that the Durbin–Watson statistic d [given by (A5)] is approximately $2(1 - \rho_1)$ where ρ_1 is the first autocorrelation of the residual series. Note that this allows us to translate the question of the significance of d to a question of the significance of ρ_1.

13. Note that formally $\gamma_j = E(x_j x_{t-j})$ if $E(x_t) = 0$. Thus for AR(1), $\gamma_1 = E(x_t x_{t-1})$. Using (7.23),

$$\begin{aligned}
\gamma_1 &= E[x_{t-1}(\phi_1 x_{t-1} + u_t)] \\
&= \phi_1 E(x_{t-1}^2) + E(x_{t-1} u_t) \\
&= \phi_1 \gamma_0,
\end{aligned}$$

since x_{t-1} and u_t are assumed independent. Hence

$$\rho_1 = \gamma_1/\gamma_0 = \phi_1.$$

Now use this approach to verify (7.24), (7.26), and (7.27).

8 Integrative Case Study

The following case study brings together all the aspects of current asset management discussed in the preceding chapters. Through the vehicle of the UTT Corporation, a fictitious firm, the various tools and techniques presented earlier can be applied. A brief narrative that describes the basic organization and funds flows is presented first. Numerous financial schedules and related operating data are also included. The case study is quite conductive to group work, and this approach is recommended.

Using the data and materials provided, prepare a comprehensive report to senior management of the UTT Corporation. Be sure to clearly show any other assumptions made in completing the study. The report, at a minimum, should

Analyze the firm's working capital position.

Evaluate existing current asset management policies.

Recommend modifications to existing practices and procedures, in implementable terms.

The Universal Truck and Tractor Corporation

The Universal Truck and Tractor Corporation (UTT) is a U.S.-based corporation with headquarters in New York City. The firm ranks in the lower half of the Fortune 1000 listing of corporations and is primarily involved with the manufacture, distribution, and sale of agricultural equipment and machinery.

Since its founding in 1904, UTT has developed a respectable market share although it is not the leader in its industry. Its products are considered to be of the highest quality, and its technical features are among the most advanced in the industry. The customers for UTT's products are regional dealers in the U.S. and major dealers in the overseas markets UTT taps through export as well as local sales efforts. Customers are extremely loyal and provide frequent suggestions for product enhancements and new market developments.

UTT has two major plants that manufacture products for worldwide marketing efforts. Both plants are located in the United States, one in upstate

New York (Syracuse) and the other in California (Turlock, a city near San Francisco). Both plants are quite large and are the leading employers in their communities. The plants have long enjoyed relative autonomy in their operations although some activities have traditionally been handled by central staff. Plants purchase supplies locally and handle their own payroll activities. Major purchases of raw materials and manufacturing equipment is made by central purchasing. Plants do not receive any customer check payments as this function is handled by a central staff credit and invoicing department.

Sales and marketing activities are performed by five local offices in the United States and a major office in Europe and Asia. The U.S. offices are located in New York City, Chicago, Atlanta, Los Angeles, and Houston. Overseas offices are in Brussels and Singapore.

The central credit and invoicing department is run by a credit manager and his staff. This department sets credit terms and policies for all customers, prepares and distributes invoices based on information from local sales orders and shipping documentation from both plants, and manages outstanding receivables, taking necessary dunning or follow-up actions. The central staff handles all export sales as well. Foreign sales representatives function in a similar manner to their domestic counterparts, making sales but then relaying all orders to New York for further processing. Any letters of credit or related types of sales are handled by the central staff group.

In the United States all customer payments are made by check, and the customers are instructed to make their payments to a central corporate lock box UTT maintains with its lead bank, Gotham Trust, in New York City. The bank delivers check copies, envelopes, and any other contents (such as invoices paid) to the credit staff daily. Local offices and salesmen receive checks from time to time but must send them to the lock box in New York for deposit.

Payables disbursements are processed by central accounting from information supplied by central purchasing and related staff departments. All checks are drawn on a disbursement account with Gotham Trust that is funded by the cash management department. Both plants maintain local disbursement accounts with large local banks in their cities, Upstate National (Syracuse) and West Coast National (California). Both accounts are funded by wire transfer weekly according to a schedule supplied to central cash management by local plant accountants.

Payrolls are handled by each plant locally with accounts at the same banks as indicated above. Funds are transferred to each account on pay day by cash management, based on a phone call one or two days prior to pay day from each plant payroll manager. The payrolls for the rest of the corporation in the United States are handled through a central payroll group with checks drawn on another New York bank, Metropolitan State Bank. The account is funded on payday by wire transfer from Gotham.

Export collections are received in two primary forms, check and wire transfer. UTT maintains four collection receiving accounts with banks in

New York City since transfers can come into any one of them. These banks are supposed to notify UTT treasury staff or credit staff when payments have been received. They typically notify the credit staff as this group has more frequent interaction with the bank's international department. The banks involved include Gotham Trust, Metropolitan State, New York National, and American International. All checks come into the credit staff and are sent to Gotham Trust for deposit or collection. A few checks have been received by the New York lock box as well. Foreign currency checks are purchased by Gotham at competitive exchange rates. Checks are usually received for payments of spare parts. Other sales are collected via wire transfer.

Daily the cash manager establishes cash positions at each major UTT bank. These include Gotham Trust, the plant banks, and all international receiving banks. Funds are moved to Gotham as a central cash "pool." Each bank is called by the cash manager or his assistant each morning to obtain the beginning balance for the current day's activity. The plants both call in any variations to their cash forecasts daily. By late morning the credit staff also provides the cash deposit figure for the current day based on a call from the lock box area of the bank. The credit staff will also usually send over a "buck slip" via internal mail to tell the cash manager of any international receipts (based on phone calls from the banks). The main account at Gotham is used to wire transfer funds to any other banks as necessary, and the cash manager completes these transfers by calling his bank account officer before noon daily with the details. International transfers are handled this way as well although they are often done in the afternoon.

Banking relations are handled by the treasurer although the credit manager must approve any changes in collections. UTT maintains lines of credit with each of its banks and keeps 10% in compensating balances. The company is not a constant borrower, doing so only as essential to fund seasonal funding needs.

In Belgium the UTT office deals with a large local Belgian bank (Bank of Belgium). All transactions are made through this bank, whose major U.S. correspondent bank is American International. The relationship is a long and valued one as the bank helped UTT set up its offices in Brussels and is quite helpful in supplying credit and other information on potential customers.

In Singapore the UTT office uses a local bank as well, the NPB Bank. As in Belgium, all transactions are made through this bank. Its major U.S. correspondent bank is West Coast National.

Spare parts inventories are maintained at both Brussels and Singapore. Each location maintains a stock of approximately 11,000 items. All items are shipped from New York City with the average time to Brussels being three weeks and Singapore six weeks. Written authorization from headquarters is required for all inventory replenishments with value more than U.S. $1 million. This sometimes (but usually) delays the order by about five days. Guidelines for inventory policies are established at headquarters. Inventory turnover targets are set at four per year on all items. Safety stocks are to be maintained at 25% of annual demand.

Receivables turnover are likewise set by headquarters and are also targeted at four per year. In Europe salesmen are paid fixed salaries while in Asia they are paid a small salary plus a commission on the U.S. dollar value of sales. Payments are to be made to Gotham or one of the other international collection banks. In the U.S. salesmen receive a regular salary plus a commission on all sales orders sent to New York.

The credit group has established standard policies for U.S. business. Overseas accounts past due are not now subject to any penalties, but each month New York sends dunning letters to major offenders. In some exceptional situations they will call the customer or even ask the local office to help. This contrasts with domestic U.S. policy which refuses to ship to any account more than 60 days past due and charges 4% over prime on those over 60 days past.

Standard terms are net 90 days in the United States and Europe. In Asia local trade credit standards are adopted, using the standard for the machinery industry.

Sales have shown only a slight increase in recent years. The sales trend during any given year tends to follow a typical seasonal pattern. The major peak is in the summer with a normal winter low point. The company's profits have been fairly stable over time. There are currently no major expansion plans.

The following exhibits provide basic data on banking, treasury, receivables, and inventory management functions.

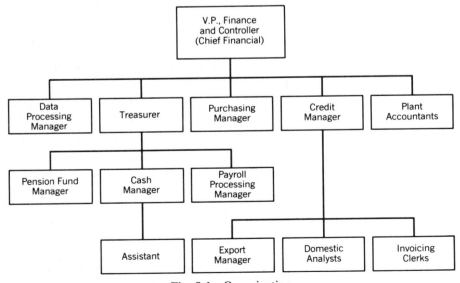

Fig. 8.1 Organization.

EXHIBIT 8.1 UTT CORPORATION FINANCIAL STATEMENTS ($ Million)

Balance Sheet

	1980	1981	1982
Cash and short-term investment	36.7	33.3	28.2
Accounts receivable	167.5	187.6	215.8
Inventory	45.5	52.5	60.5
Other current assets	2.5	2.7	2.3
Fixed assets	602.5	577.7	545.5
Total assets	854.7	853.8	852.3
Accounts payable	172.2	185.4	221.2
Notes payable	126.5	88.9	26.2
Current portion of LTD	29.1	31.2	33.2
Other current liabilities	1.7	1.9	1.8
Long-term debt	275.1	286.2	298.5
Total liabilities	604.6	593.6	580.9
Equity	250.1	260.2	271.4
Total Liabilities and equity	854.7	853.8	852.3

Profit and Loss Statement

	1980	1981	1982
Total revenues	700.0	730.0	765.0
Cost of goods sold	75.0	86.0	97.0
Total expenses	531.0	547.0	560.0
Net profit before taxes	94.0	97.0	108.0
Net interest income/(expense)	12.0	19.0	22.0
Depreciation	42.0	45.0	51.0

EXHIBIT 8.2 QUARTERLY SALES FIGURES (TOTAL COMPANY) (U.S. $ Millions)

Quarter	1980	1981	1982
1st	70	75	72
2nd	200	220	235
3rd	280	290	304
4th	150	145	150

EXHIBIT 8.3   QUARTERLY SALES FOR 1982 (US$ MILLIONS)

		Q1	Q2	Q3	Q4
United Kingdom	Spare parts	1.2	1.1	1.4	0.8
	Total sales	14.0	20.5	23.3	8.3
Germany	Spare parts	3.0	3.4	4.4	4.1
	Total sales	6.0	8.5	18.0	9.1
France	Spare parts	2.9	4.8	9.8	3.4
	Total sales	3.1	7.0	14.1	4.1
Malaysia	Spare parts	0.1	0.1	0.2	0.2
	Total sales	3.4	2.0	2.0	4.7
Australia	Spare parts	2.6	2.2	1.4	1.9
	Total sales	9.6	4.1	1.4	12.1
Korea	Spare parts	0.3	2.2	0.7	0.1
	Total sales	0.3	2.7	0.7	0.1
United States	Spare parts	20.2	29.4	40.4	25.1
	Total sales	35.6	190.2	244.5	115.6
Totals	Spare parts	30.3	43.2	58.3	35.6
	Total sales	72.0	235.0	304.0	154.0

EXHIBIT 8.4   RECEIVABLES AND SALES DATA (US$ MILLIONS)

		Receivables Aging (Year-End 1982)			
	Annual Sales	Current	0–30 Days OD	31–60 Days OD	More Than 60 Days OD
United Kingdom	66.1	13.6	5.1	0.8	0.2
Germany	41.6	10.1	0.8	0.4	0.0
France	28.3	8.2	4.3	1.1	0.6
Malaysia	12.1	4.3	0.3	0.0	0.0
Australia	27.2	5.8	0.0	0.0	0.0
Korea	3.8	0.4	0.3	0.1	0.0
United States	586.0	130.2	20.4	6.7	1.9

EXHIBIT 8.5 INVENTORY DATA

Location	Shipments	Value of Year's Shipments	Year-End Inventory Value
Singapore	16	13.1	5.4
Brussels	20	36.1	10.3

Data shown are for spare parts inventory for 1982. All figures are in millions of U.S. dollars.

EXHIBIT 8.6 DSOs FOR MACHINERY INDUSTRY

Australia	53.1
France	130.7
Germany	99.1
Korea	60.3
Malaysia	92.4
United Kingdom	112.3
United States	104.4

EXHIBIT 8.7 UTT CORPORATION CASH FORECAST ($000)

	Jan.	Feb.	Mar.	Apr.	May	June	July	Aug.	Sept.	Oct.	Nov.	Dec.	Year
Receipts													
Lock box deposits	29	28	24	22	46	47	51	75	82	73	65	53	595
Export payments	12	14	11	17	16	18	25	27	28	13	12	15	208
Total	41	42	35	39	62	65	76	102	110	86	77	68	803
Disbursements													
Accounts payable	68	83	78	64	56	47	49	47	62	51	40	71	716
Payrolls	4	4	4	4	4	5	5	5	4	4	4	5	52
Total	72	87	82	68	60	52	54	52	66	55	44	76	768
Net—in/(out)	(31)	(45)	(47)	(29)	2	13	22	50	44	31	33	(8)	35

EXHIBIT 8.8 BANKING AND TREASURY DATA

Average Bank Balances

Bank	Average ($000)	(Annual Averages)
Gotham		
Disbursement account	4400	
Lock box account	2000 (ledger)	500 (collected)
Main account	5000	
Upstate Nat'l		
Payroll	750	
Disbursement	250	
West Coast Nat'l		
Payroll	600	
Disbursement	200	
Metropolitan—Collections	2000	
New York Nat'l—Miscellaneous	1000	
American Int'l—Miscellaneous	3000	

Credit Lines	**($ millions)**
Gotham	50
Upstate	5
West Coast	5
Metropolitan	5
New York Nat'l	5
American	5

Average Payrolls	**($000)**
Syracuse	125
Turlock	100
All other	1000

EXHIBIT 8.9 FLOAT TIMES—CURRENT AND PROSPECTIVE COLLECTION POINTS

Sending Point	$Dep. ($000)	Days (Calendar)						
		Curr	Atl	Chi	L.A.	Hous	St.L.	Nwk
New York	480	4.3	4.6	4.3	4.7	4.5	4.5	4.0
Charlotte	100	4.6	3.7	3.9	4.4	4.3	4.0	4.1
Memphis	200	5.7	3.8	3.9	4.4	3.8	4.0	4.5
Cleveland	150	5.5	4.0	4.1	4.6	4.0	4.5	4.4
Atlanta	250	5.7	3.2	4.0	4.5	4.0	4.1	4.7
Chicago	280	6.2	3.8	3.1	4.2	3.9	3.8	4.5
St. Louis	190	5.6	3.9	4.0	4.3	4.1	2.9	4.2
Houston	210	6.7	3.8	4.4	4.7	2.9	3.9	4.5
Denver	230	7.1	4.3	5.0	4.1	4.0	4.3	4.8
Los Angeles	250	7.2	4.7	4.5	3.1	4.3	4.4	4.8

Volumes

Daily volume (average)	420 items for $2,300,000
Spare parts	400 items for 500,000 (Lock Box)
Equipment	20 items for 1,800,000

EXHIBIT 8.10 REQUIRED BALANCES FOR NONCREDIT SERVICES (TOTALS FOR EACH BANK)

Bank Name	Required Balance ($000)
Gotham	250
Upstate	75
West Coast	75
Metro	50
NY Nat'l	50
Amer. Intl.	50

EXHIBIT 8.11 EXPORT CHECKS AND COLLECTIONS

Checks

Source	Volume	$Dep (000)	Mail Time
U.K.	150	155	8.0
Germany	100	110	7.5
Malaysia	50	65	12.0
Australia	75	80	9.5
France	60	70	8.0

EXHIBIT 8.12 LOCAL OFFICE RECEIPTS (U.S.)

Office	$Dep (000)
New York	95
Chicago	70
Atlanta	60
Houston	80
Los Angeles	75

EXHIBIT 8.13 MONTHLY BORROWING/INVESTING ACTIVITIES

Month	Ave. Invest/(Borrow) ($000)
Jan.	(30)
Feb.	(60)
Mar.	(105)
Apr.	(125)
May	(125)
June	(110)
July	(95)
Aug.	(50)
Sept.	(10)
Oct.	20
Nov.	40
Dec.	30

Borrowings are at bank prime rate (11.0%). Investments are at 9.0%.

Case Discussions

CASE 4.1 JMP COMPANY. The primary problem dealt with here is that of maintaining local bank accounts with little control over the individual account balance levels. As a result, excess balance situations can arise. Revising systems of this sort is relatively easy to accomplish in theory but can be riddled with peripheral considerations or secondary problems. For instance, the loss of local autonomy will often create internal frictions between local financial personnel and the central cash management staff. Similarly, the maintenance of accounts for all locations with a single bank, while a logical solution to the problem, may not be possible due to branch banking regulations or the simple extent of the geographic spread of the company's operating locations. In dealing with problems like this, the need to identify pertinent data to be collected or reported on an ongoing basis is often overlooked entirely. The temptation to attempt a onetime "fix" will not be successful unless a means to monitor the future flows, levels, and so forth is properly established.

CASE 4.2 BC STORES. This case looks at the problem of concentrating funds from many diverse operating locations. The problem is, of course, similar to the retail collection problem described in Section 1.4. Any new system should improve or at least standardize current cash handling procedures while accommodating additional locations with minimal time and expense. Such a system should also be as automatic as possible so that the need for manual intervention by a central cash manager can be minimized. The setting shown is typical for firms that are just beginning to investigate cash management procedures and find no effective control over local cash management activities.

CASE 4.3 MUFFIN MAKERS INTERNATIONAL. This case offers a small-scale lock box study. Again, this is a typical setting for a firm with checks coming into its major offices. For a firm with lock boxes already in place, the methodology is still the same. For instance, if the two points in this case were considered as existing lock box points, the potential improvements for alternative sites over the present ones would be the result. For the sake of simplicity, float times are shown for mail, processing, and clearing as a combined number. The final network should be both cost-effective and simple to operate. The optimal arrangement is usually identified by heuristically adding points that should continue to improve float reduction. Also, it is useful to compute the *single*, best point in case the cash manager wishes to have just one lock box location. Further insights into the methodology of lock box studies are included in Section 2.2.

CASE 4.4 DAISY MANUFACTURING.   In this case a straightforward look at improved disbursement control is offered. Controlled disbursement services can have a substantial impact on the balances kept at a firm's operating banks, and this impact can be measured by the computation suggested in this case. This type of profile can be completed for one or more competing banks if desired. In this way, the cash manager or treasurer can effectively compare the potential benefits of the same service from one institution to another. It should be noted, also, that gathering the data to perform this sort of analysis can be somewhat time-consuming. Even if no changes are made, a better understanding of average clearance times should be obtained. This finding can then be used in planning daily cash needs on an ongoing basis.

CASE 4.5 JBK LTD.   This case provides a brief glimpse into cash scheduling and cash position management, the daily "number-crunching" activity of the cash manager. The success of the activity will be directly related to the accuracy and reliability of the short-term estimates. Also, the cash manager must develop and continually refine working rules or guidelines for handling variations in these estimates. As shown in this case, these rules should be fairly simple and conservative, favoring a "worst case" situation. They also should be developed by the cash manager based on recent experience. The cash manager should not, however, make sweeping changes without first investigating the sources of the variations. Otherwise, the rules may be in a continuous state of change and will offer little help in cash planning or cash position management.

CASE 4.6 PUFF DISTRIBUTORS.   Whatever the method of compensation, the cash manager should periodically evaluate bank service charges for the services provided by his or her banks. This case shows how this can be done. The data needed can usually be obtained from monthly account analysis statements provided by the banks, and average volumes over several months should be developed to assure comparability. An analysis of this sort can be performed to evaluate prospective services or to compare the costs of existing ones. In either case, the cash manager should be able to develop a quantitative perspective of the firm's cash management services.

CASE 4.7 TRIUMPH PRODUCTS.   Another common concern for most cash managers is the handling of short-term funding needs of the company. As shown in this case there are usually several alternative forms of this funding, each with its own limitations and rate differentials. Thus, the cash manager must establish an effective framework for the short-term funding activity and, in order to do so, must develop suitable guidelines. The accuracy and reliability of short-term cash flow projections can heavily influence these funding decisions. Wide variations can create problems for the cash manager.

CASE 4.8 JEFF-PARK, INC. This case deals with a problem that is becoming more common in occurrence as companies investigate the possible use of electronic banking services. The identification of key components and an objective appraisal of comparative costs and potential benefits are basic requirements in performing this type of analysis. The final result may not be clearcut; a conversion decision may depend on an increased payroll level, a majority of employees accepting a new electronic system, or further increases in the paper-based processing system already in place. The approach suggested by the case places these considerations in a useful framework for both current and future evaluation.

CASE 4.9 MALDWYN INTERNATIONAL. This case demonstrates the importance of effective target balance management. Target balances are especially important, of course, if compensation is on a collected balance basis. Targets will then be used in daily cash position management. Significant variations from targets should be minimized by daily monitoring of actual balances and adjusting balances accordingly. This usually entails using one key control-account at each major bank. Another aspect of target balances shown in the case is the minimum balance amount that must be maintained in any account. This can pose problems in adjusting balances for wide variations from target have occurred in that it may not be possible to reduce balances low enough to reduce the average balance to the desired target level. In such cases, the lowering must stay in place for a period of time in order to attain the average target level.

CASE 4.10 HILL-MILLS. This case deals with the question of compensating a company's banks by direct fees or collected balances. The comparative calculations are relatively straightforward. The case suggests a simple approach and deals with the question on a bank by bank basis. It also includes the consideration of non-interest time deposits as another means of compensation. It also deals with the possibility that the company may not be able to reduce its balances fully. The case deals with this issue of compensation by fee for both credit and non-credit services. Often as is shown or suggested in the case, these may be two separate questions for the cash manager to answer.

CASE 5.1 ABC BANK. Using the 1982 data:

$$x_1 = .630$$
$$x_2 = .097$$
$$x_3 = 3.407$$

so that

$$Z = 5.185$$

which is positive, indicating that XZY Corporation's application should be accepted.

While this technique offers some clear advantages (speed, simplicity, objectivity, and quantification of risk exposure), it seems a poor choice for this application. While in other cases this type of analysis has proven a very useful input to the loan granting decision, it is probably of little value here. Some of the problems that deserve mention include:

Why is there no consideration of the size, purpose, or maturity of the loan being requested? (Other aspects of the loan agreement such as pricing, collateral, etc. are also clearly pertinent.)

Classical discriminant analysis shouldn't be used since the prior probabilities of classification are not equal and neither are the costs of classification errors.

Choosing the last 100 may lead to a bias. It is too small a sample and there is no holdout sample (a test of the model on data that were not used in its estimation) to validate the model.

There is a bias in that we have estimated the model only from applicants that were previously granted loans.

A single cutoff score shouldn't be used; there should be a range of uncertainty.

CASE 5.2 NATIONAL P.B. BOARD. This case is basically an exercise in the computation of working capital ratios. A particularly significant ratio in this example is the receivables turnover ratio, indicating possible noncompliance with the stated net 30 terms. A number of the aggregate measures could also be applied here. The Altman Z-score model (see Section 7.5) is usable; see also problem 7.

CASE 6.1 THE MANAGEMENT OF BLOOD SUPPLIES.

1. The mean is 120 and the standard deviation is 33.33.
2. The policy curve extends from $R = 120$ ($S = .500$, $A = 0$) to $R = 200$ ($S = .008$, $A = .400$). The minimal value of R for which $S \leq .05$ can easily be determined from the curve. To compute it more exactly,

$$R = 120 + 1.645(33.33) \simeq 175.$$

3. We now have a "lead time" of two weeks since after an order is placed there is a lag of two weeks before any corrective action can have an affect on the blood supplies. The next opportunity to order is one week away and the newly introduced delay before delivery adds another week. To compute the revised value of the standard deviation we need to determine the variability of the two week demand. Since we have here assumed that weekly demands are independent, the variance of the two week demand is merely twice the

variance of the one week demand. Hence the standard deviation is 47.136 and

$$R = 120 + 1.645(47.136) \simeq 198.$$

CASE 7.1   EECS.

1. The regression results point out a significant positive trend in monthly revenues. The R^2 is excellent; the F and t statistics are significant at the .005 level. The only problem is the low Durbin-Watson statistic. This is partially explained in 4 below.

2. The data in Exhibit 7.8 suggest that a regression approach might be useful with inventory and accounts receivable (as well as time) as independent variables. While the correlation between capital expenditures and R_t is high, there is no sound economic reason for including this in the forecasting model. It would also be interesting to apply first differencing to the R_t series and attempt to fit a Box-Jenkins model to the data. It turns out that an MA(2) model, i.a., is reasonable.

3. The fact that the residuals are negative and the percentage errors are quite high suggests that the forecast growth is overestimating the actual growth.

4. One approach would be to rerun the regression with a dummy variable for these five months. Note that this additional information helps explain why the original Durbin-Watson statistic is so low. The five consecutive negative residuals contribute to the positive autocorrelation of the residuals which drives the d statistic down.

A Basic Statistical Concepts

This appendix gives a very brief review of the statistical definitions utilized within this book. We will use the sales data of Example 7.2 to demonstrate the basic measures.

Given a set of n observations $x_1, x_2, \ldots, x_n$ the mean (expected value, average value) of x is

$$E(x) = \frac{x_1 + \cdots + x_n}{n} = \bar{x}.$$

For the data of Example 7.2

$$E(x) = \frac{2.5 + \cdots + 3.6}{7} = 3.0.$$

So the average month of sales should be 3.0.

To obtain a concept of the variability (spread, dispersion) of x, the most important measure is the variance:

$$\text{var}(x) = E(X - \bar{x})^2 = E(x^2) - [E(x)]^2 = \sigma_x^2$$

For our example,

$$\text{var}(x) = \frac{2.5^2 + \cdots + 3.6^2}{7} - 3^2 = 0.2714.$$

Exercise. Verify this result by using the alternative form of var(x). (See notes 5 and 6 of Chapter 7.) The square root of the variance, the standard deviation, is also an important measure of dispersion.

When dealing with two random variables, x and y, we are often concerned with their "degree of association": how much information about x is contained in y. This is measured by the covariance between x and y:

$$cov(x,y) = E[(x - \bar{x})(y - \bar{y})].$$

In our example,

$$cov(x,y) = \frac{(-0.5)(-3) + \cdots + (0.6)(3)}{7} = 0.857.$$

To standardize the covariance, we define the correlation between x and y:

$$corr(x,y) = \frac{cov(x,y)}{\sigma_x \sigma_y} = \rho_{x,y}.$$

For our example,

$$\rho_{x,y} = \frac{0.857}{(0.5210)(2)} = 0.822.$$

The correlation coefficient ($\rho_{x,y}$) is always between -1 and 1. The extreme points indicate perfect predictability (knowing the value of x means that the value of y can be determined without error); a correlation near zero means approximate independence (knowing the value of x is almost useless in attempting to find the value of y).

For a given set of data it is thus simple to compute these statistical measures. We now turn to a pair of theoretical distributions that are important as models of random outcomes: the Poisson and the normal distributions.

The Poisson Distribution

The most common model for discrete demand is the Poisson distribution. For properties see, for example, Ross (1972). If the random variable X has a Poisson distribution with parameter $\lambda > 0$, the probability that $X = i$ is

$$P(X = i) = e^{-\lambda}\left(\frac{\lambda^i}{i!}\right) \qquad i = 0, 1, 2, \ldots .$$

Here $e = 2.71828$ (the base of the natural logarithm) and

$$i! = i \cdot (i - 1) \ldots 2 \cdot 1$$

if i is a positive integer. By definition $0! = 1$. (Here X is an example of counting process; its only possible values are nonnegative integers.)

Exercise. If demand has a Poisson distribution with $\lambda = 4$, verify that the probability demand exceeds 4 is 0.3712.

A great advantage of the Poisson is that

$$\lambda = E(X) = \text{var}(X).$$

This, in estimating the mean an estimate of the variance is obtained without further effort. In addition, the Poisson has been shown to be an appropriate model for approximating discrete demand; see Peterson and Silver (1979).

The Normal Distribution

The Poisson distribution is an example of a distribution where we can attach a probability to each possible outcome. For a random variable with a very large number of possibilities this becomes very cumbersome. The alternative is a continuous distribution, where we define the probabilities of an outcome between two possible values. For example, with the normal distribution, the probability of obtaining an outcome within one standard deviation of the mean is about 0.6826; see Table A, Appendix C, for the values of the normal.

The normal distribution is the most common model for a continuous distribution for a number of reasons. The normal is uniquely characterized by its mean and variance (which makes estimation easy). The sum of two normals is still normal (as is the sum of two Poissons). More precisely, if x is normally distributed with mean μ_x and variance σ_x^2 and y is normally distributed with mean μ_y and variance σ_y^2, then $x + y$ is normally distributed with mean $\mu_x + \mu_y$ and variance $\sigma_x^2 + \sigma_y^2 + 2 \text{ cov }(x,y)$. Finally, the normal distribution is a limit of many other distributions. For example, if we take a Poisson with a large mean, then it can be accurately approximated by a normal with the same mean and variance. See Figure A.1 for a sketch of a normal and a Poisson with mean and variance equal to 4.

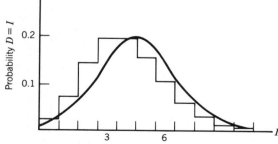

Fig. A.1 Poisson and normal distributions with mean and variance of four.

APPENDIX B Formulas for Regression

This appendix gives the formulas for the t-statistics and standard error of the forecast for a regression with one independent variable. Derivations of these and more general cases are found in, for example, Draper and Smith (1966).

We assume each u_i is independent and normally distributed with mean zero and variance σ_u^2 (notationally, $u_i \sim N[0, \sigma_u^2]$). Now $\hat{a}_0$ and $\hat{a}_1$ are also normally distributed (more exactly, the sampling distributions of $\hat{a}_0$ and $\hat{a}_1$ are normally distributed) with means a_0 and a_1, respectively, and variances

$$s_{a_0}^2 = \hat{\sigma}_u^2 \sum_{i=1}^{n} (y_i)^2 / n \sum_{i=1}^{n} (y_i - \bar{y})^2 \tag{A.1}$$

and

$$s_{a_1}^2 = \frac{\hat{\sigma}_u^2}{\displaystyle\sum_{i=1}^{n} (y_i - \bar{y})^2} \tag{A.2}$$

where

$$\hat{\sigma}_u^2 = \frac{\displaystyle\sum_{i=1}^{n} (\hat{u}_i)^2}{n - 2}. \tag{A.3}$$

Note that in (A.3) we divide by $(n - 2)$ so that $\hat{\sigma}_u^2$ is unbiased. The standard error of $\hat{a}_0$ and $\hat{a}_1$ is defined to be the square root of (A.1) and (A.2), respectively.

Thus the t-statistic is the estimate (normally distributed) divided by its standard error. The name arises from the fact that this statistic follows the t-distribution; see, for example, Hogg and Craig (1959) for discussion.

In Example 7.2, to compute t_{a_0} (the t-statistic for the constant term in the regression) we compute

$$\hat{\sigma}_u^2 = \frac{(-0.142)^2 + \cdots + (0.042)^2}{5} = 0.123$$

$$\Sigma(y_i^2) = (1^2 + 2^2 + \cdots + 7^2) = 140$$

and

$$\Sigma(y_i - \bar{y})^2 = 28.$$

Thus, using (A.1),

$$s_{a_0}^2 = \frac{0.123 \cdot 140}{7 \cdot 28} = 0.088$$

so that

$$t_{a_0} = \frac{2.144}{(0.088)^{1/2}} = 7.233$$

Comparing this value to the entries in Table B, Appendix C, with five degrees of freedom (from seven data points and two estimated parameters, a_0 and a_1), we conclude that t_{a_0} is significant at the 0.005 level.

Exercise. Compute t_{a_1}. Is it also significant at the 0.005 level? What is your interpretation of the results of the t-test?

We also utilize the concept of the standard error of the forecast. If we specify a value of the independent variable y, the standard error of the regression is

$$\hat{\sigma}_u\left(1 + \left(\frac{1}{n}\right) + \left[\frac{(y - \bar{y})^2}{\sum\limits_{i=1}^{n} (y_i - \bar{y})^2}\right]\right)^{1/2}. \qquad (A.4)$$

Here note that $\bar{y}$ is calculated "within the sample," i.e., from the data used to generate the estimated regression, and y is "out of sample," i.e., not from these data. It is clear that the best predictions are for y near $\bar{y}$; when we extrapolate further we have less confidence in the prediction. In Example 7.2, to obtain the standard error of the forecast at $y = 8$,

$$(0.123)^{1/2}\left(1 + \left(\frac{1}{7}\right) + \left(\frac{4^2}{28}\right)\right)^{1/2} = 0.459.$$

Exercise. What is the standard error calculated at $y = 10$?

The Durbin–Watson Statistic

Again, assume that the n residuals $\hat{u}_1, \ldots, \hat{u}_n$ are known. The d-statistic is computed via

$$d = \frac{\sum\limits_{t=2}^{n} (\hat{u}_t - \hat{u}_{t-1})^2}{\sum\limits_{t=1}^{n} (\hat{u}_t^2)}. \tag{A.5}$$

This statistic is closely related to ρ_1 defined in Section 7.5. If the u_t are independent, then d has an expected value of 2. [This is easy to verify:

$$(u_t - u_{t-1})^2 = u_t^2 + u_{t-1}^2 - 2u_t u_{t-1} \approx u_t^2 + u_{t-1}^2$$

since $u_t u_{t-1}$ has an expected value of zero if the u_t are independent. Then, ignoring the fact that the summations are over slightly different values of t, we find that $d \approx 2$.]

The variance of d depends on n (the number of observations) and k' (the number of independent variables). For Example 7.2,

$$d = \frac{(0.142 + 0.572)^2 + \cdots + (-0.228 + 0.042)^2}{(0.142)^2 + \cdots + (-0.042)^2}$$

$$= 2.269.$$

The critical values of d are tabulated in most forecasting texts. Since there is usually no entry for $n = 7$, we use $n = 15$, for illustration. With $k' = 1$, $d_l = 0.95$, and $d_u = 1.23$. There are three possible cases:

1. If $d < d_l$ or $(4 - d_l) < d$, then we reject the hypothesis of no autocorrelation.
2. If $d > d_u$ and $d < (4 - d_u)$, then we accept the hypothesis of no autocorrelation.
3. If neither case 1 nor 2 applies, then the test is inconclusive; we neither accept nor reject the hypothesis of no autocorrelation.

In Example 7.2, $d = 2.269 > d_l$ and $(4 - d_l) > d$, so case 1 does not apply; $2.269 > d_u$ and $2.269 < (4 - d_u)$ so that case 2 applies and we accept the hypothesis of no autocorrelation. (For another approach to this question see problem 12, Chapter 7.)

APPENDIX C Statistical Tables

TABLE A AREAS UNDER THE NORMAL CURVE

An entry in the table is the proportion under the entire curve that is between $z = 0$ and a positive value of z. Areas for negative values of z are obtained by symmetry.

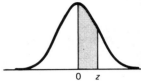

Second decimal place of z

z	.00	.01	.02	.03	.04	.05	.06	.07	.08	.09
0.0	.0000	.0040	.0080	.0120	.0160	.0199	.0239	.0279	.0319	.0359
0.1	.0398	.0438	.0478	.0517	.0557	.0596	.0636	.0675	.0714	.0753
0.2	.0793	.0832	.0871	.0910	.0948	.0987	.1026	.0164	.1103	.1141
0.3	.1179	.1217	.1255	.1293	.1331	.1368	.1406	.1443	.1480	.1517
0.4	.1554	.1591	.1628	.1664	.1700	.1736	.1772	.1808	.1844	.1879
0.5	.1915	.1950	.1985	.2019	.2054	.2088	.2123	.2157	.2190	.2224
0.6	.2257	.2291	.2324	.2357	.2389	.2422	.2454	.2486	.2517	.2549
0.7	.2580	.2611	.2642	.2673	.2703	.2734	.2764	.2794	.2823	.2852
0.8	.2881	.2910	.2939	.2967	.2995	.3023	.3051	.3078	.3106	.3133
0.9	.3159	.3186	.3212	.3238	.3264	.3289	.3315	.3340	.3365	.3389
1.0	.3413	.3438	.3461	.3485	.3508	.3531	.3554	.3577	.3599	.3621
1.1	.3643	.3665	.3686	.3708	.3729	.3749	.3770	.3790	.3810	.3830
1.2	.3849	.3869	.3888	.3907	.3925	.3944	.3962	.3980	.3997	.4015
1.3	.4032	.4049	.4066	.4082	.4099	.4115	.4131	.4147	.4162	.4177
1.4	.4192	.4207	.4222	.4236	.4251	.4265	.4279	.4292	.4306	.4319
1.5	.4332	.4345	.4357	.4370	.4382	.4394	.4406	.4418	.4429	.4441
1.6	.4452	.4463	.4474	.4484	.4495	.4505	.4515	.4525	.4535	.4545
1.7	.4554	.4564	.4573	.4582	.4591	.4599	.4608	.4616	.4625	.4633
1.8	.4641	.4649	.4656	.4664	.4671	.4678	.4686	.4693	.4699	.4706
1.9	.4713	.4719	.4726	.4732	.4738	.4744	.4750	.4756	.4761	.4767
2.0	.4772	.4778	.4783	.4788	.4793	.4798	.4803	.4808	.4812	.4817
2.1	.4821	.4826	.4830	.4834	.4838	.4842	.4846	.4850	.4854	.4857
2.2	.4861	.4864	.4868	.4871	.4875	.4878	.4881	.4884	.4887	.4890
2.3	.4893	.4896	.4898	.4901	.4904	.4906	.4909	.4911	.4913	.4916
2.4	.4918	.4920	.4922	.4925	.4927	.4929	.4931	.4932	.4934	.4936
2.5	.4938	.4940	.4941	.4943	.4945	.4946	.4948	.4949	.4951	.4952
2.6	.4953	.4955	.4956	.4957	.4959	.4960	.4961	.4962	.4963	.4964
2.7	.4965	.4966	.4967	.4968	.4969	.4970	.4971	.4972	.4973	.4974
2.8	.4974	.4975	.4976	.4977	.4977	.4978	.4979	.4979	.4980	.4981
2.9	.4981	.4982	.4982	.4983	.4984	.4984	.4985	.4985	.4986	.4986
3.0	.4987	.4987	.4987	.4988	.4988	.4989	.4989	.4989	.4990	.4990

Source: Donald J. Koosis, Business Statistics *(New York: John Wiley & Sons, 1972). Reprinted by permission.*

TABLE B STUDENT *t* DISTRIBUTION

The first column lists the number of degrees of freedom (*k*). The headings of the other columns give probabilities (*P*) for *t* to exceed the entry value. Use symmetry for negative *t* values.

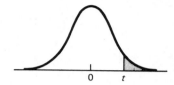

df \ P	.10	.05	.025	.01	.005
1	3.078	6.314	12.706	31.821	63.657
2	1.886	2.920	4.303	6.965	9.925
3	1.638	2.353	3.182	4.541	5.841
4	1.533	2.132	2.776	3.747	4.604
5	1.476	2.015	2.571	3.365	4.032
6	1.440	1.943	2.447	3.143	3.707
7	1.415	1.895	2.365	2.998	3.499
8	1.397	1.860	2.306	2.896	3.355
9	1.383	1.833	2.262	2.821	3.250
10	1.372	1.812	2.228	2.764	3.169
11	1.363	1.796	2.201	2.718	3.106
12	1.356	1.782	2.179	2.681	3.055
13	1.350	1.771	2.160	2.650	3.012
14	1.345	1.761	2.145	2.624	2.977
15	1.341	1.753	2.131	2.602	2.947
16	1.337	1.746	2.120	2.583	2.921
17	1.333	1.740	2.110	2.567	2.898
18	1.330	1.734	2.101	2.552	2.878
19	1.328	1.729	2.093	2.539	2.861
20	1.325	1.725	2.086	2.528	2.845
21	1.323	1.721	2.080	2.518	2.831
22	1.321	1.717	2.074	2.508	2.819
23	1.319	1.714	2.069	2.500	2.807
24	1.318	1.711	2.064	2.492	2.797
25	1.316	1.708	2.060	2.485	2.787
26	1.315	1.706	2.056	2.479	2.779
27	1.314	1.703	2.052	2.473	2.771
28	1.313	1.701	2.048	2.467	2.763
29	1.311	1.699	2.045	2.462	2.756
30	1.310	1.697	2.042	2.457	2.750
40	1.303	1.684	2.021	2.423	2.704
60	1.296	1.671	2.000	2.390	2.660
120	1.289	1.658	1.980	2.358	2.617
∞	1.282	1.645	1.960	2.326	2.576

Source: Donald J. Koosis, Business Statistics (New York: John Wiley & Sons, 1972). Reprinted by permission.

TABLE C   VALUES OF THE F-TEST

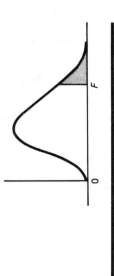

Degrees of Freedom for Numerator (df_1)

Degrees of Freedom for Denominator (df_2)	1	2	3	4	5	6	7	8	9	10	11	12	14	16	20	24	30	40	50	75	100	200	500	∞
1	161	200	216	225	230	234	237	239	241	242	243	244	245	246	248	249	250	251	252	253	253	254	254	254
	4052	*4999*	*5403*	*5625*	*5764*	*5859*	*5928*	*5981*	*6022*	*6056*	*6082*	*6106*	*6142*	*6169*	*6208*	*6234*	*6258*	*6286*	*6302*	*6323*	*6334*	*6352*	*6361*	*6366*
2	18.51	19.00	19.16	19.25	19.30	19.33	19.36	19.37	19.38	19.39	19.40	19.41	19.42	19.43	19.44	19.45	19.46	19.47	19.47	19.48	19.49	19.49	19.50	19.50
	98.49	*99.01*	*99.17*	*99.25*	*99.30*	*99.33*	*99.34*	*99.36*	*99.38*	*99.40*	*99.41*	*99.42*	*99.43*	*99.44*	*99.45*	*99.46*	*99.47*	*99.48*	*99.48*	*99.49*	*99.49*	*99.49*	*99.50*	*99.50*
3	10.13	9.55	9.28	9.12	9.01	8.94	8.88	8.84	8.81	8.78	8.76	8.74	8.71	8.69	8.66	8.64	8.62	8.60	8.58	8.57	8.56	8.54	8.54	8.53
	34.12	*30.81*	*29.46*	*28.71*	*28.24*	*27.91*	*27.67*	*27.49*	*27.34*	*27.23*	*27.13*	*27.05*	*26.92*	*26.83*	*26.69*	*26.60*	*26.50*	*26.41*	*26.30*	*26.27*	*26.23*	*26.18*	*26.14*	*26.12*
4	7.71	6.94	6.59	6.39	6.26	6.16	6.09	6.04	6.00	5.96	5.93	5.91	5.87	5.84	5.80	5.77	5.74	5.71	5.70	5.68	5.66	5.65	5.64	5.63
	21.20	*18.00*	*16.69*	*15.98*	*15.52*	*15.21*	*14.98*	*14.80*	*14.66*	*14.54*	*14.45*	*14.37*	*14.24*	*14.15*	*14.02*	*13.93*	*13.83*	*13.74*	*13.69*	*13.61*	*13.57*	*13.52*	*13.48*	*13.46*
5	6.61	5.79	5.41	5.19	5.05	4.95	4.88	4.82	4.78	4.74	4.70	4.68	4.64	4.60	4.56	4.53	4.50	4.46	4.44	4.42	4.40	4.38	4.37	4.36
	16.26	*13.27*	*12.06*	*11.39*	*10.97*	*10.67*	*10.45*	*10.27*	*10.15*	*10.05*	*9.96*	*9.89*	*9.77*	*9.68*	*9.55*	*9.47*	*9.38*	*9.29*	*9.24*	*9.17*	*9.13*	*9.07*	*9.04*	*9.02*
6	5.99	5.14	4.76	4.53	4.39	4.28	4.21	4.15	4.10	4.06	4.03	4.00	3.96	3.92	3.87	3.84	3.81	3.77	3.75	3.72	3.71	3.69	3.68	3.67
	13.74	*10.92*	*9.78*	*9.15*	*8.75*	*8.47*	*8.26*	*8.10*	*7.98*	*7.87*	*7.79*	*7.72*	*7.60*	*7.52*	*7.39*	*7.31*	*7.23*	*7.14*	*7.09*	*7.02*	*6.99*	*6.94*	*6.90*	*6.88*
7	5.59	4.74	4.35	4.12	3.97	3.87	3.79	3.73	3.68	3.63	3.60	3.57	3.52	3.49	3.44	3.41	3.38	3.34	3.32	3.29	3.28	3.25	3.24	3.23
	12.25	*9.55*	*8.45*	*7.85*	*7.46*	*7.19*	*7.00*	*6.84*	*6.71*	*6.62*	*6.54*	*6.47*	*6.35*	*6.27*	*6.15*	*6.07*	*5.98*	*5.90*	*5.85*	*5.78*	*5.75*	*5.70*	*5.67*	*5.65*
8	5.32	4.46	4.07	3.84	3.69	3.58	3.50	3.44	3.39	3.34	3.31	3.28	3.23	3.20	3.15	3.12	3.08	3.05	3.03	3.00	2.98	2.96	2.94	2.93
	11.26	*8.65*	*7.59*	*7.01*	*6.63*	*6.37*	*6.19*	*6.03*	*5.91*	*5.82*	*5.74*	*5.67*	*5.56*	*5.48*	*5.36*	*5.28*	*5.20*	*5.11*	*5.06*	*5.00*	*4.96*	*4.91*	*4.88*	*4.86*
9	5.12	4.26	3.86	3.63	3.48	3.37	3.29	3.23	3.18	3.13	3.10	3.07	3.02	2.98	2.93	2.90	2.86	2.82	2.80	2.77	2.76	2.73	2.72	2.71
	10.56	*8.02*	*6.99*	*6.42*	*6.06*	*5.80*	*5.62*	*5.47*	*5.35*	*5.26*	*5.18*	*5.11*	*5.00*	*4.92*	*4.80*	*4.73*	*4.64*	*4.56*	*4.51*	*4.45*	*4.41*	*4.36*	*4.33*	*4.31*
10	4.96	4.10	3.71	3.48	3.33	3.22	3.14	3.07	3.02	2.97	2.94	2.91	2.86	2.82	2.77	2.74	2.70	2.67	2.64	2.61	2.59	2.56	2.55	2.54
	10.04	*7.56*	*6.55*	*5.99*	*5.64*	*5.39*	*5.21*	*5.06*	*4.95*	*4.85*	*4.78*	*4.71*	*4.60*	*4.52*	*4.41*	*4.33*	*4.25*	*4.17*	*4.12*	*4.05*	*4.01*	*3.96*	*3.93*	*3.91*

Note: 5% points for the distribution of F are presented in roman type; 1% points are in italic type.

Source: Donald J. Koosis, Business Statistics (New York: John Wiley & Sons, 1972). Reprinted by permission.

TABLE C Continued

Degrees of Freedom for Numerator (df_1)

Degrees of Freedom for Denominator (df_2)	1	2	3	4	5	6	7	8	9	10	11	12	14	16	20	24	30	40	50	75	100	200	500	∞
11	4.84 / 9.65	3.98 / 7.20	3.59 / 6.22	3.36 / 5.67	3.20 / 5.32	3.09 / 5.07	3.01 / 4.88	2.95 / 4.74	2.90 / 4.63	2.86 / 4.54	2.82 / 4.46	2.79 / 4.40	2.74 / 4.29	2.70 / 4.21	2.65 / 4.10	2.61 / 4.02	2.57 / 3.94	2.53 / 3.86	2.50 / 3.80	2.47 / 3.74	2.45 / 3.70	2.42 / 3.66	2.41 / 3.62	2.40 / 3.60
12	4.75 / 9.33	3.88 / 6.93	3.49 / 5.95	3.26 / 5.41	3.11 / 5.06	3.00 / 4.82	2.92 / 4.65	2.85 / 4.50	2.80 / 4.39	2.76 / 4.30	2.72 / 4.22	2.69 / 4.16	2.64 / 4.05	2.60 / 3.98	2.54 / 3.86	2.50 / 3.78	2.46 / 3.70	2.42 / 3.61	2.40 / 3.56	2.36 / 3.49	2.35 / 3.46	2.32 / 3.41	2.31 / 3.38	2.30 / 3.36
13	4.67 / 9.07	3.80 / 6.70	3.41 / 5.74	3.18 / 5.20	3.02 / 4.86	2.92 / 4.62	2.84 / 4.44	2.77 / 4.30	2.72 / 4.19	2.67 / 4.10	2.63 / 4.02	2.60 / 3.96	2.55 / 3.85	2.51 / 3.78	2.46 / 3.67	2.42 / 3.59	2.38 / 3.51	2.34 / 3.42	2.32 / 3.37	2.28 / 3.30	2.26 / 3.27	2.24 / 3.21	2.22 / 3.18	2.21 / 3.16
14	4.60 / 8.86	3.74 / 6.51	3.34 / 5.56	3.11 / 5.03	2.96 / 4.69	2.85 / 4.46	2.77 / 4.28	2.70 / 4.14	2.65 / 4.03	2.60 / 3.94	2.56 / 3.86	2.53 / 3.80	2.48 / 3.70	2.44 / 3.62	2.39 / 3.51	2.35 / 3.43	2.31 / 3.34	2.27 / 3.26	2.24 / 3.21	2.21 / 3.14	2.19 / 3.11	2.16 / 3.06	2.14 / 3.02	2.13 / 3.00
15	4.54 / 8.68	3.68 / 6.36	3.29 / 5.42	3.06 / 4.89	2.90 / 4.56	2.79 / 4.32	2.70 / 4.14	2.64 / 4.00	2.59 / 3.89	2.55 / 3.80	2.51 / 3.73	2.48 / 3.67	2.43 / 3.56	2.39 / 3.48	2.33 / 3.36	2.29 / 3.29	2.25 / 3.20	2.21 / 3.12	2.18 / 3.07	2.15 / 3.00	2.12 / 2.97	2.10 / 2.92	2.08 / 2.89	2.07 / 2.87
16	4.49 / 8.53	3.63 / 6.23	3.24 / 5.29	3.01 / 4.77	2.85 / 4.44	2.74 / 4.20	2.66 / 4.03	2.59 / 3.89	2.54 / 3.78	2.49 / 3.69	2.45 / 3.61	2.42 / 3.55	2.37 / 3.45	2.33 / 3.37	2.28 / 3.25	2.24 / 3.18	2.20 / 3.10	2.16 / 3.01	2.13 / 2.96	2.09 / 2.89	2.07 / 2.86	2.04 / 2.80	2.02 / 2.77	2.01 / 2.75
17	4.45 / 8.40	3.59 / 6.11	3.20 / 5.18	2.96 / 4.67	2.81 / 4.34	2.70 / 4.10	2.62 / 3.93	2.55 / 3.79	2.50 / 3.68	2.45 / 3.59	2.41 / 3.52	2.38 / 3.45	2.33 / 3.35	2.29 / 3.27	2.23 / 3.16	2.19 / 3.08	2.15 / 3.00	2.11 / 2.92	2.08 / 2.86	2.04 / 2.79	2.02 / 2.76	1.99 / 2.70	1.97 / 2.67	1.96 / 2.65
18	4.41 / 8.28	3.55 / 6.01	3.16 / 5.09	2.93 / 4.58	2.77 / 4.25	2.66 / 4.01	2.58 / 3.85	2.51 / 3.71	2.46 / 3.60	2.41 / 3.51	2.37 / 3.44	2.34 / 3.37	2.29 / 3.27	2.25 / 3.19	2.19 / 3.07	2.15 / 3.00	2.11 / 2.91	2.07 / 2.83	2.04 / 2.78	2.00 / 2.71	1.98 / 2.68	1.95 / 2.62	1.93 / 2.59	1.92 / 2.57
19	4.38 / 8.18	3.52 / 5.93	3.13 / 5.01	2.90 / 4.50	2.74 / 4.17	2.63 / 3.94	2.55 / 3.77	2.48 / 3.63	2.43 / 3.52	2.38 / 3.43	2.34 / 3.36	2.31 / 3.30	2.26 / 3.19	2.21 / 3.12	2.15 / 3.00	2.11 / 2.92	2.07 / 2.84	2.02 / 2.76	2.00 / 2.70	1.96 / 2.63	1.94 / 2.60	1.91 / 2.54	1.90 / 2.51	1.88 / 2.49
20	4.35 / 8.10	3.49 / 5.85	3.10 / 4.94	2.87 / 4.43	2.71 / 4.10	2.60 / 3.87	2.52 / 3.71	2.45 / 3.56	2.40 / 3.45	2.35 / 3.37	2.31 / 3.30	2.28 / 3.23	2.23 / 3.13	2.18 / 3.05	2.12 / 2.94	2.08 / 2.86	2.04 / 2.77	1.99 / 2.69	1.96 / 2.63	1.92 / 2.56	1.90 / 2.53	1.87 / 2.47	1.85 / 2.44	1.84 / 2.42
21	4.32 / 8.02	3.47 / 5.78	3.07 / 4.87	2.84 / 4.37	2.68 / 4.04	2.57 / 3.81	2.49 / 3.65	2.42 / 3.51	2.37 / 3.40	2.32 / 3.31	2.28 / 3.24	2.25 / 3.17	2.20 / 3.07	2.15 / 2.99	2.09 / 2.88	2.05 / 2.80	2.00 / 2.72	1.96 / 2.63	1.93 / 2.58	1.89 / 2.51	1.87 / 2.47	1.84 / 2.42	1.82 / 2.38	1.81 / 2.36
22	4.30 / 7.94	3.44 / 5.72	3.05 / 4.82	2.82 / 4.31	2.66 / 3.99	2.55 / 3.76	2.47 / 3.59	2.40 / 3.45	2.35 / 3.35	2.30 / 3.26	2.26 / 3.18	2.23 / 3.12	2.18 / 3.02	2.13 / 2.94	2.07 / 2.83	2.03 / 2.75	1.98 / 2.67	1.93 / 2.58	1.91 / 2.53	1.87 / 2.46	1.84 / 2.42	1.81 / 2.37	1.80 / 2.33	1.78 / 2.31
23	4.28 / 7.88	3.42 / 5.66	3.03 / 4.76	2.80 / 4.26	2.64 / 3.94	2.53 / 3.71	2.45 / 3.54	2.38 / 3.41	2.32 / 3.30	2.28 / 3.21	2.24 / 3.14	2.20 / 3.07	2.14 / 2.97	2.10 / 2.89	2.04 / 2.78	2.00 / 2.70	1.96 / 2.62	1.91 / 2.53	1.88 / 2.48	1.84 / 2.41	1.82 / 2.37	1.79 / 2.32	1.77 / 2.28	1.76 / 2.26
24	4.26 / 7.82	3.40 / 5.61	3.01 / 4.72	2.78 / 4.22	2.62 / 3.90	2.51 / 3.67	2.43 / 3.50	2.36 / 3.36	2.30 / 3.25	2.26 / 3.17	2.22 / 3.09	2.18 / 3.03	2.13 / 2.93	2.09 / 2.85	2.02 / 2.74	1.98 / 2.66	1.94 / 2.58	1.89 / 2.49	1.86 / 2.44	1.82 / 2.36	1.80 / 2.33	1.76 / 2.27	1.74 / 2.23	1.73 / 2.21

TABLE C Continued

Degrees of Freedom for Numerator (df_1)

Degrees of Freedom for Denominator (df_2)	1	2	3	4	5	6	7	8	9	10	11	12	14	16	20	24	30	40	50	75	100	200	500	∞
25	4.24 / 7.77	3.38 / 5.57	2.99 / 4.68	2.76 / 4.18	2.60 / 3.86	2.49 / 3.63	2.41 / 3.46	2.34 / 3.32	2.28 / 3.21	2.24 / 3.13	2.20 / 3.05	2.16 / 2.99	2.11 / 2.89	2.06 / 2.81	2.00 / 2.70	1.96 / 2.62	1.92 / 2.54	1.87 / 2.45	1.84 / 2.40	1.80 / 2.32	1.77 / 2.29	1.74 / 2.23	1.72 / 2.19	1.71 / 2.17
26	4.22 / 7.72	3.37 / 5.53	2.98 / 4.64	2.74 / 4.14	2.59 / 3.82	2.47 / 3.59	2.39 / 3.42	2.32 / 3.29	2.27 / 3.17	2.22 / 3.09	2.18 / 3.02	2.15 / 2.96	2.10 / 2.86	2.05 / 2.77	1.99 / 2.66	1.95 / 2.58	1.90 / 2.50	1.85 / 2.41	1.82 / 2.36	1.78 / 2.28	1.76 / 2.25	1.72 / 2.19	1.70 / 2.15	1.69 / 2.13
27	4.21 / 7.68	3.35 / 5.49	2.96 / 4.60	2.73 / 4.11	2.57 / 3.79	2.46 / 3.56	2.37 / 3.39	2.30 / 3.26	2.25 / 3.14	2.20 / 3.06	2.16 / 2.98	2.13 / 2.93	2.08 / 2.83	2.03 / 2.74	1.97 / 2.63	1.93 / 2.55	1.88 / 2.47	1.84 / 2.38	1.80 / 2.33	1.76 / 2.25	1.74 / 2.21	1.71 / 2.16	1.68 / 2.12	1.67 / 2.10
28	4.20 / 7.64	3.34 / 5.45	2.95 / 4.57	2.71 / 4.07	2.56 / 3.76	2.44 / 3.53	2.36 / 3.36	2.29 / 3.23	2.24 / 3.11	2.19 / 3.03	2.15 / 2.95	2.12 / 2.90	2.06 / 2.80	2.02 / 2.71	1.96 / 2.60	1.91 / 2.52	1.87 / 2.44	1.81 / 2.35	1.78 / 2.30	1.75 / 2.22	1.72 / 2.18	1.69 / 2.13	1.67 / 2.09	1.65 / 2.06
29	4.18 / 7.60	3.33 / 5.42	2.93 / 4.54	2.70 / 4.04	2.54 / 3.73	2.43 / 3.50	2.35 / 3.33	2.28 / 3.20	2.22 / 3.08	2.18 / 3.00	2.14 / 2.92	2.10 / 2.87	2.05 / 2.77	2.00 / 2.68	1.94 / 2.57	1.90 / 2.49	1.85 / 2.41	1.80 / 2.32	1.77 / 2.27	1.73 / 2.19	1.71 / 2.15	1.68 / 2.10	1.65 / 2.06	1.64 / 2.03
30	4.17 / 7.56	3.32 / 5.39	2.92 / 4.51	2.69 / 4.02	2.53 / 3.70	2.42 / 3.47	2.34 / 3.30	2.27 / 3.17	2.21 / 3.06	2.16 / 2.98	2.12 / 2.90	2.09 / 2.84	2.04 / 2.74	1.99 / 2.66	1.93 / 2.55	1.89 / 2.47	1.84 / 2.38	1.79 / 2.29	1.76 / 2.24	1.72 / 2.16	1.69 / 2.13	1.66 / 2.07	1.64 / 2.03	1.62 / 2.01
32	4.15 / 7.50	3.30 / 5.34	2.90 / 4.46	2.67 / 3.97	2.51 / 3.66	2.40 / 3.42	2.32 / 3.25	2.25 / 3.12	2.19 / 3.01	2.14 / 2.94	2.10 / 2.86	2.07 / 2.80	2.02 / 2.70	1.97 / 2.62	1.91 / 2.51	1.86 / 2.42	1.82 / 2.34	1.76 / 2.25	1.74 / 2.20	1.69 / 2.12	1.67 / 2.08	1.64 / 2.02	1.61 / 1.98	1.59 / 1.96
34	4.13 / 7.44	3.28 / 5.29	2.88 / 4.42	2.65 / 3.93	2.49 / 3.61	2.38 / 3.38	2.30 / 3.21	2.23 / 3.08	2.17 / 2.97	2.12 / 2.89	2.08 / 2.82	2.05 / 2.76	2.00 / 2.66	1.95 / 2.58	1.89 / 2.47	1.84 / 2.38	1.80 / 2.30	1.74 / 2.21	1.71 / 2.15	1.67 / 2.08	1.64 / 2.04	1.61 / 1.98	1.59 / 1.94	1.57 / 1.91
36	4.11 / 7.39	3.26 / 5.25	2.86 / 4.38	2.63 / 3.89	2.48 / 3.58	2.36 / 3.35	2.28 / 3.18	2.21 / 3.04	2.15 / 2.94	2.10 / 2.86	2.06 / 2.78	2.03 / 2.72	1.98 / 2.62	1.93 / 2.54	1.87 / 2.43	1.82 / 2.35	1.78 / 2.26	1.72 / 2.17	1.69 / 2.12	1.65 / 2.04	1.62 / 2.00	1.59 / 1.94	1.56 / 1.90	1.55 / 1.87
38	4.10 / 7.35	3.25 / 5.21	2.85 / 4.34	2.62 / 3.86	2.46 / 3.54	2.35 / 3.32	2.26 / 3.15	2.19 / 3.02	2.14 / 2.91	2.09 / 2.82	2.05 / 2.75	2.02 / 2.69	1.96 / 2.59	1.92 / 2.51	1.85 / 2.40	1.80 / 2.32	1.76 / 2.22	1.71 / 2.14	1.67 / 2.08	1.63 / 2.00	1.60 / 1.97	1.57 / 1.90	1.54 / 1.86	1.53 / 1.84
40	4.08 / 7.31	3.23 / 5.18	2.84 / 4.31	2.61 / 3.83	2.45 / 3.51	2.34 / 3.29	2.25 / 3.12	2.18 / 2.99	2.12 / 2.88	2.07 / 2.80	2.04 / 2.73	2.00 / 2.66	1.95 / 2.56	1.90 / 2.49	1.84 / 2.37	1.79 / 2.29	1.74 / 2.20	1.69 / 2.11	1.66 / 2.05	1.61 / 1.97	1.59 / 1.94	1.55 / 1.88	1.53 / 1.84	1.51 / 1.81
42	4.07 / 7.27	3.22 / 5.15	2.83 / 4.29	2.59 / 3.80	2.44 / 3.49	2.32 / 3.26	2.24 / 3.10	2.17 / 2.96	2.11 / 2.86	2.06 / 2.77	2.02 / 2.70	1.99 / 2.64	1.94 / 2.54	1.89 / 2.46	1.82 / 2.35	1.78 / 2.26	1.73 / 2.17	1.68 / 2.08	1.64 / 2.02	1.60 / 1.94	1.57 / 1.91	1.54 / 1.85	1.51 / 1.80	1.49 / 1.78
44	4.06 / 7.24	3.21 / 5.12	2.82 / 4.26	2.58 / 3.78	2.43 / 3.46	2.31 / 3.24	2.23 / 3.07	2.16 / 2.94	2.10 / 2.84	2.05 / 2.75	2.01 / 2.68	1.98 / 2.62	1.92 / 2.52	1.88 / 2.44	1.81 / 2.32	1.76 / 2.24	1.72 / 2.15	1.66 / 2.06	1.63 / 2.00	1.58 / 1.92	1.56 / 1.88	1.52 / 1.82	1.50 / 1.78	1.48 / 1.75
46	4.05 / 7.21	3.20 / 5.10	2.81 / 4.24	2.57 / 3.76	2.42 / 3.44	2.30 / 3.22	2.22 / 3.05	2.14 / 2.92	2.09 / 2.82	2.04 / 2.73	2.00 / 2.66	1.97 / 2.60	1.91 / 2.50	1.87 / 2.42	1.80 / 2.30	1.75 / 2.22	1.71 / 2.13	1.65 / 2.04	1.62 / 1.98	1.57 / 1.90	1.54 / 1.86	1.51 / 1.80	1.48 / 1.76	1.46 / 1.72

TABLE C Continued

Degrees of Freedom for Numerator (df_1)

Degrees of Freedom for Denominator (df_2)	1	2	3	4	5	6	7	8	9	10	11	12	14	16	20	24	30	40	50	75	100	200	500	∞
48	4.04 / 7.19	3.19 / 5.08	2.80 / 4.22	2.56 / 3.74	2.41 / 3.42	2.30 / 3.20	2.21 / 3.04	2.14 / 2.90	2.08 / 2.80	2.03 / 2.71	1.99 / 2.64	1.96 / 2.58	1.90 / 2.48	1.86 / 2.40	1.79 / 2.28	1.74 / 2.20	1.70 / 2.11	1.64 / 2.02	1.61 / 1.96	1.56 / 1.88	1.53 / 1.84	1.50 / 1.78	1.47 / 1.73	1.45 / 1.70
50	4.03 / 7.17	3.18 / 5.06	2.79 / 4.20	2.56 / 3.72	2.40 / 3.41	2.29 / 3.18	2.20 / 3.02	2.13 / 2.88	2.07 / 2.78	2.02 / 2.70	1.98 / 2.62	1.95 / 2.56	1.90 / 2.46	1.85 / 2.39	1.78 / 2.26	1.74 / 2.18	1.69 / 2.10	1.63 / 2.00	1.60 / 1.94	1.55 / 1.86	1.52 / 1.82	1.48 / 1.76	1.46 / 1.71	1.44 / 1.68
55	4.02 / 7.12	3.17 / 5.01	2.78 / 4.16	2.54 / 3.68	2.38 / 3.37	2.27 / 3.15	2.18 / 2.98	2.11 / 2.85	2.05 / 2.75	2.00 / 2.66	1.97 / 2.59	1.93 / 2.53	1.88 / 2.43	1.83 / 2.35	1.76 / 2.23	1.72 / 2.15	1.67 / 2.06	1.61 / 1.96	1.58 / 1.90	1.52 / 1.82	1.50 / 1.78	1.46 / 1.71	1.43 / 1.66	1.41 / 1.64
60	4.00 / 7.08	3.15 / 4.98	2.76 / 4.13	2.52 / 3.65	2.37 / 3.34	2.25 / 3.12	2.17 / 2.95	2.10 / 2.82	2.04 / 2.72	1.99 / 2.63	1.95 / 2.56	1.92 / 2.50	1.86 / 2.40	1.81 / 2.32	1.75 / 2.20	1.70 / 2.12	1.65 / 2.03	1.59 / 1.93	1.56 / 1.87	1.50 / 1.79	1.48 / 1.74	1.44 / 1.68	1.41 / 1.63	1.39 / 1.60
65	3.99 / 7.04	3.14 / 4.95	2.75 / 4.10	2.51 / 3.62	2.36 / 3.31	2.24 / 3.09	2.15 / 2.93	2.08 / 2.79	2.02 / 2.70	1.98 / 2.61	1.94 / 2.54	1.90 / 2.47	1.85 / 2.37	1.80 / 2.30	1.73 / 2.18	1.68 / 2.09	1.63 / 2.00	1.57 / 1.90	1.54 / 1.84	1.49 / 1.76	1.46 / 1.71	1.42 / 1.64	1.39 / 1.60	1.37 / 1.56
70	3.98 / 7.01	3.13 / 4.92	2.74 / 4.08	2.50 / 3.60	2.35 / 3.29	2.23 / 3.07	2.14 / 2.91	2.07 / 2.77	2.01 / 2.67	1.97 / 2.59	1.93 / 2.51	1.89 / 2.45	1.84 / 2.35	1.79 / 2.28	1.72 / 2.15	1.67 / 2.07	1.62 / 1.98	1.56 / 1.88	1.53 / 1.82	1.47 / 1.74	1.45 / 1.69	1.40 / 1.63	1.37 / 1.56	1.35 / 1.53
80	3.96 / 6.96	3.11 / 4.88	2.72 / 4.04	2.48 / 3.56	2.33 / 3.25	2.21 / 3.04	2.12 / 2.87	2.05 / 2.74	1.99 / 2.64	1.95 / 2.55	1.91 / 2.48	1.88 / 2.41	1.82 / 2.32	1.77 / 2.24	1.70 / 2.11	1.65 / 2.03	1.60 / 1.94	1.54 / 1.84	1.51 / 1.78	1.45 / 1.70	1.42 / 1.65	1.38 / 1.57	1.35 / 1.52	1.32 / 1.49
100	3.94 / 6.90	3.09 / 4.82	2.70 / 3.98	2.46 / 3.51	2.30 / 3.20	2.19 / 2.99	2.10 / 2.82	2.03 / 2.69	1.97 / 2.59	1.92 / 2.51	1.88 / 2.43	1.85 / 2.36	1.79 / 2.26	1.75 / 2.19	1.68 / 2.06	1.63 / 1.98	1.57 / 1.89	1.51 / 1.79	1.48 / 1.73	1.42 / 1.64	1.39 / 1.59	1.34 / 1.51	1.30 / 1.46	1.28 / 1.43
125	3.92 / 6.84	3.07 / 4.78	2.68 / 3.94	2.44 / 3.47	2.29 / 3.17	2.17 / 2.95	2.08 / 2.79	2.01 / 2.65	1.95 / 2.56	1.90 / 2.47	1.86 / 2.40	1.83 / 2.33	1.77 / 2.23	1.72 / 2.15	1.65 / 2.03	1.60 / 1.94	1.55 / 1.85	1.49 / 1.75	1.45 / 1.68	1.39 / 1.59	1.36 / 1.54	1.31 / 1.46	1.27 / 1.40	1.25 / 1.37
150	3.91 / 6.81	3.06 / 4.75	2.67 / 3.91	2.43 / 3.44	2.27 / 3.13	2.16 / 2.92	2.07 / 2.76	2.00 / 2.62	1.94 / 2.53	1.89 / 2.44	1.85 / 2.37	1.82 / 2.30	1.76 / 2.20	1.71 / 2.12	1.64 / 2.00	1.59 / 1.91	1.54 / 1.83	1.47 / 1.72	1.44 / 1.66	1.37 / 1.56	1.34 / 1.51	1.29 / 1.43	1.25 / 1.37	1.22 / 1.33
200	3.89 / 6.76	3.04 / 4.71	2.65 / 3.88	2.41 / 3.41	2.26 / 3.11	2.14 / 2.90	2.05 / 2.73	1.98 / 2.60	1.92 / 2.50	1.87 / 2.41	1.83 / 2.34	1.80 / 2.28	1.74 / 2.17	1.69 / 2.09	1.62 / 1.97	1.57 / 1.88	1.52 / 1.79	1.45 / 1.69	1.42 / 1.62	1.35 / 1.53	1.32 / 1.48	1.26 / 1.39	1.22 / 1.33	1.19 / 1.28
400	3.86 / 6.70	3.02 / 4.66	2.62 / 3.83	2.39 / 3.36	2.23 / 3.06	2.12 / 2.85	2.03 / 2.69	1.96 / 2.55	1.90 / 2.46	1.85 / 2.37	1.81 / 2.29	1.78 / 2.23	1.72 / 2.12	1.67 / 2.04	1.60 / 1.92	1.54 / 1.84	1.49 / 1.74	1.42 / 1.64	1.38 / 1.57	1.32 / 1.47	1.28 / 1.42	1.22 / 1.32	1.16 / 1.24	1.13 / 1.19
1000	3.85 / 6.66	3.00 / 4.62	2.61 / 3.80	2.38 / 3.34	2.22 / 3.04	2.10 / 2.82	2.02 / 2.66	1.95 / 2.53	1.89 / 2.43	1.84 / 2.34	1.80 / 2.26	1.76 / 2.20	1.70 / 2.09	1.65 / 2.01	1.58 / 1.89	1.53 / 1.81	1.47 / 1.71	1.41 / 1.61	1.36 / 1.54	1.30 / 1.44	1.26 / 1.38	1.19 / 1.28	1.13 / 1.19	1.08 / 1.11
∞	3.84 / 6.64	2.99 / 4.60	2.60 / 3.78	2.37 / 3.32	2.21 / 3.02	2.09 / 2.80	2.01 / 2.64	1.94 / 2.51	1.88 / 2.41	1.83 / 2.32	1.79 / 2.24	1.75 / 2.18	1.69 / 2.07	1.64 / 1.99	1.57 / 1.87	1.52 / 1.79	1.46 / 1.69	1.40 / 1.59	1.35 / 1.52	1.28 / 1.41	1.24 / 1.36	1.17 / 1.25	1.11 / 1.15	1.00 / 1.00

References

ABA Banking Journal, "Cash Management Will Change in the 80's—with or without the Banks," December 1980.

Altman, Edward I., "Financial Ratios, Discriminant Analysis and Prediction of Corporate Bankruptcy," *Journal of Finance*, **23**, No. 4, 1968.

Altman, Edward I., "Commercial Bank Lending: Process, Credit Scoring, and Costs of Errors in Lending," *Journal of Financial and Quantitative Analysis*, November 1980.

Altman, Edward I., Robert B. Avery, Robert A. Eisenbeis, and Joseph F. Sinkey, Jr., *Application of Classification Techniques in Business, Banking, and Finance*, JAI Press, Greenwich, Conn., 1981.

American Institute of Certified Public Accountants, "Audit Considerations in Electronic Funds Transfer Systems,' 1980.

Andrews, V. L., "Cash Management: An Overview for the Corporate Treasurer," *Cash Management Forum*, January 1975 (Supplementary Report).

Ang, James S., Jess H. Chua, and Ronald Sellers, "Generating Cash Flow Estimates: An Actual Study Using the Delphi Technique," *Financial Management*, Winter 1979.

Armstrong, J. Scott, *Long Range Forecasting: From Crystal Ball to Computer*, Wiley, New York, 1978.

Austin, Larry M., "Project EOQ": A Success Story in Implementing Academic Research," *Interfaces*, **7**, No. 4, August 1977.

Babbit, Roy, "Discussion: Are Changes Needed in the Bankruptcy Act?" in *The Changing Universe of Retail Credit*, **2**, NYU Institute of Retail Management, New York, 1982.

Basu, Shankar, and R. G. Schroeder, "Incorporating Judgements in Sales Forecasts: Application of the Delphi Method at American Hoist and Derrick," *Interfaces*, **7**, No. 3, May 1977.

Beardsley, George, and Edwin Mansfield, "A Note on the Accuracy of Industrial Forecasts of the Profitability of New Products and Processes," *Journal of Business*, **51**, No. 1, September 1979.

Beehler, P. J., *Contemporary Cash Management*, Wiley, New York, 1983.

Beehler, P. J., "Crocker's Automated Money Transfer System," *Bank Administration*, April 1979.

Benton, J. B., "Electronic Funds Transfer: Pitfalls and Payoffs," *Harvard Business Review*, July–August 1977.

Beranek, William, "Financial Implications of Lot-Size Inventory Models," *Management Science*, **13**, No. 8, April 1967.

Berry, Bryan H., "Detroit Automakers Slim Down Inventories to Beef Up Profits," *Iron Age*, August 20, 1982.

Bierce, A. H., "Retail Cash Management at J. C. Penney Co. Inc.," *Journal of Cash Management*, October 1981.

Bock, Robert H., "Measuring Cost Parameters in Inventory Models," *Management Technology*, **4**, No. 1, June 1964.

Bonocore, J. J., "Getting a Picture of Cash Management," *Financial Executive*, May 1980.

Box, G. E. P., and G. M. Jenkins, *Time Series Analysis, Forecasting, and Control*, Holden-Day, San Francisco, 1970.

Boyd, K., and Vincent A. Mabert, "A Two Stage Forecasting Approach at Chemical Bank of New York for Check Processing," *Journal of Bank Research*, Summer 1977.

Business Week, "Making Millions by Stretching the Float," November 23, 1974.

Business Week, "Cash Management: The New Art of Wringing More Profit from Corporate Funds," March 13, 1978.

Business Week, "A New Expense: Clearing Checks," August 3, 1981.

Canen, Alberto Gabbay, and Roberto D. Galvao, "An Application of ABC Analysis to Control Imported Material," *Interfaces*, **10**, No. 4, August 1980.

Carfang, A. J., "What Bank Deregulation Will Cost Treasurers," *Cashflow*, June 1982.

Carfang, A. J., "How Treasurers Can Cope with Deregulation," *Cashflow*, July–August 1982.

Cashflow, "Commercial Collectors Find Boom and Bust as Recession Hits," May 1982.

Chace, S., "Checkless Banking Gains with Spread of Electronic Funds-Transfer Network," *Wall Street Journal*, December 26, 1980.

Chambers, John C., Satinder Mullick, and Donald D. Smith, "How to Choose the Right Forecasting Technique," *Harvard Business Review*, July–August 1971.

Churchhill, Gilbert A., Jr., John R. Nevin, and R. Richard Watson, "The Role of Credit Scoring in the Credit Decision," *The Credit World*, March 1977.

Churchill, Gilbert A., Jr., John R. Nevin, and R. Richard Watson, "Developing a Credit Scoring Model," *The Credit World*, April 1977.

Cole, Robert H., *Consumer and Commercial Credit Management*, 6th Ed., Richard D. Irwin, Inc., Homewood, Ill. 1980.

Connelly, J., "Is Aggressive Cash Management a Myth?" *Institutional Investor*, May 1978.

Corcoran, A. W., "The Use of Exponentially-Smoothed Matrices to Improve Forecasting of Cash Flows from Accounts Receivable," *Management Science*, **24**, No. 7, March 1978.

Cyert, R. M., H. J. Davidson, and G. L. Thompson, "Estimation of the Allowance for Doubtful Accounts by Markov Chains," *Management Science*, **8**, August 1962.

DeSalvo, A., "Cash Management Converts Dollars into Working Assets, *Harvard Business Review*, May–June 1972.

Dory, John P., and Robert J. Lord, "Does TF Really Work?" *Harvard Business Review*, November–December 1970.

Draper, N. R., and H. Smith, *Applied Regression Analysis*, Wiley, New York, 1966.

Dudick, Thomas S., and Ross Cornell, *Inventory Control for the Financial Executive*, Wiley, New York, 1979.

Eisenbeis, Robert A., "Selection and Disclosure of Reasons for Adverse Action in Credit-Granting Systems," *Federal Reserve Bulletin*, September 1980.

Erdevig, E., "Deposit Service—New Tool for Cash Management," *Business Condition*, April 1980.

Fama, Eugene F., "The Behavior of Stock Market Prices," *Journal of Business*, **38**, January 1965.

Federal Reserve Bank, "Pricing of, and Access to, Federal Reserve Bank Services," Staff Memo, December 5, 1980.

Federal Reserve Bank of Kansas City, "Security and Control of Fund Transfer," undated publication.

Federal Reserve Bank of Richmond, "The Federal Reserve at Work," undated publication.

Federal Reserve Bank of San Francisco, "Regional Check Processing Centers," undated publication.

Fetter, Robert B., and Winston C. Dalleck, *Decision Models for Inventory Management*, Richard D. Irwin, Homewood, Ill., 1961.

Fisher, D. I., "Cash Management," *The Conference Board*, 1973.

Flowers, A. Dale, and James B. O'Neill II, "An Application of Classical Inventory Analysis to a Spare Parts Inventory," *Interfaces*, **8**, No. 2, February 1978.

Frydman, Halina, J. G. Kallberg, and D. L. Kao, "The Application of Markov Chain and Mover-Stayer Models to an Empirical Analysis of Credit Behavior," NYU, Faculty of Business Administration, Working Paper, 1983.

Gage, T. J., "Desktop Computers Enter Cash Management," *Cashflow*, September 1982.

Gardner, Everette S., Jr., "Box-Jenkins vs. Multiple Regression: Some Adventures in Forecasting the Demand for Blood Tests," *Interfaces*, **9**, No. 4, August 1979.

Gardner, Everette S., Jr., "Inventory Theory and the Gods of Olympus," *Interfaces*, **10**, No. 4, August 1980.

Gardner, Everette S., Jr., and David G. Dannenbring, "Using Optimal Policy Surfaces to Analyze Aggregate Inventory Tradeoffs," *Management Science*, **25**, No. 8, August 1979.

George, John A., "Discounting a Slow-Moving Stock Item," *Interfaces*, **12**, No. 4, August 1982.

Giannotti, J. B., and R. W. Smith, *Treasury Management*, Ronald Press (Wiley), 1981.

Gitman, L. J., E. A. Moses, and I. T. White, "An Assessment of Corporate Cash Management Practices," *Financial Management*, Spring 1979.

Goodman, L., "Talking Computers—Where Cash Management Services are Going," *Cashflow*, September 1981.

Grandinetti, J. F., "Netting Boosts Multinational Cash Flow," *Cashflow*, January–February 1983.

Granger, C. W. J., *Forecasting in Business and Economics*, Academic Press, New York, 1980.

Greguras, F. M., "Corporate EFT: Vulnerabilities and Other Audit Considerations," *Presentation*, December 10, 1980.

Groff, Gene K., "Empirical Comparison of Models for Short-Range Forecasting," *Management Science*, **20**, No. 1, September 1973.

Hadley, G., and T. W. Whitin, *Analysis of Inventory Systems*, Prentice-Hall, Englewood Cliffs, N.J., 1963.

Haley, Charles W., and Robert C. Higgins, "Inventory Control Theory and Trade Credit Financing," *Management Science*, **20**, No. 4, December 1973.

Hall, R. A., "Where EFT in Wholesale Banking Stands Today, and Where It's Going," *Banking*, May 1978.

Harvey, J. C., "Direct Pricing vs. Compensating Balances," *Financial Executive*, October 1974.

Helmer, Olaf, "The Utility of Long-term Forecasting," in *Forecasting: TIMS Studies in the Management Sciences*, Vol. 12, S. Makridakis and S. Wheelwright, eds., North-Holland, Amsterdam, 1979.

Herron, David P., "Managing Physical Distribution for Profit," *Harvard Business Review*, May–June 1979.

Hershauer, J. C., "A Productivity Audit of Lock Box Service Quality: First National Bank of Chicago," *Bank Administration*, October 1978.

Hettenhouse, George W., and Jack R. Wentworth, "Credit Analysis Model—A New Look for Credit Scoring," *Journal of Commercial Bank Lending,* December 1971.

Hill, Ned C. and K. D. Riener, "Determining the Cash Discount in the Firm's Credit Policy" *Financial Management,* Spring 1979.

Hill, T. W., Jr., "A Simple Perturbed Demand Inventory Model with Ordering Cost," *Management Science,* **23,** No. 1, September 1976.

Hodgson, Vincent, "Cash Forecasting by Box-Jenkins," paper presented at the TIMS/ORSA meetings, May 1979.

Hoeffer, E., "GM Tries Just-in-Time American Style," *Purchasing,* August 19, 1982.

Hoel, A., "A Primer on Federal Reserve Float," Federal Reserve Bank of New York, undated publication.

Hogg, Robert V., and Allen T. Craig, *Introduction to Mathematical Statistics,* Macmillan, New York, 1959.

Jannis, C. Paul, Carl H. Poedtke, Jr., and Donald R. Ziegler, *Managing and Accounting for Inventories,* Wiley, 1980.

Johnson, Robert W., "Economic Characteristics of Department Store Credit," National Retail Merchants Association, New York, 1969.

Kallberg, Jarl G., "Discussion of Sartoris and Hill," *Journal of Finance,* **38,** No. 2, May 1983.

Kallberg, Jarl G., and Anthony Saunders, "Innovations in Accounts Receivable Financing for General Merchandise Retailers," in *The Changing Universe of Retail Credit,* Vol. 2, NYU Institute of Retail Management, New York, 1982

Kallberg, Jarl G., and Anthony Saunders, "Markov Chain Approaches to the Analysis of Payment Behavior of Retail Credit Customers," *Financial Management,* Summer 1983.

Kallberg, Jarl G., R. White, and W. T. Ziemba, "Short-Term Financial Planning Under Uncertainty, *Management Science,* **28,** No. 4, 1982.

Karson, Marvin J., and W. J. Wrobleski, "Confidence Intervals for Absorbing Markov Chain Probabilities Applied to Loan Portfolios," *Decision Sciences,* **7,** No. 2, 1976.

Krieger, G. R., and E. C. Kramer, "How to Reduce the Bureaucratic Float," *Cashflow,* October 1981.

Kutler, J., "Check Volume Fails to Rise as Expected, Fed Study Finds," *American Banker,* *1980.*

Larson, Glenn G., "Discussion Is Retail Credit Still a Feasible Merchandising and Promotional Tool?" in *The Changing Universe of Retail Credit,* Vol. 2, NYU Institute of Retail Management, New York, 1982.

Leahy, J. J., "Special Report on Controlled Disbursement Banking Services," *Leahy Financial Services,* March 1982.

Lewin, W., and D. V. L. Taylor, "CHIPS: An Evolving Funds Transfer System," *Bank Administration,* November 1979.

Lieber, Zvi, and Yair E. Orgler, "An Integrated Model for Accounts Receivable Management," *Management Science,* **22,** No. 2, October 1975.

Liu, Lon-Mu, "Analysis of Time Series with Calendar Effects," *Management Science,* **26,** No. 1, January 1980.

Lordan, J. F., "A Profile of Corporate Cash Management: The Role of the Bank; The Money Mobilization Bank—Criteria for Providing Services; and Bank Compensation," *Bank Administration,* series of three articles, April–June 1972.

Love, Stephen F., *Inventory Control,* McGraw-Hill, New York, 1979.

Maier, S. F., and J. H. Vander Weide, "A Decision Support System for Managing a Short Term Financial Instrument Portfolio," *Journal of Cash Management,* March 1982.

Maier, S. F., and J. H. Vander Weide, "What Lockbox and Disbursment Models Really Do," *Journal of Finance*, **38**, No. 2, May 1983.

Maier, S. F., "Insulated Controlled Disbursing," *Journal of Cash Management*, November 1982.

Maier, S. F., and D. M. Ferguson, "Disbursement System Design for the 1980," *Journal of Cash Management*, November 1982.

March, R. T., "Cash Management—Ready or Not," *The Bankers Magazine*, July–August 1979.

Marks, L. A., "Sampling Techniques in Lockbox Modeling," *Cash Management Forum* (First National Bank of Atlanta), November 1980.

Marquardt, D. W., "An Algorithm for Least Squares Estimation of Nonlinear Parameters," *SIAM Journal*, **11**, 1963.

Martino, Joseph P., "Technological Forecasting—An Overview," *Management Science*, **26**, No. 1, January 1980.

Mathur, I., and P. J. Luisada, "The Future of EFT," *Bankers Monthly Magazine*, March 15, 1980.

McGillivray, Russell, and Edward A. Silver, "Accounting for Substitutable Demand in Inventory Control," Working Paper 101, Department of Management Science, University of Waterloo, August 1976.

Meek, P., "U.S. Monetary Policy and Financial Markets," Federal Reserve Bank of New York, 1982.

Mehta, Dileep R., *Working Capital Management*, Prentice-Hall Englewood Cliffs, N.J., 1974.

Miltko, S. E. (Project coordinator), "An Analysis of Floating the Commercial Banking Industry," Bank Administration Institute, New York, 1982.

Morgan, James I., "Questions for Solving the Inventory Problems," *Harvard Business Review*, **41**, July–August 1963.

Morris, R. D., and T. O. Johnson, "A Case Study in Corporate EFT," *Bank Administration*, September 1978.

Myers, E., "Electronic Cash Management," *ABA Banking Journal*, August 1979.

Myers, John E., R. E. Johnson, D. Egan, and H. J. Schleef, "Determining Optimal Drug Purchase Quantities under Conditions of Increasing Prices," *American Journal of Hospital Pharmacy*, **29**, December 1972.

Naddor, Eliezer, *Inventory Systems*, Wiley, New York, 1966.

Nauss, R. N., and R. E. Markland, "Solving Lock Box Location Problems," *Financial Management*, Spring 1979.

Nelson, Charles R., *Applied Time Series Analysis*, Holden-Day, San Francisco, 1973.

Newbold, Paul, "Time Series Model Building and Forecasting: A Survey," in *Forecasting, TIMS Studies in the Management Sciences*, Vol. 12, S. Makridakis and S. Wheelwright, eds., North-Holland, Amsterdam, 1979.

O'Connor, William J., Jr., "The Equal Credit Opportunity Act and Business Credit—Some Problems Reconsidered," *The Journal of Commercial Bank Lending*, January 1979.

Orr, B., "An ACH Growing Pain: What Caused It, What Will Relieve It," *ABA Banking Journal*, August 1980.

Osterman, W. J., "An Integrated System for Cash Management," *ABA Banking Journal*, May 1979.

Pan, Judy, Donald E. Nichols, and O. Maurice Joy, "Sales Forecasting Practices of Large U.S. Industrial Firms," *Financial Management*, Fall 1977.

Parkinson, K. L., "Bank Account Analysis: Compensation Tools," *Cash Newsletter*, March 1981.

Parkinson, K. L., "Multilateral Netting: International Cash Management Technique," *Cash Newsletter*, August–September 1981.

Parkinson, K. L., "Commercial Paper on the Rebound," *Pensions—Investment Age*, September 28, 1981.

Parkinson, K. L., "Companies Look Overseas for Idle Cash Savings," *Pensions—Investment Age*, April 26, 1982.

Parkinson, K. L., "Dealing with the Problems of International Cash Management," *Journal of Cash Management*, February–March 1983.

Peterson, Rein, and Edward A. Silver, *Decision Systems for Inventory Management and Production Planning*, Wiley, New York, 1979.

Phillips, John P., "Yet Another Digression on Systems Analysis: The Great Spare Parts Fiasco," *Interfaces*, **8**, No. 3, May 1978.

Plossl, G. W., and O. W. Wight, *Production and Inventory Control*, Prentice-Hall, Englewood Cliffs, N.J., 1967.

Rawlings, B. R., "Will the ACH Ever Grow Up?" *Transition*, November 1982.

Ray, W. D., "ARIMA Forecasting Models in Inventory Control," *Journal of Operational Research Society*, **33**, 1982.

Reuterskiold, C., "S.W.I.F.T.—The Next 10 Years," *The World of Banking*, March–April 1982.

Rideout, T. P., "Fed's Pricing Proposals Raise Many Questions," *ABA Banking Journal*, October 1980.

Ross, Sheldon M., *Introduction to Probability Models*, Academic Press, New York, 1972.

Saltzman, C., "The Floating Check Game," *Forbes*, March 5, 1979.

Sartoris, William L., and Ned C. Hill, "Evaluating Credit Policy Alternatives: A Present Value Framework," *The Journal of Financial Research*, **4**, No. 1, Spring 1981.

Sartoris, William L. and Ned C. Hill, "A Generalized Cash Flow Approach to Short-Term Financial Decisions," *Journal of Finance*, **38**, No. 2, May 1983.

Schwartz, B. L., "Optimal Inventory Policies in Perturbed Demand Models," *Management Science*, **16**, No. 8, April 1970.

Schwartz, Robert A., and David K. Whitcomb, "The Trade Credit Decision," in *Handbook of Financial Economics*, James L. Bicksler, ed., North-Holland, New York.

Searby, F. W., "Use Your Hidden Cash Resources," *Harvard Business Review*, March–April 1968.

Shain, J. H., P. McFeely, and O. Jakubowska, "Check Truncation: Ahead of Its Time?" *Bank Administration*, April 1981.

Shim, Jae K., "Estimating Cash Collection Rates from Credit Sales: A Lagged Regression Approach," *Financial Management*, Winter 1981.

Showers, J. L., and L. M. Chakrin, "Reducing Uncollectable Revenue from Residential Telephone Customers," *Interfaces*, **11**, No. 6, December 1981.

Silver, E. A., and H. C. Meal, "A Simple Modification of the EOQ for the Case of a Varying Demand Rate," *Production and Inventory Management*, **10**, No. 4, 1969.

Simpson, H. C., Jr., "Toward a Global Banking System," *The World of Banking*, March–April 1982.

Smith, Keith V., *Guide to Working Capital Management*, McGraw-Hill, New York, 1979.

Smith, Keith V. (ed.), *Readings on the Management of Working Capital*, 2nd Ed., West Publishing, St. Paul, 1980.

Snedecor, G. W. and W. C. Cochran, *Statistical Methods,* 6th ed., Iowa University Press, Ames, Iowa, 1967.

Snyder, Arthur, "Principles of Inventory Management," *Financial Executive,* **32,** No. 4, April 1964.

Sokol, M. D., and Associates, *The System Approach to Cash Management,* MDS Publication, White Plains, N.Y., 1981.

Sparkes, C., "Establishing an Account Analysis System," *Bank Administration,* Arpil 1977.

Spurlock, Ted, "Discussion of Hirschman and Assael," in *The Changing Universe of Retail Credit,* Vol. 1, NYU Institute of Retail Management, New York, 1980.

Starr, M. K., and D. W. Miller, *Inventory Control: Theory and Practice,* Prentice-Hall, Englewood Cliffs, N.J., 1962.

Steece, Bert M. and Steven D. Wood, "An ARIMA-Based Methodology for Forecasting in a Multi-Item Environment," in *Forecasting, TIMS Studies in the Management Sciences,* Vol. 12, S. Markridakis and S. C. Wheelwright, eds., North-Holland, Amsterdam, 1979.

Stigum, M., *The Money Market: Myth, Reality and Practice,* Dow-Jones Irwin, Homewood, Ill., 1978.

Stone, B. K., "The Payments Pattern Approach to the Forecasting and Control of Accounts Receivable," *Financial Management,* Spring 1976.

Stone, B. K., and N. C. Hill, "Alternative Cash Transfer Mechanisms and Method: Evaluation Frameworks," *Journal of Bank Research,* Spring 1982.

Stone, B. K., and R. A. Wood, "Daily Cash Forecasting: A Simple Method for Implementing the Distribution Approach," *Financial Management,* Fall 1977.

Sullivan, A. Charlene, "Consumers' Use of the Bankruptcy Option," in *The Changing Universe of Retail Credit,* Vol. 2, NYU Institute of Retail Management, New York, 1982.

Sullivan, C. F., "Reviewing Bank Account Analysis: Ramada's Approach," *Journal of Cash Management,* November 1982.

Thunell, L., "The American Express Formula," *Euromoney,* March 1980.

Wasilewsky, J., "Bank-Corporate Cash Information Systems," *Presentation,* Fall 1980.

Weberman, B., "Cash Like a Flash," *Forbes,* April 1, 1977.

Wecker, William E., "Predicting Demand from Sales Data in the Presence of Stockouts," *Management Science,* **24,** No. 10, June 1978.

Wecker, William E., "Predicting the Turning Points of a Time Series," *Journal of Business,* **51,** No. 4, 1979.

Wentworth, H. B., "The Monetary Control Act and Account Analysis," *Bank Administration,* January 1982.

Weston, J. Fred, and Pham D. Tuan, "Comment on Analysis of Credit Policy Changes," *Financial Management,* Winter 1980.

Wheelwright, Steven C., and Darral G. Clarke, "Corporate Forecasting: Promise and Reality," *Harvard Business Review,* November–December 1976.

White, G. C., Jr., "Development in Payment Systems in the USA." *Presentation,* October 8–10, 1979.

White, G. C., Jr., "Electronic Banking and Its Impact on the Future," *Bank Administration,* December 1979.

White, G. C., Jr., "Development in the United States Payment Systems," *Journal of Bank Research,* Winter 1981.

White, G. C., Jr., "The Conflicting Roles of the Fed as a Regulator and a Competitor," *Journal of Bank Research,* Spring 1983.

Whitin, Thomas M., *The Theory of Inventory Management,* 2nd Ed., Princeton University Press, Princeton, N.J. 1957.

Winters, Peter R., "Forecasting Sales by Exponentially Weighted Moving Averages," *Management Science*, **6**, 1960.

Wittebort, S., "The Frantic New Pace of Cash Management," *Institutional Investor*, June 1981.

Woolsey, R. E. D., and H. S. Swanson, *Operations Research for Immediate Application: A Quick and Dirty Manual*, Harper and Row, New York, 1974.

Zanakis, Stelios H., L. M. Austin, D. C. Nowading, and E. A. Silver, "From Teaching to Implementing Inventory Management: Problems of Translation," *Interfaces*, **10**, No.6, December 1970.

Zick, H. F., "The Investment of Idle Cash Funds," *Management Accounting*, February 1974.

Index